SUFFERING SOLDIERS

mpy577

NH5531

T. Badger pinx. et del.   Lith. of Pendleton.

John Resch

SUFFERING SOLDIERS

Revolutionary War Veterans, Moral Sentiment, and Political Culture in the Early Republic

UNIVERSITY OF MASSACHUSETTS PRESS   AMHERST & BOSTON

This book is published with the support and cooperation of the University of Massachusetts Boston and with the assistance of a grant from the University of New Hampshire at Manchester.

First paperback printing 2010
ISBN 978-1-55849-788-7

Designed by Sally Nichols
Printed and bound by Lightning Source, Inc.
Typeset in Adobe Caslon by Keystone Typesetting, Inc.

Library of Congress Cataloging-in-Publication Data

Resch, John Phillips, 1940–
Suffering soldiers : Revolutionary War veterans, moral sentiment, and political culture in the early republic / John P. Resch.
  p. cm.
Includes bibliographical references (p.) and index.
ISBN 1-55849-232-1 (cloth : alk. paper)
  1. United States—History—Revolution, 1775–1783—Veterans. 2. Military pensions—United States—History—18th century. 3. Military pensions—United States—History—19th century. 4. United States. Continental Army—Public opinion. 5. Public opinion—United States—History. 6. Veterans—Government policy—United States—History. 7. Veterans—United States—Social conditions. 8. Veterans—New Hampshire—Peterborough—Social conditions. 9. New Hampshire—History—Revolution, 1775–1783—Veterans. 10. Political culture—United States—History.
I. Title.
E259.R47 1999
305.9´0697´097309033—dc21
                                                    99-33065
                                                    CIP

British Library Cataloguing in Publication data are available.

Frontispiece: Colonel James Clark of Lebanon, Connecticut, age ninety-five. At the time the lithograph was made, Clark was the oldest survivor of the Battle of Bunker Hill. *Courtesy, American Antiquarian Society.*

FOR
JOHN, GRIFF, AND JANE

Contents

Preface

IN 1818 CONGRESS granted pensions to Revolutionary War veterans who had served at least nine months in the Continental Army and who were in "need of assistance from their country."[1] In 1820, following a scandal that tarnished the program, Congress approved an amendment that removed all pensioners from the rolls and that required veterans to pass a means test before receiving their pensions.[2] The two acts appeared to be no more than minor and obscure measures to aid impoverished soldiers. Their historical value, so it seemed, was the generation of nearly twenty thousand claims that contained untapped information about applicants' military service, wealth, and households.[3] Following an exploratory study of one hundred claims, I concluded that a systematic, quantitative analysis of those records could shed new light on the young soldiers who fought in the Continental Army and would create a novel view of them as elderly, impoverished veterans. I envisioned a narrow, focused, and limited project to portray pension claimants and their households.

The project broadened, however, into a study of political culture and public policy after I discovered, to my surprise, bitter opposition in the Senate to the 1818 pension bill. Opponents denounced the bill for breaching the Founders' republican principle that pension establishments were aristocratic and vice-ridden institutions that undermined civic virtue. Adhering to this principle, the Continental Congress and subsequent Congresses had refused to grant service pensions, except to disabled veterans. In 1818, however, the vast majority of congressmen in the House and Senate swept aside opponents' principles and overturned the Founders' policy against awarding military pensions. Moreover, in 1820, Congress saved the pension program despite a national scandal caused by corruption and runaway costs. The program withstood renewed attacks by traditionalists who viewed the scandal as vindication of their dire warnings.

The overturn of an established creed, the reversal of public policy opposed to awarding service pensions, and the preservation of a program disgraced by scandal posed several questions: Why did a new generation of leaders eagerly credit the once maligned Continental Army with securing independence? Why did Congress readily abandon the Founders' policy to create and sustain a pension establishment? How did the program withstand a scandal that appeared to confirm its critics' prediction of declension if Founders' principles were abandoned? More fundamentally, what did the creation of a pension establishment reveal about the forces transforming political culture and public policy in the Early Republic?

Part of the answer to these questions is contained in changed memories of the Revolutionary War. At the turn of the nineteenth century, Americans viewed the Revolution as a people's war won by a virtuous citizenry. Within twenty years Americans conceived the Revolution as a people's war won by the Continental Army. This new memory of the war was fostered by the romantic image of the suffering soldier. That image portrayed regulars as heroic warriors who embodied the republican ideals of militant patriotism and civic virtue. It also portrayed aging veterans as infirm, impoverished, and disadvantaged benefactors to whom the nation owed a debt of gratitude.

What had given rise to this new image? Why was it so successful in shaping political culture and public policy, as well as in transforming the notion of the Revolution as a people's war? This project expanded to address these questions. In part the answers were found in the evocative power of the image of the suffering soldiers. The image became a conventional rhetorical device to sway public opinion and political leaders. But feelings are fleeting and the words that evoke strong emotions can quickly lose their power to arouse public sentiment.

Could the power of the image have resulted from more than rhetorical evocation of patriotism and feelings of empathy? To answer that question, I studied the lives of the Revolutionary War soldiers and veterans from Peterborough, New Hampshire, to discover if their lives corresponded with the image of the suffering soldier.[4] I chose Peterborough because of its rich his-

torical sources (See appendix A, *Peterborough Sources*). Jonathan Smith's *Peterborough New Hampshire in the American Revolution* included service records
and biographical sketches for every Revolutionary soldier credited to Peterborough or who claimed residence in the town. Albert Smith, another town
historian, chronicled Peterborough's growth and constructed a genealogy of its
early settlers. Town meeting records, lists of town officers, a 1776 militia list,
state papers, family narratives, ecclesiastical records, wills and deeds, tax records, and recollections of early settlers were among the many sources available
to reconstruct the lives of Peterborough's soldiers within the context of their
community. Thus the lives of soldiers and veterans became an integral part of
this study of changes in political culture and public policy in the Early Republic. As the study evolved, it blended different areas of historical research.
I used methods from cultural, political, legislative, institutional, social, and
quantitative history, and prosopography to reveal the complex interplay of
partisanship, memory, war, nationalism, nostalgia, political leaders, bureaucracy, ordinary veterans, and the sentiment of gratitude.

There are many people to thank. Before I do that I wish to express my
appreciation to the National Endowment for the Humanities. Without support from NEH this book would not have been possible. The project began at a
National Endowment for the Humanities Summer Seminar conducted by
John Shy. Under John's auspices I pilot-tested the feasibility of a quantitative
analysis of the Revolutionary War pension records. His work on Long Bill
Scott and his interest in social dimensions of military service led me into the
subject of this book, especially the study of Peterborough's soldiers. I am indebted to John for initiating this project and for his continued support and
guidance. I also wish to thank David Hackett Fischer and Richard Herr. Their
NEH Summer Seminars, and my colleagues who participated in them, contributed significantly to my understanding of political and rural culture. In
addition to these summer seminars, a fellowship from NEH made possible an
enriching year of research at the American Antiquarian Society. I wish to thank
the staff of that society, in particular John Hench and Joanne Chaison, for their
help and encouragement. I also thank Georgia Barnhill for her assistance in
finding many of the illustrations used in this book.

Staffs at many other libraries and repositories have aided my research. I
especially want to thank the following: the staff at the Newberry Library; Mike
York, Judy Romein, and Mary Jean Chaput of the Oudens Library at the
University of New Hampshire at Manchester; Bill Copeley of the Tuck Li-

brary at the New Hampshire Historical Society; Frank Mevers, director and
state archivist of the New Hampshire Division of Records Management and
Archives; and Tod Butler at the National Archives.

Many colleagues have provided valuable instruction, insights, and helpful
criticisms of work while it was in progress. I want to thank Daniel Scott Smith
and Richard Jensen for teaching me quantitative methodology and demography. I am grateful to Jim Oeppen of the Cambridge Group for the History of
Population and Social Structure for helping me analyze the demographic
biases in Albert Smith's genealogy of Peterborough residents. My thanks also
to Richard Wall and colleagues at the Cambridge Group for allowing me to
spend a semester at their offices working on this project. I want to thank
Jonathan Chu, Tom Pervis, and Eldon Turner for their comments on early
versions of the manuscript written while we were at the American Antiquarian
Society. Connie Schulz and Ted Crackel, early pioneers in doing systematic
studies of the pension files, shared their work on applications from women and
veterans' geographic mobility. Sarah Purcell provided valuable criticisms at the
1998 annual meeting of the Society for Historians of the Early Republic. In
addition, her dissertation enriched my own work. I want to thank Jonathan
Shay for guiding me through the technicalities and controversies related to
post-traumatic stress disorder. I wish to thank Bob Cray, whose comments and
scholarship increased my understanding of the role of class in the formation of
memory. Wayne Franklin offered valuable suggestions and encouragement.
My thanks also to Judith Moyer, whose editorial help improved the manuscript's organization and readability. I wish to thank the anonymous reviewers
of my manuscript, in particular the individual who provided numerous pages of
corrections, criticisms, and suggestions for improving the text. Finally, Paul
Wright, editor of the University of Massachusetts Press, and the staff of the
University of Massachusetts Press have been very helpful in the final stages of
this project.

I wish to express my appreciation to the University of New Hampshire,
which has provided generous financial support of this project through research
fellowships and sabbatical leaves. A number of my colleagues at the university
have aided my efforts in a variety of ways, not the least important being their
encouragement, interest, and friendship. In particular I wish to thank Tom
Birch, who shared his interest in Adam Smith's work; John Cerullo, for our
many conversations about historiography and scholarly standards; and Karla
Vogel, for putting up with my endless questions about computer applications. I

especially want to thank Terry Savage, with whom I've team-taught a humanities course for over twenty years. As a philosopher, Terry was well equipped to guide me through the intricacies of David Hume and Adam Smith and to ask probing questions that led to a clearer and deeper understanding of the issues in this book.

I am particularly grateful to Ellen Derby, director of the Peterborough Historical Society, who gave me access to its wonderful collection of manuscripts. Ellen has assisted this project through her knowledge of the history of Peterborough, her support and encouragement, and her enthusiasm for local history. Lucy Blair, a volunteer at the society and a descendant of one of the veterans in this book, offered insights into her own family's history, as did Mrs. Roland Hemmett, a descent of the Scott and Robbe families of Peterborough.

Al Young deserves special recognition. He fostered this project with thoughtful guidance and encouragement by connecting researchers working on the pension files and by sharing his wealth of information. His prize-winning essay on George Robert Twelves Hewes stands as a model of how to reconstruct the lives of Revolutionary War veterans not only to see them for what they were but also to understand the significance of ordinary people in shaping American society.

Bob Bremner's thoughtful, subtle, and insightful scholarship created a model of historiography that has guided my work. I feel fortunate to have Bob as a mentor, and Bob and Kay as friends.

My interest in studying the families of Peterborough in part reflects my own family's interest in learning about its past. Talk about our family was part of the conversation of my youth. My parents, Robert and Nelle Resch, aunts Helen Louise Resch and Eleanor Resch Helman, and uncles Albert, Charles, Art, Ozzie, and Paul Resch spun tales of pranks, adventures, and personalities. My sister, Judy Resch Adams, and brother, Robert Resch, have added to the lore. Studying the history of Peterborough's families became an extension of an interest in my own.

My wife, Carol, has shared in this work, and our children, to whom this book is dedicated, have grown up with it. This project has been a source of great pleasure and many adventures, not the least being memories of our summer in Cambridge, England.

JOHN RESCH

Manchester, New Hampshire

SUFFERING SOLDIERS

Introduction

THROUGHOUT 1783 THE Continental Army dissolved. It officially disbanded that December. As they had throughout the war, discharged men, alone or in small groups, drifted back to their communities. In November William Alld returned home from the army's encampment at Newburgh, New York. Alld stopped at his father's house in Peterborough, New Hampshire, before continuing his journey to Maine, where he had moved in 1777.[1] No homecoming ceremony celebrated the veteran's return to New Hampshire. Rather, he found townsmen tired of war and struggling to subsist. Years of inflation and taxation had reduced the community to penury; in 1782, unable to pay a teacher's salary, Peterborough voted to suspend its school.[2] Observers would later recall that veterans like Alld "returned to the bosom of their country, objects of jealousy, victims of neglect."[3] Many were "destitute."[4] The country greeted them with indifference; it quickly forgot them. Proud veterans felt betrayed.

The nation's ingratitude toward the Continental Army disillusioned Peterborough's "Short Bill" Scott. Throughout the war the army had lacked supplies, was often without pay, was undermanned, and was treated by its citizens with a level of hostility that seemed more appropriate for enemy troops.[5] Moreover, in 1783 Congress reneged on its 1780 promise to Scott and his fellow officers that they would receive half-pay pensions for life. In place of a pension, Scott received a commutation certificate worth five years of full pay. By the time Congress was able to pay its obligation in 1790 many officers, desperate for cash, had sold their certificates to speculators for a fraction of their value. Scott had fought for seven years at great personal cost and had little to show for it except a disfiguring injury. He left the service "unfit for labor" because his left hand had been mutilated in 1777 by a British musket ball and a surgeon's knife. By war's end his mangled hand resembled a bird's claw. For all of these reasons Scott considered himself part of "that class [regular soldiers] whose hardships" in the Revolutionary War "are exceedingly disproportionate to any other citizens of America." Uprooted by years of service, in 1783 Scott departed Peterborough.[6] Hoping to start a new life, Scott settled in Greenfield, New York, probably as much for sentimental as for economic reasons. There he could relive his valor as a soldier in the victory over Burgoyne.

In 1792 Scott's anger at the nation's mistreatment of veterans boiled over in his application for a disability pension. He wrote with bitter irony about the injustice he and others like him endured: "many of those who aided in conquering [the enemy] are suffering under the most distressing penury" while many "who deserted and bore arms against their country live in splendor and affluence."[7] Scott subsequently received a modest disability pension. In death Scott chose to be close to the ghosts of Saratoga. In 1815 he was buried near the camp where his troops had assembled before engaging the British. A headstone was the only memorial to his patriotism and courage. Veterans like Scott were embittered by the nation's failure to recognize the extraordinary sacrifice they had made to secure independence from Great Britain. Continental Army veterans felt the sting of the nation's ingratitude.[8]

Americans declined to memorialize the Continental Army because they conceived the Revolution to be a people's war, not a conflict won by regular troops. John Adams, in May 1776, put the concept of the people's war simply: "We must all be soldiers."[9] That concept appealed to Americans because it conformed to the Revolutionary generation's opposition to regular armies. The concept also reinforced the republican ideal that military service was a citizen's duty and that fighting for the cause of liberty was its own reward. Accounts of a virtuous and patriotic citizenry, voluntary service, and family sacrifice, such as the story told about the Holmes family of Peterborough, helped to create the memory of the Revolution as a people's war.

According to local lore, early in 1776 Nathaniel Holmes, just turning sixteen and a member of a prominent family, returned to Peterborough after serving in Cambridge, Massachusetts, as a waiter for fellow townsman Lt. Henry Ferguson. That fall Washington appealed for more troops. In October, Holmes responded by enlisting in Nahum Baldwin's regiment, which fought in the battle of White Plains. In December, Holmes returned home. The next fall family members urged young Holmes to reenlist, but he refused "on the ground that his clothes were worn out" and because he did not want to lose wages while under arms. Brother-in-law William Moore offered to compensate Holmes for lost wages, and Moore's wife volunteered to make her brother a uniform; she told Moore to provide shoes. The next morning she sheared four lambs and within "twenty days the wool was colored, spun, woven and made into cloth, and when Captain (Joseph) Findlay came along on his way to Saratoga, the boy joined the army."[10] Members of the Holmes family personified the concept of a people's war. Holmes's sister had labored to make a uniform. His brother-in-law provided shoes and presumably made up the wages lost by the young soldier. Nathaniel Holmes, an amateur citizen-soldier from a prominent local family, repeatedly volunteered to risk his life to serve his country. In their own way they were all soldiers.

At the turn of the nineteenth century, Fourth of July orators reinforced this concept of a people's war with rhetorical images of the sacrifice, suffering, and patriotism of heroic mothers, sisters, and young men like Holmes.[11] Orators honored "citizen-soldiers" as a "band" of the people, and as "hardy yeomen" who endured a "painful" struggle against great odds to defeat a superior force. Orators acclaimed "the people" who, along with the troops, "suffered" injuries, endured great "hardships," and "paid an awful price" to win independence and liberty. Citizen-soldiers and the people were one. Celebrants apotheosized Washington, praised the patriotic citizenry, and singled out for tribute Revolutionary leaders such as Greene, Montgomery, Warren, and Franklin. The young republic venerated civilians and citizen-soldiers alike for their sacrifices, suffering, valor, honor, and glory in securing independence and gaining liberty. Few Americans shared Scott's belief that the Continental Army had won the war. Nor did most Americans share Scott's conviction that regular soldiers deserved special honors and reward. Exceptional leaders and militant people had created an American "David" to defeat the English "Goliath."[12]

Not confined to the narrow meaning of guerrilla warfare, the concept of the people's war depicted a fundamentally cultural, ideological, and nationalistic conflict. The concept dramatized the Revolution as an epochal uprising of a virtuous citizenry against corruption and tyranny. It transformed the Revolutionary generation into a mythic people who embodied the spirit of '76, a combination of civic virtue and militant patriotism. The concept of a people's war affirmed the Revolutionary generation's ideological distrust of a standing army, including, ironically, the Continental Army. The belief that the Continental Army enlisted social dregs and instilled corruption reinforced that distrust. Continuing demands after the war by Continental Army officers for service pensions strengthened public hostility toward the regular army. Those demands buttressed the conviction that service pensions created "placemen," that dreaded class that signified old-world corruption and aristocratic privilege. The concept of the Revolution as a people's war confirmed reliance upon militia for the nation's defense. It justified the government's refusal to single out for preferment veterans like Peterborough's Scott. Special tribute was reserved for the pantheon of exceptional leaders, such as Washington, Montgomery, Warren, Green, Wooster, and Mercer. The anonymous people, such as the Holmes family, were praised for their spirit of '76.[13]

By 1818, however, the nation embraced a new view of the Revolutionary War. The occasion was the passage of the 1818 Revolutionary War Pension Act. The act awarded pensions to Continental Army veterans who were "in reduced circumstances" to memorialize, reward, and comfort them. Americans acclaimed regular soldiers for delivering the United States from tyranny and celebrated Continental Army veterans as the nation's benefactors. Throughout the summer of 1818, aged veterans, mustering before special courts to submit their applications for pensions, released a public outpouring of gratitude that decades before had been denied veterans like Alld and Scott.

Typical of Fourth of July orators in 1818, Austin Denny (1795–1830), a lawyer and later the editor of the *Massachusetts Spy*, praised veterans for their valor as young soldiers. He told Independence Day celebrants in Worcester, Massachusetts, that the nation took pride in its "Revolutionary Army . . . its fortitude in suffering, its courage in danger . . . How large the debt of gratitude which was due from their country to this band of heroes." Celebrating the pension act for paying that debt, Denny said, at last "something has been done to cheer the last days of the surviving soldiers of the Revolution . . . the doors of the National Treasury have been thrown open to relieve their wants and to mitigate their woes."[14]

Continental Army soldiers emerged from obscurity to eminence. They were no longer dangerous "hirelings and mercenaries" who posed a threat to liberty.[15] Instead, the pension act honored them as virtuous republican warriors. The act also transformed the meaning of the people's war, and with it the memory of the Revolution. The act overturned the inherited belief that the

Continental Army, like all regular armies, was inherently corrupt. In place of that belief, the Continental Army became a republican institution composed of citizen-soldiers. Regular soldiers and the people were made one. Moreover, Continental Army veterans became symbols of patriotism and archetypes of national character. The public viewed them as benefactors owed a debt of gratitude by a grateful nation. In awarding pensions, a new generation reversed the Founders' creed that rewarding benefactors promoted moral declension and social privilege by creating placemen who subverted civic virtue. So strong was the new generation's conviction to memorialize and reward veterans with pensions, that the program survived a national scandal caused by corruption and high cost. It withstood congressional challenges to its constitutionality. It survived sectional conflict caused by resentment arising from the northeastern states receiving most of the benefits.

The image of the suffering soldier was the catalyst for legitimizing the Continental Army as a republican institution, and for reversing the Founders' policy against service pensions. The image elevated veterans to an esteemed social status. The image contained two mutually reinforcing characteristics. One feature romanticized the patriotism of Continental soldiers through accounts of bravery and heroic suffering endured in combat and camp. This part of the image apotheosized regular soldiers as republican warriors, as exemplars of the spirit of '76, and as models of national character. The second feature of the image depicted aging veterans' deprivation, poverty, infirmity, and despair as badges of honor, valor, and rectitude. This feature not only underscored the veterans' virtue, but also accentuated the nation's vice for its ingratitude toward the old soldiers. In passing the pension act, Congress codified the image of the suffering soldier in the political culture and public policy.

Although the image of the suffering soldier had appeared after the Revolutionary War, it was not until Jefferson's second administration that it emerged as an integral part of the nation's celebratory rites of self-affirmation and renewal.[16] In civic and political orations, the image expressed a new view of the Revolution. It helped to shape national identity during the congressional and public debate over the pension bill. The image reinforced the elevation of the common man and the spread of democracy that later characterized the Jacksonian Era. Yet, it also retained the republican ideal of civic virtue. Capable of symbolizing the new vision of the Revolution and able to arouse the public's moral sentiment of gratitude, the image of the suffering soldier became a powerful force forging the nation into a democratic republic.[17]

By 1818 the image became part of what historian David Waldstreicher called "the cult of sentiment," in particular the sentiment of gratitude as historian Sarah Purcell has ably shown.[18] The sentiment of gratitude exerted an increasingly powerful influence on politics and nationalism in the early republic. David Hume's and Adam Smith's theories of moral sentiment are useful for understanding the emergence and effect of the image of the suffering soldier. Unlike general concepts of gratitude from classical philosophy or religion, Hume and Smith focused on the role of gratitude in a liberal, market-based society like that developing in the Early Republic.[19]

Hume's *Enquiry Concerning the Principles of Morals,* published in 1751, reconciled sentiment and reason, and self-interest and public welfare in forming a moral and just society. Hume stated that "benevolence," or a feeling of empathy and goodwill toward others, was the "natural sentiment" that bound society by overcoming the divisive effects of self-interest. He believed that benevolence, when felt collectively, was a force that uplifted public morality and led to just laws. Hume also wrote that virtue and justice were determined by their "utility" to promote society's "happiness." Happiness did not mean hedonistic pleasure, but what he termed the highest sentiments, such as honor, dignity, and patriotism. He claimed that a person intuitively recognized virtue and justice because their effects were "agreeable" to an individual's feelings. Hume conceived collective sentiment to be a social bond, the arbitrator of civic virtue and public justice.[20]

Smith carried these ideas further as he developed his view that liberal society fostered public morality. Smith's *The Theory of Moral Sentiment* (1759) announced his belief that civic virtue ought not to be based on a fixed moral doctrine, as many traditionalists claimed it should, because doctrine prohibited individuals from rising above its rules.[21] Indeed, Smith, who embraced Hume's ethical principles, claimed that virtue was not a fixed behavior. Rather, virtue consisted of motives and actions "which deserved approbation" because their merit aroused real feelings such as compassion and gratitude. Smith concluded that civic virtue and justice would improve if they were "not confounded by misplaced intervention of human reason" and if society were to base "morality on a phenomenon of the passions alone."[22] Smith's precepts assured social cohesion and public virtue in an expanding market economy of individualism and self-interest.

Smith's concept of the "impartial spectator" was central to his idea of formulating civic virtue and justice in a liberal society. It was part of his "system of natural liberty."[23] According to Smith, the impartial spectator was not the actual spectator but the voice of conscience from an observer or observers far removed from actual events and their parties.[24] Smith described the impartial spectator as "the great inmate of the breast, the great judge and arbiter of conduct" that exercises "self command" over passions through "respect . . . for the sentiments of others." Smith wrote that impartial spectators derive moral authority "from a combination of well informed, impartial and accurate . . . imaginative representation of the situation being assessed." Over time a few spectators may find their sentiments shared by a mass of people who are increasingly sympathetic to them. Smith stated that "sympathy" or empathy may result in compassion, "the emotion which we feel for the misery of others." According to Smith, when our imaginations transport us to a situation where another person is suffering (Revolutionary War veterans, for example), our senses respond to "what we ourselves should feel" in these circumstances. These feelings are not a "copy" of what people at another time felt in response to the same circumstances. The result, he said, is "fellow feeling," a real sensation as if the imagining person were actually experiencing the effects of another person's misery. Smith stated that all people, "even the greatest ruffian," are capable of "fellow feeling."[25] Smith wrote that mass sympathy of "beating hearts" applauding motives and actions of distant "agents" excited "feelings of approval" for their virtue that defined a new standard, a presumably higher one, of personal and public morality.[26]

Smith wrote that fellow feeling discerns "merit" in other people's motives and actions, and that it may produce gratitude, the "sentiment which most immediately and directly prompts us . . . to recompense, to remunerate, to return good for good received . . . [un]til we ourselves [beneficiaries] have been instrumental in promotion [of] his [benefactor's] happiness" by paying our debt of gratitude. The objects of gratitude are those "persons" who cause the "heart" of every "impartial [and] indifferent spectator" to "feel" that their "merit" is the "cause of our good fortune." When that feeling is widespread (as it was with the public's gratitude toward Revolutionary soldiers), Smith said "every human heart is disposed to beat time to, and thereby applaud" the object of gratitude, which "enhances and enlivens fellow feeling" of the community as a whole. In such cases every citizen participates in moral advancement that derives from fellow feeling.[27]

Smith stated that paying a debt of gratitude begins as a free choice by beneficiaries to fulfill their moral obligation to reward their benefactors. A beneficiary who refused to pay his debt of gratitude was subject to the "highest disapprobation" for "the blackest ingratitude," especially ". . . when he has it in his power [to do so], and when his benefactor needs his assistance." The benefactor, however, relied on the beneficiary's good conscience and moral sentiment to obtain payment of that debt of gratitude. He could not compel payment "by force" without "dishonoring" himself and dissolving his moral claim to the reward.[28]

There were rare instances, Smith conceded, in which a moral obligation had to be enforced rather than relying on the voluntary reward to a benefactor. In these instances exceptional merit roused "another virtue," the "sentiment" of justice that elevated a voluntary obligation to a duty that is compelled by law. Smith wrote that justice allowed that "our own wills may be extorted by force" to fulfill our moral obligation.[29] In other words, "justice is literally . . . enforceable virtue." Smith believed that converting justice into law—replacing individual free will with collective force—required "the greatest delicacy . . . propriety and judgment" because ignoring civic duty led to "gross disorders" and "to push it too far is destructive of all liberty, security and justice."[30] Smith conceived the degree of moral obligation as directly related to the degree of merit. The greater the merit, the greater the obligation. He believed that the fulfillment of moral obligations was best left to free will. In some instances, however, society could compel payment of its debt of gratitude in the names of virtue and justice, defined by moral sentiment.

Revolutionary War veterans played an essential role in arousing the sentiment of gratitude within a new generation of Americans. By the time of Madison's administration, veterans began to present themselves to the public as suffering soldiers. Their applications for increases in disability pensions contributed heartrending accounts of privation that aroused compassion and guilt. Growing sympathy toward aged, poor, and disabled veterans, coupled with a budget surplus following the War of 1812, contributed to the passage of the 1818 Pension Act. Sanctioned by the act, the image of the suffering soldier became a more powerful rhetorical device. It blended what historian John Bodnar has called "official" and "vernacular" cultures.[31] The act made pensions a memorial honoring veterans. Veterans responded both with the verve of patriot-warriors and with the humble appreciation of grateful recipients. By the fall of 1818 nearly 20,000 men applied for pensions, often as part of musters of old soldiers celebrating the Fourth of July.

The public's esteem for veterans remained unscathed despite the scandal in 1819 over the pension program's high cost and corruption. Moreover, veterans reinforced that esteem after Congress amended the pension act in 1820 to require proof of poverty in order to receive a pension. Appearing in public court to prove their poverty, veterans affirmed the public's image of them as suffering soldiers who deserved the nation's honor and gratitude. Old and poor, yet proud and dignified, their appearance belied the fear and the distrust the Revolutionary generation had shown them in their youth. Pension applicants confirmed the new view of the army as a republican institution, one whose ranks were filled by citizen-soldiers. By 1818 the Continental Army had become central to the memory of the Revolution as a people's war.

Nor did veterans' poverty mark them with the shame and vice that sometimes accompanied a person's slide into dependency. Impoverished Continental Army veteran, Benjamin Alld of Peterborough, no doubt felt disgraced in 1816 when selectmen auctioned him to the lowest bidder willing to care for him at town expense; the low bid was ninety-six cents per week.[32] Under the 1820 amended pension act, veterans proudly displayed their infirmities and poverty as badges of honor and patriotism; their applications for pensions reflected such. Not dregs to be loathed and not among the poor to be shunned, hoary-headed veterans affirmed their place in communities as citizen-soldiers and republican-warriors worthy of the nation's gratitude and liberality.

These veterans did not fit the profile ascribed to them either by the Revolutionary generation or by modern historians. Most historians conclude that Continental soldiers came largely from society's poor, propertyless, transient, and marginalized.[33] Historian Charles Neimeyer stated that position most forcefully: "[I]t is apparent that the social origins of the majority of men who comprised the Continental army (where records can be found) were lower class. . . . The New Jersey regular, for instance, was neither 'a yeoman nor a middle class soldier—just as New Jersey was not a predominately yeoman society.' The same can now be said of Concord, Massachusetts; Peterborough, New Hampshire; and Prince George's County, Maryland." He concluded that the view of the Revolution, as a war fought by "the well-to-do and 'yeomen farmers,'" is a bewitching myth.[34]

Neimeyer claimed that the lowborn status of Continental Army soldiers revealed the American colonies to be a class-ridden and exploitative society. He asserted that the "propertied" class "lured" the "'lower sort'" from "low paying jobs" into the army with bounties, repressed these "military workers" out of fear they would turn on "their oppressors," and used this "'surplus population'" as cannon fodder. The "disempowered" soldiers, he stated, resisted through "work stoppages" in the form of "insubordination . . . desertion . . . refusal to reenlist," and by "mutiny." He concluded that military service in the Continental Army was another venue for class conflict. Relying on John Shy's study of Peterborough's "Long Bill" Scott ("Short Bill" Scott's cousin) and Jonathan Smith's *Peterborough New Hampshire in the American Revolution* (1913), Neimeyer stated that the low status of Peterborough's soldiers supported his claims. Few of them, he wrote, "could be termed 'yeoman soldiers'; rather, the large majority were 'an unusually poor, obscure group of men, even by the rustic standards of Peterborough'"; they were young, "owned no property, paid no taxes, and did not vote."[35]

However, an examination of the lives of all of Peterborough's soldiers—Continental and non-Continental—within the context of their households and community led to a different conclusion. Their lives conformed to the memory of the Revolution as expressed in the image of the suffering soldier and as codified in the 1818 Pension Act. Rather than being segregated by class, enlistments from Peterborough throughout the war represented a cross section of the town's society. In Peterborough, social rank did not determine military service. Some men served at one time in the Continental Army and at another time in militia and state regiments. Moreover, many of the townsmen who enlisted in 1775, whom historians agree were the most representative of society, supplied the core of Peterborough's recruits to the Continental Army throughout the war. For Peterborough the Revolution was a people's war not a poor man's war. Moreover, Peterborough's veterans reified the image of the suffering soldier that would transform nation's memory of the Revolution, its political culture, and its public policy.

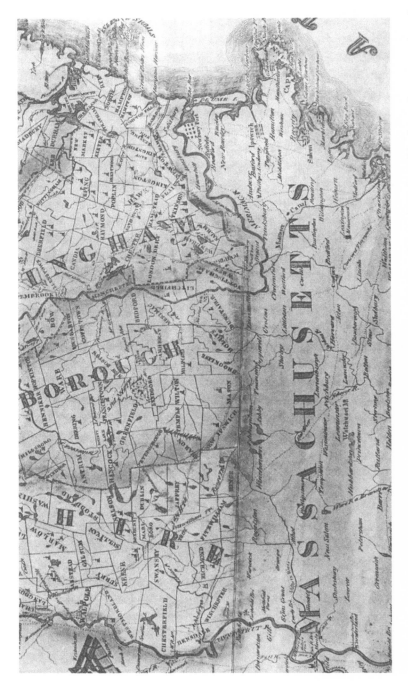

Map of New Hampshire and northern Massachusetts by Edward Ruggles (1817). Peterborough township is located in the southwestern section of Hillsborough County. The townships of Greenfield, Temple, Sharon, Jaffrey, Dublin, and Hancock are contiguous to Peterborough. The Massachusetts towns of Townsend and Lunenburg are located about thirty miles south and east of Peterborough. *Courtesy, American Antiquarian Society.*

CHAPTER I

Peterborough in the Revolutionary War

DURING THE REVOLUTION Peterborough engaged in a people's war. Most men of military age fought, if for only brief periods. Noncombatants supported the war effort by contributing supplies and money and by encouraging men from their households to fill ranks. Civilians suffered the effects of the long war—inflation, disruption of trade, and dislocation of society. The town shared the grief of families whose sons were wounded, or whose sons died in battle or from disease contracted in camp. About a third of the town's soldiers served in the Continental Army. Many served for years, a few for the entire war. Not from the dregs of society, these soldiers represented a cross section of the town, especially its middle and upper ranks.

PETERBOROUGH, NEW HAMPSHIRE, 1738–1775

Peterborough was one of the hundreds of new towns formed in eighteenth-century New England to accommodate a burgeoning population that was doubling in size about every twenty years.[1] Peterborough was also one of many towns founded by speculators who hoped to profit from the development and sale of frontier land. In 1738 four Massachusetts investors colluded with fifty Concord residents to obtain a free township of land from the province's General Court, which still controlled some land grants in New Hampshire. The Concordians, for their part of this scheme, pledged to the legislature that "they were all eager to leave the old home town and improve the wilderness for the public good."[2] After receiving the grant, the Concordians sold it to the speculators. The township was located on the frontier's edge in the Monadnock region, about twenty miles north of the Massachusetts towns of Lunenburg and Townsend and thirty miles west of the Merrimack Valley towns of Londonderry and Derryfield (now Manchester) in New Hampshire. Fertile hilltops made the Monadnock region a prime area for settlement by land-hungry residents from Massachusetts and New Hampshire towns, and by newly arrived Scotch-Irish immigrants.

The speculators surveyed the tract, divided it into ranges of one-hundred-acre lots, split the lots among themselves, staked themselves to choice five-hundred-acre farmlands, and promoted sale of the rest. They attracted settlers through low prices for land and through homestead agreements that guaranteed a fifty-acre lot to anyone who built a house and raised a crop within five years. The proprietors gambled that once the township was partly settled, the demand for remaining land would increase. They retained their five-hundred-acre farms as capital assets, expecting prices to rise substantially as good land in the town became scarce. Peterborough turned out to be a risky investment, however. Only a few people moved to the township, because of its vulnerability to Indian raids during King George's War (1740–48). In 1748 those early settlers deserted Peterborough.[3]

In 1750 the proprietors promoted resettlement. They attracted couples and young families who sought economic independence by establishing farms on New Hampshire's frontier. One group, possibly a third of the settlers, appeared to be recent Scotch-Irish immigrants. Generally, they were landless husbandmen and artisans temporarily residing in northern Massachusetts towns awaiting an opportunity to homestead or buy frontier land.

Another group, about a third of the settlers, came from Londonderry, New Hampshire. They were transplants from an established Scotch-Irish community that had been bitterly divided by the Great Awakening. In 1739 Londonderry had split into conservative "Old Side" and evangelical "New Side" Presbyterian parishes. According to the town historian, Edward Parker, "This unhappy division continued for nearly forty years [and] was productive of evils long felt in the town, occasioning alienation of feeling, and often bitter animosities between members of the religious societies." Neighbors attending different parishes stopped socializing. The conflict left deep social scars that remained for years and led some families to migrate to other towns. Most settlers who moved to Peterborough from Londonderry were Old Side Presbyterians.[4] The last third of the town's founders, for whom no information was found, were probably similar in background to settlers from Londonderry and northern Massachusetts.

Although sharing a common ethnic heritage, Peterborough's settlers came from different economic ranks. Some came from well-to-do parents who had purchased farmland for them. Others were poor men who moved to the frontier as homesteaders. Still others were self-made men who had accumulated some capital to purchase land from Peterborough's proprietors. William Scott, John Ferguson, and Samuel Miller's sons illustrate these features of the town's founders.

In the 1750s Samuel Miller of Londonderry, New Hampshire, purchased land in Peterborough for each of his sons—Matthew, John, William, and James. They were young men in their teens and twenties. Backed by their father, the four boys settled in town, established their farms, and assumed prominent roles in building the community. William Scott (1713–95), on the other hand, was a poor homesteader. In the 1740s the proprietors promised Scott one hundred acres if he settled "a good family" and "built them a dwelling house eighteen feet square" and "cultivate[d] six acres." Scott took possession of his land in the late 1750s. John Ferguson's economic status lay between the well-to-do Millers and the homesteader Scott. In the mid-1730s Ferguson emigrated from Ireland to Lunenburg, Massachusetts, where he established a "temporary residence." He purchased land in Peterborough at bargain prices and was among those who tried to settle the area in the 1740s. In 1750 Ferguson, after some fifteen years of residence in Lunenburg, returned to Peterborough with his wife and six children to reestablish his farm. They and young families like them formed an economically stratified agricultural settlement that had strong ethnic ties to other Scotch-Irish towns in New Hampshire and Massachusetts.[5]

Growing slowly at first, town population increased from a few score settlers in 1750 to 549 people by 1775. Just prior to the war with England, Peterborough's population growth surged. Between 1767 and 1775 town censuses revealed a 20 percent increase in population. In 1767 Peterborough was also home to one slave, a number that would increase to eight "Negroes and slaves for life" by 1775.[6]

Population growth was partly due to natural increase. Typical of the period, Peterborough couples had large families. Peterborough households contained an average of six children, and a third of Peterborough families had seven to nine children. The town also grew because it attracted many young families through the emerging kinship networks that linked Peterborough to Scotch-Irish communities in northern Massachusetts and New Hampshire's Merrimack valley.

By 1775 many Peterborough families orbited around two large kin networks. One of these networks centered on the Cunningham, Robbe, Taggart, and Scott families, which had strong ties to communities in Massachusetts. The other centered on the Miller, Morison, Moore, and Smith families, which were linked to communities in the Merrimack Valley, in particular Londonderry. The town's social fabric was strengthened first by marriages within these two networks, and then, during the Revolution and following it, between them.

Peterborough remained a youthful community in the pre-Revolutionary period. In 1750 the average age of a Peterborough resident was nineteen and the median age was fifteen; more than 80 percent of the population was less than thirty-one years of age. From 1760 to 1770, a period of rapid population growth, the average and median ages continued to hover around nineteen and fifteen, respectively, and the proportion of people under age thirty-one remained steady at about 80 percent. The town sustained its youthful character by attracting young families and by retaining the founders' children.[7]

Between 1754 and 1763, Peterborough was deeply involved in the imperial struggle in North America between Great Britain and France. Townsmen built a stockade on Ritchie Hill to defend themselves against raiding parties rather than desert the settlement, as they had in 1748. During the French and Indian War, thirty-two men volunteered for military service. Most of them served under "'ambitious and violent'" Maj. Robert Rogers of Amherst, New Hampshire, and his lieutenant, John Stark, from nearby Derryfield.[8]

Peterborough suffered dearly. The French and Indian War extracted the highest proportion of deaths for any war in the town's history. Nearly half of Peterborough's soldiers died while in service—nine were killed in battle and four died of dysentery contracted in camp. Six of those men were slaughtered in one engagement on 13 March 1758, when 600 or 700 Indians ambushed Rogers's company of 180 men near Lake George, New York. Samuel Cunningham and Alexander Robbe of Peterborough were among the 25 survivors. They and other veterans John Taggart, Short Bill Scott, and his cousin Long Bill Scott would later become captains in the Revolutionary army.[9]

Despite the war's heavy toll, the community continued to prosper. From the late 1750s through the 1760s Peterborough became part of the region's economy.

Mary Hodge Wilson's cloak. Mrs. Wilson wore it when she rode her horse with goods to trade and sell in Boston. *Courtesy, Peterborough Historical Society.*

Townsmen built roads, supported schools, sold farm surpluses and linen goods in area markets. Albert Smith, the town's historian and a descendant of a founding family, later wrote that every home was equipped for weaving for the household and market.[10] General James Wilson, a grandson of a town founder, recalled stories of his grandmother, Mary Wilson, marketing farm goods. Twice each year, dressed in her bright scarlet cloak, she led her packhorse loaded with butter, linen, and other farm products along forest trails to markets in Boston.[11] In the 1760s, although still part of New England's frontier, Peterborough's men and women actively promoted the town's economic development by linking it to the region's economy.

Townsmen were politically ambitious as well as industrious. In 1760 the settlers established home rule by removing the proprietors from power and incorporating the town. They used their newfound independence and authority to promote Peterborough's prominence. In 1767 the town petitioned New Hampshire's governor Benning Wentworth to create a new county. Petitioners complained that traveling east over Temple Mountain to Amherst, the shire town, to conduct their legal business was difficult and inconvenient. Wentworth denied their petition but there is little doubt that townsmen hoped to make Peterborough a shire town in the proposed county. In 1774 they petitioned Governor Wentworth to redraw town borders to include land belonging to the neighboring town of Jaffrey. Although Wentworth also denied this petition, townsmen remained eager to add good farmland to the town even at the expense of neighboring communities.[12]

The town's most difficult problem, one encountered by many New England communities, was securing a minister. Settling a minister was a central issue because church doctrine and polity largely shaped a community's political culture. Peterborough's leaders subscribed to Calvinist belief in human depravity, patriarchy, deference, covenant, and self-rule. Ideally, a minister embodied these principles and would propagate and legitimize them through daily examples and from the pulpit. Creating a stable and effective church, rather than protesting British tyranny, occupied the attention of Peterborough's early settlers as they built the community.

Not until 1766 was the town successful in hiring its first minister, the Reverend John Morrison. Possibly the shortage of ministers, the town's frontier character, and residual tensions between Old Side and New Side settlers who came from Londonderry had made the hiring of a minister difficult. Morrison was a twenty-three-year-old graduate of the University of Edinburgh who had arrived in Boston in 1765. Peterborough was his first pulpit.[13]

Morrison's tenure began auspiciously. In 1767 he married Sarah Ferguson, the daughter of John Ferguson, one of Peterborough's founders who was active in town government. By 1771, however, townsmen had accused Morrison of swearing, drunkenness, and lewd behavior. They petitioned the Londonderry Presbytery to remove Morrison for misconduct. Although the Presbytery tried to mediate a compromise to retain Morrison, the town continued to seek the discredited minister's dismissal. In 1771 the town's selectmen petitioned the New Hampshire General Court to dissolve its contract with Morrison. The General Court refused Peterborough's petition, stating that its complaint was an ecclesiastic not a civil matter. In March 1772, the town succeeded in forcing Morrison's resignation, and he left town without his family. Peterborough's ecclesiastic problems persisted, however. Town leaders were unsuccessful in attracting a new minister and had to rely on itinerant preachers until 1775 when Morrison returned to Peterborough, possibly to make amends and to regain his pulpit. Nevertheless, he remained at odds with the town. In 1775 Morrison defected from his militia unit prior to the battle of Bunker Hill. He remained in Boston to preach against the Revolution until the British evacuated the city in 1776. Later, Morrison fought with the British in the southern states where he died in 1782.[14]

On the eve of the Revolutionary War, Peterborough had grown from a precarious aggregation of Scotch-Irish settlers under proprietor rule to a thriving, self-governing community of farmers and traders. Although bloodied by the French and Indian War, the town had continued to grow and prosper. The population grew rapidly as new settlers migrated to town and young families added more children to their households. The emerging social and economic ranks were composed of former homesteaders, self-made men, recent immigrants, and children of well-to-do families from nearby towns. Despite these diverse backgrounds, residents were bound, if not united, by the principles of Old Side Presbyterianism. Emerging kin networks also stabilized the community and connected it to neighboring towns in New Hampshire and Massachusetts. No longer a frontier town, its artisans and farmers traded in the region's economy. The presence of one slave in Peterborough's first census of 1767, increasing to six slaves by 1773 and to eight by 1775, attested to the growing wealth and rising social status of some residents.[15]

PETERBOROUGH'S MOBILIZATION

When word of the battles of Lexington and Concord reached Peterborough on April 19, Short Bill Scott closed his store, mustered about a third of the townsmen of military age into a company of troops, and marched them to Boston.[16] Peterborough residents were once again deeply engaged in war. Between 1775 and 1783, 100 residents (64 percent) out of a total of 156 males served in the army. The total number of males included men of military age, sixteen to fifty, and those few boys and elders who enlisted. For each year of the war there were about one hundred townsmen at risk of service. In each of those years, the number of men under arms and the number of days they served varied (table A). During the war, twenty of the one hundred soldiers became casualties. Eight died as a result of their service, including five or six who succumbed to disease. Another twelve were wounded. Once again war bloodied town families.

Peterborough's mobilization was part of the country's war-making machinery. Like other communities, the town served as a recruitment center and eventually like a draft board. In the fall of 1775 the New Hampshire General Court divided the state into twelve military districts to recruit and mobilize

Table A
Peterborough Residents
1775–1783

Year	Number of Men at Risk of Service Each Year	Number of Men in Service Each Year	Percent of Men Who Served	Total Potential Days of Service for Men at Risk	Total Days Served Each Year	Percent of Potential Days Served Each Year
1775	100	42	42.0	25,365	8,547	33.7
1776	99	29	29.3	34,996	5,533	15.8
1777	106	66	62.3	37,237	7,780	20.9
1778	104	47	45.2	36,063	9,642	26.7
1779	97	26	26.8	35,040	8,841	25.2
1780	103	23	22.3	36,415	6,031	16.6
1781	102	16	15.5	37,048	4,096	11.1
1782	97	9	9.3	35,349	2,959	8.4

The number of men at risk of service for each year was compiled from Albert Smith's genealogical information in his *History of Peterborough,* Jonathan Smith's *Peterborough New Hampshire in the American Revolution,* and other sources such as militia lists. The at risk are able-bodied male residents of Peterborough between sixteen and fifty years of age, and residents in service for each year of the war regardless of their age. This age division is based on the New Hampshire Assembly's requirement that all able-bodied males between the ages of sixteen and fifty be mustered in the militia, and the less able and older men, ages sixteen to sixty-five, be included on the Alarm list. The at-risk population was recalculated for each year of the war by deleting men who exited because they died, departed, or turned fifty-one years of age, and by adding men who entered the town, and boys, not in service, who turned sixteen years of age. The number of potential days of service for each individual on this list was calculated for each year of the war. To illustrate, based on the above sources there were one hundred men at risk of service between 19 April and 31 December 1775. This number nearly matches the 102 men recorded in Peterborough's 1775 census.[17] The total potential days of service for 1775 accounted for the death of one soldier and the desertion of another in June 1775. Their exit reduced the male population at risk of service through the remainder of 1775, consequently reducing the potential days of service for that year.

The number of men in service for each year was compiled from Jonathan Smith's *Peterborough New Hampshire in the American Revolution.* Smith's book contains the names, service records, and biographical information of the 176 soldiers for whom there is any reference of association with Peterborough. Those 176 soldiers are divided into four categories: 102 of the men were residents of the town sometime during the Revolutionary War. One soldier, Samuel Treadwell, moved to town during the war after completing his service. He was included in the at-risk category, but deleted from the list of soldiers because he did not serve while he was a resident of Peterborough. Peterborough resident Daniel Mack served in the militia after he moved from Peterborough. He was included in the at-risk category while a resident, but not included in the list of resident soldiers. Thus, with the exclusion of Treadwell and Mack, the figure of 100 resident soldiers, rather than 102, is used in this study. In addition to those residents, twelve soldiers in Smith's account had no association with town until they moved there sometime after the Revolutionary War; the remaining sixty-two were not residents of town, and most had no association at all with Peterborough.

Smith's study contains enlistment and discharge dates for each of Peterborough's one hundred soldiers and their units. This information was quantified and the number of days of military service per year for each soldier derived from the enlistment reocrds. Thus the forty-two men who enlisted in 1775 served a total 8,547 days from 19 April through 31 December 1775.

troops. Peterborough belonged to Col. Enoch Hale's regimental district, which included the towns of Rindge, New Ipswich, Jaffrey, Temple, Stoddard, and Sharon. Hale counted on fielding a portion, or all, of Peterborough's able-bodied men as the need arose.[18]

In April 1775, thirty-four of one hundred Peterborough residents of military age organized into companies formed through kinship and friendship, and were led by local officers seasoned in the French and Indian War. Twenty-seven of those thirty-four men served in fellow townsman Capt. Short Bill Scott's unit, which included his cousin Lt. (and later Capt.) Long Bill Scott, Sgt. James Hockley, and Cpls. Andrew Bailey and Charles White. This unit included family members such as John Scott, Thomas Scott, William Scott Jr., and David White. The unit also included friends and family from the nearby New Hampshire towns of Dublin, Sharon, New Ipswich, and Stoddard, and from Massachusetts towns such as Townsend and Lunenburg, where the Scotts and other townsmen had resided before settling in Peterborough. Other residents enlisted in units raised from towns where they had previously lived. For example, Peterborough's Hugh Gregg and James Miller joined John Stark's militia company, which contained men from their hometown of Londonderry, New Hampshire.[19] Recruits to other units came from the town's kin groups, such as three members of the Morison family, their cousin John Smith, and three members of the Taggart family. In May and June five more townsmen enlisted, and between October and December 1775, three more Peterborough residents joined the army, raising the total number of enlistments that year to forty-two men (see table B). These forty-two men represented a cross section of the town's population structure. They averaged thirty years of age, two years younger than the average age of the one hundred men at risk of military service in 1775. They ranged in years from seventeen-year-old Ebenezer Perkins to sixty-nine-year-old John Scott. John Scott was the unmarried uncle of Long Bill and Short Bill as well as the brother of the homesteader William Scott who had helped settle Peterborough in the 1750s. Nearly 40 percent of the soldiers were in their thirties or forties, about the same age distribution for all of Peterborough's males.

Many of the town's political leaders marched to war. Eleven of the forty-two soldiers (26 percent) had held or were holding a town office. They included former selectman James Taggart and Selectman Charles Stuart who had been elected to office in March 1775. The large number of town officials was remarkable given that 20 percent of the troops were not eligible for office because

TABLE B

RESIDENTS OF PETERBOROUGH AT THE TIME OF THEIR ENLISTMENT

1775–1782

N=100

New Enlistees Each Year	NUMBER ENLISTING, CONTINUING, OR RETURNING TO SERVICE EACH YEAR							
	1775	1776	1777	1778	1779	1780	1781	1782
1775: N=42	42	18	23	19	12	10	7	4
1776: N=11		11	9	3	3	2	1	1
1777: N=34			34	16	5	5	2	2
1778: N= 9				9	4	5	4	2
1779: N= 2					2	0	0	0
1780: N= 1						1	1	0
1781: N= 1							1	0
1782: N= 0								0
TOTALS=100	42	29	66	47	26	23	16	9

they had not reached the age of twenty-one. The troops also included sons of town leaders, such as Samuel Mitchell Jr., age twenty-three. Samuel's father, "Gentleman" Samuel Mitchell, was a deacon in the town church, a selectman from 1762 to 1767, and the town clerk from 1775 through 1780. Town leaders promoted community mobilization either by volunteering for duty or by sending their sons.[20]

The soldiers represented the town's economic structure. Although some were propertyless, they were not part of a rural proletariat. They were young sons of Peterborough farmers, such as Samuel Moore Jr., and William Smith Jr., both age nineteen. Nor were the older men who enlisted part of a proletariat. Some were identified as "yeomen" who owned average-size farms. Henry Ferguson, age thirty-nine, who was the son of founder John Ferguson, and Long Bill Scott and his cousin Short Bill Scott, ages thirty-three and thirty-two respectively, were part of this group. Others were among the town's largest landholders. The three Taggarts—John, Lt. James, and James, ages twenty-five, thirty-three, and thirty-seven, respectively—owned large farms as did James Miller, age thirty-seven. To recall, Miller's father had given farms in Peterborough to his son James and his three brothers. James McKean, age thirty-six, who owned about 150 acres, was also among this group.[21]

The *rage militaire* unified Peterborough's social, economic, and generational ranks behind its seasoned soldiers. Short Bill and Long Bill Scott totaled nearly two years of military service in the French and Indian War. Other townsmen gathered under John Stark of Derryfield. Although not a resident, Stark had served with Peterborough men in the French and Indian War, had a distinguished combat record with Rogers's Rangers, and had organized a company that included kin and former neighbors of Peterborough settlers.

Most of the recruits were soon engaged in combat. Over half of the men, twenty-two of thirty-nine then under arms, probably fought at Bunker Hill.[22] Most, such as William Graham, age twenty-two, were in Scott's company under the command of Paul Dudley Sargent. Others, such as James Miller, fought with Stark's troops, who stopped the British light infantry's attack on the Mystic River beach. In the battle of Bunker Hill, one Peterborough soldier, Joseph Taylor, age eighteen, was killed and two were injured, including Long Bill Scott who was "severely wounded." Scott was shot five times and was found on the battlefield bleeding from "nine orifices."[23] A British officer saved Scott from troops who were executing wounded rebels. Nevertheless, Scott was left on the field overnight, presumably to die. Still alive the following day, he was nursed back to health and was later imprisoned in Nova Scotia. In June 1776, with the help of John Morison, who was a resident of Nova Scotia and whose brothers lived in Peterborough, Scott and six companions broke out of prison and escaped by ship to Boston. After a brief return to his home, Scott rejoined the Continental Army in New York.[24]

Peterborough's soldiers suffered hardships. In August 1775, John Blair Sr., age fifty-eight, detached from Short Bill Scott's company to join Benedict Arnold's force marching through Maine to attack Quebec. Arnold's troops endured harsh weather, lacked provisions, and were ravaged by sickness. One soldier recalled that starving men were "obliged to kill a dog and eat it for our breakfast."[25] Blair was captured on 31 December 1775, after the failed assault on Quebec. He spent the next six months imprisoned in a "French Convent . . . on rations of bread and a jill of rum a day." He was paroled in August 1776 and returned to Peterborough where he received his enlistment bounty, a new coat. Hardships in camp appeared to have contributed to the deaths of James McKean, age thirty-six, and John Ritchie, age twenty-six. Both succumbed to illness early in 1776 shortly after returning from duty in Boston.[26]

Twenty-nine (76 percent) of the thirty-eight surviving soldiers who first enlisted in 1775 either continued in service in 1776 or reenlisted at other times during the war. For example, in August 1777 six men reenlisted in John Stark's state regiment, which defeated German mercenaries and British troops at

TABLE C

PETERBOROUGH SOLDIERS

	ALL ENLISTEES 1776–1783		ONLY MEN WHO FIRST ENLISTED IN 1775 N=42		
Year	Total in Service	Total Days Served	Enlisted in 1775: The Number Who Continued in Service or Reenlisted after 1775	Enlisted in 1775: The Number of Days Served Each Year after 1775	Percent of Total Days Served
1776	29	5,553	18	3,538	63.9
1777	66	7,761	23	4,080	52.6
1778	47	9,642	19	4,709	48.8
1779	26	8,841	12	4,328	49.0
1780	23	6,031	10	2,966	49.2
1781	16	4,096	7	2,019	49.3
1782	9	2,959	4	1,193	40.3

$$\text{Percent of total days served} = \frac{\text{Total days served for each year of the war for men who first enlisted in 1775}}{\text{Total days served for all men enlisted for each year of the war}}$$

Bennington, Vermont. In 1778 cousins Charles and David White, veterans of 1775, reenlisted in Enoch Hale's state regiment, which joined Continental troops in the campaign to drive the British from Rhode Island. Soldiers who enlisted in 1775 accounted for half of the town's service days for the entire war—22,833 days of service out of total of 44,883 days of service for all of the soldiers from Peterborough. Furthermore, they contributed from a third to a half of the town's soldiers under arms each year of the war (see table C).

Those who enlisted in 1775 participated in many of the Revolution's major engagements. By war's end, many could boast of participating in the war's two greatest militia victories, Bunker Hill and Bennington. Some had witnessed the British evacuation of Boston in 1776 after a siege that lasted nearly a year. Many were part of Washington's victories at Trenton and Princeton. Others witnessed Burgoyne's surrender in 1777. A handful participated in major engagements that occurred between 1778 and 1781, including Yorktown. Some who first enlisted in 1775 could recall the grueling campaign in Quebec, captivity as prisoners of war, winter encampments at Valley Forge in the winters of 1777 and 1778, and mutiny. Collectively, they represented the town's most militarized population, the heart and soul of its war effort, and the war's richest legacy for future generations. Warfare itself probably stiffened their resolve to fight for independence and probably politicized these citizen-soldiers into hard-core troops. Nearly half of the town residents who later served in the Continental Army had first enlisted in 1775.[27]

Peterborough's contribution to the war effort dropped substantially in 1776 following American defeats in Canada and British evacuation of Boston. About 60 percent of the men who had served in 1775 returned home in 1776. Only eleven new recruits, just over 14 percent of the men of military age remaining in town (eleven of ninety-nine), took up arms for the first time (see tables A and B). They were younger than the men who first enlisted in 1775; they averaged twenty-seven years of age compared to the average of thirty for recruits in 1775. Eight of the ten new enlistees whose birth dates are known

By order of Congress, the list of trainable men under the command of Alexander Robbe of Peterborough, dated 13 January 1776. The list contains the names of men between 16 and 50 years of age then in town who were eligible for service. These men drilled eight times a year. There is also the Alarm List, which contains the names of men between 16 and 65 years of age who were available for service in case of emergency. These men trained twice each year. The list was printed in Jonathan Smith, *Peterborough, New Hampshire, in the American Revolution*, 27–28. The original list is in the Peterborough Historical Society. *Courtesy, Peterborough Historical Society.*

were under thirty years of age; none were in their thirties or forties; two were in their fifties.[28] By contrast, nearly 40 percent of the men who first enlisted in 1775 were between thirty and forty-nine years of age. After the conflict shifted from New England to the middle states in 1776, an increasing number of Peterborough men in their thirties and forties left distant fighting to younger recruits, a few battled-hardened soldiers in their thirties, and a couple of old warriors.

The town's reduced war effort also reflected the changing character of the conflict. The war had begun as an uprising of citizens who had mobilized under community leaders. These citizen-soldiers had expected a quick victory in a localized conflict. By 1776 America had entered a new stage of the war. The war had spread from Canada to Georgia. Throughout 1776, states organized regiments for local operations, and Washington created his national army by recruiting veterans such as Long Bill Scott and Short Bill Scott and by appealing to citizens who had yet to bear arms to enlist for a year's service.[29]

Townsmen were enlisted through Hale's formal mechanism and through an informal network of kin, friends, and former residents who lived within a roughly thirty-mile radius of Peterborough. This area extended beyond Hale's regimental district into northern Massachusetts and south-central New Hampshire. In addition, Peterborough was directly linked to the Continental Army through Capts. Short Bill and Long Bill Scott. These two officers bypassed the state's recruitment mechanism to enlist men directly through Peterborough's kin networks.[30] They enlisted men to meet Peterborough's troop quota and the quotas of the other towns. By the end of the war, about half of the thirty-one Peterborough residents who served in the Continental Army credited their service to towns other than Peterborough. These men would appear to later historians as transients and lower sorts because there was no record of them in those towns.[31]

Despite the decline in enlistments, the town's leading families continued to contribute their children to military service. The new recruits either joined kin then in service or replaced them, as was the case for Benjamin Mitchell. Benjamin's father was Deacon Samuel Mitchell, a town founder, owner of a saw mill and a grist mill, and a former selectman. Benjamin's brother Samuel had served through 1775 and returned home at the end of that year. In July 1776 Benjamin Mitchell, age twenty, enlisted for six months in Nahum Baldwin's state regiment which was attached to Continental Army forces at White Plains, New York. Two other recruits, Benjamin Alld and John Todd, came from prominent families. Alld's father was a substantial landowner in the Merrimack Valley who had recently purchased land in Peterborough. Todd was related to the Morisons, Smiths, and Taggarts who had collectively contributed eight men in 1775.[32] Military service apparently politicized kin networks and turned the war into a family matter.

Town leaders continued to set a patriotic example for other citizens by serving in the army. For example, Captain Alexander Robbe, age fifty, enlisted for the first time in 1776. He was a selectman, a member of the Committee of Safety in 1775, commander of the town's militia, and a relative of the Taggart and Scott families, which had contributed many men in 1775. He served four months in a regiment raised from local militia to reinforce America's army in Canada.[33]

Service stiffened the resolve to fight among many men who first enlisted in 1776, as it had for many who had enlisted in 1775. Nearly all of Peterborough's new recruits, ten of twelve, either continued in service beyond 1776 or reenlisted in subsequent years.[34] Most became part of the core of volunteers that the army relied on for soldiers. Such was the case for Benjamin Alld. In 1776, Alld, age seventeen, enlisted in Nahum Baldwin's state regiment, which was recruited to reinforce Washington's troops in New York. Alld fought in the battle of White Plains and returned to Peterborough after his three-month enlistment expired. In July 1777 he reenlisted for three years in Long Bill Scott's company. Others reenlisted for short terms in state regiments that were hastily formed to reinforce Washington's army. John Todd, age twenty-one, spent six months in 1776 as part of David Gilman's state regiment guarding Portsmouth, New Hampshire. At the conclusion of this enlistment, in December 1776, he reenlisted for six months in Gilman's regiment, which was ordered into the field to reinforce one of New Hampshire's Continental Army regiments. Todd returned to Peterborough in June 1777 and promptly reenlisted in July for two months' service under John Stark at Bennington.[35] Young men such as Benjamin Mitchell, Benjamin Alld, and John Todd responded to wartime emergency, kin pressure, and examples set by town leaders. Some, like Alld, became hard-core troops who served for years in the Continental Army.[36]

In 1777, Burgoyne's invasion of New York produced a general mobilization. The highest proportion of Peterborough men at any period of the war carried arms that year. Many were engaged in combat. On 1 July 1777, British troops began their siege of Fort Ticonderoga, the "Gibraltar of the North," which was defended by two thousand Continental troops—including a company under the command of Peterborough's Short Bill Scott—and by one thousand state troops who reinforced the Continental Army.[37] On July Fourth British troops mounted cannon on Mt. Defiance, overlooking "Ti," and forced its commander, Gen. Arthur St. Clair, to evacuate the fort under cover of darkness. American troops divided into two groups and made a fighting retreat. Captain Short Bill Scott's company of the First New Hampshire Regiment engaged in rear-guard action against pursuing Redcoats commanded by Simon Fraser. Surprised by advancing British troops, commanders ordered Scott's troops to retreat. Interpreting the order to suit himself, Scott ordered his men to take "three paces" toward the rear and form battle lines. In the skirmish that followed, Scott's neighbor John Taggart, age seventeen, whom Scott had recruited for Continental service that April, was killed in a hail of musket balls.[38]

Lieutenant Thomas Blake of the First New Hampshire Regiment recorded in his journal that "everything [was] in great confusion" as troops retreated through Vermont.[39] Ticonderoga fallen, the American army in retreat, and loyalists mobilizing to aid the British, Burgoyne appeared ready to recapture New England. Panic followed. New England states ordered their militia forces mobilized to repel Burgoyne's invasion. New Hampshire commissioned Gen. John Stark, who had resigned from the Continental Army in April in a dispute over seniority, to raise troops for an "independent command." From 19 July to 24 July, about 1,500 New Hampshire men, one out of ten male residents of voting age, enlisted under Stark. Stark's victory at Bennington on August 16 marked the campaign's turning point in favor of the patriots. Stark recalled that the battle "became a confused melee [and] the hottest I ever saw in my life." His 1,500 New Hampshire militia, including many Peterborough men, along with 150 Continental Army soldiers defeated 550 Brunswicker, Tory, and Canadian troops, and routed 640 troops sent as reinforcements. The victory was one-sided. Stark lost thirty men. British forces suffered 150 men killed and 700 troops taken prisoner. Major Robert Wilson of Peterborough was one of twenty-three Peterborough soldiers at the battle. Wilson served on Stark's staff and later commanded the troops in charge of prisoners.[40]

Burgoyne's invasion marked the high point of Peterborough's contribution to the military effort. In 1777 a total of sixty-six townsmen, or 62 percent of the male residents of military age that year, carried arms (see table A). Over half, thirty-four of the sixty-six men, fought for the first time (see table B). These new enlistees differed from those who had enlisted for the first time in either

1775 or 1776. The crisis forced the community to mobilize all able-bodied soldiers.

About a third of the first-time recruits (ten of thirty-four) had moved to town sometime between 1775 and 1777. Generally, these newcomers, such as David Ames and John Kennady, were in their early twenties. Nothing is known about Ames prior to his move to Peterborough. Having settled in town, in 1776 Ames signed the town's Association Test and joined Alexander Robbe's militia company. In May 1777 Ames, age twenty-five, enlisted in Jonathan Chase's state regiment which reinforced the Continental Army at Fort Ticonderoga. He returned to town in mid-June, at the conclusion of his enlistment, only to be called out at the end of June when the fort came under attack. Ames marched with Robbe and other townsmen as far as Charlestown, New Hampshire, near the Connecticut River, but returned home after four days in the field after learning that Ticonderoga had fallen to the British. That was the last of Ames's service for the war, a total of forty-five days. He apparently had his fill of duty or was possibly weakened in the field and could not continue under arms. In 1782 Ames moved to nearby Dublin, but he retained his ties to Peterborough, where he died in 1834.

Another newcomer, John Kennady (birth date and birth place unknown), arrived in town by 1775 and like Ames joined Robbe's militia company. In 1777 he mustered for five days' service in John Taggart's militia company based in the neighboring town of Sharon. This company was composed of men recruited from towns such as Peterborough and New Ipswich. If Kennady followed established patterns, he enlisted with Taggart rather than Robbe because Kennady had kin or friends in that unit. While serving in the militia, Kennady was "hired" by the town of Attleboro, Massachusetts, to serve three years as one of its Continental soldiers. Kennady enlisted in Henry Jackson's Massachusetts regiment which contained Long Bill Scott's company and many local men from New Hampshire and Massachusetts. Already under arms, Kennady may have been enticed by bounties and a chance to improve his station in the world. He succeeded in rising to the rank of sergeant and remained in service until the war's end. He did not return to Peterborough after the war.[41]

Two other newcomers, Jonathan Wheelock, age fifty, and his son Jonathan Jr., age twenty-three, had moved to Peterborough in 1775. The elder Wheelock had joined Alexander Robbe's militia, had become one of its sergeants, had signed the 1776 Association Test, and, in 1777, had been elected to Peter-borough's Committee of Safety. In the spring of 1777, Jonathan Wheelock Jr. enlisted in Short Bill Scott's company for a term of three years. That summer Wheelock's father mobilized two different times in the town's militia to repel Burgoyne's invasion. In 1778 the elder Wheelock enlisted a third time in Enoch Hale's state regiment, which was attached to Continental troops attacking British forces around Newport, Rhode Island. Although new to the commu-nity, the Wheelocks quickly became involved in the town's war effort, began to establish themselves in its military and political hierarchy, and, in 1777, volun-teered for duty in accord with community expectations that town leaders serve their country. The Wheelocks continued to play a leading role in town until 1790 when they moved to Cavendish, Vermont, where they became prominent community members.[42]

Of the ten newcomers who first enlisted in 1777, only Samuel Houston remained in Peterborough for the rest of his life. Houston was born in Dun-stable (now Nashua), New Hampshire, in 1745 and moved to Peterborough prior to the war to practice his blacksmith trade. Like Ames and Kennady, he joined Robbe's militia company, which also contained Houston's younger brother Isaac, age eighteen, who seems to have lived variously among the New Hampshire towns of Dunstable and Bedford. The brothers marched for four days with Robbe to and from Charlestown, New Hampshire. Later that sum-mer they returned to the field to fight with John Stark at Bennington. In August of the following year, Samuel Houston spent a month with Enoch Hale's state regiment in Rhode Island. After this enlistment Houston re-turned to Peterborough, where he practiced his blacksmith trade until his death in 1824.[43]

In general, the newcomers were young single men. They were part of the migration to Peterborough that had contributed to the town's 20 percent in-crease in population between 1767 and 1775. They did not appear to be tran-sients or strangers pressed into service. Rather, they were recent arrivals to Peterborough who were in various stages of establishing themselves in the community. The general mobilization to repel Burgoyne swept them into the town's war effort. For a few, as in the cases of the Wheelocks and Hous-tons, service may have been another step toward affirming their status as town leaders.

Two thirds of the new recruits in 1777 (twenty-four of thirty-four) came from the town's established households. The invasion mobilized families, especially those that had not contributed men to the army. Two established Peterborough families, McCoy and Davison, contributed soldiers for the first time in the war. In 1777 Charles McCoy, age sixteen, the second son of town founder William McCoy, was the first member of his family to serve in the war. He engaged the enemy under John Stark's command at Bennington. As of 1777 neither Charles's father, then age fifty, nor his first son, Andrew, then age twenty-four, had ever left town under arms. In 1777 Deacon Thomas Davison, age fifty, sent the first member of his family to war. His oldest son, Thomas Davison Jr., age nineteen, enlisted, but his younger son, Charles Davison, age seventeen, remained at home as a reserve in Robbe's militia. Between 1778 and 1779, the two Davison brothers alternated in the service.[44]

The crisis forced some town leaders who had yet to serve to leave town under arms. In 1777 Samuel Cunningham, age thirty-nine, who had fought in the French and Indian War, and William Nay, age thirty-seven, mobilized for the first time. Cunningham and Nay were cousins by marriage. They were also related by marriage to Peterborough's Taggart and Swan families. In addition, Cunningham was the brother-in-law of militia captain Alexander Robbe, as well as the brother of James Cunningham, former town selectman and, later in 1779, a member of the Committee of Safety. Nay, the son of town founder Deacon William Nay, was elected a selectman in 1775 and 1776 and elected church elder in 1778, a post he held until his death in 1810. Nay and Cunningham may have been responsible for persuading William McKean, a newcomer to town, to join the fight against Burgoyne. McKean was Cunningham's brother-in-law and the brother of James McKean, who had died in early 1776 after serving in Washington's army holding Boston under siege. Military service rendered by Cunningham and Nay illustrated both the community's expectation that town leaders serve and the role of kin networks in recruiting soldiers.[45]

Many families that had already provided men for the army in 1775 and 1776 contributed more soldiers in 1777. Jeremiah Smith, and brother James, ages seventeen and twenty-one, respectively, followed their brothers John and Robert, who had served successively in 1775 and 1776, into the militia; Jeremiah and James were joined by their cousin Thomas Smith, age twenty-one, also a new recruit. Other established families such as the Swans, Whites, and Scotts contributed more family members to the military, including twelve-year-old John (known later as "Honorable John") Scott, the son of Long Bill Scott, who enlisted as a fifer in his father's company. Also in 1777, homesteader William

Pay Roll of part of Col Enoch Hale Regiment which Regiment Marched from the State of New Hampshire June 29th 1777 Under the command of Lt Col Thomas Heald to reinforce the Garrison at Ticonderoga

Names	Rank			Rate pr Month	Amount							
Alexander Robbe	Capt	June 29 July 3	5	12.0.0	2.0.0	15	0.10.0	2.10.0				
Sam Cunningham	Sergt	do	do	5	4.18	16.4	50	1.0.10	1.17.2			
Charles Stuart	do	do	do	5	4.18	16.4	50	1.0.10	1.17.2			
John White Sen	private	do	do	5	4.10	15	50	1.0.10	1.15.10			
Jonathan Wheelock	do	do	do	5	do	15	50	1.0.10	1.15.10			
James Mitchell	do	do	July 4	14	do	2.2.0	100	2.1.8	4.3.8			
Adam Gragg	do	do	3	5	do	15	50	1.0.10	1.15.10			
Robert Swan	do	do	3	5	do	15	50	0.0.0				
William Swan	do	do	3	5	do	15	50	1.0.10	1.15.10			
Thomas Bell	do	do	3	5	do	15	50	1.0.10	1.15.10			
David Ames	do	do	3	5	do	15	50	1.0.10	1.15.10			
Saml Mitchel	do	do	3	5	do	15	50	1.0.10	1.15.10			
Saml Morse	do	do	3	5	do	15	50	1.0.10	1.15.10			
Joseph Miller	do	do	3	5	do	15	50	1.0.10	1.15.10			
James Smith	do	do	3	5	do	15	50	1.0.10	1.15.10			
William Scott	do	do	3	5	do	15	50	1.0.10	1.15.10			
Saml Houston	do	do	3	5	do	15	50	1.0.10	1.15.10			
Isaac Houston	do	do	3	5	do	15	50	1.0.10	1.15.10			
John Morrison	do	do	3	5	do	15	50	1.0.10	1.15.10			
Thomas Morrison	do	do	3	5	do	15	50	1.0.10	1.15.10			

The payroll for the men from Peterborough who enlisted in Captain Alexander Robbe's company, Colonel Enoch Hale's regiment which marched to reinforce the garrison at Ticonderoga. They mobilized on 29 June and disbanded on 3 July when it was learned that the fort had fallen to the British. This was the second time that year that John White Sr. mustered to fight the British. He would march again that fall. Jonathan Wheelock Sr. enlisted for the first time under Robbe. *Courtesy, New Hampshire Division of Records, Management and Archives.*

Scott, age sixty-four, bore arms for the first time as he marched with Robbe's militia company to Stillwater, New York.[46]

The crisis attracted some youths to service whose parents had sheltered them from the war. In July Jeremiah Smith left the safety of his studies at Harvard to fight Burgoyne. His father, William Smith, a town founder and leading citizen, forbade Jeremiah to enlist. William probably believed that the family had contributed enough men to the war effort. One of his sons had served briefly in 1775. In 1776 another son was in the battle of White Plains. In late June 1777, a third son spent five days marching to and from Charlestown, New Hampshire expecting to join the fight against Burgoyne.

Despite his father's objections, Jeremiah enlisted in Col. Moses Nichols's state regiment. Nevertheless, William refused to let Jeremiah leave home until his son's captain promised "that if the company went into action the boy should be excused" from battle. Disobeying his father's wishes and his captain's orders, Jeremiah fought in the battle of Bennington. He was part of an advanced guard that was ambushed by the side of a brook while filling their canteens. Four men were riddled with musket balls and a fifth, John Robbe of Peterborough, was badly wounded. Jeremiah was nearly killed by a shot that gashed his throat and left a scar that lasted for years. After Jeremiah returned from Bennington, none of William's sons left town under arms, possibly because of Jeremiah's brush with death and because of his father's belief that having sent four sons to war, the family had done enough fighting.[47]

The crisis in 1777 failed to produce the same resolve among new recruits as had comparable crises in 1775 and 1776. Measured by the number of days served (see table A), and despite a British invasion lasting nearly eight months, Peterborough's new enlistees served an average of two and a half months in 1777. By contrast soldiers who first enlisted in either 1775 or 1776 had served an average of seven and six months, respectively, during their first enlistments. Moreover, proportionately fewer men who first enlisted in 1777 reenlisted after the crisis ended that fall, and most of those who reenlisted responded to the "alarms" (British raids and threatened attacks that continued through 1780) close to home. Just over 50 percent (eighteen of thirty-four) of the first-time enlistees in 1777 remained in service after 1777 or reenlisted in subsequent years. By contrast nearly 80 percent of the townsmen who first enlisted in either 1775 or 1776 continued in service or reenlisted in subsequent years.

The crisis, which swept up newcomers and forced families to dig deeper into their kin networks for soldiers, may have enlisted many men who were the least physically or psychologically fit for soldiering. Some youths, such as Jeremiah Smith, probably enlisted from a sense of patriotism, adventure, and from anxiety resulting from Burgoyne's invasion. Following his brief adventure as a soldier Jeremiah resumed his studies in preparation for a career as a lawyer. In general, Burgoyne's invasion mobilized new recruits who fought to repel the attackers and who then returned to civilian life after the immediate British threat to their homes ended. Most of these recruits reenlisted only when the threat was close to home. By the end of 1777, the majority of townsmen who had taken up arms had seen their last action. Those who formed the hard-core troops beyond 1777 consisted of a band of veterans who had enlisted in 1775 or 1776 and a handful of men who first enlisted in 1777.

Between 1778 and 1780, as the war shifted to the middle and southern states, only thirteen Peterborough residents became new recruits, bringing the town's total to one hundred servicemen by war's end (see table B). Kinship, friendship, birth order, and links to military units continued to determine enlistment patterns, as illustrated by recruits John Scott, David Scott, and Samuel Spear. The town relied upon such youths from established families to fill military ranks. In 1778, two Scott cousins enlisted in the Continental Army. Capt. Short Bill Scott recruited his son, John, age fourteen or fifteen, to serve as his company's fifer. In 1778 Capt. Long Bill Scott recruited his son David, age fifteen, to be his company's drummer, and Samuel Spear, age sixteen, likely David's friend, to serve in the infantry. David was reunited with his brother, Honorable John, and his cousin Thomas Scott in Long Bill's company.[48]

Community expectations that its leaders serve in the army continued to produce recruits. James Cunningham felt these pressures. In 1774 Cunningham was elected to the office of tithingman. In 1775 he advanced in Peterborough's political structure by being elected one of its selectman. The absence of military service, however, diminished his status as a leader. He held no town office between 1776 and 1778, despite a general pattern of townsmen reelecting officials. In 1778 Cunningham, age thirty-four, enlisted under his brother Samuel who commanded a company of New Hampshire troops sent to Rhode Island to reinforce Continental regiments near Newport. Samuel, age forty, was a veteran of the French and Indian War and a prominent town leader. He had served as selectman in 1768 and in 1776. In 1775 Samuel was Peterborough's representative to the Provincial Congress. Samuel had fought at Bennington and had been present at Burgoyne's surrender near Saratoga. In August 1778 Samuel and James returned from Rhode Island after three weeks' service. In

1779 James resumed his rise among town leaders when he was elected to Peterborough's Committee of Safety.[49]

New recruits continued to come from established families that contributed sons who came of military age or who had previously been spared service. For example, in 1777 Thomas Davison first enlisted at age nineteen to defend Fort Ticonderoga. In 1779 his brother Charles, age nineteen, enlisted for the first time. Charles served for three weeks in Rhode Island. In 1780 Thomas, then age twenty-two, returned to service for three months with the Continental Army at West Point while Charles stayed home. Other men such as John White Jr., age thirty-one, took their turn under arms. White's brother and four cousins had marched with Samuel Cunningham in 1778. A fifth cousin had served in the Continental Army in 1776 and had enlisted in a state regiment that engaged Burgoyne the following year. In 1779 John White Jr. enlisted for the first time for three weeks' service in Rhode Island.[50] Households continued to serve as recruiting agencies that rotated sons in and out of service.[51]

By 1780 most men with military experience chose to stay close to home as the war moved to the southern states. Fighting far from home was left to the hard-core soldiers who first saw action in 1775, 1776, and 1777. Rarely did the town hire strangers, as it did in 1779 when it recruited "transhant" Zaccheus Brooks, to help fill the town's quota of Continental soldiers.[52] By war's end Peterborough had sent nearly two thirds of its available manpower into service for various periods of enlistment either to the credit of their own town or to the credit of other communities. And yet, it was a smaller group of hard-core soldiers in the Continental Army who formed the mainstay of the country's war effort. A closer examination of the Scott, Blair, Alld families reveals deeper insights into the connections between households, kin networks, Peterborough's culture, and military service.

SCOTT FAMILY

The Scotts were self-made men who had become well established in the middle ranks of their communities before the war. In the 1730s the Scott brothers—John (1706–98), William (1713–95), and Alexander (c. 1715–87)—migrated from Ireland to Massachusetts. They were followed in the 1750s by a nephew, William (1743–1815), who was later known as Short Bill Scott. The Scotts first settled in Lancaster, Massachusetts, where Alexander married Margaret Robbe, whose family helped to settle Peterborough and whose brother, Alexander Robbe, later became the town's militia captain. Between 1734 and 1758, the

Scott brothers lived variously between the Massachusetts towns of Lancaster, Townsend, and Lunenburg and the New Hampshire towns of Dublin and Peterborough.[53]

Although beginning modestly, the Scotts succeeded economically. In the 1740s William (1713–95) had homesteaded land which by 1775 had become a thriving farm. His brother Alexander was even more successful. In 1758 and 1759, after living for a time in Dublin, a town bordering Peterborough, he bought 220 acres in Peterborough. In 1761 he sold one hundred acres, possibly indicating that Scott was either speculating in land or raising capital for his Peterborough farm.[54] Alexander's son William (1742–96), nicknamed Long Bill Scott, added to the family's success. In 1762, at age twenty, he married Phoebe Woods, age twenty, of Groton, Massachusetts. She was a descendant of one of Massachusetts's founding families. The newlyweds lived briefly with Phoebe's parents in Groton, where their first child, David, was born in 1763. By 1765 they moved to Dublin, New Hampshire, where they lived on John Gleason's farm. Long Bill and likely his father, Alexander, were among the men who founded Dublin. While in Dublin Phoebe and Bill had their second child, John (later Honorable John), born in 1765. In 1783 Phoebe's tenth and last child was born on the family farm in Peterborough.[55]

Alexander's nephew Short Bill Scott contributed to the family's growing prominence in Peterborough. In 1760, Short Bill moved from Dublin to Peterborough where, in 1763, he married Rosanna Tait. The following year they had the first of their four children, John. In the 1760s Short Bill and the other Scotts, including cousin Long Bill, bought and sold land in Peterborough. Generally they were identified as yeomen, although in 1767 William (probably Short Bill) was also referred to as a "Schoolmaster" in his deed for fifty acres of land in Peterborough.[56]

The Scotts established themselves as military leaders. Two brothers, Alexander and William, fought in the French and Indian War, the former with Rogers's Rangers and the latter in the expedition to Crown Point, New York. Long Bill Scott served two enlistments in that war. In 1760 Long Bill served with his brother David, age sixteen, who died the same year from smallpox contracted while in service. In 1761 Long Bill enlisted a second time for eight months, possibly in the same regiment as his cousin Short Bill Scott.[57]

The Scotts were enterprising, ambitious, and active in Peterborough. Short Bill ran a store from his house and was a leader in the local militia. Long Bill was a farmer and shoemaker anxious to make his mark in the world. They were involved in running and building the town. Between 1762 and 1775, William Scott, possibly one of the two "Bills," and John Scott held six minor town offices, including constable and hogreeve.[58] John, Alexander, and William (probably their brother) were among the town's signers of a 1767 petition to Governor Benning Wentworth to create a new county and shire town. John and William were also among the residents who petitioned Governor Wentworth in 1774 to enlarge town borders by taking land belonging to the town of Jaffrey.[59]

Just before the war, Alexander Scott moved about twenty miles west to Stoddard, New Hampshire, taking two of his sons, Alexander and James, with him. They were among Stoddard's founders. Once again the Scotts were involved in developing a new town as they had been in Dublin and Peterborough. Alexander's son Long Bill remained on the family's Peterborough farm. Despite the move, father and sons kept close ties as did all the Scott kin.

In April 1775 Short Bill Scott led the town's militia company to Boston. His cousin, Long Bill Scott, later recalled that he agreed to join Short Bill's company only if appointed an officer. Ambition for military rank, desire for higher social status, and possibly revolutionary ideals inspired Long Bill to take up arms. He told chronicler Peter Oliver after the war: "I was very ambitious & did not like to see [neighbors] . . . who were no better than myself . . . above me. I was asked to enlist, as a private Soldier. My Ambition was too great for so low a Rank; I offered to enlist upon having a Lieutenants Commission; which was granted." Scott stated that he would risk death in battle for a "Chance to rise higher [in rank]."[60] Community prominence as active citizens, military leadership, and, for one brother at least, the ambition to rise higher in the world led the two Scotts to war.

Both cousins served for the entire war. Their long service resulted from a combination of factors: high status as officers, the war's politicizing effect, and attraction to military life. Long Bill Scott, the shoemaker and yeoman farmer, became Captain Scott "Esquire" or "Gentleman." He continued to use this title after the war. His cousin Short Bill also raised his social status. In 1769, when selling fifty acres of land, Short Bill was identified as "yeoman" Scott. In 1777 when he sold his shop and a small parcel of land he was Capt. Scott, "Gentleman."[61] The ambitious Scotts had achieved greater prominence in town as Continental officers, patriots, and military leaders.[62]

In all, twelve of thirteen Scotts of military age, representing three generations living in Peterborough and nearby towns, took up arms; seven Scotts served in the Continental Army. In 1775 Long Bill's son Honorable John, age ten, and Short Bill's son John, age eleven, served their fathers as waiters. Later, both boys enlisted on their own in the Continental Army.[63] Other family members served in the army as well. In 1777 David Scott, age fifteen, enlisted in his father's (Short Bill's) company as a drummer for the town of Attleboro, Massachusetts. In 1781 he reenlisted for a second three-year term for Townsend, Massachusetts. David was described as a "farmer," who was 5'9" in height with "blue eyes," a "light complexion," and "dark hair." He died in 1782, possibly of camp fever, after six years of service.

Judging from their enlistments, the Scotts made no distinction between service in the Continental Army and other military units. Some family members, such as Alexander Scott of Stoddard, New Hampshire, and his son James served only in local militia companies and state regiments. In 1777, Peterborough's William Scott, age sixty-four, the homesteader, marched with Alexander Robbe's militia company to repel Burgoyne's invasion. In September 1777, William reenlisted in Col. Daniel Moore's state troops, which reinforced the army opposing Burgoyne at Stillwater. His son David had served in 1775 under Short Bill and later as a sergeant in the state unit raised in 1780 to repel a Tory raid on Royalton, Vermont. William's two other sons, Thomas and William Jr., served in the Continental Army.[64]

By war's end twelve Scotts had collectively contributed about forty years of military service in Continental, state, and militia units. They were hard-core fighters from well-established and aspiring families who were mobilized into service through their kin network. For some, military service became one more avenue to improve their social status and standing as community leaders. For most, the war was a family affair involving fathers, sons, and cousins serving, often together, in militia, state, and Continental Army units. Furthermore, the Scotts' service was part of the enlistment pattern of their kin network, which included the Robbes, Cunninghams, Nays, Taggarts, and Swans. Three men from the Taggart family and two from the Swan family, both part of Peterborough's establishment, contributed soldiers to the Continental Army.[65] Republican creed differentiating regulars and militia had no meaning to the Scotts and their kin. Whether serving in the Continental Army or in other units, the Scott clan appeared to perceive themselves as citizen-soldiers.

THE BLAIR FAMILY

The Blairs, in contrast to the Scotts, were on the fringe of Peterborough's society. Although the Blairs had arrived in Peterborough in 1763, John Blair remained a landless artisan who had apparently not secured a place in town society by the start of the war. In 1775 the Blair family occupied Peterborough's lower social layer.

John Blair Sr., was born in 1717 and in his youth lived in Groton, Massachusetts, where he worked as a cooper. His 1744 marriage to Nancy Brown of Boston produced three children: Mary (1749–1833), William (1750–1825), and John "2d" (1763–1824). In 1753, John Sr. tried to settle in New Hampshire. He agreed to purchase a sixty-four-acre lot from the proprietors of New Ipswich, a town a few miles south of Peterborough. The deal apparently collapsed.[66] About 1763 John moved to Peterborough where he continued his cooper's trade and farmed rented land. Following his wife's death, possibly during childbirth in 1763, John remarried and had at least five more children by his second wife, Mary Freeman.[67]

Prior to the Revolution, neither John nor son William held a town office. John was not among the town signers of 1767 and 1774 petitions to Governor Wentworth to establish a new county and to add to town land at Jaffrey's expense. He did not sign the 1771 petition censuring the Reverend John Morrison.[68] John Blair Sr. was an artisan who resided in Peterborough but had not yet planted deep roots.

The Revolutionary War was a family affair for the Blairs as it was for most Peterborough households. John Blair Sr. and his sons, William and John 2d served a total of 2,876 days in the militia, various state regiments, and the Continental Army. John Sr.'s patriotism, or zest for combat, and hardy constitution were evident in his service record. On 19 April 1775, he marched under Short Bill Scott's command to Boston and reenlisted on 23 April in Captain Scott's company of state troops. Although not at Bunker Hill, Blair volunteered to join Benedict Arnold's expedition against Quebec. John left his son William, age twenty-five, in charge of his father's household, which consisted of his other son, John 2d, age twelve, and John Sr.'s young wife, Mary, age twenty-six, and their three daughters who ranged in age from four to ten. Leaving his sons at home, John Sr. faced the risks of war without jeopardizing the economic survival of his household. William and his younger brother could sustain their father's household in case John was disabled or killed. Thus, father and sons were partners in war—John Sr. was freed from household duties to be a soldier and his sons were his insurance policy.

Military service strengthened ties between the Blairs and the community. In 1776 William, age twenty-five, became a member of Alexander Robbe's "training band," and his brother, John, a member of Robbe's "Alarm List." In June

1776 one of the Blairs signed the town's Association Test.[69] Military service also strengthened family ties. In 1777 the Blair family mobilized for war. John Sr. and William mustered into the local militia to repel Burgoyne's invasion. John Sr. age sixty, volunteered. William, age twenty-seven, was "hired" either by the town of Sharon or by a draftee unwilling to march with Sharon's militia. William received ten pounds, ten shillings for his brief service. Father and son were comrades at Bennington and witnessed Burgoyne's defeat at Stillwater.[70] In July 1777, John Blair 2d, age fourteen, followed his father and brother's example. He enlisted in Long Bill Scott's company as a drummer and credited his service, which lasted until the end of the war, to Peterborough's quota of troops. William's and John 2d's decisions to enlist were likely the result of the examples set by their father and by sons from leading town families who served in the army.

Bounties were another factor. It is probable that William used his first bounty as a down payment on land in Peterborough. In December 1777, after returning from duty, William purchased one hundred acres in Peterborough for £105.[71] A few months later he enlisted again for nine months' service in the Continental Army serving for the town of Townsend, Massachusetts (Peterborough's quota was filled). After returning home he probably applied his second bounty toward the purchase of his farm.

The Blair sons, possibly feeling family and community pressure to serve, combined patriotic duty with economic gain. One hired himself as a substitute in the militia, and both received bounties for serving in the Continental Army. After the war, John 2d moved to Newburgh, New York, where he had been stationed during the war. There he became an established member of the community.[72] William remained in Peterborough on his newly purchased farm.[73]

BENJAMIN ALLD

Benjamin Alld was a Continental Army veteran who had served four years during the darkest days of the war. In 1816, having separated from his wife and child and failing to sustain himself as a day laborer, Alld, age fifty-seven, became a pauper.[74] That year Peterborough's selectmen auctioned Alld to a local resident who agreed to receive ninety-six cents a week from the town toward the veteran's care. Possibly for this reason, John Shy cited Alld as one of the town's soldiers who was "near the bottom of the socioeconomic ladder" when he enlisted.[75] Despite impoverishment in his fifties, Alld was not born poor. Rather, he was from a wealthy and prominent local family. By 1816 the veteran Alld became a déclassé relic of the Revolutionary War, having fallen from high status and wealth to pauperism.

Benjamin's father, William Alld, was born in 1723 in Armagh, Ireland. In 1740 his family was among the thousands of Scotch-Irish immigrants who moved to New England. The Allds settled in Dunstable, Massachusetts. In 1746 William, age twenty-three, married Lettice Caldwell, age eighteen, and the following year the couple moved to Merrimack, New Hampshire, one of the many Scotch-Irish communities established in the south-central portion of the province. A brother, David Alld, and another relative, John Alld, and their families also moved to Merrimack. In 1747 William Jr., the first of William's ten children (five males and five females), was born. The last of William's children, Samuel, was born in 1766.

By 1767 William had acquired substantial holdings in the region and was known as "Gentleman" William Alld. In 1767 he ranked in the top 10 percent of Merrimack's ratepayers (fourth out of sixty-four). In addition to farming, William appeared to be a land speculator. Farming and land sales kept Alld at the top of the town's growing list of ratepayers. In 1773 he ranked ninth out of Merrimack's 113 taxpayers. William was also a leader of the town. He held numerous public offices including that of selectman. In 1775 he became the captain of the town militia, which added military prestige to his esteemed social rank of Gentleman. William Alld was at the top of Merrimack's social, political, economic, and military structure.[76]

William provided amply for his children to sustain their high status. By 1775, at age fifty-two, he had accumulated land for his children, including Benjamin, then age sixteen. Throughout the war, William apparently strengthened his economic position by liquidating some of his holdings to purchase other property at bargain prices. In 1777, he sold his Merrimack farm, which included a sawmill, for £1,500. The following year he sold one of his farms in nearby Amherst for £150. He also sold his church pews in Amherst and Merrimack when he moved to Peterborough, where he had purchased farms for himself, his sons, and his daughters.[77]

In 1778 William purchased more land in Peterborough by buying property the town had confiscated for back taxes and then sold at rock-bottom prices at public auction.[78] Throughout the war, William Alld and son James bought and sold land in Peterborough and in nearby towns. William included his other sons in the family land business when they came of age. Just after the war, his youngest son, Samuel, became involved in the family's extensive land dealings.[79]

In 1779 the Alld family solidified their status in Peterborough when William's daughter Jean married Robert Swan, the son of town founder Gustavus Swan. Robert was also well established in Peterborough. He had inherited his father's farm and was considered a man "of superior abilities [who became] one of the most influential men in town."[80] In 1783 William insured financial security for another daughter, Hannah, and her husband, Michael Dalton of Londonderry, New Hampshire, by giving her two hundred acres of land in Peterborough for "goodwill and affection." William and his wife, Lettice, had provided for their children by giving them farms and other advantages expected from a prosperous and prominent family.[81]

Besides being a successful businessman and generous parent, William was one of Peterborough's officials. In 1779 and 1781, townsmen appointed him to settle the wages it owed soldiers. In 1782 the town made Alld part of the committee reviewing the proposed state constitution. In 1783 and 1784 he was elected as the town's treasurer and then, in 1785 and 1786, was elected tithing-man; he also served for a number of years as surveyor of roads.[82]

True to the pattern exhibited by community leaders, the Alld family contributed sons to the war effort. Two of its four sons of military age, Benjamin and William Jr. (1747–90), served in the Continental Army. Two other sons of military age, James and John, did not serve. James was probably the family's insurance policy to sustain its enterprises in case his brothers Benjamin and William Jr. were killed or disabled while in service. Throughout the war, James (1751–?) assisted his father on their farm and with land purchases, which added to the family's fortunes. John, however, age eighteen in 1775, may have been incapable of service, possibly because he was weak or disabled. John never received land, was not involved in any land transactions, and he lived at home, unmarried, until his death in 1790 at the age of thirty-three. William's last son, Samuel, was too young to fight. He was only nine years old in 1775.

Coming from a wealthy family, neither Benjamin nor William, Jr. enlisted for economic reasons as had the Blairs. Their service probably reflected the combination of community expectations that prominent families contribute manpower to the war, politicization while in service, and the influence of the Scotts. Benjamin served in the same regiment as Long Bill Scott who attracted many townsmen into the army.[83]

Benjamin Alld, like many townsmen, served several enlistments in various units of the Revolutionary army. In the fall of 1776 he mustered into one of New Hampshire's state regiments that was sent to New York to reinforce Washington's beleaguered army. Benjamin returned in December, a veteran of the battle at White Plains. Shortly thereafter, Alld became a hard-core soldier. In July 1777 he enlisted for three years in Henry Jackson's Massachusetts regiment, which included Long Bill Scott's company. With other Peterborough residents in that regiment, such as John Blair 2d and Hon. John Scott, Alld participated in the army's 1778 campaigns at Philadelphia and Monmouth, in its 1779 Rhode Island campaign, and its 1780 defense of New Jersey.[84]

The brutality and hardships of war apparently troubled Alld. In May 1779 he deserted but returned to service that October under a pardon. He completed his service in July 1780 and was honorably discharged.[85] In October 1781 he mustered for the last time in a New Hampshire state regiment that spent two months reinforcing Continental troops at West Point. By war's end, Alld had spent nearly four years under arms in either the Continental Army or state regiments. He had fought in some of the war's major engagements and had experienced the hardships of combat and the miseries common among Continental troops.

IN SUMMARY, THE town's war effort was most intense in 1775. In 1775 about 40 percent of the men at risk of service were under arms sometime that year. More important, those men who first enlisted in 1775 accounted for nearly half of the total days served by Peterborough's soldiers between 1776 and 1783 (see table C). Most representative of the community in 1775, those soldiers continued to shape the character of Peterborough's contribution to the Revolutionary army throughout the war. Fourteen of the town's thirty-one Continental soldiers were part of that *rage militaire.*

In general, Peterborough's war effort varied with the ebb and flow of the war. New enlistments declined in 1776 following the British evacuation of Boston. Enlistments peaked in 1777 after scores of townsmen rushed into the field that summer to repulse Burgoyne's invasion of New York and Vermont. After 1778 the town's war effort depended upon retaining men already in service and persuading veterans to reenlist. Only thirteen of the town's one hundred soldiers enlisted for the first time between 1778 and 1782. Beginning in 1780, the year that enlistments expired for most who joined the Continental Army in 1777, the town's war effort dropped precipitously. By 1782 the war was virtually over and only the most hardened troops remained in service. By war's end, many townsmen had served alternately in militia companies, in state regiments, or in Continental Army units.[86]

The view prominent in the Revolutionary generation, and in claims made by modern historians, that the Continental Army was unrepresentative of society fails to materialize when all of Peterborough's soldiers are examined within the context of their households and community.[87] Whether serving in the Continental Army, state regiments, or militia, Peterborough's enlistees represented a cross section of the community. Some men were on the margin of the town's society, a few were transients, and two were possibly former slaves.[88] Most recruits, however, came from families such as Smith, Morison, Miller, Ferguson, Scott, Blair, and Alld. These soldiers were sons of well-to-do farmers, immigrant settlers, and homesteaders who by the time of the Revolution had established positions in the town's social, political, and economic structure.[89] That the young soldiers would lack wealth or property was a function of their age or perhaps their lower position in the birth order among males in their households, not their class.

Service was not stigmatized by class. Many townsmen served alternately in militia companies, in state regiments, or in Continental units. Six factors accounted for enlistments. First, kinship was probably the most important factor. Enlistments followed family lines. Once a family member left town under arms, others, including fathers, sons, brothers, cousins, and in-laws, could be expected to enlist. Second, high social status influenced enlistment. Town leaders or their children and those aspiring to leadership were expected to serve in the military.

Third, confidence in local commanders produced enlistments. Many Peterborough residents served either with Captain Short Bill Scott or with his cousin Captain Long Bill Scott. Many mobilized under the town's militia captain, Alexander Robbe.[90] All three captains were town founders, veterans of the French and Indian War, and seasoned officers. Thus townsmen clustered around experienced and trusted officers whose units contained relatives, friends, and neighbors. Bounty payments did not cause Peterborough enlistments to shift to the lower sorts in the community. Rather, financial rewards were conventional, and thus expected, when responding to kin, peer, and community expectations to serve.

Fourth, demography affected enlistments. The army recruited young men. Peterborough had a large pool of men between ages sixteen and twenty-five, the prime military ages. Consequently, fathers and older townsmen of military age were under less pressure to enlist because they could send young sons to war. Fifth, the war's changing character motivated townsmen to enlist. Conflict close to home aroused many men to arms. During both the *rage militaire* in 1775 and the British invasion of New England in 1777, a large portion of the men in the community bore arms. As the conflict became a long and dirty war, from 1777 to 1782, recruits came from the manpower pool of newcomers, veteran soldiers, and young men from the town's established families. A handful of "hired" men came from the manpower pool of friends, relatives, transients, and possibly former slaves. Sixth, the war politicized soldiers and stiffened their resolve, particularly those who fought in 1775 and 1776. Many of the men who saw action early in the war became hard-core troops. They frequently re-enlisted when there was a call to arms. To recall, over half (eighteen of thirty-one) of the town residents who served in the Continental Army first enlisted in either 1775 or 1776.

Viewed as a whole, Peterborough mobilized households, kinship networks, and the community to fight a people's war.[91] Nevertheless, Peterborough's Continentals carried the brunt of the town's war effort. They averaged 1,369 days of service compared to an average of 190 days of service for the town's sixty-nine soldiers who did not enlist in the army. The meaning of the people's war was quite different to these two groups. Peterborough's Continental soldiers were in the thick of the conflict. Most served in Captain Long Bill Scott's company, in Henry Jackson's Massachusetts regiment, or in Short Bill Scott's company in the First New Hampshire Regiment, which participated in Washington's victories at Trenton and Princeton in December 1776. Both Jackson's and the First New Hampshire regiment took part in the 1777 northern campaign that included the American loss of Fort Ticonderoga and Burgoyne's surrender at Saratoga. They suffered casualties. In the victorious battle of Bemis Heights, September 1777, Short Bill Scott's left hand was wounded by a rifle shot. His little finger was surgically amputated and his left hand grotesquely maimed. Peterborough's soldiers endured exposure and malnutrition at Valley Forge in the winters of 1777 and 1778. They engaged in Washington's 1778 Pennsylvania campaign and the June 1778 battle at Monmouth, New Jersey. In August 1779 New Hampshire troops fought the Iroquois at the Battle of New Town where four men from their regiment were killed and seventy-two wounded. After 1779 the Massachusetts and New Hampshire regiments encamped in the Hudson Highlands to protect that vital juncture against English attack and raids by outlaws.

Some experienced the virtual collapse of military discipline that resulted from the government's neglect of the army. In 1778, following the battle of Monmouth, Short Bill Scott was wounded during a mutiny by Pennsylvania troops who rioted against the government's failure to provide food, clothing, shelter, and pay. Scott was bayoneted in the back, "the bayonet penetrating to the lumbar vertebra." The offender was sentenced to death but Washington rescinded the sentence at Scott's request.[92]

Scott, like many officers and men, deeply resented the disdain, suspicion, and hostility toward them that resulted from republican anti-army ideology. They were outraged by the government's withholding of supplies from the army. A 1779 petition to the state legislature from New Hampshire's Continental officers, including Short Bill Scott, claimed that the public's failure to adequately pay troops, especially officers, threatened to undermine the war effort. Scott and the other officers stated in the petition that they had "patiently endured the Loss of Domestic Happiness and the Pleasures of social Life neglecting their own private Interest . . . [and had] endured Losses, Sickness and every Species of Hardship" to secure "Peace, Liberty and Safety" for future generations. The petition stated that the officers were forced to choose between duty to support their families and duty to their country. They demanded additional pay to continue the struggle against Great Britain. They grieved that, "Pay once liberal is become of little Value [and] our Families [are] starving. . . ." Without additional compensation, Scott and the other officers concluded, they would be "compelled to sacrifice our all, beggar our Families, ruin our constitutions, and hasten old Age upon ourselves. . . ." They swore loyalty to the cause and pleaded with the legislature for "Justice, Equity" to save them from poverty and to prevent them from being "morally condemned" because they had failed to support their families.[93]

Scott and the other officers blamed their plight partly on venal citizens. The petition accused profiteers of endangering the army's fight for independence by weakening its ability to buy supplies. Scott and his comrades complained that "Gentlemen of Rank" refused to accept Continental currency and plotted to depreciate it further for their own gain. The officers charged that such "People who would be thought virtuous, honest and religious" were corrupt.[94] The officers feared that the profiteers' venality and self-interest were spreading to the people as whole. After the war, some, like Scott, harbored bitter memories of the neglect and hostility they had suffered at the hands of the people they had sought to free from British rule. Officers like Scott came to believe that only the army's few, brave, hard-core troops stood between victory and defeat. In their minds they had saved the people from their own vices and had won the people's war.

CHAPTER 2

Revolutionary War Veterans in Peterborough

VETERANS RETURNING TO Peterborough, or moving there following the war became part of a rapidly growing community. Peterborough's population increased 300 percent between 1767 and 1800, from 443 to 1,333 inhabitants. Most of that growth occurred between 1790 and 1800. Shortly after 1800 the town's population began to stabilize at about 1,500 people.[1]

In addition to rapid growth, the town's population changed in three other ways. First, the proportion of the younger population declined relative to the middle and older population groups. For example, in 1790, people age thirty and younger composed 66 percent of the population compared to 82 percent of that group in 1750. By 1800 the share of that age group dropped to 60.9 percent.[2]

Second, Peterborough experienced a large population turnover. Census and tax data show that a majority of household heads who appeared in these records in 1790 failed to appear on tax and census lists in 1800. For example, the 1790 federal census (the nation's first) recorded 134 Peterborough household heads. In 1800, eighty-three of those heads or 63 percent failed to appear in the 1800 federal census for the town. A comparison of the 1792 tax list (the first found for the town) and the 1800 tax list revealed an attrition rate nearly that recorded in the federal census. Specifically, 97 of 189 ratepayers found on the 1792 tax list were not found on the 1800 list, an attrition of 51 percent.

Third, by 1800, three distinct population strata appeared. One stratum, about a quarter of the household heads, was composed of town founders or

early settlers. A second stratum, which represented about a third of the household heads, consisted of newcomers who moved to town sometime between
1790 and 1800. The remaining group, about 40 percent, consisted of the sons of
household heads recorded in the 1790 census. They had become household
heads in 1800 because of the deaths of their fathers, possession of the family
homestead, or acquisition of farms of their own. By 1800 the founders and their
heirs continued to dominate the town's population structure.[3]

Beside population growth and the creation of a more complex social structure, veterans witnessed a new liberal spirit in the religion of the town. At the
turn of the century, most townsmen abandoned their Presbyterian church to
embrace Congregationalism, antinomian doctrine, and then, in 1826, Unitar-
ianism. In the 1820s, other denominations, Baptists, Methodists, and Presbyterians, established churches in town. Religious pluralism replaced the founders'
sectarian conformity.[4]

Furthermore, the Revolutionary generation and their heirs abandoned the
founders' localism to embrace nationalism. In 1788 the town had voted against
the ratification of the federal Constitution. By 1800 townsmen were deeply
involved in the partisan politics of state and national government. Veterans
lived in a community where the Federalist party dominated.[5]

Veterans were part of an increasingly prosperous community. Townsmen
embraced rural capitalism. Following the postwar depression, Peterborough
residents resumed their trade in Boston's agricultural, commodity, and financial markets. In 1796 small manufacturing shops opened, which stimulated
economic diversity. The full weight of the economic changes was felt in the
early nineteenth century. Peterborough's principal capital assets—its developed
farms—were used to secure liquid capital for major investments in textile mills.
These mills, begun in 1808, exploited the town's river power, provided employment for the town's growing population, and encouraged specialization of
mechanical, commercial, and manufacturing talents. By 1820 the town was
deeply enmeshed in the region's expanding manufacturing economy.[6]

Within this context of great change Peterborough's veterans made their
lives. By the turn of the nineteenth century, in terms of their economic and
social characteristics, those veterans who served briefly were indistinguishable
from their peers who had not served. Generally, these two groups occupied the
upper strata in town society. On the other hand, the town's Continental Army
veterans generally occupied a lower economic level than others in their generation (see appendix B, table 1). These veterans generally occupied a tax bracket
that was one-third or one-half lower than their contemporaries. Furthermore,

between 1792 and 1807 about 50 percent of the town's Continental veterans paid taxes below the town's annual average of $5.50 per ratepayer. By contrast, only 10 percent of their age cohort paid less than that amount.

Although not a monolithic economic class—Honorable John Scott became and remained wealthy most of his life—most Continental veterans, such as Benjamin Alld and William Blair, tended toward the lower end of Peterborough's economic ladder. Furthermore, the personal and real wealth of Continental Army veterans, as measured in taxes paid, drooped considerably after 1813 in contrast to only a slight economic decline for others in their age cohort. By 1815 the taxable wealth of army veterans had declined to about half that reported by others in their cohort. By 1820 the economic gap had widened even more as Continental Army veterans dropped farther down the economic ladder while most men in their cohort retained their high rank among Peterborough's taxpayers. Nearly all of the Continentals (88 percent) had fallen below the town average in taxable estates. Through the second decade of the nineteenth century, Continental Army veterans were moving down the economic ladder while others in their cohort generally retained their place on its upper rungs (see appendix B, table 1).

Peterborough's Continental Army veterans were less involved politically in their community than were other members of their cohort. On the whole, army veterans occupied proportionately fewer town offices. Moreover, the few Continental veterans who held offices occupied minor positions such as a hogreeve or fence viewer. Veterans who had served only in the militia or state regiments and those who had not served at all were often elected to major town offices such as selectman, moderator, and representative to the General Court. For example, in 1801 more than 91 percent of the offices held by men from the Revolutionary generation were divided between former militiamen (39 percent) and peers who did not serve (52 percent). (See appendix B, table 2.) In 1801 men from these two groups also shared the town's major offices. Continental Army veterans, by contrast, held only two minor offices. This pattern of office holding remained constant throughout the early nineteenth century.

Differences in household structure also distinguished Peterborough's Continental veterans from others in their cohort. Although men of that generation married in their early and mid-twenties, Continental Army veterans had fewer children (see appendix B, tables 3 and 4). Their households contained an average of six children compared to an average of more than seven children in households of men who served briefly or not at all (appendix B, table 4).

Thus, Peterborough's veterans were roughly divided into two groups. Veterans who had served only in the militia or state troops were virtually indistinguishable from their cohort who never enlisted. They sired about the same number of children. They occupied the same economic bracket, which was well above the average townsman. They were actively involved in the community as measured by elected offices, including leadership positions.

Continental Army veterans differed from that group in several ways. These veterans sired fewer children. They held fewer town offices. They occupied a lower economic bracket, and, as they aged, they slipped farther and more rapidly down the economic ladder. The lives of Peterborough's Continental Army veterans—Benjamin Alld, William Diamond, William Blair, Randall McAllister, Christopher Thayer—illustrated these features. Their lives, when contrasted with veterans from the Smith and Morison families who served in the militia and state regiments, would confirm the belief that military service had disadvantaged Continental Army veterans. Moreover, as we will see, the lives of Peterborough's Continental veterans would validate the image of the suffering soldier and the public's sentiment of gratitude. Aging, infirm, and sliding into poverty, these men would also affirm the justice of honoring, rewarding, and comforting them with pensions.

BENJAMIN ALLD

Following the war Benjamin Alld remained in Peterborough, where he enjoyed the advantages of his family's growing wealth and prominence. He appeared to be on the same track toward success enjoyed by his father and brothers. In 1784 Benjamin, age twenty-five, identified himself as a "husbandman," successfully petitioned the state compensation for his depreciated soldiers' pay, and began dabbling in real estate. However, within a few years Alld's life crumbled. As a result Alld's father lost confidence in his son's ability to sustain the family's property.[7]

William refused to entrust Benjamin with his estate when a series of family misfortunes made the veteran the heir apparent to his father's wealth and business. In 1790, two of William Alld's sons died, William Jr., who had married in 1788 at age forty-one and had moved to Maine, died in an accident. In 1790, Benjamin's other brother, John, age thirty-three, died at his father's home, possibly after a lifetime of infirmity. Also about this time, James Alld, age thirty-nine, who had been his father's principal associate, moved from Peterborough. The reasons for the move are unknown. In 1795 William retired, but instead of deeding his farm to Benjamin, he granted it to his youngest son,

Samuel, age twenty-nine. William appeared to believe that Benjamin was incapable of providing for his parents' support. The deed required that Samuel keep the farm in good order, provide his parents with one-third of the farm's produce, enough wood "for one fire," and pay two-thirds of the household's taxes owed the town.[8]

Together, William and Samuel retained the family's high economic and political standing in town. In 1796 Samuel Alld and his father ranked in the town's top 10 percent of ratepayers. They were taxed $19.73 for five horses, twenty-five cows, four oxen, 6 planted acres, 12 acres mowed for fodder, 20 acres in pasture, 350 acres of undeveloped land, and £100 lent at interest. The loan indicated that they were involved in the region's expanding capital market. At the turn of the century, the Allds were successful at farming, investing, and speculating. After William's death in 1805 at age eighty-two, Samuel continued at the top of Peterborough's ratepayers as did other members of the family, except for Benjamin. Samuel's brother-in-law Robert Swan enjoyed an equally high economic rank and social prestige. In the early nineteenth century, the Allds were firmly placed in the upper tier of the town's economic, social, and political structure.

Benjamin, unlike brother Samuel, failed to live up to his inherited social and economic advantages. Nevertheless, Benjamin continued to enjoy his parents' love and financial support while they lived, and he was remembered in their wills. His father's will, prepared in 1790, and his mother's bequest following her death in 1807 named him as a beneficiary.[9] Despite these blessings, Benjamin's life shattered.

Benjamin's marriage dissolved. He had married Nancy White, daughter of John and Molly Wallace White, two of the town's early settlers, and had fathered a daughter. For unknown reasons, Benjamin separated from his wife and child. Beginning in the 1790s, Benjamin—then in his mid-thirties— apparently moved among several communities in New Hampshire and Maine. He remained a legal resident of Peterborough, where he may have lived with kin and worked as a day laborer. His transient life suggests alienation. By 1816 Benjamin, then on the verge of pauperism, was disowned by his family. By law and custom, either his brother Samuel or his sister Jean Alld Swan was required to support him. They were financially able to do so. Instead, they cut their ties with him and allowed Peterborough's selectmen to place Benjamin on the pauper's auction block, up for bid for the lowest cost for his care. Benjamin, once part of a wealthy and prominent family, once a Continental soldier, had sunk to the ignominy of an outcast and pauper. Alld's case was extreme, but such shattered lives would reinforce the public's sentiment that impoverished veterans deserved justice.[10]

PERHAPS MORE TYPICAL of the long-term effects of military service were the lives of Continental Army veterans William Diamond, who moved to Peterborough after the war; William Blair; and Randall McAllister. Unlike Alld, they came from modest origins and were successfully climbing the social and economic ladder prior to the Revolution. However, their wartime experiences appeared to change the course of their lives. None fell to the depths of Alld, however. Nevertheless, despite improvement in their economic rank, they remained below the level of their cohort. They did not become part of the town's political hierarchy. Although not alienated from society, as happened to Benjamin Alld, they tended to segregate themselves from the community. They occupied lower economic strata in the town and gravitated toward other veterans like themselves. Finally, they appeared to be more vulnerable to economic misfortune than other men their age.[11]

WILLIAM DIAMOND

William Diamond was born in 1755 in Boston. He apprenticed as a wheelwright, and at age nineteen moved to nearby Lexington where he presumably practiced his trade.[12] Diamond was the drummer under John Parker's command at Lexington. During Diamond's flight from the engagement he lost his drum, an episode immortalized in a poem and in the folklore of the battle. Diamond returned to action at Bunker Hill and remained in service through 1775. Diamond served long and numerous enlistments throughout the war. In January 1776 Diamond enlisted as a musician for one year in Washington's newly formed Continental Army. The roster reported that he was a small man, five foot five inches tall, and "dark." In the fall of 1776, he was with Washington's army during its defeats in New York and its retreat through New Jersey. Possibly he was among the troops who were stirred by Thomas Paine's immortal words, "These are the times that try men's souls," written on a cold and dreary day in December when the army was on the verge of collapse and the cause appeared to be lost. Diamond participated in Washington's spectacular victories at Trenton and Princeton that December. Diamond's patriotic fervor was probably heightened as a result of those triumphs. He remained under arms through July 1777. In July 1780 he was "raised" by the town of

Lexington to reinforce the Continental Army stationed in New York. Diamond served six months under the command of Capt. Daniel Shays. This was Diamond's last enlistment in the Revolutionary army. By war's end, Diamond had compiled an exemplary record as a soldier and patriot.

After completing his service with Shays, Diamond returned to Lexington, Massachusetts. In March 1783, he married Rebecca Simonds of Lexington, and six months later the first of their six children was born. Diamond had married into a well-established family. Rebecca's great-grandfather was a founder of Lexington and a substantial landowner. Many of her kin held town offices. The Simonds family were patriots who contributed soldiers to the Revolutionary War.

In 1795 the Diamond family moved to Peterborough. For three years Diamond worked as a laborer, living as a tenant on Asa Carley's farm. Diamond's last child was born there. Diamond retained his ties to Lexington through the Simonds family. In 1798 Diamond purchased sixty acres of wild land for $200 lent to him by his brother-in-law. For the next eight years Diamond appeared to work as a farm laborer and as a wheelwright while converting those sixty acres of wild land into a farm capable of sustaining his family. By 1806 Diamond had become a husbandman and was aided by his two sons, William Jr., age twenty-one, and John, age sixteen.

Despite their success, the Diamonds ranked in the lowest third of Peterborough's ratepayers. In 1811, at age fifty-six, yeoman William Diamond paid the mortgage on his farm to his wife's brother and sold a small portion of his land to a Peterborough resident, possibly for profit or to help pay off the mortgage. In 1817, at age sixty-two, Diamond retired. He divided his farm between his two sons, William Jr., age thirty-three, and John, age twenty-seven, both unmarried. In accord with common practice to insure filial support, titles to the farms were not formally transferred to the sons. William Jr. received title to the land in 1821 and John received his title in 1828. Although a few men of similar economic standing held minor town posts, the Diamonds never held a town office. Diamond and his sons remained outside the community's mainstream of self-government.

JOHN BLAIR FAMILY, RANDALL MCALLISTER, AND CHRISTOPHER THAYER

The Blair family was among Peterborough's founders, but the Blairs had lived on the edge of the town's society until they became actively involved in the town's war effort. John Blair Sr. and his two sons, William and John Jr., had collectively served nearly three thousand days in militia, state regiments, and Continental Army units.[13] In 1780 John Blair Sr. died at age sixty-three leaving his second wife, Mary Blair, and four young children. In 1781 Mary purchased a small farm where she lived with her children until 1791, when she sold it and left town.[14] In 1784 John Blair Jr., age twenty-one, moved to Newburgh, New York, where he remained until his death in 1824. His last association with the town was in 1786 when he received eleven pounds, thirteen shillings, four pence as final payment of the town's promised compensation for soldiers' depreciated pay.

In 1787 William Blair, age thirty-seven, married Elizabeth Little, age thirty-one, of Peterborough. Her father, Thomas Little, had settled early in town and participated in the siege of Boston in early 1776. In 1777, Little marched with future son-in-law, William Blair and William's father to Bennington under the command of John Taggart. William Blair remained on his Peterborough farm, which he had purchased during the war. He shared it with his sister Mary and brother-in-law, Randall McAllister, a disabled Continental Army veteran.

War, marriage, and economics bound the Blair and McAllister families. McAllister served with John Blair Sr. at Bunker Hill where he had been maimed by a bullet that ripped open his mouth and shattered his jaw. McAllister then served three years with John's sons, John Jr., in Long Bill Scott's company. He returned to civilian life a partial invalid as a result of his war wound and weakened health. In 1785, at age thirty-five, Mary Blair, John's daughter, married Randall McAllister, age forty. McAllister then became the co-owner of the Blair farm on which he, Mary, and William Blair's family lived.

In 1800 the Blair-McAllister households were firmly established in the lower half of the town's ratepayers.[15] In 1800 William paid $4.08 in taxes, which included a $1.30 poll tax. Randall paid $2.14 in taxes, which included a poll tax of $1.30. William's taxes had increased slightly over the rate paid in previous years because in 1798 he had purchased fourteen acres of land from Samuel Brackett. Blair's and McAllister's tax inventories revealed modest holdings. William owned two oxen, two cows, one acre of land planted in crops, two acres planted in feed grain, four acres in pasture, and seventy-five acres in wild land. McAllister owned one acre of land planted in feed grain, four acres of pasture, and fifty acres of wild land. His tax had declined from previous years because of the sale or the slaughter of his two cows. In 1808 McAllister retired from farming after receiving an invalid pension from the federal government.[16] That year McAllister's daughter, Mary, married William Field, the son of John Field, a tanner who had moved to town in 1786. By the turn of the century, John Field was in the top half of Peterborough's ratepayers.

The marriage to Field linked the Blairs and McAllisters to the family of Deacon Christopher Thayer, another Continental Army veteran, who had moved to town from Braintree, Massachusetts. Thayer had enlisted in 1775, served throughout that year, and reenlisted in 1776 in Colonel Joseph Cilley's First New Hampshire regiment of the Continental Army, which contained Short Bill Scott's regiment. In 1786 Thayer had moved from Braintree to Peterborough with his brother-in-law John Field.[17] The four families interlocked through marriage and finance. In 1808 William Field paid William Blair $200 for part of the farm where McAllister lived, and then, for $200, Field gave McAllister a lifetime lease on the house and plot where McAllister remained for the rest of his life, living on the income from his disability pension. Blair, Field, and Thayer also engaged in land transactions among themselves.[18]

Throughout his life, Blair remained just below the median of Peterborough ratepayers and slightly below the economic rank occupied by Christopher Thayer. In 1813, Blair's economic position began to decline. He mortgaged his seventy-acre farm to James Wilson for $510, a fact reflected in a 22 percent drop in his tax from $4.20 in 1813 to $3.30 in 1814. This decline placed him among the lowest quarter of town ratepayers. The decline was particular to the Blairs because the average and median taxes of the town as a whole increased from 1813 to 1814. The following year, 1815, William Blair retired and turned over his farm to his unmarried son, William Jr., age twenty-six. By 1818, with their farm mortgaged, the Blairs—father and son—were reduced to near bankruptcy. Their taxable estate had declined to $1.70, which included a poll tax of $1.30 and the tax on one ox. The family appeared on the verge of losing their farm. They could expect little help from their in-law, Christopher Thayer, whose estate had also diminished. In 1814 Thayer had sold twelve acres of his homestead to Moses Dodge of Peterborough for $410.[19] Thayer may have faced financial difficulties or have been trying to raise cash to help his sons purchase their own farms.[20] The economic fortunes of William Blair, Randall McAllister, and Christopher Thayer were rapidly declining. They appeared to be in jeopardy of losing their grasp on the modest estates they had acquired through years of labor.

By 1818 Blair, McAllister, and Christopher Thayer occupied economic positions among the lower half of the town's ratepayers. For the most part, these Continental Army veterans, except for Thayer, appeared on the fringe of the town's social and political life. Neither Blair nor McAllister ever held a town office. Thayer, on the other hand, was elected tithingman three times between 1786 and 1818 and held the position of church deacon. None of the three were actively engaged in the town's economic expansion, which began in 1808 with the establishment of its first textile mill; none of them bought stock in the town's locally owned mills. They seemed content to transact land among family members, and generally keep to themselves.

By the time of Monroe's administration, these aging veterans were slipping down the economic ladder. Their relatively lower economic rank stood in sharp contrast to higher positions enjoyed by others in their cohort, such as members of the Smith and Morison families who had spent only a few weeks or months under arms. In Peterborough, at least, the image of the suffering soldier, disadvantaged by service and sinking into poverty during old age, has a ring of truth when applied to former Continental Army soldiers such as Alld, Diamond, Blair, McAllister, and Thayer.

SMITH AND MORISON FAMILIES

William Smith, his brother-in-law Thomas Morison, and their kin formed an interlocking directorate that virtually ran the town well into the 1820s.[21] They were linked by marriage to a number of other prominent Peterborough families, such as the Moores, Fergusons, and Ritchies, and they were connected by friendship to the Scotts. Members of this large kin group had served in the Continental Army, as did sons from other prominent families such as the Allds. Most, however, served in the militia and state regiments.

William Smith, one of the founders of the Peterborough clan, was born in Ireland in 1723. In 1736 he migrated with his family to Lunenburg, Massachusetts. His father, Robert Smith, was a tanner who "brought considerable property with him" when he emigrated.[22] In 1751 William Smith married Thomas Morison's sister, Elizabeth, from Londonderry, New Hampshire. Two years later, possibly with his father's support, William purchased a 177-acre tract in Peterborough and began establishing his farm on New Hampshire's frontier. In 1761 he purchased a second tract of 164 acres, which made Smith one of the town's major landholders. He was active in town and church affairs. William served as selectman, tithingman, treasurer, moderator, town clerk, representative to the Provincial Congress in 1774, justice of the peace, and a deacon in the town's Old Side Presbyterian church.

His brother-in-law, Thomas Morison, the other founder of the clan, was born in 1710 in Ireland and at age nine accompanied his family to Londonderry, New Hampshire. The Morisons and Smiths were probably acquainted with each another in Ireland. In 1739 Thomas married William's sister, Elizabeth Smith, age seventeen. In 1744 they moved from Londonderry, New Hampshire, to Lunenburg, Massachusetts, where the Smiths lived. In 1750 Thomas settled in Peterborough. Between 1750 and 1759, he began his Peterborough farm and built the town's first saw mill. He was also active in town affairs. He was elected frequently to the office of selectman.

By 1775 Thomas Morison and William Smith had developed their farms and had provided land for their grown children. At the outbreak of war, Thomas's two oldest sons, John (1740–1818) and Robert (1744–1831), had married, were living on their own farms, and were beginning their families. Eight of Thomas Morison's children—four boys and four girls who ranged in age from thirteen-year-old Ezekiel to Elizabeth, age thirty-three—lived with him at home. In 1775 nine of William Smith's children—seven boys and two girls who ranged in age from ten-year-old Samuel to twenty-one-year-old Robert— resided in his household.

Both families supported the war with manpower. Seven out of thirteen men of military age in the Smith and Morison families fought in militia and state regiments. In late 1775, John Smith, age twenty-one, was raised by the town's Committee of Safety for a state regiment to replace Connecticut troops that had returned home that December, despite Washington's plea that they remain in Boston. After three months of service, John returned to Peterborough where he remained for the rest of the war. In the fall of 1776, John's brother Robert Smith, age twenty-two, mustered into Enoch Hale's regiment, which was formed to reinforce Washington's army in New York. Robert served three months, was probably in the battle of White Plains, and then returned home where he remained for the rest of the war.

Following the enlistment pattern in which kin rotated service, two more brothers, James Smith, age twenty-one, and Jeremiah Smith, age eighteen, mustered in 1777 to repel Burgoyne's army. James served a total of five days. He marched to Vermont in late June under the command of fellow townsmen Alexander Robbe and returned home after encountering the retreating American army. That exercise marked the end of James's military service for the war. As seen above, in July 1777, Jeremiah left his studies at Harvard and, contrary to his father's command, enlisted in John Stark's forces. Jeremiah was nearly killed in an ambush near Bennington. By war's end, four of William Smith's sons— Robert, John, James, and Jeremiah—had spent a total of 246 days in military service.[23]

The Morisons were more deeply involved in military service than were their Smith cousins. Collectively, the three older Morison brothers spent a total of 1,180 days or just more than three years in the army. In 1775 John, Robert, and Thomas Morison, ages thirty-five, thirty-one, and twenty-four respectively, joined Washington's army at Boston. John and Robert served in John Stark's regiment at Bunker Hill. Thomas may also have been in that battle. In December 1775, after eight months of service, the brothers returned to Peterborough. In the fall of 1776 Thomas and Robert mustered a second time. Thomas joined Colonel Nahum Baldwin's regiment and Robert enlisted in Colonel Thomas Tash's regiment. They marched with their cousin Robert Smith to reinforce Washington's army in New York. Thomas Morison and Robert Smith fought in the battle of White Plains that October. In 1777 the three oldest Morison brothers answered the call for troops to repel Burgoyne. John and Thomas Morison mustered, as did their cousin Robert Smith, in Alexander Robbe's company, which spent five days in June marching to and from the Connecticut River. Later that summer, John and Thomas reenlisted, as did their brother Robert and their cousin Jeremiah Smith, under John Stark's command. The Morisons and Jeremiah Smith fought at the battle of Bennington. After 1777 the Morison family's military service virtually ended, except when John joined Enoch Hale's regiment in Rhode Island.[24] The Smiths and Morisons fulfilled local expectations that leading citizens serve, and yet they were careful not to let the war disrupt their lives through long enlistments and service far from home.

After the war Thomas Morison and William Smith, like William Alld, continued to groom places for their children and strengthen their kin networks. In 1791 William Smith deeded one of his farms to his son Jonathan, age twenty-eight. William deeded another farm, purchased in 1761, to his oldest son, Robert, age thirty-eight. These transactions merely formalized ownership; Smith's sons had been living on these farms for more than fifteen years. William provided legacies to his four other sons: John, James, Jeremiah, and Samuel. Like William Alld, William Smith wanted his children to live near him. John settled on a farm near his father, married in 1791, and began fathering his children—three girls and five boys. Veterans James and Jeremiah Smith moved from town, but they kept close ties with their family. In 1790 James moved to Cavendish, Vermont, married the following year, and within a few years fathered five children. James was a "highly respected" member of the community who held various town offices, was a justice of the peace, and served as a state legislator for thirteen years. In 1797 Jeremiah Smith moved to Exeter, New Hampshire, although he retained property and investments in Peterborough.[25] William Smith remained titular head of his family until his death in December 1808 at age eighty-five, a little more than three months after the death of his wife, Elizabeth Morison Smith, who was also eighty-five.

Thomas Morison continued to live on his farm until his death in 1797 at the age of eighty-seven. His sons, veterans John and Robert Morison, remained in Peterborough. Both had large families, seven and ten children, respectively. After the war veteran Thomas Morison Jr. married and moved to Buxton, Maine, where he died in 1796 after falling from a bridge he had built. Samuel Morison (1758–1837), who had not served in the war, remained in Peterborough and married his first cousin Elizabeth Smith. All of their six children, except for a son who died at age seven, were deaf mutes. Two other brothers, Jonathan (1749–?) and Ezekiel (1762–?) Morison, remained in town for some years and then moved away.[26]

The Smith and Morison children remained at the top of the town's economic ladder. They were leaders in promoting the town's economic growth within the region's expanding market economy of agriculture, finance, and manufacturing. In 1794, for example, Samuel Smith built a 200-foot-long building to house a paper-making mill, a trip-hammer shop, and machinery to make wool cards. The Smiths ranked in the top 10 percent of Peterborough's taxpayers, a position they shared with the Allds. Jeremiah and Samuel were taxed for their "stock in trade," which included Samuel's 1794 factory building, rents collected from tenants, and interest on Jeremiah's loans and mortgages. The other Smiths had prosperous farms. The four Morison brothers—John, Robert, Samuel, Ezekiel—like their cousins the Smiths, were quite successful. All were in the top 25 percent of Peterborough taxpayers in 1796, and two brothers, Samuel and Ezekiel, were in the top 20 percent and 2 percent of taxpayers, respectively.

The two families cooperated to expand their wealth. In 1808 the Smiths and Morisons converted equity in land into capital to invest in Peterborough's new spinning mills, including one started by Samuel Smith. Successful investments helped to keep John, Jonathan, and Samuel Smith in the top 10 percent of Peterborough taxpayers through the first decade of the nineteenth century. Three Morison brothers (Ezekiel had left Peterborough by 1808), either sustained or improved their top position in the town's wealth structure. The Smiths and Morisons were part of the growing entrepreneurial spirit that changed Peterborough's economy and strengthened their families' prominence in the community.[27]

The Smiths and Morisons were active in town government and involved in state and national politics as staunch Federalists. Beginning in 1791, John and Jonathan Smith held town offices, alternately serving as representatives to the New Hampshire General Court for almost forty years. Their brother Jeremiah Smith was a state representative (1788–90), a member of the state's constitutional convention (1791 and 1792), a member of Congress (1790–97), and U.S. attorney for New Hampshire (1797–1800) after he moved to Exeter in 1797. In 1800 President Adams appointed him to the U.S. circuit court. He later served on the state's superior court until elected New Hampshire's governor in 1809 and 1810. Between 1813 and 1816 he was chief justice of New Hampshire's supreme court. In 1820 Jeremiah retired from law and politics to begin a business career as president of the Exeter Bank. He was also the treasurer of Phillips Exeter Academy. His brother, Samuel Smith, served in Congress (1813–15), but left politics to devote himself full time to his cotton mill, which he had established in 1808. Robert Morison joined his uncle William Smith, cousin Jonathan Smith, and father-in-law, Nathaniel Holmes, as deacons in the town church. Collectively, the Morison brothers could count thirty-one community offices among themselves during the period 1772–1806. When combined with their cousins, the Smiths, and other kin, they dominated the town government, church, and economy.[28] Military service may have disrupted the lives of the Smiths and Morisons, but it did not dislocate them. After the war, they and their kin expanded the strong economic and political foundations laid by their fathers.

By contrast, few of Peterborough's Continental Army veterans, Honorable John Scott being an exception, matched the success of either the town's elite like the Smiths and Morisons, or men of lesser status in their age cohort. Although army veterans were part of the town's middle rank, they were, as a group, less prosperous than their contemporaries. For some, relatively lower economic status was a continuation of humble origins. These men started

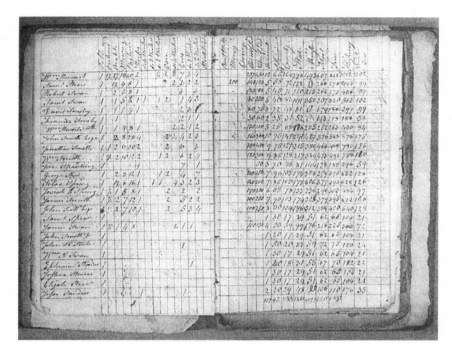

Peterborough, New Hampshire, tax list for 1821. The tax list shows that Continental Army veteran John Scott owned farmland and farm animals. He was taxed $8.00, which included his poll tax of $1.30. Scott's tax exceeded the average rate by about 30 percent. Continental Army veteran Samuel Spear was assessed only a poll tax of $1.30. Spear had transferred his property as part of a retirement contract. Even though he received support as a result of this contract, he was technically propertyless and thus eligible for the pension. The War Department accepted such contracts as evidence that veterans were no longer self-supporting. Such contracts generally provided a low level of subsistence in the form of a room in the homestead's farmhouse, a share of the food raised on the farm, and fuel. *Courtesy, Peterborough Historical Society.*

lower and didn't rise as high as those who began with the advantages enjoyed by the Smith and Morison children. Some men slipped farther and faster down the economic ladder than others in their generation, possibly as result of declining health that accompanied increased age. For still others, misfortune could account for their lower status. At the extreme, possibly the result of the shattering wartime experiences, Benjamin Alld became rootless and alienated from society. Alld fell from high status to society's fringe.

Studies of veterans of the Civil War and twentieth-century war, used cautiously, suggest that wartime trauma may have contributed to the social and economic differences between Continental veterans and others in their cohort.

Intensive research on veterans of World War I shows that many combat veterans who returned to civilian life were unfit "to shoulder the burden of individual adult responsibility." Warfare had disrupted "the natural development of youth, altering in many cases, not only the emotional growth, but the vocational aptitude and social attitude as well."[29] Systematic studies of World War II veterans corroborate the residual and adverse effects of combat on some men. According to one finding, nearly 75 percent of the men who suffered mental breakdowns under the strain of combat, "were not entirely free of psychoneurotic illness" five or six years after their release from medical treatment. Most of these men reported that their health became "worse" or "much worse" in the years following their discharge from the army. Moreover, a third of these veterans did not make a "satisfactory occupational adjustment" in civilian life. They reported difficulty cooperating with co-workers, irregular employment, occupying menial jobs beneath their abilities, and slack work habits. These attributes, researchers concluded, resulted not from veterans' social status, age, or education, but rather from the psychological effects of combat, which impaired normal personality development and hampered readjustment to civilian life.[30]

Similar characteristics appeared among thousands of Vietnam veterans. According to a study by Josefina Card, as late as 1981, 20 percent of Vietnam veterans reported symptoms of post-traumatic stress disorder (PTSD), also known as shell shock or battle fatigue in previous wars. Veterans with severe symptoms recounted "nightmares, panic attacks, emotional numbing, withdrawal from the external environment, hyperalertness, anxiety and depression. . . ." An additional 24 percent suffered symptoms resembling PTSD. They reported not "getting along with friends," "feeling life is not worth living," "feeling lonely," and "feeling things won't be better tomorrow." The severity of PTSD symptoms, Card concluded, resulted from the "intensity of the combat experience. . . . the more severe the soldier's exposure to combat and injury during the Vietnam War, the greater the number of PTSD-related problems as a civilian more than a decade later." In addition to the effects of intense combat, Card attributed these characteristics to service in units plagued by poor leadership, low morale, and disunity, and to the absence of a hero's welcome home, which accentuated the traumatic effects of war. According to Card, those attributes were "equally applicable to whites and nonwhite, individuals of low and high academic ability, and economically advantaged and disadvantaged individuals." Thus the damaging psychological effects of war cut across race and across social and economic classes.[31]

In extreme cases, those effects produced anomie and social atomization. In less extreme cases, veterans experienced various degrees of neurosis and social alienation, which stunted their personal development, ambitions, and efforts to rise in the world. These characteristics were most prominent among those who served long enlistments and who engaged in combat. When compared to peers who lacked such experiences, these veterans showed one or more of the following traits: the fathering of fewer children, having a higher rate of divorce, occupational instability, reduced aspirations for material success, greater cynicism and pessimism, more detachment from the community, and a tendency to cluster around veterans who shared similar experiences and outlooks. In such cases, military service diminished the capacity of veterans to keep pace with the economic and social gains of their peers. These veterans formed the lowest social and economic strata of their class. In a few instances, veterans became misfits, fell to a lower class, and some were marginalized.

Some clinicians and scholars debate whether PTSD is a political statement in opposition to the Vietnam War or a medical diagnosis that is contrived to secure veterans' benefits.[32] Nevertheless, there is general agreement that individuals are traumatized by extreme circumstances that are far beyond the range of normal human experience. Going beyond the older ideas of "shell shock," this broader view encompasses soldiers who witness death and the destruction of war, and who have extreme feelings of helplessness. These experiences have been characterized as "war-zone stress."[33] Historian Eric T. Dean has argued that the stress of war produced symptoms of social maladjustment and serious psychological trauma among veterans of the Civil War.[34]

Clinicians can use medical records, and historians of modern wars can interview veterans or, as Dean did, study the records of veterans committed to asylums for the insane to support their conclusions. The evidence that Revolutionary War veterans experienced trauma is inferential. Yet, given increased understanding of the effects of warfare on personality, regardless of weaponry, the traumatic effect of being in a war zone on men like Alld or Blair, especially over a prolonged period of time, cannot be dismissed. Alld's desertion may have resulted from war-zone trauma. Dean contends that many of the 300,000 men who deserted the Union and Confederate armies did so because of stress.[35] While Benjamin Alld could have been the black sheep of his family, and Blair and Diamond, who rose from humble origins, less able than their peers to build a substantial estate, their lower fortunes may have also reflected the traumatic effects of war.

In towns such as Peterborough, the sight of aging, infirm army veterans who were poor or sinking toward poverty would strengthen the emerging sentiment that the nation owed a debt of gratitude to its suffering soldiers. Such men would also reinforce the revisionist view that made Continental soldiers the symbol of a people's war.

CHAPTER 3

The Image of the Suffering Soldier

AT THE TURN of the nineteenth century, the concept of the Revolution as a people's war was a defining element of the political culture. It portrayed the Revolutionary generation as mythic people who embodied the spirit of '76, a combination of civic virtue and militant patriotism. The suffering endured by the people in the war against British tyranny attested to their heroism. The concept reinforced ideological distrust of a standing army by portraying it as a menacing, vice-ridden institution that was apart from the people. Thus, by elevating the people to mythic status, the concept diminished the Continental Army in the memory of the Revolutionary War.[1] Within two decades, however, partisan conflict over defense policy, sentimental and revisionist histories of the Revolutionary War, the War of 1812 and humiliating military defeat, a surge of nationalism during and following that war, and appeals from disabled and poor Revolutionary War veterans for assistance created the image of the suffering soldier. That image transformed the memory of the Revolutionary War and the army.

By 1818 the image of the suffering soldier dominated the concept of the Revolution as a people's war. That image, while including all veterans, gave special credit to Continental soldiers for winning independence. Continental ranks, once imagined as filled with dregs and mercenaries, were portrayed as filled with citizen-soldiers from all ranks of society such as occurred in Peterborough. Ordinary men, especially those who fought under Washington, like

Peterborough's Scotts, Alld, Blair, Diamond, and McAllister, were accorded honored status within the mythic people. Veterans, particularly regular troops, became the principal symbols of the spirit of '76 and models of national character. The image evoked the sentiment of gratitude that was expressed in appeals to memorialize soldiers' valor and to assist veterans in need. A new generation sought to affirm its place as worthy heirs of the Revolution by removing the stain of ingratitude that tarnished the republic.

IN 1798 REPUBLICANS used the concept of a people's war to oppose Hamilton's plan to create a new army of potentially fifty thousand men during the quasi war with France.[2] On July Fourth of that year, with conflict appearing imminent, George Clinton Jr. reminded members of New York City's Tammany Society, a Jeffersonian organization, that "in a republic every citizen should be a soldier. . . . The means of the national defense should rest in the body of the people. . . ." Clinton warned against relying on regular troops to defend the nation because "[s]tanding armies are not only expensive but dangerous to the liberty of the state." Clinton moralized that the "armies of liberty have ever triumphed over the armies of despotism."[3] Clinton expressed a widely shared faith in the vitality of the people's spirit of '76. His views echoed popular opinion that regular armies enlisted rabble. His remarks probably reminded listeners of the 1783 Newburgh Conspiracy, which had discredited the Continental Army in the minds of many. Clinton's views illustrated the continued strength of radical Whig anti-army sentiments in the Republican party and the party's belief in the legendary prowess of the militia.[4]

Jeffersonians used the concept of a people's war to portray themselves as guardians of Revolutionary ideals. Once in power, Republicans used that concept to justify reliance upon the militia and a small regular army for national security. Praising the people's valor in the Revolution, George Eacker, a 1793 graduate from Columbia College, speaking before the New York City Tammany Society on 4 July 1801, venerated the selfless spirit of "our brave and virtuous countrymen [who] flew to arms" to deliver the nation from tyranny. He described the soldiers as having "no other reliance than in their own bravery. . . . Their zeal compensated the want of discipline, their military ardor supplied the defects of experience." He lauded citizens for their bravery, determination, and militancy despite the "plunder of habitations; the conflagration of towns . . . rapine and devastation of every description. . . ."[5] Jeffersonians assured a new generation that the nation, endowed with the spirit of '76, was capable of defending itself in future conflicts by waging a people's war. Political culture and defense policy reinforced each other.[6]

Despite such assurances, Federalists, joined by a few Republican "malcontents," continued to criticize Jefferson's defense policy.[7] Federalists used the "murder" of John Pierce to accuse Republicans of leaving the nation helpless. Pierce was a crewman on the schooner *Richard*, which was intercepted on 25 April 1806 near Sandy Hook, Long Island, by a squadron of British warships blockading New York Harbor against vessels trading with France, then at war with England. When the *Richard*'s captain, presumably upholding the right of a neutral nation to trade freely, refused to heed British orders to be boarded and searched for contraband, the captain of HMS *Leander* ordered his ship's cannon to fire. A shot hit the fleeing *Richard*, killing crewman Pierce.

The Federalist paper, the *Boston Columbian Centinel*, reported that Pierce's death "excited a righteous indignation" against Jefferson because he had left New York City "defenseless by the removal of our ships of war into the mud docks of the Potomac." The paper called Jefferson's defense policies "penny wise and pound foolish [because] they deprived our country of a navy."[8] The New York City Common Council condemned the "treacherous murder" of John Pierce and the British "aggression upon our national rights." Eulogizing Pierce at a public funeral, city officials criticized Republicans for letting the navy, coastal fortifications, and army deteriorate. Taking matters into their own hands, city officials confiscated supplies purchased for British ships and appointed a delegation, led by the Federalist stalwart Rufus King, to submit their demand to Jefferson to rearm the nation.[9]

Federalist Fourth of July orators used the Pierce incident to attack Jefferson for weakening the nation's defense and for subverting the spirit of '76.[10] Daniel Webster (1782–1852) told Federalists gathered in Concord, New Hampshire, that the death of innocent men in the Boston massacre had "roused America," but the murder of John Pierce only produced a "Proclamation" from Jefferson who ordered the arrest of the *Leander*'s captain and halted American supplies to that vessel.[11] Webster declared that Jefferson's actions "never sprang from the altar of 'Seventy-Six'," but from "corrupt opinions" that lacked "regard to national honour. . . ." Webster sarcastically concluded that under Republican leadership "Patriotism hath given place to the more laudable spirit of economy," a reference to the administration's meager allocations for defense. He asserted, "so long as we are rich and defenseless, rapacity will prey upon us. . . .

Daniel Webster (1782–1852), at age 22 or 23. Young men such as Webster were often chosen to give Fourth of July orations. *Courtesy, Dartmouth College Library.*

IF WE WILL HAVE COMMERCE, WE MUST PROTECT IT." To the public at large, Webster promised that the Federalist party would stop the "'torrent flood' of disunion and factions" caused by the Republican party's submission to England. He proclaimed that Federalists would revive ". . . our VIRTUE and . . . PATRIOTISM"—the foundations of "public LIBERTY."[12] By advocating rearmament, Federalists portrayed themselves as defenders of the Revolution, guardians of the spirit of '76, and accused Republicans of betraying both.

Federalist attacks intensified following Jefferson's embargo enacted in December 1807. Jeremiah Perley (1784–1834), a classmate of Webster's at Dartmouth and a fellow lawyer, told Federalists celebrating the Fourth of July in Hallowell, Maine, that under Jefferson's leadership America was "in danger of running the same career that all free people have trodden . . . [which] shall blast that liberty and independence which are so dear to us." Unless the nation rearmed, he warned, "we must desert our seaports . . . and retreat to the mountains. . . . Is this the spirit of seventy-six?" he asked. Perley claimed that

America, this "last best hope of a despairing humanity," was on the verge of ruin. Knowing his audience full well, Perley inflamed fears that Republican defense policy sapped patriotism and made the nation a prey to its enemies.[13]

Although both parties had traditionally honored veterans in public celebrations, increased partisan conflict over defense led both parties to focus on the veteran as a symbol of the spirit of '76. The locks of "hoary-headed" soldiers and their infirmities became emblems used by orators to remind audiences that these men had once been young, heroic patriots. Partisan orators also used veterans as metaphors with which to attack opponents and to justify their own positions. In 1807 Republican orators paid special attention to veterans to refute Federalist attacks on their defense policy. By honoring the aging soldiers they assured the public that the nation could rely upon the spirit of '76 to defend itself in case of war.

Benjamin Gleason (1777–1847), a recent graduate of Brown and a schoolmaster in Charlestown, Massachusetts, expressed these sentiments in his 4 July 1807 speech to Republicans in Hingham, Massachusetts. Gleason portrayed veterans of the Revolution, militia and regulars, as mythical warriors: "Your old age is rewarded with all the honors your patriotism deserves . . . you knew no fear. . . . You were more than mortal."[14] In 1807 in Pittsfield, Massachusetts, Republican Congressman Ezekiel Bacon (1776–1870) also romanticized those veterans who participated in the town's Independence Day celebration. Bacon, speaking with a rhetorical flourish typical of Fourth of July orators, honored and praised the old soldiers for their Olympian heroism: "those aged citizens, whose venerable countenances, and locks silvered with lapse of years, bespeak them to have been Patriots of the days sacred to Liberty, and Heroes of the Battles of our Independence. Permit me to offer them the homage of that respectful veneration, which is due from the present generation to the veteran defenders of their country's rights."[15] Gleason and Bacon celebrated heroic soldiers, rather than the people, for personifying the spirit of '76 and for securing independence.[16] In 1808 New York's Tammany Society moved beyond rhetoric. In April some thirty thousand people celebrated the laying of a cornerstone for a monument to honor the troops "who perished on board the British prison ships." Republicans sought to affirm the vitality of the spirit of '76 by honoring veterans through both word and monument.[17]

Federalists responded by also honoring veterans, but as a way to attack Republicans for failing to strengthen the nation's military. For example, in 1809 Solomon Kidder Livermore (1779–1859), a Harvard graduate, lawyer, and Federalist, proclaimed on the Fourth of July in Temple, New Hampshire, that Republicans undermined the spirit of '76 by defaming Washington and soldiers of the Revolution. Livermore told his listeners that Republican zealots had "pronounced [Washington] a traitor and monarchist," denounced John Adams as a "hoary-headed incendiary," and reproached the "veteran soldier" for "want of patriotism." The crowd did not have to be told that Republican denigration of Revolutionary leaders and veterans, as Livermore alleged, undermined patriotism and thus weakened the nation's moral fiber. He urged the partisan crowd to "consult history" by listening to veterans' accounts of the Revolutionary War to inspire their own patriotism. "The war worn soldier," Livermore told the celebrants, "will recount his marches, his retreats, his encounters, his dangers and his escapes. . . . forgetting his infirmities he will assume the vigor and activity of youth." He closed with an appeal to "bring back the glory and dignity and felicity which have departed" by following the example of Revolutionary soldiers.[18] Similarly, on 4 July 1809, August Alden proclaimed to Federalists of Augusta, Maine, that the Revolutionary War soldier embodied the spirit of '76. Alden (1780–1850), a Dartmouth graduate and lawyer, instructed celebrants to "mind the *glorious achievements* of our Ancient Heroes! *Their* examples will fire your mind to emulation . . . animated with the *glorious spirit* of '76 you will *grasp* your arms *rush* into the field and fight *valiantly* for your *Country,* for your *Liberty* and for your *Independence.*"[19] Federalists, sounding the alarm of the declension under Republican leadership, called for the nation to renew its patriotism by emulating Revolutionary soldiers.[20]

As tensions with England and France increased, Republican opposition to creating a regular army softened. Party rhetoric venerating military leaders and soldiers intensified.[21] Charles Caldwell (1752–1853), a physician and former medical officer in the federal army that quelled the 1794 Whiskey Rebellion, assured party faithful and the public that "Americans will be true to themselves" and will meet any aggression with the "spirit of '76." He told the American Republican Society in Philadelphia on 4 July 1810 that "[t]he patriotism of our fathers is not yet extinguished in the bosoms of their descendants. The spirit of Seventy-six only sleeps for a season." Caldwell hoped to awaken the spirit of '76 with homage to "Warren, Montgomery, Mercer" and to "our Revolutionary heroes" whose valor in battle had achieved victory and independence. Caldwell said that celebrating their achievements ". . . exalts the civic virtues and gives a higher lustre to the character of the patriot." Caldwell called upon the country to immortalize Revolutionary War soldiers and their leaders in art, song, and print. Civic festivals "calculated to awaken our gratitude . . . to the heroes who achieved our revolution" are insufficient to "exalt the civic virtues and give higher lustre to the character of the patriot." Caldwell appealed for a "Reynolds, a West or a Trumbull" to paint the courage and devotion to liberty of our "Revolutionary heroes." He pleaded for a "modern Homer" to celebrate "them in a song as deathless as themselves."[22] Similarly, in 1810 Selleck Osborn (1783–1826), the Republican journalist who had been jailed in 1806 for libeling Federalists, told celebrants gathered on the Fourth of July in New Bedford, Massachusetts, that he "acknowledged with all possible deference to [*sic*] the virtues of the veteran hero." While he still paid tribute to the "Spartan heroism and constancy" of mothers and daughters, Osborn singled out veterans for praise because they exemplified the classical republican ideal of "heroic self-denial which never places private fortune in competition with public interest."[23]

Thus Republicans and Federalists used the image of the heroic soldier, personified by veterans, to assure the public that their respective parties would uphold the revolution's militant patriotism. Republicans, still clinging to anti-army doctrine, celebrated veterans to affirm the ideal of the citizen-soldier. Federalists, on the other hand, celebrated veterans to attack Republicans for being soft on defense. Federalists also sought to assure the public that a regular army posed little danger to the republic. Their demands to build a strong navy and a standing army were aided not only by threats of war but also by recently published histories of the Revolutionary War that distinguished the Continental Army from standing armies in Europe.

Revisionist histories of the Revolution published after the turn of the century, written mainly by Federalists, removed the stigma of vice and treason from the Continental Army. These histories made regular troops part of a people's war. Their portrayals of the suffering experienced by Continental troops, as Short Bill Scott had recounted, glorified the heroism of regular soldiers. Their descriptions of naked, cold, hungry, bloodied, and mistreated troops underscored the courage, virtue, fortitude, and patriotism of the regular army.[24]

John Marshall's *The Life of George Washington* (1804) sentimentalized the troops' miseries at Valley Forge. Those men were, Marshall wrote, "without food" and clothes and decimated by "a violent fever [that] raged among them" and killed many.[25] Mercy Otis Warren's children's history of the Revolution, published in 1805, added to the sentimental accounts of soldiers' bravery and fortitude at Valley Forge by romanticizing their suffering. She wrote that the encampment had the "gloomy appearance of a hutted village in the woods, inhabited only by a hungry and half naked soldiery" who patiently awaited supplies "amidst penury, hunger, and cold . . . [while forced to lay] on the cold ground [and] wet earth."[26]

Dr. David Ramsay, a former Continental Army officer, devoted ten pages in his *The Life of George Washington* (1807) to a romanticized description of the heroic suffering at Valley Forge. By contrast, in 1789, Ramsay's *History of the American Revolution* contained only a few impassioned lines about their plight at Valley Forge: men "suffered . . . without shoes" and marched "over frozen ground, which so gashed their naked feet, that each step was marked with blood."[27] In 1807, adding to that earlier account, Ramsay wrote that the soldiers at Valley Forge were "barefooted and otherwise naked" because selfish civilians refused to aid the army. He disclosed that Washington had been forced "to extort supplies" from civilians "at the point of the bayonet" to feed, cloth, and house his troops. Ramsay moralized that virtuous soldiers not only suffered from war and the elements, but also at the hands of corrupt officials and a vice-ridden public. In Ramsay's account, the lesson of Valley Forge was clear: the patriotic army had overcome civilian corruption and neglect to carry on the war against Britain.[28]

Revisionist histories of the Revolution also removed the black mark of the Newburgh Conspiracy. In the spring of 1783, Continental Army officers at the encampment in New York had threatened rebellion to obtain back pay for their troops and to enforce Congress's promise to award officers lifetime pensions at half pay. The Newburgh Conspiracy never became a rebellion, however. Indeed, it was more a political bluff than a serious attempt at a coup d'état. Nevertheless, it reinforced popular perceptions that the Continental Army, like all regular armies, was filled with riffraff and was corrupt, that it threatened liberty, and that it deserved to be treated as a necessary evil. Newburgh affirmed Revolutionary leaders' fears of military tyranny, their contempt for the Continental Army, and their anti-army creed.[29] Sensitive to their views, in 1789 Ramsay wrote a twelve-line apology for the troops' rash action.[30] By contrast, his *The Life of George Washington* contained fifteen pages on Newburgh to celebrate the army's virtues.[31]

Ramsay's *The Life of George Washington* praised the army at Newburgh for its forbearance and patriotism despite the fact that it was mistrusted by the public and mistreated by civil authorities. Ramsay wrote that officers were "smarting under past sufferings, and present wants. . . ." As a consequence, "their expectations became violent and almost universal" because they were "provoked at the apparent neglect with which they had been treated." Ramsay stated that an "artful" officer exploited these feelings. In 1789 he had called that officer "seditious." Ramsay's revised account included Washington's letter to Congress that portrayed Newburgh not as a conspiracy, but as a testament to the army's patriotism and virtue. Washington told Congress that the troops' refusal to rebel ought to be viewed as "the last glorious proof of patriotism which could have been given by men who aspired to the distinction of a patriot army; and will not only confirm their claim to justice, but will increase their title to the gratitude of their country."[32]

Ramsay concluded that Newburgh revealed the Continental Establishment to be an "army of free republicans."[33] His history portrayed Continental troops as patriots, not mercenaries, and as virtuous citizen-soldiers, not vice-ridden dregs. One measure of the popularity of Ramsay's revisionist history was the reprinting of his biography of Washington in 1811, 1814, 1815, and 1818.[34] For a new generation of Americans, Ramsay's histories, as well as Marshall's and Warren's, transformed the stigma of Newburgh into a symbol of patriotism and republican virtue. Such histories challenged anti-army doctrine by revising portions of the history of the Revolutionary War that supported those beliefs.[35] These histories popularized Valley Forge as a symbol of the Continental Army's valor and patriotism, especially when contrasted with recreant and selfish civilians who allowed troops to suffer. Furthermore, new histories of the war removed the stain of treason from the Continental Army. These histories incorporated regular troops into the concept of the Revolution as a people's war. More than that, revisionist histories made regular troops symbols of the ideals of republican virtue and militant patriotism previously reserved for civilians and militia. Thus, these histories contributed to the image of the suffering soldier by praising the exceptional virtue, valor, and patriotism of regular troops made evident by their loyalty at Newburgh and by their miseries at Valley Forge.

Valley Forge, in particular, distinguished regular troops from the militia because of the severity of suffering experienced there. That suffering attested to their patriotism and valor. By May 1812, echoing the rhetoric of partisan orators, Virginia's *Monthly Magazine and Literary Journal* proposed that Valley Forge be preserved as a memorial to the heroic suffering of ennobled patriotic soldiers encamped there. Going further with its proposal, *Monthly Magazine* stated that Americans ought to pay "tribute to those places [Valley Forge being foremost] which have been rendered memorable during the revolutionary war by the toil, sufferings and conflicts of our countrymen or consecrated by the blood of heroes." Valley Forge and other hallowed sites, it intoned, would become "classic ground to posterity," which would inspire histories of the epoch, "the song of Muses," and legendary scenes for "painters." *Monthly Magazine* reminded readers that the Greeks had honored their warriors at Marathon, Thermopylae, and Plataea with monuments to memorialize their courage and sacrifice. The editors moralized that Americans ought to follow that example because monuments were a "voice from the grave" to inspire valor and patriotism in later generations. The editors predicted that commemorating America's soldiers would be "a bond of union which bind[s] the community together and stamps the character of the nation as a whole."[36] Efforts to make Valley Forge into a memorial separated soldiers from the mythic people and honored the exceptional valor of regular troops as compared to the militia. Valley Forge was becoming a fixture in American culture as a symbol to evoke the image of the heroic, suffering soldier.[37]

When war broke out with England in June 1812, Republicans employed both the new image of heroic soldiers and the old concept of a people's war to arouse the spirit of '76, to unite the nation and to promote enlistments. Samuel Brower Romaine romanticized the Revolutionary War veteran to inspire a new generation to arms. Romaine (1789–1861) was particularly suited to make such an appeal to members of the New York City Tammany Society. He was a Columbia College graduate and a rising politician with bloodlines to the Revolution. His father, Benjamin Romaine, had served several enlistments in the New Jersey Revolutionary militia and bore a reputation as "zealous in preserving memory of the patriots." Samuel Romaine paid "reverential homage [to the] lofty spirit" of the Revolutionary era. He appealed for a renewal of patriotism and militancy inspired by the example of Revolutionary War veterans such as his father. Romaine praised the soldiers' heroic suffering to inspire patriotism among his listeners. He paid tribute to "the miseries and privations [soldiers had] endured in the momentous struggle" to encourage perseverance in the new struggle with England. "Is there not," Romaine asked, "a revolutionary veteran who hears me, staring from the crutch which supports his aged limbs and pointing to his scars, [who] will exclaim," Americans unite to defend their independence? Romaine concluded that the patriotism of the "Heroes of '76" ought to inspire a new generation to defeat the British.[38] On 4 July 1812 Richard Rush (1780–1869), who was chosen by President Madison to give the Independence Day speech to Congress, assured the nation that "war in a just cause produces patriotism." He stated that Americans would not "dishonor" the "noble achievements" of the Revolutionary generation by failing to heed their country's call to arms.[39] Rush called for a people's war.

Confidently and defiantly, the *Military Monitor and American Register,* a journal founded in August 1812 to report the war, proclaimed in its first edition that Americans would rise to the defense of their country as they had in the Revolution. Invoking the concept of a people's war, the *Military Monitor* reminded readers that "the spirit of the people" lay behind victory in the Revolutionary War. To question victory in the current war, the *Military Monitor* stated, "would be to doubt the patriotism, courage, good sense and virtue of the citizens of the United States; and to suppose them destitute of these qualities would be to proclaim them unfit to be free and unfaithful trustees of the invaluable legacy bequeathed by their ancestors for the benefit of posterity." The *Military Monitor* concluded, "this country cannot be again enslaved, it cannot be conquered—we have numbers, we have virtue, we have patriotism and courage."[40]

To assure skeptical readers that the spirit of '76 had revived in the people, the *Military Monitor* reported the bravery and selflessness of a "female patriot," Mrs. John Pruitt of Georgia. The *Military Monitor* stated that Mrs. Pruitt exemplified the "heroic firmness of public virtue of Spartan females" as she sent two of her sons to war in 1812. Upon their departure to the state militia, the stoic Pruitt told her boys that she would not "regret" their deaths "if they fell for their country. . . ." The *Military Monitor* moralized from Pruitt's example: "Let those of you who think lightly of female virtue and patriotism read this and blush for shame. In the Revolutionary War our females acquitted themselves well and so will their daughters of the present day." Early in the war, Republican leaders hoped that the American "David," spiritually renewed, would again defeat "Goliath."[41]

Spectacular American military defeats, increasingly bitter sectional conflict over the legitimacy of the war, and failure to fill ranks, dashed hopes for victory in a people's war. After the surge of recruits at the beginning of the war subsided, men declined to volunteer for service; federal ranks remained unfilled; states rebelled against Madison's efforts to mobilize their militia as part of a federal army. For example, in 1813 Vermont's governor Martin Crittenden withdrew the state's militia from New York because he believed that Madison lacked constitutional authority to nationalize the militia.[42]

Furthermore, military defeats cast doubt on the courage and character of America's amateur soldiers, that "band" of the people. British victories disproved the republican verity, put forcefully by George Clinton Jr. in 1798, that the "armies of liberty have ever triumphed over the armies of despotism." Unfilled ranks and defeat, added to sectionalism and intense partisan conflict, confirmed fears of a moral declension raised repeatedly in previous years by Federalist orators. In 1812 the nation appeared sapped of the spirit of '76. Defeat and division discredited the traditional concept of a people's war.

In 1813 Port Folio, the country's "pre-eminently . . . national magazine," responded to this crisis by championing military virtues, particularly those associated with regular forces.[43] In January 1813, Port Folio expanded its "American Gallantry" series by publishing accounts of heroic soldiers and sailors in the War of 1812 as well as stories about heroes in the Revolution. In this series, the American soldier, not the spartan mother, became the principal symbol of civic virtue. The editors, Nicholas Biddle and Charles Caldwell, used stories of valor and selflessness to counter dissension, disunion, and the "violence of our political animosities [by fostering] a national feeling" of pride, patriotism, and unity. Caldwell wrote these stories "in colors as glowing . . . [and] as complimentary to our arms and as flattering to the pride of the nation as I was able to command. . . ."[44] In the hands of nationalists like Caldwell and Biddle, the image of the heroic, suffering soldier expanded to include the ideal of the republican warrior who personified not only the spirit of '76, but also American character.

Biddle and Caldwell intended to "excite the high and honorable feeling of patriotism [and to] add honour or distinction to the national character . . . [through] instances of bravery. . . ." Looking beyond the war, they told readers that America needed, "certain rallying points in our habits and manners . . . [to produce] a higher and more generous sentiment . . . which identifies our pride with its glory—which makes us blush for its failings, or weep for its misfortunes, or swell with its triumphs. . . ." The editors urged the nation to "unite in celebrating our own institutions, our own manners, our own statesmen, *our own soldiers* [my italics]." They stated that the United States must not be "condemned, as we now are, . . . [only to hear of the] triumphs of foreign heroes . . ." but must celebrate their own heroes whose valor and character would swell the country's pride.[45]

Port Folio venerated heroes such as Nathan Hale because he had given his life for his country from "a sense of duty, a hope that he might in this way be useful to his country. . . . Neither expectation of promotion nor pecuniary reward induced him" to serve his country. *Port Folio* observed that Hale "has remained unnoticed" although the nation "has celebrated the virtues and lamented the fate of Andre," the British spy executed in 1780 on Washington's orders. *Port Folio* stressed the irony of the monument to Andre, but "not a stone has been erected [to Hale's memory] nor an inscription to preserve his ashes from insult." *Port Folio* hoped that Hale's valor and virtue would arouse pride in America's patriot soldiers as well as illustrate the genius of American character. The journal urged the public to erect a monument to Hale to teach future generations the lessons of honor and bravery.[46] *Port Folio* also proposed that the nation build a "National Burial Ground" in "reverence for dead heroes . . . [including] our Revolutionary heroes. . . ."[47] In doing so, *Port Folio* echoed earlier appeals to strengthen the conviction that "if [such] works were multiplied they would . . . do much toward forming a national character."[48]

Throughout 1813 *Port Folio* published accounts of gallantry in the Revolutionary War and the War of 1812 to popularize the image of the heroic soldier. *Port Folio* "fearlessly" concluded that the nation's soldiers in the Revolution and War of 1812 revealed courage, enterprise, and patriotism deeply embedded in the American character.[49] *Port Folio*'s editors appealed to the country's artists, poets, historians, and political leaders to honor and preserve the gallantry of soldiers in both the Revolution and the War of 1812; the nation's military heroes should not die "unsung." Moreover, *Port Folio* raised doubts about the nation's virtue because the nation failed to honor its soldiers. "Are republics necessarily framed to be, in all respects, ungrateful? Will they bestow on their champions neither riches nor honours, gratification nor fame? Must their warriors fight in the character of amateurs, purely for the sake of killing and dying and when they fall must Oblivion receive them to her blighted embrace? . . . posterity must never be allowed to blush for their forefathers, from finding unperformed a task which primarily and peculiarly belongs to those of the present day." Such appeals to moral sensibilities idealized the republican-warrior as a model of national character. They also challenged a new generation of Americans to prove their worth as heirs of the Revolution by memorializing the gallantry and courage of American soldiers.[50]

Port Folio's editors assured readers that tributes to America's fighting men would form a "new moral bond" uniting the American people. Sounding a theme heard at Fourth of July celebrations, the editors predicted that America's soldiers would inspire American writers and poets to immortalize military "virtues and achievements." Biddle and Caldwell claimed that Americans "will acquire" from these future epics, "what we have heretofore wanted, and without which we can never be respected as a people—a national character." They proclaimed that "the triumphs of our arms . . . [including] the glorious achievements of our navy . . . have kindled a new and holy spirit of nationality. . . ."[51] *Port Folio* sought to transform platitudes into a civic ritual by sponsoring a competition for "the two best naval songs" to immortalize the navy's "brilliant deeds and heroism." The journal promised each winner a prize of $100.[52]

Port Folio criticized the military value of the militia to explain American losses on the battlefield. In November 1812, following a summer of military debacles, *Port Folio* published Washington's letter to Congress, dated 18 October 1780, because "our own subsequent experience" of defeat in war "should stamp an additional value with deliberate opinion of one who so often conducted the soldiers of America to victory." Washington criticized the practice of "temporary enlistments" and denounced the militia for doing little more than consuming food needed by the army. "It is time," Washington wrote, "we should get rid of our errour [*sic*] which the experience of all mankind had exploded and which our own experience had dearly taught us to reject:—the carrying on a war with militia . . . against a regular, permanent and disciplined force . . . The idea is chimerical."[53] Criticisms of the militia supported appeals to build a regular army and base the nation's security on it.

In December 1812, *Port Folio* used the publication of General Henry Lee's Revolutionary War *Memoirs* for "diffusing more correct notions of our military policy than have hitherto prevailed among us." The *Memoirs*' primary lessons were twofold: the militia failed to win the Revolutionary War; and, far worse, the militia thwarted victory. Lee's memoirs showed, *Port Folio* stated, that "after the first gallant stand at Breed's hill . . . the militia were quite as injurious as they were beneficial to the public service." In addition to Lee's condemnations, *Port Folio* blamed the militia for Montgomery's defeat at Quebec in 1775.

The Nation's Bulwark: A Well Disciplined Militia (1829)
While Americans celebrated the myth of the militia as formidable fighting band with references
to the soldiers' heroics at Concord, Lexington, and Bunker Hill, the militia was also the object of
ridicule. Training days were notorious for their slovenly discipline and drunken revelry, and the
military performance of these troops subject to severe criticism. *Courtesy, American Antiquarian
Society.*

Furthermore, it criticized the militia for retreating "in disorder before the first
fire of the British at Princeton [and for throwing] away their arms and flee[ing]
in a body on the first fire at the battle of Camden." The journal concluded, "the
great and radical vice in our modes of thinking on military matters is the
reliance we are disposed to place in the militia."[54]

In December 1813, *Port Folio* further attacked the militia by printing Washington's previously unpublished letter, dated 24 September 1776, to John Hancock, president of the Continental Congress. In that letter Washington complained to Hancock that militant patriotism quickly evaporated in a people's
war. Washington wrote that "when men are irritated, and the passions inflamed, they fly hastily and cheerfully to arms, but after the first emotions are
over, a soldier reasoned upon the goodness of the cause he is engaged in, and
the inestimable rights he is contending for, hears you with patience, and ac-
knowledges the truth of your observations, but adds that it is of no more
importance to him than others." Washington informed Hancock that "to place

any dependence upon militia is assuredly resting upon a broken staff: just dragged from tender scenes of domestic life; unaccustomed to the din of arms; totally unacquainted with every kind of military skill . . . makes them timid and ready to fly from their own shadows." Washington closed his letter to Congress with an appeal for a regular army—"[t]he jealousies of a standing army, and the evils to be apprehended from one are remote. . . . the consequences of wanting one . . . is [sic] certain and inevitable ruin."[55] *Port Folio* concluded that America must not rely on the militia, but on regular troops for defense. It told readers in its February 1814 edition that the "passion" for war must be disciplined by the "science" of war. The editors wrote that "[m]ilitary science" must be taught; it is knowledge gained through study not a "talent falsely thought to be a gift of Nature."[56] For a new generation of Americans, revelations of the failure of amateur soldiers in the Revolution explained the nation's failures in the War of 1812. These revelations further elevated the reputation of the Continental Army. Explanations of American defeats in the War of 1812 were transforming American memory of the Revolutionary War.

Americans also learned that their forefathers' fears of the Continental Army were unfounded. In November 1812, a writer using the pen name Civis wrote a letter to *The Military Monitor* explaining that the Continental Army was an exception to the rule found in classical republican principles. Civis conceded that, as a rule, "standing armies are dangerous to civil liberties," and that generally they are inherently corrupt and tools of tyrants because they are "school[s] for vice" which attract men, "without patriotism and virtue," who become "privileged robbers" in camp. Civis claimed, however, that the Continental Army had departed from this rule because it recruited patriotic, virtuous, and courageous citizens from all social ranks. Moreover, once disciplined in the art of war, these soldiers became formidable troops. This argument reinforced revisionist histories that portrayed the Continental Army as a republican institution whose soldiers deserved credit for gaining independence. Civis's view that the Continental Army enlisted citizen-soldiers would also resonate in Peterborough. Furthermore, Civis concluded that any future American army would be neither corrupt nor a tool for tyranny because it would be composed of virtuous men imbued with the spirit of '76. The recruits' character would insulate the army from the degenerate effects normally found in professional armies. Civis's conclusion reassured readers familiar with revisionist histories and nationalist rhetoric that the regular army then being formed could be trusted to defend the nation and not feared as an instrument of tyranny.[57]

By 1813 Fourth of July orators from both parties celebrated the prowess and virtues of regular soldiers, both in the Continental Army and the army then being formed. Gouverneur Morris (1752–1816), a Federalist party stalwart, told members of New York's Washington Benevolent Society on 5 July 1813 that Washington's army was composed of "patriot soldiers engaged to defend their rights against forces of aggression. They were in truth the army of liberty. . . ." Morris said, "we had often been told that standing armies are dangerous to republics . . ." but experience in the current war taught another lesson—"no people however brave can prudently rely for defense on militia alone."[58] On 4 July 1813 Samuel Harrison Smith, editor of the *National Intelligencer*, reassured administration supporters that Madison had strengthened the army and navy. They were now on a "solid and permanent basis which cannot be shaken or undermined by returning peace."[59] Anti-army sentiment eroded under the weight of defeat and the new legacy of the Continental Army as a republican institution.

The Continental Army, stigmatized and tarnished during the Revolution, was now viewed as a model republican institution and precursor for the nation's new regular army. Political leaders, revisionist historians, and nationalists had transformed the Continental Army into "the patriot army" or "army of republican freeman." No longer was it portrayed, as it had been by republican theorists during and following the Revolution, as an army of social dregs and mercenaries. Rather, its soldiers were venerated as warriors who represented a cross section of society. They were motivated by the spirit of '76 and had not succumbed to the inherent vices of a professional army. They became trained, disciplined, and fierce fighters who retained their virtue. The Continental Army, and by implication the regular army being formed during the War of 1812, embodied the spirit of '76. As a result, the public's view that the Revolutionary War was won by regular soldiers was strengthened.

After the war mythmaking flourished around the nation's military prowess.[60] The war over, the debate over the value of the militia subsided and the distinctions between them and regulars blurred in public discourse. Nevertheless, the Continental Army had gained a new stature. American celebration of its soldiers added to the euphoria of peace and outpouring of nationalism. In September 1815, the ceremony to lay the cornerstone for a battle monument honoring soldiers who defended Baltimore against British attacks in 1814 occasioned an effusion of nationalism and gratitude toward soldiers of the War of 1812 and, more broadly, toward veterans of the Revolutionary War. Commenting

BATTLE MONUMENT

The Corner Stone of which was laid in Baltimore at the Solemnity of the 12th of Sep. 1815, in commemoration of the Defenders of this City who fell on the XII of Sep. 1814. at the Battle of North Point & the XIII during the Bombardment of Fort McHenry

"Battle Monument" was dedicated in September 1815 in Baltimore, Maryland, to the memory of the soldiers who had defended that city in 1814. At the dedication, the public expressed its gratitude not only to soldiers in the War of 1812 but also to Revolutionary War veterans. "Battle Monument" made the absence of memorials at Revolutionary War battlefields even more disgraceful because it reminded the public of their neglect in memorializing the troops that had secured the nation's independence. *Courtesy, American Antiquarian Society.*

on the dedication, *Port Folio* explained that Baltimore's monument signified much more than a memorial to a single battle. It was a "public act of justice and honour to those who have fallen in defence of their country and it sets forth an example that is altogether invaluable—an example, which if followed, will soon wipe from the page of history one of the foulest charges against republics—that of ingratitude to their best benefactors." By honoring dead heroes with monuments, *Port Folio* stated, the nation awakened "merit among the living: that people who can thus honour the fallen and perpetuate the memory and achievements of the valiant will never want heroes to fight their battles." In the future, predicted *Port Folio,* courageous men who rush to their country's defense will have "confidence that should they fall, their deeds will be rewarded by acts of public justice and that their memory will survive in the gratitude of their country." Speakers and writers reassured old soldiers that their heroism would be rewarded and remembered. Nationalists also assured the public that the veneration of soldiers would uplift public virtue.[61]

Young men caught this new spirit that romanticized heroic soldiers as archetypes of American character. So said a young scholar in an "Oration in Defense of the American Character" he delivered in 1815 before the Philomathean Society, a University of Pennsylvania student organization. The orator told his listeners that "American prowess and enterprise and talents in war" proved false the claim made by Europeans that Americans were "totally destitute of a natural character [and] love of glory [and only] . . . absorbed in a dishonest and grovelling cupidity of gain." He said that in the Revolutionary War American soldiers had displayed "the best and most exalted qualities of human nature." The victory of the "yeoman" at Bunker Hill produced "deeds [of] patriotism, valour and firmness [that] rank with those of the heroes of Thermopylae." Battles fought by the Continental Army at Trenton, Princeton, and Monmouth revealed American "talents and heroic virtues . . . [which] shone with a lustre almost superhuman." These battles, he continued, produced a "brotherhood of heroes more daring and accomplished [than] the brightest period of the most warlike nation. . . ." Taking liberties with history, the young orator observed that the War of 1812 "throws still brighter lustre around the moral and military reputation of the United States." He concluded that man for man the American soldier and sailor had no equal for daring, valour, virtue, and fighting ability. Postwar Americans romanticized their fighting men as heroic soldiers who were imbued with the spirit of '76.[62]

I sing the birth of black INGRATITUDE!
INGRATITUDE! The fiend accurst!
By guilt from hell's dark entrails torn,
When from its horrid womb, the fury burst,

. . . .

All hail! the Monster Vice is born!

POLYANTHUS 3

DURING AND AFTER the War of 1812, veterans' impoverishment, infirmities, and age added to their new status as republican-warriors. Their deprivations prompted a new generation to recall that these hoary-headed men were once young heroic soldiers who had suffered in the cause of liberty. Their miseries as aging veterans produced feelings of guilt and shame in the new generation for its ingratitude toward them. Fictional stories such as the one about the old soldier below, and pleas from invalid veterans for increased benefits or for aid in the form of pensions, aroused the public's moral sentiment of gratitude toward the aging soldiers.

The sentimental story, "The Old Soldier: An Affecting Narrative," was published in 1812 in the first edition of Thomas Condie's *Juvenile Port Folio and Literary Miscellany.*[63] Condie, the fourteen-year-old editor, regularly published didactic, melodramatic stories where "morality abounds and at length, selfishness, cruelty and injustice are punished."[64] The story begins with the maudlin scene of a poor, disabled Revolutionary War veteran, dressed in a "tattered military coat," begging for food on a busy street. Pedestrians preoccupied with their own business ignore him until a youth stops to aid the old soldier. The veteran entreats the young man to hear his tale of patriotism and sacrifice before accepting charity. A tear appears in the "old soldier's" eye as he begins to recount his life. Attracted to this emotional scene, a crowd of curious onlookers gathers around the veteran and youth.

The veteran recalls that he had left the loving arms of his bride to join the army and had endured the "various distresses of the body and mind" during the war for liberty. He recollects that his suffering continued after leaving the service because he returned home "a cripple, dependent on his country." To make matters worse, the veteran learned that his dear brother had died and that his wife was "untrue to her vow [and] was in the arms of another." His listeners learn that the veteran's service to his country cost him his health, self-sufficiency, and marriage, and left him stricken with grief. The old veteran was reduced to a beggar. His only shred of dignity was his tattered uniform and his memories of patriotism, heroism, and sacrifice.

As the story continues, the old man is transformed from a beggar, shunned and possibly despised, into a heroic soldier who deserves the public's compassion and gratitude. The veteran's tale causes the boy to confess to a passerby, he "softens my heart to pity and disposes me to acts of benevolence." The youth rewards the begging soldier with alms. Other people on the street, following the boy's example, "opened the liberal hand of charity" and "smiled . . . in approbation" upon the suffering soldier. The story concludes with a moral: "It is the business of all of us to make the countenance of this man smile with our blessings [wealth]; and chase away, if it be but for a moment, the lines of sorrow from the face of misfortune." Young readers were instructed to follow their hearts, to be compassionate and generous toward needy old soldiers because their poverty was evidence of the heroic suffering they had experienced in their youth.

The story had an even larger lesson: infirm, impoverished, and aging Revolutionary War veterans were not to be shunned as paupers; they were worthy of acclaim, gratitude, and reward. Their decrepitude was not evidence of moral failure, but a badge of honor and merit as patriotic republican-warriors. Moreover, young and old, civilian and soldier, revolutionary and postrevolutionary generations would be bound by feelings of empathy, gratitude, and charity toward suffering soldiers; the nation would be united and morally uplifted.

Veterans contributed to the public's sentimental image of themselves as heroic, disadvantaged soldiers who deserved the nation's gratitude. In their petitions for increased disability benefits or for service pensions, they often described themselves in ways that resembled both the beggar in Condie's tale of the "Old Soldier" and the heroes venerated by Fourth of July orators, nationalists, and revisionist historians. Their pleas added credibility to oratorical images and sentimental stories of suffering soldiers.

Abraham Davis's petition claimed a moral right to benefits. In December 1816, Davis, from Louisa County, South Carolina, petitioned Congress's Committee on Claims in support of a private bill submitted by his congressman to increase his invalid pension from forty dollars a year to sixty dollars annually, the maximum allowed by law. Davis resorted to a special bill after the War Department refused to increase his pension because the veteran had not submitted medical evidence to verify that his disability had become worse. Instead Davis had submitted an affidavit describing the deprivation and mental anguish that resulted from his deepening poverty, aging, and an inadequate pension.

The affidavit reported that the veteran was "aged and infirm and . . . at times suffering for want of the necessities of life." It explained that on 15 June 1815 the overseers of the poor for Louisa County voted to provide Davis ten dollars a year because the invalid pension "was not sufficient to answer the demands of his family." It explained that as his "years advance his infirmities increased [and] the extraordinary rise [in costs] in every species of subsistence" made Davis a pauper. In Davis's mind he was a heroic and disadvantaged soldier who deserved a higher benefit. Despite this heartrending appeal, the Committee on Claims rejected Davis's bill because he had based his claim on a plea to moral sentiment rather than on medical proof as required by law.[65] Nevertheless, impoverished veterans increasingly petitioned Congress for pensions. In general these veterans claimed that wartime sacrifices had either caused their poverty or were imperiling their ability to remain self-sufficient. Self-portrayals further reinforced the popular image of them as heroic and disadvantaged soldiers.

Some claimants, like John Montgomery from Chillicothe, Ohio, urged Congress to treat impoverishment as a military disability. He told Congress that his poverty resulted from infirmities that he traced to hardships while serving in the army. Montgomery claimed that his leg was amputated in 1814 because of a disease contracted as a result of "exposure and privations" while in the army. Montgomery tried to arouse Congress's empathy. He plaintively reported other miseries. The veteran wrote that his son, on whom he had relied for help, had been crippled after losing his left hand. Continuing his tale of woe, Montgomery claimed that deprivation and misfortune had compelled him to "recur to the humanity of his fellow citizens and solicit their charity in behalf of his distressed and afflicted family," a wife and their eight children.[66] Similarly, Henry Martin, from Green County, North Carolina, appealed to Congress's compassion to get a pension. His petition, submitted in February 1816, begged Congress for aid because he was "crippled by infirmities naturally incident to great age, combined with the pangs of severe wounds which he received in defense of his country's rights. . . ." Martin reported that he was "entirely unable to earn by labor a reasonable sustenance; and therefore [he] begs to be considered a pensioner on a grateful and beneficent public."[67]

The Committee on Claims rejected both Montgomery's and Martin's petitions and all others like them. The law made no provision to aid poor veterans.

The committee recited classical republican principles when it proclaimed that "Congress cannot undertake the support of paupers merely because they may have been at some period of their lives engaged in the public service." In the committee's view, soldiers served their country from a sense of patriotic duty rather than from expectations of preferment.[68] Despite resistance to their pleas in Congress, Revolutionary War veterans continued to lobby for pensions.

In 1816, taking advantage of the public's esteem and its deepening sentiment of gratitude toward Revolutionary War veterans, Continental Army officers resubmitted a petition for half-pay pensions, first introduced to Congress in 1810.[69] (See appendix A, *Officers' Claims*, for a summary of this controversy.) That petition used the image of the suffering soldier to build support for passage. No doubt many officers, certainly Short Bill Scott as we've seen, believed that they were a disadvantaged class because of the nation's mistreatment of them as soldiers and because of its neglect of them as veterans.[70] Their petition stated that they had entered the army "without regard to personal or pecuniary considerations . . . to persevere through the hardships and vicissitudes of a long and arduous war . . ." until victory was achieved. The annals of the war, the petition asserted, contained "unequivocal testimonies to their services, and privations . . ." during and following the conflict. They had "retired patiently to their homes . . . [under] the most humiliating and embarrassing circumstances" and had awaited "the justice of their country." The officers concluded that they "have an equitable claim" for pensions and appealed to the "justice and magnanimity [of Congress] for remuneration."[71]

By 1816 growing moral sentiment toward aging, infirm, and impoverished veterans created broad public support for the officers' petition, which Congress had rejected in 1810. The *Philadelphia True American* stated that the country was "indebted . . . to the fortitude, fidelity and long sufferings of those meritorious men . . ." and that a sympathetic Congress ought to be "disposed to relieve the urgent necessities of the thinned remnant of that veteran band. . . ." The *True American* printed a letter by a person identified as "Citizen," a pseudonym probably meant to convey Democratic-Republican ideals and the writer's self-professed civic virtue. Citizen told readers that "no men ever deserved to be well rewarded more than our revolutionary officers and men; for it is admitted by all that they not only risked life, limb, and property but their suffering during the contest from 1776 to 1780 was such as no people during a revolutionary struggle ever endured. . . ."[72] Despite such appeals, in 1816 Congress again rejected the officers' petition on legal grounds. Congress stated that the nation's obligation to these officers had been met in 1783 with the award of commutated pensions. Nevertheless, the officers' claims, along with claims from rank-and-file troops, reinforced the image of the suffering soldier in the public's mind.[73]

The groundswell of nostalgia for the Revolution that swept the country in 1816 strengthened the view that the nation owed a debt of gratitude to suffering soldiers such as Montgomery and Peterborough's Alld. In November 1816, Benjamin Elliot, a young lawyer and author from a prominent South Carolina family, urged Hezekiah Niles, editor of the *Niles Weekly Register*, to collect the "speeches and orations of revolution." Elliot wrote Niles that "the present is a most propitious period: the feelings and sentiments of '76 were never so prevalent as present. . . . the events of the late war have imparted a flow of national feeling for every thing republican." The death notices of Revolutionary leaders and soldiers, which appeared more frequently, added a sense of urgency to honor Revolutionary War veterans.[74]

Elliot's appeal reflected and energized public sentiment. "Posterity will ask the record of this age," a supporter of Elliot's project wrote Niles, "and wonder that the immediate successors of the people of '76 should have so degenerated in forty years as to forget to estimate the importance of that period, and the virtues of those who stamped its character. I do not believe that the age will continue to risk the imputation."[75] We must "keep alive," a friend wrote to Niles, "the sentiments and principles that inspired the bosoms of our fathers, and urged them to put on the armour of resistance to curb tyranny and arrest oppression. There never was a more favorable juncture, for instilling those sentiments, than the present. . . ."[76] Expressing a similar view, the editor of the *Boston Patriot* added that it was the "duty of the present generation" to show that "the founders of our liberties were as deserving of their admiration as fiction has made a Romulus or Aeneas in Italy or an Alfred in England: men who want nothing but the future greatness of their country. . . ." The Revolutionary era, he said, was unique in the history of mankind and "will be remembered by remote generations as one whose importance makes all other eras of comparative insignificance."[77] Projects honoring soldiers gained widespread and enthusiastic support because the post–revolutionary generation was eager to affirm its own virtue by expressing gratitude to the Revolutionary veterans.

July Fourth orators further popularized this sentiment. Mordecai Noah's powerful oration to New York's Tammany Society on 4 July 1817 urged his listeners to honor Revolutionary War veterans. Noah, the former United States consul to Tunis and editor of the *National Advocate,* told celebrants that Revolutionary soldiers had endured the "privations" of war, and yet "the fire of patriotism burned bright in their hearts; it warmed them to deeds of heroism never exceeded in the annals of the world; they struggled and conquered—they suffered but were victorious." Noah concluded, "never let us forget the gratitude we owe to the noble spirits who died in this contest nor neglect the warworn soldier or Patriot of the Revolution. We have but few left—let us cherish them in their declining years and smooth their passage to the grave by the liberality and confidence of a free and enlightened people."[78] Animated by sentiment, America hastened to preserve the spirit of '76 by awarding pensions to its suffering soldiers.

The flood of petitions from veterans seeking pensions coupled with the public groundswell of moral sentiment toward infirm, impoverished, and aged veterans resulted in easy passage in Congress of a bill in 1816 to substantially increase disability benefits. Disability pensions rose by 60 percent for privates, from a maximum of five to eight dollars a month, and by 30 percent for officers at or below the rank of captain to twenty dollars per month.[79] That same year, Congress considered creating an "invalid corps" that would provide pensions to "invalid, disabled and superannuated" soldiers of the Revolution, like Montgomery, Martin, and Alld.[80] Giving their full support to the idea, the editors of *Port Folio* implored the public to "preserve and increase [the nation's] reputation" through preferment to those "by whom it has been achieved. Let honours ennoble them, and opulence open her coffers to excite the emulation of contemporary or succeeding ambition." *Port Folio* claimed that the proposed pension would pay the nation's debt of gratitude to its heroic and disadvantaged veterans.[81] Despite Congress' rejection of the invalid corps, public pressure increased to compensate veterans as an expression of gratitude.[82]

In 1817 Pennsylvania doubled its pension to impoverished Continental Army veterans who had served in its state's regiments.[83] Legislators justified the increase from forty to eighty dollars a year both as a reward and as a compensation to the "old and infirm soldiers of '76" whose sufferings had achieved the blessings of independence, liberty, and prosperity enjoyed by their heirs. Legislators stated that Pennsylvania ought to share "a trifle out of our abundance" to ease the last days of these soldiers and to show their "services are appreciated by a grateful country." Legislators proclaimed that the increase in benefits "is not only demanded by considerations of gratitude and justice to these venerable patriots . . . but is also required by the dictates of a liberal and enlightened policy." They asserted that a forty-dollar annual annuity was "inadequate to supply their wants or alleviate their sufferings. . . . it is a pittance equally unworthy [of] the giver and those to which it is given [especially since] the public treasury [is] flourishing."[84]

Pennsylvania lawmakers described the recipients as elderly and poor, "the youngest of whom cannot indeed be less than sixty years of age [and] borne down under the accumulated weight of age, infirmity and want, with not a house or home. . . ." Appealing to the public's conscience and compassion, lawmakers rhetorically asked, "shall we . . . cast these veterans on the charity of the world and leave them to pine, to sicken and to die in misery and want?" Answering their own question, they declared, "Justice, gratitude and patriotism forbid it." Legislators concluded that republics must "reward" those who "render distinguished and meritorious" public service. In Pennsylvania, legislators used the image of the suffering soldier to shape state policy affecting veterans.[85]

BY 1817 THE image of the suffering soldier had become a part of the country's political culture. Partisan politics helped to create the image. Between 1806 and 1812, partisan conflict over defense policy expanded into a rhetorical battle over which political party could preserve the spirit of '76. Republican and Federalist orators romanticized soldiers to evoke that spirit among their listeners. By ennobling soldiers, party spokesmen helped to change the concept of the Revolution as a people's war by accentuating the role of soldiers.

Sentimental and revisionist histories of the Revolutionary War, which appeared after the turn of the century, contributed to the image by transforming the meaning of a people's war. New histories romanticized the miseries endured by troops to glorify their heroism, patriotism, and merit. They removed the stigma of treason from the Continental Army by transforming its Newburgh Conspiracy into an example of civic virtue. Revisionist histories credited the army, not the mythical people, with winning the war.

The new image gained strength partly because the nation failed to wage the kind of people's war in 1812 that they had believed had been fought in the Revolution. When the War of 1812 began leaders expressed faith in a resurgence of patriotism and a *rage militaire* against England. American military defeats and bitter factionalism over the conflict dashed those hopes. As defeats and disunion discredited the concept of a people's war, leaders from both political parties and nationalists increasingly glorified ordinary soldiers to rouse militant patriotism and to restore national unity. Going even further, they portrayed regular soldiers in the Revolution and in the War of 1812, rather than the amateur citizen-soldier, as republican-warriors and as exemplars of American character. During the War of 1812 Americans used the image of the suffering soldier to redefine defense policy and their political culture.

Veterans' self-portrayals as anguished, aging, infirm, impoverished, and neglected heroes also fostered and strengthened the image. Their appeals for aid to Congress aroused the public's compassion toward veterans and inspired a new generation to venerate, reward, and succor the old soldiers. Veterans pleading for assistance also roused the nation's feelings of guilt for its ingratitude toward them. Their supplications helped to convince a new generation that regular soldiers, as Short Bill Scott had claimed, deserved to be rewarded for their heroic service and aided for their deprivations.

Thus, Fourth of July orations, revisionist histories, the lessons of the War of 1812, nationalism, veterans' pleas for aid, sentimental tales of veterans' hardships, and an outpouring of nostalgia for the Revolution had created the image of the suffering soldier. The image romanticized the patriotism of American soldiers through accounts of bravery and heroic suffering endured in combat and camp. This feature of the image made battlefields and military encampments, especially Valley Forge, hallowed symbols of soldiers' nationalism and civic virtue. This part of the image apotheosized soldiers as republican-warriors, as exemplars of the spirit of '76, and as models of national character. The image also depicted aging veterans' deprivation, poverty, infirmity, and despair as badges of honor, valor, and rectitude. This feature not only underscored the veterans' virtue, but it also accentuated the nation's vice for its ingratitude toward the old soldiers. These two features were synergetic. Together they heightened the power, utility, and durability of the image in public discourse and political debate. The image continually unleashed the moral sentiment of gratitude. It enlivened Americans to follow their hearts, rather than received beliefs, to shape their political culture and public policy. Soldiers, such as those from Peterborough, New Hampshire, were elevated to an esteemed cultural status as heroes owed a debt of gratitude. As a result, the Revolution could no longer be portrayed as a people's war if that image excluded the Continental Army. The people and the army were one.

The image transformed perceptions of the Continental Army. No longer did Americans view it as an army filled by large numbers of transients, social dregs, former slaves, greedy bounty jumpers, draftees, paid substitutes, and power-hungry officers who many Revolutionary leaders feared and despised. No longer did Americans perceive the army as frequently plagued by the desertions, riots, and insurrections that had nearly crippled it. Newburgh no longer tarnished the army with the stain of treason. A new generation apotheosized the army's troops as brave, heroic, patriotic citizens who came from all ranks of society as they had in Peterborough. Revolts in the army came to be viewed as reflections of its suffering, not measures of its vice. Valley Forge and other such sites became hallowed ground, and Newburgh a symbol of civic virtue.

Thus, Americans rejected a central tenet of republicanism and received wisdom. They conceived the Continental Army as an exception to the doctrine that regular armies were filled with a vice-ridden rabble inclined toward tyranny, and that regular armies were antithetical to republican ideals. Americans were poised to choose between two memories of the Revolutionary War. One celebrated only the militant patriotism of the people and their militia. The other included regular troops and gave special credit to the Continental Army, for the nation's independence, and to its soldiers, as models of national character. In 1817 that choice moved to Congress.

WHERE THERE ANY STORIES of
SUCCESSFUL CONTINENTAL VETERANS?

CHAPTER 4

Suffering Soldiers and Public Policy

The 1818 Revolutionary War Pension Act

IN THE SUMMER of 1817, President Monroe made a triumphant tour of the Northeast to unite the recently divided nation. He animated nationalist feelings, kindled nostalgia toward the Revolution, honored the new status of veterans, and aroused the sentiment of gratitude toward the old soldiers. Proudly wearing his military cocked hat, Monroe reminded citizens that he had "profusely shed his blood more than 40 years ago" to help win independence. With great feeling, the president pledged never to "be indifferent to the merit of those who" fought in the Revolution.[1] Within a few months, Monroe proposed legislation that would codify the image of the suffering soldier in the nation's political culture and public policy. In doing so he shifted the venue for transforming the nation's memory of the Revolution and the status of veterans from celebratory fetes to congressional debate. The sentiment of gratitude, linked to democratic ideals, would play a significant role in that debate.

During his tour Monroe praised and sentimentalized veterans before cheering crowds. He sanctified the Revolutionary War battlefields he visited by declaring them hallowed ground.[2] On one occasion on 2 July, while inspecting the run-down earthen ramparts of Fort Griswold in New London, Connecticut, Monroe greeted Parke and Ebenezer Avery. The Avery brothers were possibly the last survivors of the vicious battle that had cost, by historian Mark Boatner's estimate, the lives of most of Griswold's 145 defenders.[3] Parke and Ebenezer were the sons of Capt. Parke Avery, whose family was prominent in

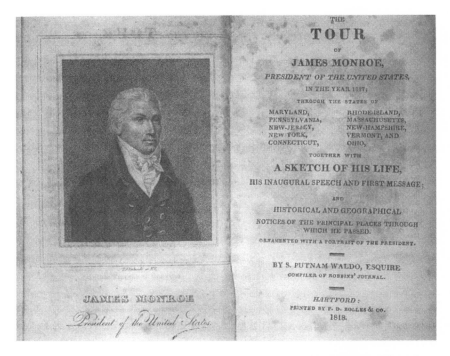

Frontispiece of the account of President James Monroe's 1817 tour of the Northeast. Monroe's tour was intended to diminish the sectional and political conflict that had erupted over the War of 1812. Monroe used the tour to promote feelings of nationalism by paying homage to soldiers and veterans of the Revolutionary War. He visited battlefields and joined in the Fourth of July Celebration at Bunker Hill. It was during this tour that Monroe reminded the public of its debt of gratitude to Revolutionary War veterans and spoke of the need to aid those veterans who were destitute. *Courtesy, American Antiquarian Society.*

Groton and New London. Parke (1741–1821) was a lieutenant in the local militia. In 1776 and 1778, he had served with troops attached to the Connecticut line of the Continental Army. Parke's brother, Ebenezer (1747–1828), served as an ensign in the First Groton Company of the militia. The social background and military experience of the Avery brothers conformed to the new image of the heroic suffering soldier. Like most of the soldiers from Peterborough discussed above, the Avery brothers came from an established family whose service crossed generational lines and military organizations. Like Peterborough's Randall McAllister, the brothers bore the scars of war.

No doubt the three veterans spoke about that bloody and legendary engagement where, thirty-six years earlier, Benedict Arnold, the "infamous Judas," commanded the British force.[4] The Avery brothers probably recalled that on 6 September 1781, as British troops burned the towns of Groton and New London, militia and veterans of the Continental Army gathered in the broken-down fort to protect citizens fleeing from the enemy. Ebenezer, Parke, and their brothers Jasper (1743–81) and Elisha (1755–81) rushed to defend the fort. Parke brought his teenage son Thomas. Arnold ordered the fort taken. Maj. William Montgomery, who led the assault force, warned the Americans that if they did not surrender they would be put to the sword. Although outnumbered five to one, the defenders stubbornly resisted, "with the greatest resolution and bravery," numerous British assaults against the fort. After a half hour of bitter and intense combat, the superior British force overwhelmed the Americans. Jasper, Elisha, and Thomas Avery were killed during the assault. Thomas, who was standing by his father's side, died firing at the attackers storming the rampart. Parke's face was horribly disfigured in the assault. An onrushing

"A REPRESENTATION of the FIGURES exhibited and paraded through the Streets of Philadelphia," 1780. Benedict Arnold was a symbol of treachery and ingratitude. In this representation,
he is depicted as an agent of the Devil whom the people have condemned to infamy for his treason
and greed. The reference to him made at Fort Griswold had a double meaning for the new
generation of Americans. As a symbol of evil, Arnold's role in the attack accentuated the virtue of
the fort's defenders. As a traitor, he also symbolized the vice of ingratitude. *Courtesy, American
Antiquarian Society.*

GROTON HEIGHTS MONUMENT.

To commemorate the defence of Fort Griswold by Col. WILLIAM LEDYARD and his brave companions, September 6, 1781. Corner-stone laid September 6, 1826; dedicated September 6, 1830. Material, granite ; 26 feet square at the base, 24 feet square on the die, 22 feet square at base of the shaft, and 11 feet at the top ; whole height 127 feet. It stood thus till the Centennial, in 1881, when the height was increased to 135 feet.

Monument dedicated in 1826 to the memory of Colonel William Ledyard and the defenders of Fort Griswold. Especially during and following the War of 1812, nationalist publications urged the construction of monuments to memorialize the hallowed battlefields of the Revolutionary War and the soldiers who fought there. *Courtesy, American Antiquarian Society.*

British soldier plunged his bayonet into Parke's eye socket above the brow, tore out his eye, and left a hideous inch-deep gash the length of his forehead. British troops left the profusely bleeding patriot for dead. Attackers bayoneted Ebenezer in his shoulder and neck and left him writhing on the ground to bleed to death.[5]

Heavy casualties and Montgomery's death in the final assault sent British troops into a frenzy after they occupied the fort. A British officer used Col. William Ledyard's sword moments after it was given as a token of surrender to rip open the American commander's chest, killing him instantly. British troops ran amok. They executed many of the wounded and committed atrocities. British troops loaded wounded defenders in a wagon and pushed it down a "long and very steep hill," firing at it "while it was running." The impact of the wagon against a tree "was so great to those faint & bleeding men that part of them died instantly."[6] Following the war Parke enjoyed the reputation of a "'true patriot.'" He cherished his scar as a mark of valor. His brother Ebenezer was equally proud of his service. He refused to remove the bloodstains on the floor of his house where wounded and dying defenders of Fort Griswold had been nursed. The old soldier was delighted to show those stains to visitors who were curious to learn about the battle from one of its few survivors.[7]

Monroe and the Averys probably recalled that in 1781 the battle became a symbol of American valor and honor, which patriots contrasted with British villainy. They may have recollected that the cry, "remember Griswold," was shouted at Yorktown to inspire American troops. While the three veterans reminisced, a reporter observed that onlookers stood in awe as if watching a mystical civic rite. The *Hartford American Mercury* reported that the president, deeply moved by the wounds borne by the Avery brothers, caressed their scars: "under the impulse of the moment [Monroe] laid his hands on the traces of their wounds." Monroe's touch, according to the *Mercury,* anointed the two veterans: "[T]hese venerable patriots realized that THEIR COUNTRY BLESSED THEM [for their] valour [and] sufferings" to secure its liberty. The symbolism of a civic blessing escaped no one watching the scene. The reporter, overwhelmed by nostalgia, wrote that Fort Griswold "becomes again distinguished in the annals of our country. There we behold the NATION'S CHIEF and *at his side* the *hoary* veteran who *on that spot* . . . stood as *volunteer* in defense of his COUNTRY and his HOME." Monroe, the former Continental Army officer who could still feel his wounds, paid homage to fallen heroes and valiant survivors of the Revolutionary War. To observers, the Avery brothers and their commander in chief personified the image of the heroic suffering soldier.[8]

Monroe's tour created a crescendo of nationalism and nostalgia as it moved toward Massachusetts.[9] Nearly forty thousand people cheered him as he entered Boston and a huge crowd joined him to commemorate the Fourth of July at Bunker Hill. He told the multitude that the site had been consecrated by the blood of the men who had fought and died there. "It is impossible," he said, "to approach Bunker Hill, where the war of the Revolution commenced, with so much honor to the nation, without being deeply affected. The blood spilt here roused the whole American people, and united them in a common cause in the defense of their rights; that union will never be broken." Later, the president used the meeting of the Massachusetts Society of the Cincinnati to praise the Continental Army and urge compassion for disadvantaged veterans. Monroe told the officers that they shared the "honor [of] the common toils and perils of the war for our Independence. We were embarked in the same sacred cause of liberty, and we have lived to enjoy our common labors." Noting that only a few of their comrades were still alive, he pledged to preserve their example of "manly patriotism . . . political integrity . . . social concord and public virtue" for future generations to emulate. The welfare of those few remaining men was never far from his mind. Possibly in hushed tones, he told his fellow veterans that some old soldiers were "less fortunate than ourselves" and deserved the nation's compassion and assistance. The officers responded to Monroe's words of charity by handing him their petition for half-pay pensions for themselves. Ignoring the objects of Monroe's charity, they appealed for his "intercession" with Congress to secure its passage.[10]

Monroe refused, however, to single out officers for special treatment. He returned from his tour intent on honoring and aiding "less fortunate" veterans. Monroe had in mind a sweeping and liberal program of service pensions for aged, infirm, and impoverished veterans. Monroe's stature as a patriot and war hero added credibility to his sentiments. Monroe had fought at Harlem Heights, White Plains, Brandywine, Germantown, and Monmouth, and had been badly wounded at Trenton. After his election to the presidency, newspapers had published excerpts from James Wilkinson's recently published *Memoirs* to remind the public of Monroe's heroism at Trenton, where he led a successful attack on a British battery. Had it failed, Wilkinson wrote, American forces *"might have* [been] *compelled to retreat which would have been fatal to us."*[11]

Politically as well, Monroe was ideally suited to propose a radical departure from the Founders' public policy. At age fifty-eight the president projected the visage of a virtuous republican. He looked like a "plain country gentleman"— hardy and vigorous, benign, and above suspicion with a "countenance [that] exhibits lineaments of great severity." His public manner complemented this humble appearance. Though an awkward speaker, he was capable of shedding tears at the sight of old comrades suffering from infirmities and poverty. Monroe's shyness added to his "affable, unaffected and dignified" demeanor. He dressed the part of a Founder and war hero by wearing clothes stylish in that era, especially "an outfit reminiscent of [a Continental Army] uniform." People fondly referred to him as the last of the "cocked hats."[12] During his summer tour Monroe had worn a black-bowed ribbon cockade, the emblem of the Federalist party, in his hat to symbolize that he stood above party. Monroe was a patriot leader and war hero who strove to preserve the spirit of '76 and to secure the nation's honor by paying the debt of gratitude to Revolutionary War veterans. Memorializing and aiding ordinary soldiers would not only bind generations, but would also set a new standard of civic virtue.[13]

On 2 December 1817, in his opening address to the Fifteenth Congress, Monroe proposed that the federal government aid impoverished Revolutionary War veterans. Monroe appealed to Congress's spirit of nationalism, liberality, compassion, and gratitude. Never before, he told Congress, had the nation been so "prosperous and happy. . . . Local jealousies are rapidly yielding to more generous, enlarged and enlightened views of national policy," which draws "our attention . . . with peculiar interest to the [few] surviving officers and soldiers of our Revolutionary army. . . ." Monroe said that some of the survivors were reduced to poverty and "even to real distress. . . ." He continued, "These men have a claim on the gratitude of this country, and it will do honor to their country, to provide for them." He urged prompt action because in a few years "the opportunity will be forever lost. . . ."[14] Monroe's proposal marked a watershed between the Revolution's republican principles and the new generation's emerging political culture. Supported by an outpouring of nostalgia and moral sentiment of gratitude, Monroe proposed to elevate veterans to a privileged social rank and to grant them preferment. In doing so, he asked Congress to incorporate the image of the suffering soldier in the political culture.[15]

Monroe expected little opposition, because of the growing sentiment to reward and aid Revolutionary War veterans. He was not disappointed. The public applauded Monroe's proposal. The *Boston Columbian Centinel* voiced its approval that the "war worn relics of the army which acquired Independence" were objects of Congress's "beneficence."[16] Monroe's address was warmly received by a Congress that was filled with a new generation of legislators who were part of the massive turnover of representatives in the 1816 election.[17] The debate on the pension proposal in the House of Representatives disclosed the power of the image of the suffering soldier to shape the political culture and public policy.

The House appointed five former Continental Army officers to a special seven-member committee, headed by Joseph Bloomfield (1753–1823) of New Jersey, to prepare pension legislation.[18] Bloomfield, himself a war hero and now a political sage, strongly supported Monroe's proposal. Bloomfield had risen to the rank of major in the Continental Army, had been wounded at Brandywine, and had fought at Monmouth. His public career covered the spectrum of American politics. After the war, he joined the Federalist party and was a member of the Society of the Cincinnati. In 1800 Bloomfield embraced Jeffersonian Republicanism. He was elected the governor of New Jersey from 1803 to 1812. In June 1812, Bloomfield resigned the governorship to accept a command of American troops to wage war against British forces. Like many others during that war, Bloomfield became an ardent nationalist. In 1817 Bloomfield entered Congress "wealthy, respected," a leader in the Republican party, an elder statesman, a nationalist, and a Revolutionary War hero who showed great "pride in his military service." Bloomfield's leadership was expected to quash any controversy over the bill and to ensure its passage.[19]

On 12 December 1817 Bloomfield's committee reported a liberal bill to award half-pay pensions to every soldier "who served in the revolutionary war" and who was either "reduced to indigence" or who was unable to "procure subsistence by manual labour" for any reason such as "age" or "sickness." The bill required applicants to present proof of "service and incapacity" under an oath to federal district judges. The bill provided that after a court certified a veteran's eligibility, the secretary of war was to place him on the pension rolls without further investigation. Pensioners were to be paid semiannually in the "same manner as pensions to invalids." The bill made veterans ineligible if they sold or transferred property after the bill's passage to meet its indigence requirement. It made it illegal to transfer the pension or its benefits from the veteran.[20] This bill contained the traditional half-pay principle. It incorporated the concept of an invalid corps by including infirm and impoverished soldiers. It was also democratic. The bill would award pensions to veterans regardless of the length or type of service.²¹ Potentially, the bill provided a pension to every superannuated man who ever carried a musket against the British. Estimating from the proportion of Peterborough's veterans still alive in 1817, approximately a third of the soldiers who fought in the Revolutionary War, perhaps as many as seventy thousand men were potential recipients of the pension proposed by the House. Congress, however, operated on the assumption that the number of surviving veterans was small.²²

The public's support for the House's liberal bill was widespread, bipartisan, and a reflection of the "good feelings and sense of justice" Americans had for their veterans.²³ Endorsing the bill, the *Boston Columbian Centinel*, a leading Federalist paper, reported that its "timely benevolence" would help veterans. The paper cited an artillery captain who had served throughout the Revolutionary war and was an "aged man (say of 65) . . . who was destitute of a cent," and who was discovered begging for his food.²⁴ Like Thomas Condie's tale of the old soldier told to youthful readers to arouse feelings of empathy and gratitude, newspapers used the image of the impoverished soldier to express support for Bloomfield's bill.

The *Federal Republican and Baltimore Telegraph* praised "Our Revolutionary Patriots" and applauded the bill for paying the nation's debt of gratitude to them. The paper stated that the veterans had witnessed "the success of their exertion; that [they] have lived to see their country honored and respected abroad and prosperous at home . . . while they have been suffering all the horrors of poverty and want." The *Federal Republican* scorned the nation's past ingratitude toward veterans: "the benefits are received and the benefactors forgotten." The *Federal Republican* asked rhetorically, "If a patriot when dead deserves a marble monument at the expense of his country, how much more does he deserve during life, a subsistence from his country?" The proposed pension, the paper stated, would permit every veteran to enjoy "the comfort and repose of his declining years . . . [without suffering further] all the horrors of old age and poverty, [and] . . . he would have closed his eyes in benedictions on his native land." The paper concluded that veterans deserved the nation's justice and gratitude, and until that debt was paid the country's honor and virtue were tarnished. The paper urged Congress to pass the bill "to wipe away this stain [of ingratitude] upon the national character."²⁵

Republican papers expressed similar views. William Duane, editor of the *Philadelphia Aurora*, one of the country's leading Republican newspapers, published a letter from an "old soldier," possibly a pseudonym for Bloomfield, in support of the bill. The old soldier reminded his readers of the "unparalleled sufferings of the patriotic heroes . . . [who] established our independence, our freedom, prosperity and happiness, and rescued this great republic from British bondage." He observed that many veterans were now "war worn [and] bowed down by penury . . . begging their bread." A generous pension, the old soldier continued, will "bear testimony for future history that [the] country [has] not entirely lost [its] sense of justice, honor and humanity."[26] An outpouring of moral sentiment favoring the pension bill was sweeping away traditional republican ideals that stood nearly forty years in opposition to service pensions.

The bill's principles provoked little controversy in the House, although concern over program costs led Rep. John Linn of New Jersey to propose that the pension be restricted to Continental Army veterans.[27] Responding to this restriction, Bloomfield urged the House to reject Linn's proposal because Bloomfield believed that the country could afford to give every veteran a pension because the government enjoyed a huge surplus. Based upon "personal knowledge," Bloomfield estimated that 90 percent of the Revolutionary veterans had died, and that only "one sixth" of those alive would apply for the pension. As a further response to Linn's proposal, Bloomfield urged Congress to spend more money on the program by increasing the amount of the pension. In response to Bloomfield's appeal, Congress voted "without objection" to raise monthly pensions from $3.33 to $8.00 for the rank and file and to award $20.00 a month to all officers. The proposed rates were the same as those paid to totally disabled soldiers and officers holding the rank of captain. Thus, Congress equated poverty with disability. Moreover, by changing the rate, the House differentiated the measure from the repugnant half-pay principle that was associated with the discredited officers' lobby that was then petitioning Congress for their own pensions.[28]

Ohio's William Henry Harrison, however, ignited an acrimonious battle when he proposed that pensions be awarded only to Continental Army veterans who had served at least three years or until the end of the Revolutionary War. Unlike Linn, Harrison was not interested in saving money. Harrison wanted to reward hard-core troops such as Peterborough's Scotts and Alld, not soldiers like the Morisons and Smiths who mobilized for only a few days, weeks, or months. He told the House that pensions ought to be awarded to men who saw "serious service . . . [who were] covered with scars and borne down by lengthened service, [and not to] those who had been called out for an hour or a day." Harrison's remarks drew sharp and angry replies.[29]

Virginia's George F. Strother, seething from Harrison's effort to exclude the militia, advised the House that it was neither "just [nor] politic . . . to discriminate between the Continental line and state troops and the militia," and that it was impossible to measure the "peril" faced by each soldier with a "cool arithmetical calculation [and to] draw a line of discrimination." His blood boiling, Strother defended the militia's valor and its military value. He recalled that the militia, "half armed and undisciplined [helped to] meet the invading foe and [to] assist in repelling him from your shores." He called their victories at Bunker Hill and Guilford Court House, North Carolina, "monuments" to their "valor." Strother glorified the militia's militant patriotism. Those troops, he proclaimed, were motivated by "that love of liberty and country, which elevates man to the highest destiny, [which] was the sole emulating principle which gave courage to their hearts and strength to their arms in the hour of battle. Here were motives as pure and achievements as brilliant as illustrate the proudest nations of antiquity." Possibly carried away by this panegyric or by his anger, Strother denigrated the Continental Army. Strother said that the army "had a mixed and compound motive" for fighting. He stated that the "holy flame that then electrified the country no doubt burnt bright in their bosoms; but they were surrounded by all the pride, pomp, and circumstance of glorious war; ambition had his prize in view, and avarice his reward." His angry speech resonated with his generation's resentments against regulars who were believed to be tainted with self-interest, political ambition, and greed.[30]

Strother and Harrison were about to embroil the House in the divisive controversy over the relative merit of militia and regular troops. Strother, however, stopped his tirade. Possibly his anger cooled as he realized that this old controversy was out of line with the nation's moral sentiment and the new status accorded Continental Army veterans. Strother suddenly ceased the verbal attack on the army and appealed for conciliation: let "national pride [and] national gratitude obliterate [the] invidious distinctions" and reward all "who contributed to build up our magnificent political fabric . . . [and embrace them] in the wide circle of gratitude." Strother urged Congress to extend "national beneficence" to every veteran who "wasted his health and shed his blood in freedom's cause" and who was now forced "with desponding heart and palsied limbs to totter from door to door, bowing his yet untamed soul to melt the frozen bosom of reluctant charity." He continued his appeal: the nation "should seek out these noble ruins of that splendid period and spread its charity around to warm and cheer them . . . in the evenings of their days." Having made his point to Harrison, Strother beseeched Congress to put Revolutionary War veterans above politics and to reward all of them as the nation's benefactors.[31]

Richard M. Johnson of Kentucky supported Strother's appeal for a liberal bill with a plea for justice and humanitarianism. Johnson stated that in this "age of philanthropic undertakings" when missions go abroad to save and aid the "Hindoos," the nation ought to offer its "benevolence" to the "poor and needy" Revolutionary soldiers whose "happiness or misery . . . awaits the fate of this bill." He criticized Americans for aiding heathens abroad while neglecting their suffering soldiers at home. Responding to such appeals, the House put aside the conventional conflict over the military value of the militia and regulars. Feeling generous because of the huge surplus in the Treasury, the House extended the bill's benefits to sailors and naval officers who served in either the United States Navy or navies authorized by the states.[32]

Some representatives were troubled by the bill's indigence provision, however. In their view, it tainted the pension's expression of gratitude with the stigma of pauperism. Congressmen Edward Colston of Virginia and Benjamin Orr of Massachusetts proposed that the indigence provision be removed from the bill. Colston said that it was "degrading" to require a veteran, "by whose bravery and sufferings we are entitled to hold seats in this floor . . . to expose his poverty to the world, and exhibit the proof of it, to entitle him to relief . . ." He stated that removing references to indigence would reflect the House's "liberal spirit" and its view that the pension was an "act of justice [rewarding] those meritorious men [who] having suffered . . . have remained for years unrewarded." He was "ashamed" to hear the bill called an "act of benevolence," when, in his mind, it was an act of justice.[33]

John Forsyth of Georgia also objected to the indigence provision, but he believed that the bill's indigence provision was only a legislative formality to be ignored in practice. Its liberal spirit, he believed, removed the taint of pauperism. In Forsyth's view, the bill paid the public's debt of gratitude to aged and meritorious suffering soldiers. In his mind, the pension was not poor relief because veterans "inspired the [public's] most grateful emotions [and] desire to relieve them" of their "want." Forsyth was not bothered by the prospect that some wealthy veterans would exploit the law's liberal spirit. He preferred "that the government should lose a few hundred dollars" in payments to rich soldiers rather than impose a means test that would deter "a single suffering officer or soldier of the pittance proposed." Although he agreed that a liberal pension program established a "dangerous precedent," nevertheless, Forsyth urged its passage to pay the nation's debt of gratitude to its suffering soldiers.[34]

Continued debate over eligibility and the bill's spirit resulted in a motion to recommit the proposal to Bloomfield's committee for clarification. Kentucky's Johnson said that the bill's supporters faced an "awful crisis . . . amid the diversity of opinions" over eligibility. Johnson observed: "Some would confine the benefits of the bill to the Continental troops; others would extend them to the State troops and militia. Some would embrace in its provisions the rich as well as the poor; others would limit the bounty to the needy. Some would provide for those only who served during the war; some for those who served three years; some would limit the terms of service at one year, and some at six months. . . . Amidst these jarring opinions, if we recommit the bill, it may be lost forever." Johnson urged the House to defeat the motion to recommit the bill to the committee. He pleaded with members to pass the bill that would award the nation's "bounty and generosity" to its "war-worn" veterans.[35]

In his appeal to Congress to stop bickering over the bill's provisions, Johnson invoked sentimental feelings toward General Bloomfield, its principal advocate, who was absent from the chamber, "exhausted with fatigue." Possibly in the melodramatic voice of a Fourth of July orator, Johnson told the House that "Divine Providence" had made Bloomfield, a man "with the frost of seventy winters upon his head, [God's agent] to plead the cause of those who breasted the storm of the Revolution." Continuing his emotional appeal, Johnson made opposition to the bill a personal affront to Bloomfield. The old general, Johnson said, exemplified the "venerable patriot" whose service to his country and "modesty" in retirement had "excited the deepest sensibility." Johnson declared that few of these "worthies now remain" and urged passage of the bill in the name of the "founders of American independence." The motion to recommit the bill was soundly defeated by a margin of nearly three to one.[36] Soon after, on 24 December 1817, by a voice vote, the House approved a pension of eight dollars a month to every soldier and of twenty dollars a month to every officer "who served in the Revolutionary War in any of the regiments" or navies raised either by Congress or the states, and who were "reduced to indigence and incapable of procuring subsistence."[37]

The House's liberal bill included practically all aged, poor, or infirm veterans who fought against the British in the Revolutionary War.[38] By adopting the benefit rates paid to invalid veterans, the House bill made "incapacity" and

"indigence" comparable to a service-related disability. It incorporated the presumption that aged veterans' poverty and infirmities resulted partly from military service. Between 1812 and 1817, many veterans petitioning Congress for
pensions had made this claim, and for some soldiers, such as Peterborough's
Benjamin Alld, this appeared to be true. By removing the half-pay principle
from its measure, the House separated its bill from the officers' lobby that was
tainted with self-interest and elitism. The House bill also removed the controversial issue of the relative value of the militia and regulars. The bill accorded
equal merit to all veterans who had fought in the war. The House bill was
aimed at satisfying the public's moral sentiment of gratitude. Representatives
were eager to spend part of the federal surplus to pay the nation's debt of
gratitude to its heroic soldiers and to do justice by aiding disadvantaged veterans. The bill proposed to codify the image of the suffering soldier through a
new public policy bestowing preferment and an honored social rank on all
veterans. Debate on the bill revealed that the metaphors and images found in
partisan oratory, in revisionist histories of the Revolution, in nationalist publications, and even in claims from invalid veterans for more benefits had per-
meated the ideas and language guiding the formation of public policy.

The public celebrated the passage of the pension bill in the House. An
editorial in Baltimore's *Federal Republican* endorsing the measure stated that "a
paltry panegyric on the fourth of July" was no longer sufficient to express
the nation's gratitude to the "poor, emaciated, hoary veterans whose scars are
yet manifest. . . ." The paper claimed that until the bill became law, a self-
indulgent nation treated its veterans unjustly. It protested that "had only a
small portion of the money now expended in such idle mirth and festivity
[Fourth of July celebrations] been devoted to the support of our suffering"
veterans there would be no need "to complain about the ingratitude of Americans." The editor assured readers that almost every veteran could tell Fourth of
July celebrants that "[I had] laid my weary limbs on frozen ground . . . for you I
have left prints of my bloody feet upon the snows of winter—for you I have
braved death in the battle field as these scars can testify. . . ." Without the
pension, the paper warned, veterans will continue "tottering to the grave with
no other legacy to leave [their] children than . . . poverty and our country's
ingratitude. . . . Indeed our revolutionary sympathies seem to have deadened:
in the hurry & lustre of the world our oldest benefactors have been forgotten."
The paper urged the Senate to remove this stain by passing the House's bill.[39]

Despite public enthusiasm and overwhelming support for the bill in the

House, the bill was severely attacked in the Senate. The conflict began when its Committee on Military Affairs radically changed the House's bill. The Senate's version limited benefits to Continental Army veterans who had served for at least three years or until the end of the Revolutionary War. It eliminated any suggestion of charity by substituting the phrase "in reduced circumstances" for the House's wording, "reduced to indigence; or by age, sickness, or other cause, rendered incapable to procure subsistence by manual labor"; and, the Senate's bill did not require veterans to prove financial need to be eligible for the pension.[40]

The bill faced impassioned and articulate opponents who were determined to uphold inherited republican principles opposed to service pensions. They attacked the bill for granting preferment to a class of citizens. They upheld a strict interpretation of the Constitution that would deny government the power to create a pension establishment. They fought to preserve the earlier concept of the Revolution as a people's war. The Senate debate contained, as nowhere else in the public discourse, a direct confrontation between received beliefs and new ideals fostered by the image of the suffering soldier. Dispute occurred over which memory of the Revolutionary War would be sanctioned by public policy. This dispute was linked to sectional conflict over the restriction of eligibility to Continental Army veterans.

Virginia's James Barbour (1775–1842), a traditional Jeffersonian Republican, greeted the Senate bill with a motion to kill it. He was joined by conservatives Nathaniel Macon (1758–1837) of North Carolina and William Smith (1752–1840) of South Carolina. Macon and Smith attacked the bill for subverting constitutional principles. Macon reminded fellow senators that giving "preference" to individuals "for the rank they hold in society . . . is a language unknown to our Constitution . . . [and] repugnant to the principles of our Government, and at war with good sense and public justice." Smith urged colleagues to uphold the "first principles," which had been established "by the Revolutionary Congress," by defeating the bill. Smith warned that by passing the bill, the Senate would undermine the protection of a "written constitution in which all the powers of the government are expressed and limited." He predicted that the bill's passage would allow Congress to govern by "prerogative" and "precedent," and that would result in "omnipotent" power for the national government to "do anything" it wanted. Smith reminded the Senate that the Revolutionary War had been fought, the Republic established, and the Constitution ratified "for shaking off that [kind of omnipotent] government [by getting] rid of pensions and placemen" He asked, "what avail is the Constitution if precedent is to govern?" He warned that once precedent is established as the basis of legislation "you have no control over Congress but the discretion of its members; and like the British Parliament, it will now become omnipotent." Alarmed, Smith saw the bill undermining the Constitution. In his mind the pension would dangerously expand the authority of the national government by exercising implied powers. Departing from strict construction of the Constitution, he feared, would erode state sovereignty, and expose a free people to a despotic government.[41]

Macon ridiculed use of moral sentiment to justify passage of the bill. He compared sentiment to a "sweet poison," that "pleases at first, but kills at last." Smith concurred. He stated that feelings were "miserable guide[s] to a legislator . . . [because] they are as changeable as any other human passion"; they belonged in private life and ought not be used as motives for public policy. Smith added that the nation had generously paid its debt of gratitude to those who served and suffered. It had provided for disabled soldiers, war widows, and orphans, and it had awarded public honor and office to former Continental soldiers who requested it. In Smith's view, only the Europeans who "reproach" Americans for all their actions and institutions, and the would-be pensioners, claim that the nation is "ungrateful to our armies." Smith said that the people who pay the tax, the "farmer and mechanic," are not heard criticizing the republic's ingratitude toward its veterans. Macon claimed that the nation did not owe soldiers a debt of gratitude. He said that throughout history such claims were self-serving: they have "been promulgated by the flatterers and sycophants of kings and despots to become their favorites and [by] pensioners, to live sumptuously on their folly or weakness or both, on the profits of the labor of those who were more virtuous and better than themselves. The opinion [that republics were ungrateful] is founded in idleness and hatred to free governments where every man ought to live by the sweat of his own brow— where no man ought to be paid to do nothing." Thus, Macon expressed the old warning against placemen and fear of corruption and declension.[42]

Smith invoked the traditional belief that pension establishments corrupted virtue. He mocked the fashionable notion that pensions for Revolutionary War veterans would uplift public virtue. He reminded his colleagues that "the wisdom of ages" had shown that pensions were the cause of corruption, the foundation of aristocracy and despotism. He stated that Oliver Cromwell and Napoléon Bonaparte had begun their road to power along the same path by claiming that military merit elevated soldiers above the citizenry. He warned that the United States was not immune from such ambitions by recalling that officers in the Society of the Cincinnati had aspired to create a hereditary aristocracy. Smith concluded that pension establishments threatened public morality because they enticed citizens to exchange self-sufficiency for an entitlement and because they rewarded social rank rather than individual merit. Smith feared that Americans "are imitating nations nearer our own time," and predicted that "when we are gone to rest posterity will writhe beneath the yoke borne down by hearth money, excises, and taxes to support pensions and places—the curse of a nation." Smith urged defeat of the bill to uphold the ideal of "true Roman virtue" where the veteran "maintained himself by the sweat of his brow after he had laid down the pursuit of a soldier." Admitting that his objections to the bill were "unfashionable," Smith lamented that traditional republican virtues had lost their "charm" for a new generation.

Smith scoffed at his opponents' claim that because the Revolution was a unique epoch, pensions for Revolutionary War veterans would not create a precedent for veterans of future wars. Smith said that in "some thirty-five years hence, when the veil of time shall have thrown a veil over all the minute circumstances" of the War of 1812, those soldiers will be credited with giving the military "new character, [making] it worth maintaining, [because it released] your country from its degraded state of impressments, paper blockades, royal orders in council and imperial decrees, and [War of 1812 will be given] as high a grade in the scale of nature as your independence." Taunting his opponents, he predicted that the "brave men" who fought in the War of 1812 will have a claim "as great" as the Revolutionary veterans "and the precedent you are about to make will be followed." He concluded, "This will be the beginning of a military pension system that all posterity may regret."[43]

Smith and Macon tried to rally opposition to the bill by denigrating the Continental Army. To prove his point, Smith told the Senate that Continental troops were "defeated as soon as they came [south]" and that they "gave no sort of security to the property, the persons or the lives of the inhabitants." In contrast, Smith asserted that the militia and fighting bands of volunteers, which he called "the body of the people," had been "inspired with an invincible love of liberty," and that they, not the Continental Army, won the Revolutionary War. Smith and Macon claimed that the bill rewarded self-seeking and greedy officers who had lobbied unsuccessfully to secure pensions only for themselves.[44]

IT IS NOT A REGRET, BUT IT HAS INFLUENCED THE GOVERNMENT TO REWARD "LAZINESS"

Smith and Macon celebrated the Revolution as a people's war as it had been conceived at the turn of the century. Smith lauded militiamen "for their bravery, perseverance and sufferings." He praised them as intrepid "warriors" who left their "shops" and fields to fight the British before there was a Continental Army. He compared them to the "electric spark" that touched off the war at Lexington, Concord, and Bunker Hill and sustained resistance throughout the south. They were "gallant men . . . inferior to none." Smith stated that many of these troops, like those under Marion, "never cost their country so much as a single charge of powder; they furnished even their own arms and used them like heroes." Allegations that "the militia cannot be relied on" because they lacked bravery and honor, he proclaimed, were slanderous. Smith described the war as an ideological conflict "for liberty and independence," fought by an entire nation whose people exchanged "affluence and comfort" for "penury and want with no other consolation than that of dying poor in the cause of their country." Macon apprized young senators that the conflict had been a vicious "neighborhood war," especially in the south, where "rich and poor and those who wished to be neutral suffered alike."[45]

Smith recalled that British and Tories had "plundered indiscriminately from all who refused to take protection . . . turned loose the savage Indians upon the defenseless frontiers who butchered them without regard to age or sex. . . . the Tory parties . . . plundered, burned and murdered wherever they went; and the whole country became a perfect scene of internal warfare." He said that the entire population was engaged in merciless, savage guerilla warfare. Smith, continuing his vivid portrayal of the war in the south, recalled that wanton murders, scorched earth policies, and plundering had reduced many people to work "like slaves" in the fields "amidst their families with their wives and children around them begging in vain for mercy." The countryside had been laid "waste; nothing presented itself but ruins, poverty and disease." He remembered civilians suffering from starvation because their crops and farms had been destroyed by enemy forces. Faced with devastation and tyranny, men left their families to fight in small guerilla bands like partisans, harassing the British army and striking foraging parties. With great pride he remembered that they fought "without one Continental officer or soldier among them" to defeat the "British army" at battles such as King's Mountain.[46]

Macon and Smith asserted that irregular troops had fought under more difficult circumstances and suffered greater hardships than had the Continental Army. Smith recalled that the militia lacked "camp utensils, unless they carried them from their homes. . . . In wet and stormy days it was not uncommon to see tents formed by two or three or more men putting together, not their blankets, for but few of them had them, but bed covers, which had been spun and worn at home. . . ." Smith concluded that the "Government is as much indebted to them for their bravery, perseverance and sufferings, and owes them as much protection and support, as any portion of the Continental army." Thus Macon and Smith argued against awarding pensions to army veterans because it misrepresented the character of the war and because it excluded the militia who they asserted were more deserving of reward than regulars.[47]

Smith and Macon derided the bill's charitable spirit because they thought it would make the federal government an almsgiver to the "thousands of poor who are unable to work." Smith charged that the bill undermined the principle of charity because it did not exclude the undeserving poor and because the aid was not given as a "neighborly" act. He warned that the bill's indiscriminate charity departed "from any principle" of benevolence practiced in the United States. Macon scorned the presumption that a veteran's impoverishment resulted from military service. Self-righteously, he declared that poverty is a product of individual character and not public service. He moralized that it has always been true "among every class of men—some will get rich, while others do not . . . the industrious and careful will either get rich or comfortable while those who are not so will neither be rich nor comfortable." The nation ought not to support those "who will not provide for themselves [because] on experiment, [it will] be found an endless task; it may suit other countries, but does not this; it will drain any treasury, no matter how full . . ." Macon warned that the pension will undermine public morality by encouraging those who "know their failings" to decrease their efforts to be self supporting.[48]

In summary, these opponents believed that the bill undermined the foundation of the nation's political culture. It would corrupt republican virtue by creating a class of "placemen, flatterers and sycophants" through preferment and entitlement. It would repudiate the republican principle that "every man ought to live by the sweat of his own brow." In their view it weakened the Constitution's restraint on federal authority by strengthening Congress's implied powers. It set a dangerous precedent of relying on sentiment rather than on republican principles to create public policy. They believed that by singling out the Continental Army for preferment and reward, the bill distorted history by overturning the traditional view that the mythic people had won the Revolutionary War. One can only speculate as to whether Smith's and Macon's objections would have been as passionate had the Senate's bill, like the House's, included the militia.[49]

Supporters of the Senate's bill swept aside the objections of Smith and Macon by applying the image of the heroic and disadvantaged soldier only to Continental Army veterans. Taking a cue from Smith and Macon, New Hampshire's David L. Morril portrayed army veterans as citizen-soldiers, "heroes of the country [who] flew to arms", who repelled "the invading foe . . . with undaunted determinism." Morril stated that these troops sacrificed the comforts and security of their homes. They had suffered anxiety from leaving their families to "laboring in the field to procure subsistence." They had suffered physically and psychologically from the "noisome camp, the fatigues of an army, and the dangers of battle." They had survived the "distresses of that day" to see the nation safe, prosperous, and independent, "though [they were] in indigence and want" while serving their nation. Morril asked, "Will you suffer the gray hairs of these veterans of the Revolution to come down with sorrow to the grave?" Morril urged his colleagues to view the "Revolutionary Patriots . . . [these] war worn soldiers of the Revolution hovering round their dwellings, round this Capitol, asking for a pittance . . . to supply the cravings of nature, and repair their tattered garments." Morril was referring to the vigil by veterans who had gathered in Washington.

Morril attributed veterans' poverty not to personal failings, as Smith and Macon had done, but to the effects of arduous military service. He might have had soldiers such as Peterborough's Benjamin Alld, William Diamond, and Samuel Spear in mind when he used this principle to defend the bill. Morril asserted that hard-core veterans, defined in the bill as those who served three years or until the end of the war, were entitled to aid because military service had disadvantaged them. Morril stated, "I conceive many of the infirmities under which they are now groaning, are in consequence of the privations and exposures endured while in the service of their country. In camp and the field their constitutions were broken down; the natural effects of which are infirmity and distress in advanced years." Morril asserted, "They, sir, have a claim upon your benevolence and humanity—nay, more your justice." Morril concluded there were "few remaining" soldiers and that they were "bowed down with infirmity and age, [and deserving] the interposing hand of the National Government for their relief for the mitigation of their wants in their declining years." He said that the nation was sufficiently wealthy to pay its debt of gratitude to these men. He urged the Senate to treat veterans as national benefactors, to reward their merit, to relieve their poverty, and to aid them because of the disadvantages caused by wartime service.[50]

Federalist Robert Goldsborough of Maryland also defended the bill, but as an expression of "national feeling and national character." Goldsborough stated that the nation ought not to "add another instance for those whom 'the ingratitude of Republics' is a maxim . . . [by abandoning] the veterans of the army of Independence whose wants and infirmities arise from having devoted the best portion of their lives to the service of their country [to] languish in penury." National character, he believed, would be uplifted by "doing honor to my country by doing justice to her brave defenders. . . ." Public virtue would be weakened by abandoning veterans "in the advanced age and infirmities, to the precarious offerings of public charity; to the protection of the almshouse and such receptacles of human wretchedness whilst the treasury of the country is ample to relieve them." Referring to the outpouring of moral sentiment toward veterans, he said that the public favored making "some remuneration to the worthy and indigent men" who served in the Revolutionary war. He continued, the "motives . . . of national feeling and national character . . . are strong and coercive in the adoption of this measure." He concluded that rewarding and assisting these men had become the nation's "high and solemn duty," and that failing to do so would shame the nation.[51]

The views expressed by Morril and Goldsborough reflected the public's sentiments and the Senate's views. By an overwhelming vote of thirty to three, the Senate rejected Barbour's motion to kill the bill. Only Barbour, Smith, and Macon supported the motion. In doing so, the Senate resoundingly rejected republican principles opposed to creating a pension establishment. With a heavy heart, Macon accepted defeat. He realized that a new generation was transforming America's political culture. Consoling Rufus King, the advocate of half-pay pensions exclusively for Continental Army officers, Macon stated that passage of the bill "would prove that . . . both [of them] were a little out of fashion." Philosophical in defeat, Macon told King, "each generation would govern itself," and that their day had ended.[52] Former leaders such as King, Barbour, Macon, and Smith were now on the political fringe in defining republican principles and cultural ideals for the young nation.[53]

Ideological issues aside, the Senate turned its attention to the cost of the program. The dilemma, Goldsborough said, was that the "merits of all [veterans] have been exhibited to view," and yet he and others believed that the nation could not afford to give each of them a pension. He supported the bill's provision to limit pensions to Continental Army veterans because they had suffered most and because the restriction would save money. Goldsborough estimated that by restricting eligibility to army veterans less than two thousand men would receive the pension and that the cost of the program in its first year "would not exceed $115,480." Goldsborough, as commonly done, grossly underestimated the number of men who had served in the Continental Army and the number of survivors. Often repeated portrayals of hoary-headed veterans had apparently led legislators to believe that death had greatly diminished the ranks of Revolutionary War soldiers. Nevertheless, his estimate strengthened support for the bill, especially among economy-minded senators.[54]

The predicament, according to Goldsborough, was how to "discriminate" among meritorious veterans without doing an "injustice."[55] James Barbour had claimed that to discriminate justly between "the [merit of] different classes" of soldiers was impossible. Goldsborough answered Barbour by asserting that the degree of suffering was a measure of the degree of merit. Irregular troops, he stated, had suffered far less than Continental soldiers because they had served shorter enlistments and fought closer to home. Furthermore, he opposed awarding pensions to guerrilla fighters and civilians caught in the war's cross fire. Goldsborough argued that it is "impossible to estimate" the suffering, and therefore their merit, of those who experienced "misfortunes" at the hands of British troops or enemies in "their neighborhood war" and that their "case is remediless."[56]

Goldsborough invoked sentimental images common in revisionist histories of the war to underscore the Continental Army's suffering: "Half starved, half naked, tracked in their course by the blood from their unshod feet, they followed their Heaven directed leader with heroic constancy and courage. . . ." Goldsborough concluded that those "most worthy of our gratitude . . . are the officers and soldiers of the Revolutionary Army. . . . If they are infirm, we ought to sustain them, if they are indigent, we ought first to help them." Goldsborough concluded that the Continental Army had fought for the "nation at large . . . [and] it was for the country they encountered all their hardships and it is from the national treasury they ought to be reimbursed."[57] The army's severe suffering was a measure of its extraordinary merit. Central to Goldsborough's argument was a kind of ratio of sacrifice to social worth: the greater the degree of suffering, the greater the merit. Thus, the Continental Army's extraordinary heroism and misery justified the elevation of its veterans to the front rank of America's soldiers.

Despite such eloquent and emotional pleas to limit benefits to those who suffered most, political conflict erupted over service eligibility as senators scrambled to include as many of their constituents as possible. The debate over benefits produced a political fissure caused by shifting political alliances and sectionalism. Party and sectional interests defined the bill's provisions and determined its fate. Republicans led the way toward broader coverage by successfully overcoming Federalist opposition to an amendment that lowered the service requirement from three years to two years (see appendix B, table 5). Subsequently, party alliances shattered and regional alliances formed on an amendment to reduce the service requirement from two years to nine months. Generally, senators from New England, the Middle Atlantic states, and the upper South supported the amendment. More particular, most support for expanding eligibility came from senators whose states had been required to contribute 80 percent of the men to the Continental Army. These states expected to have most of the recipients. Senators from the western states and lower South, which expected few pensioners, opposed it. The hotly contested amendment to expand eligibility passed by one vote. By the slimmest of margins, sectional politics shaped a key feature of the bill. (For votes on the amendments see appendix B and tables 6, 7, and 8).

Conflict over the bill continued when Isham Talbot of Kentucky (Independent) touched off a partisan battle by proposing that each applicant pass a means test, one for privates and another, presumably higher, for officers. Talbot wanted to prevent wealthy veterans from receiving the pension.[58] Federalists supported the amendment. Some, such as Rufus King, may have hoped to denigrate the pension program by portraying it as relief for poor veterans so as to distinguish it from his often rejected proposal to award officers half-pay pensions. Others may have supported the means test to safeguard the program against fraud and imposition. Regardless, by insisting on including a means test Federalists showed continued political insensitivity to popular will and thus contributed to their reputation as an elitist party.

Opposition to a humiliating means test was good politics for Republicans who were always eager to attack Federalists for their aristocratic pretensions. Republicans used Talbot's amendment to bolster their claim as the party of "honor and patriotism" and as a party of the people.[59] Republicans understood that the public did not view impoverished veterans as paupers, but viewed them instead as objects of compassion, gratitude, and honor. Moreover, Republicans did not want their administration stained by a charge that it mistreated veterans. In making reference to Belisarius in their support of pensions, party leaders may have wished to avoid the black mark placed on ancient Rome for humiliating and impoverishing the legendary Roman general. Belisarius had become a popular symbol of the "vicissitudes of fortune" at the hands of an ungrateful and crass nation as a result of Edward Gibbon's *History of the Decline and Fall of the Roman Empire* (1776). Gibbon's history was first printed in the United States in 1805 and again in 1816. The symbol of Belisarius probably made lawmakers wary of appearing greedy and coldhearted, particularly after they felt the public's recriminations for voting a substantial increase in their own pay in 1816. The influence of this symbol was evident in the conflict over awarding a pension to Gen. Arthur St. Clair. (The controversy was also fueled by challenges to the general's competency in the Revolutionary War and later engagements.) While the Senate was debating the pension bill for veterans, Congress considered a special bill awarding St. Clair an annual pension of $750.00. That bill stirred controversy over whether it was charity or an award for merit.[60]

In the winter of 1818, St. Clair was on the verge of imprisonment for debt. He was reported being pursued by his creditors, and at one point a tavern keeper confiscated the general's clothes for payment of debt.[61] The *New Hampshire Patriot,* a Republican newspaper, reported that when the bill to award St. Clair a pension was discussed in Congress, the general left the gallery "rather than hear the soul chilling words, *charity,* etc., which were muttered from the cold unfeeling gentry of Congress." Besides attacking Federalist haughtiness, the paper declared that St. Clair's claim for a pension was not an appeal for charity. It was a "just demand" due him for services he had rendered to the country.[62] Defending the bill, the influential *Philadelphia Weekly Aurora* indignantly reminded Congress that it would disgrace the nation if, after increasing "their own pay comfortably," Congress would not award "the worn out revolutionary veteran, gen. St. Clair, a miserable pittance." Congress treated him, the *Weekly Aurora* continued, as if St. Clair had "no claims either on our compassion or liberality [and] would be left to seek his subsistence like 'old and blind' Belisarius" who had to beg for alms in the last years of his life. Similarly, the *New York Evening Post* stated that ". . . the ancient Bellisarius [*sic*] [St. Clair] is a standing reproach on his country . . ." for its ingratitude toward those who gained its independence and suffered in poverty. The Maryland House of Delegates and Executive Council met in a special session to protest St. Clair's humiliation in Congress and to urge passage of his pension. The Council's resolution stated that the nation owed the old general a "debt of gratitude" that ought to be paid to remove a "blot" on the nation's honor by proving "that the stale charge of ingratitude, against republics, is without foundation."[63] The resolution concluded with a sweeping assertion that any citizen whose poverty resulted from public service had a right to claim assistance from his country in his old age, once he could not longer support himself.

Mindful of the public uproar over St. Clair, Republicans defeated Talbot's motion to require Revolutionary War veterans to pass a means test (see appendix B, table 9). This vote ensured that the bill would be an expression of gratitude not charity. In March, under Republican leadership and aided by sectional politics, the Senate passed by a vote of twenty-four to eight a liberal measure aimed at rewarding and aiding survivors of the Continental Army. The Senate's bill, compared to the House's version, restricted eligibility to men who had served at least nine months in the army. The measure removed any suggestion that the pension was a form of poor relief by inviting veterans who considered themselves in "reduced circumstances" to apply for the pension. To qualify for the pension those who accepted this invitation needed only submit proof of their service in a court of record.[64]

Although the House opposed the Senate's limitation of the pension to Continental troops, it failed to restore the state troops and militia to the Senate bill, despite widespread sympathy to do so. Dividing along sectional lines, nearly nine out of ten representatives from New England and the Middle Atlantic states voted against restoring those benefits while almost eight out of ten southern representatives voted to include them (see appendix B, table 10). John Holmes of Massachusetts, who had advocated including the militia in the original bill, explained that he had voted against restoring benefit to them because the bill had been so "severely opposed and criticized" in the Senate that "its friends feared to propose any alterations, lest, on disagreement between the two Houses, the bill should be lost." Holmes assured his colleagues that agreeing to the Senate bill would set a precedent for "a supplementary act" in the next Congress to provide "for others who have claims on the justice of their country for Revolutionary service." Holmes reasoned that a partial loaf was better than none. The House, however, rejected his resolution to instruct the Military Affairs Committee to prepare a "supplementary act" to expand eligibility.[65] The conflict over the bill had drained Congressional interest in the subject. Yielding to pragmatic and sectional politics the House ceased debate on veterans' pensions.[66]

ON 18 MARCH 1818, President Monroe signed the compromise bill into law. The act stated that any officer, soldier, mariner, or marine who served for a "term of nine months . . . on the continental establishment" or who served until the war ended and was "in reduced circumstances" was eligible for the pension. Testimony of service had to be certified by a court of record. The court submitted the claimant's application to the War Department for service verification only. Enlisted men received $96 per year while officers received $240.[67] The act signified a fundamental change in public policy. It reversed a policy established by the Founders and nearly forty years of opposition to the creation of a pension establishment.

More than a momentary product of the War of 1812,[68] postwar partisan and sectional politics, liberal spending of the federal surplus, exuberant nationalism, a wave of nostalgia, and Monroe's compassion, the pension act resulted from a deeper transformation of the political culture. The act incorporated the views of revisionist histories, sanctioned the new memory of the Revolutionary war, and made soldiers central to the concept of a people's war. Moreover, the act ratified Continental troops as citizen-soldiers, republican-warriors, and as symbols of the people and the spirit of '76. Furthermore, the act codified the image of the suffering soldier and the public's sentiment of gratitude to honor, reward, and aid Revolutionary War veterans. In so doing, the act blended democratic ideals with republican principles by elevating ordinary men such as Peterborough's Alld, Blairs, Diamond, McAllister, and Scott to a special cultural rank that entitled them to preferment. Conferring this status presumed that a democratic-republic could create a privileged class and award entitlements without creating placemen or an aristocracy. Inspired by fellow feeling and gratitude, the most sanguine congressman and nationalist could believe that the young nation had transformed the venal Old World convention of a pension establishment into a virtuous democratic-republican institution; that they had established a new standard of public morality and justice; and that the law itself was an expression of "enforceable virtue."

CHAPTER 5

The Pension Scandal, 1818–1820

Moral Sentiment and Public Policy on Trial

THE PENSION ACT was hailed for its prudence, its cultivation of virtue, its sentiment of gratitude, its expression of justice, its democratic principles, and its spirit of nationalism. Throughout the country, Fourth of July orators celebrated the act as a symbol of the nation's renewal and rectitude. On 4 July 1818, in Norristown, Pennsylvania, celebrants toasted Congress's "liberality towards the surviving heroes of the American Revolution [which] dispels the aspersions of national ingratitude and receives the approbation of the American people." *The National Intelligencer* observed in its editorial that public virtue had been elevated to new heights by "renewed gratitude" toward its "noble spirits" who had gained the nation's liberty and laid the foundations for its "blessings."[1] In early July 1818, the interment of Gen. Richard Montgomery's remains from Quebec to New York City added to the nation's celebration of its Revolution and its deliverance from the vice of ingratitude. Montgomery's funeral symbolically linked honored Revolutionary warriors to the advancement of national virtue. Montgomery's funeral procession, according to the *New York National Advocate,* created a "brilliant display" never before seen in New York City. It was, Governor Clinton said, an "act of piety" that restored the nation's honor through a spiritual reunion with a Revolutionary hero. The nation expressed self-satisfaction for having ended the "ingratitude of republics" toward their benefactors.[2]

The appearance of aged veterans, mustering before special courts to submit

Broadside: Poem by an old revolutionary soldier composed for Fourth of July 1818. The poem commemorates the Revolutionary War as deliverance from tyranny. It apotheosizes Washington and honors the Continental Army:

> But heaven decreed great WASHINGTON
> The saviour of our land
> To lead our troops till victory won
> By Columbia's little band. . . .

> My friends remember them who bled
> In freedom's glorious cause
> As well the living and the dead.

Courtesy, American Antiquarian Society.

their applications for pensions, added to the celebration. One squad was de-scribed as composed of "venerable, honorable and ancient" men who were "poor, old, lame, blind, deaf, and forgetful [and] bandied about from pillar to post." One soldier who had lost his discharge papers used his "age, poverty [and] scars" of faithful service in the Revolution as evidence of eligibility. Veterans, who appeared old, stooped, and "woeworn," were recalled as once being young, straight, strong, and vigorous republican-warriors. Following the report of 220 soldiers submitting pension applications in Boston, the *Weekly Register* stated that "it is grateful to believe that the few years left to such may be smoothed by the justice of this country. A little while, and no one will remain to tell the story of the revolution."[3] The appearance of hoary-headed veterans reinforced the public's feelings of gratitude because these men con-formed to the public's image of them as suffering soldiers.

The public's feelings of benevolence and justice were made more satisfying by the gratefulness of the recipients. One New Hampshire veteran publicly gave thanks to the president and Congress for making "ample provision for the poor who jeopardized their lives . . . in defense of the sacred rights of America." As young soldiers, once treated with suspicion and hostility, aged veterans had come to be cherished as the spiritual relics of the Revolution whose emergence and reward uplifted the nation's public morality and dignity.[4] Among the beneficiaries were eight of Peterborough's ten Continental Army veterans. To the public, the pension "certificate" symbolized America's compassion, recti-tude, and justice by paying its debt of gratitude to suffering soldiers.[5] The act was praised, especially in the northeast, for elevating heroic and disadvantaged soldiers to a publicly honored cultural status and privileged rank. A new gener-ation viewed the program as an expression of its virtue for paying the debt of gratitude to suffering soldiers. That generation also took pride in the program as their contribution to the nation's emerging greatness.

The euphoria was, however, short lived. In little more than a year the pension act, hailed after its passage for expressing prudence, virtue, justice, gratitude, and national honor, was attacked for creating a costly, corrupt, and disgraceful program. The resulting pension scandal produced partisan, sec-tional, class, and ideological conflict over the program. Pressure grew to repeal the act, especially after the Panic of 1819 wiped out the Treasury's surplus and the program's enormous cost deepened the federal deficit.

THE SCANDAL CAME as a shock to the War Department. In the spring of 1818, the War Department's modest pension office appeared adequate to process

Samuel Spear's pension certificate signed by John C. Calhoun. Veterans had to submit the signed claim to pension agents to receive payment. Use of such certificates was part of the War Department's efforts to deter fraud and thus reduce the possibility of scandal. *Courtesy, Peterborough Historical Society.*

the small number of claims that were expected under the new pension act. Prior to the passage of the pension act the office employed three clerks who worked in two rented rooms near the Capitol. Clerical work was light. For example, in 1817 clerks processed about two hundred inquiries for pensions besides corresponding with congressmen and their constituents about benefits. The office's administrative duties had become routine and easily managed. Clerks supervised payment of $350,000 in benefits annually to about 5,000 recipients: 3,300 disabled veterans, including 2,200 Revolutionary War soldiers; 1,681 war widows and orphans; and a handful of veterans granted pensions through private bills passed by Congress.[6]

The War, Treasury, and Justice Departments had developed a smooth working relationship so as to minimize pension fraud. The War and Treasury Departments kept duplicate accounts and applied strict reporting rules for their agents and recipients to follow in order to ensure accurate records. To facilitate administration and payment, the War Department divided the country into pension districts. In September and March the Treasury Department deposited federal notes in branches of the Bank of the United States to pay the pensioners listed in district pay books. War Department field agents, often branch bank presidents who received a commission for each payment plus expenses, drew on these funds for the pensioners' semiannual installments. To receive payment a beneficiary had to be registered with the agent in his district and had to present a pension certificate in person or through a legally authorized individual. To deter fraud by counterfeiters and to discourage pensioners from trying to collect from agents in different districts, agents sent copies of pension receipts to both the War and Treasury Departments for verification. Pension agents also reported the deaths and dates of death of pensioners so as to prorate the balance of the pension to be paid to the deceaseds' estates.

The pension office operated free of scandal because of its diligence. The office used its pension agents, local sheriffs, and federal attorneys to investigate questionable claims and to prosecute suspected swindlers in federal courts. For example, to discourage charlatans the department required veterans seeking an invalid pension to submit affidavits from two physicians describing the nature and extent of their service-related disabilities. To prevent swindlers from masquerading as pensioners, clerks carefully tracked recipients. To prevent fraud clerks required pension agents to immediately report the names of deceased claimants. A more common tracking procedure occurred when pensioners moved to a new district. After relocating to a new district, the department withheld payment to the pensioner until his name was removed from the list of his former district, added to the new district's list, and until Treasury Department payroll accounts were revised to reflect the veteran's change in residency.

This procedure, created to prevent fraud, often produced hardships for veterans moving to new districts because it delayed payment of their pensions. Nevertheless, the War Department refused to bend or break its procedures to accommodate angry veterans or their complaining congressmen. In one case,

Secretary of War John C. Calhoun explained to Sen. John J. Crittenden of Kentucky that to loosen the rules "would not only be destructive of everything like order and regularity . . . but would expose the department to continued cavil and create and unnecessary labor. . . ." On the whole, by 1818 the pension administration's sluggish and meticulous routine operated efficiently. After the passage of the pension act in March, the War Department, in anticipation of a few thousand applicants, added two clerks to process claims. Clerks prepared to enroll eligible applicants, initiate payroll records, track recipients, and order investigations in cases of suspected fraud.[7]

The act, however, produced a mass of applications that overwhelmed the department. The opening of special courts to process applications became an invitation to nearly every Revolutionary War veteran and hundreds of impostors to get a pension. Moreover, many courts, engulfed by applicants and guided by the law's liberal spirit, ignored the department's orders that veterans submit their commissions or discharge papers as proof of service. The department hired a dozen clerks who carelessly and rapidly admitted applicants to the rolls, some without proof of service, except for their word. Between March and July, about one thousand claims poured into the pension office each week.[8]

Throughout the spring and early summer of 1818, as the public celebrated its generosity and justice toward old soldiers, Calhoun became aware that corruption, fraud, and runaway costs were creating a scandal that could discredit the program. In April Congressman Heman Allen of Vermont reported to Calhoun that the pension business had put his state "in motion like a bee hive" with the prospect that "there will be about as many claimants . . . as there were soldiers in the Revolutionary War." Enterprising individuals, including government pension agents, turned the pension program into a thriving and profitable business. Allen told the secretary that an agent and judge had cooperated to enroll sixty men at a charge of forty-eight dollars each.[9] Allen predicted that the pension rolls would be bloated by massive fraud and ineligible veterans because the law was "very loose" and "little is required to establish a claim under it." He reported to Calhoun that a "respectable gentleman" from Burlington, Vermont, was "convinced that there will be a greater deception" to get the benefits under the 1818 act "than any which has been passed."[10] Corruption even spread to the department's pension office. Allen alleged that clerks in Calhoun's pension office received kickbacks for admitting ineligible applicants to the pension rolls.[11] In July 1818, Calhoun replaced the head of the pension office with James L. Edwards who fired the offenders. So effective was Edwards's administration that in 1832 he became the first commissioner of pensions, a post he held until 1850.[12]

Apart from actual cases of fraud, the law's ambiguous provisions created an appearance of corruption when wealthy veterans received pensions. Many of them, such as Hon. John Scott of Peterborough, believed that the law rewarded courageous soldiers. Some officials, however, such as Judge John Fisher of Delaware, believed that the pension was restricted to poor veterans.

In a confidential letter to Calhoun that May, Fisher complained that two officers in his community, "gentlemen of distinguished revolutionary merit" were "unable to resist the temptation" to exploit the act. Fisher wrote that one of the officers owned a large estate valued between "$15 to $20,000 dollars." The other veteran, according to the judge, owned a large tract of land and had a "lucrative [physician's] practice." Fisher wrote that he was "mortified and surprised" that these two veterans had received a benefit "designed only for the beggarly." Fisher feared that these two cases indicated widespread "impositions" that could produce more pensioners than "effective regular forces in the field at any time during the war of Independence." Allen's and Fisher's warnings confirmed Calhoun's suspicion that the law's ambiguities invited fraud, abuse, and corruption. He feared that the program and its costs were uncontrollable because of conflicting interpretations of eligibility.[13]

Calhoun was dismayed by the law's shortcomings. Congress had not defined the composition of the Continental Army and it had not specified the minimum term of service in the army as either nine consecutive months or a total of nine months. Furthermore, Congress did not delineate standards for the law's provision, "in reduced circumstances" and "in need of assistance from his country." To many veterans, Congress's refusal to require a means test confirmed the law's liberal spirit. The law's loose construction prompted militiamen, soldiers who served in state regiments, deserters, allied soldiers who later became United States citizens, men who hired substitutes to serve for them, seamen who served on privateers, teamsters, and quartermasters to apply for pensions. Most of these claimants probably viewed themselves as suffering soldiers who deserved the nation's bounty for their valor.[14]

As early as May, Calhoun began to close loopholes in the law. The department tightened application procedures by requiring veterans who had lost their military papers or whose names could not "be found on the rolls" to submit depositions affirming their service from "two disinterested witnesses" whose "credibility" was certified by a magistrate. As a further guard against fraud, the department required that a clerk of court verify the "official character and signature" of the magistrate taking the depositions. Calhoun hoped to stop collusion between fraudulent claimants and charlatans masquerading as magistrates.[15]

To restrict eligibility and improve administration of the act, the department defined the Continental Army as only those troops "paid, clothed, armed and subsisted by Congress and whose officers were commissioned" by Congress. This regulation disqualified applications from troops raised by the states, but attached to Continental Army. The department also ruled that the Continental Army was established in December 1775, thereby disqualifying those veterans who served in Washington's first army, June to December 1775, and who had volunteered to extend their enlistments through the spring of 1776.[16]

To further restrict eligibility, the department specified the minimum length of service as nine consecutive months in the army. It also ruled that militia drafted into Continental service who had served nine consecutive months were ineligible for the pension because "the drafted men were not placed on the same footing as the regular troops." Finally, the department ruled that deserters, foreign troops allied with the Continental Army, civilian staff such as wagon masters attached to the army, men who served on privateers, and those who paid substitutes to serve for them were ineligible for pensions. Despite the risk of alienating veterans and the public, the department used its rule-making authority to close loopholes to lower the program's cost and to deter fraud. It hoped to halt corruption and the looming scandal before these tarnished the program.[17]

To apply these rules, Edwards demanded that states send him copies of their enlistment and payroll records for those Continental Army regiments credited to their states. Many federal service records had been destroyed by fires in 1800 and 1804. Showing his toughness and independence, Edwards told officials from the nine states that refused to comply with his orders that he would not process claims from their states until they complied with his demands for records. The resulting delays brought criticism from veterans and congressmen. Edwards coolly and firmly answered critics that without documentation, "great impositions are likely to be practiced upon the government (without the possibility of detection . . .)." States quickly obeyed Edwards's directive.[18]

After compiling a more complete set of service records, the pension office purged ineligible recipients from the rolls. Clerks revoked Alex Atkins's pension, for instance, after discovering that his unit was not part of the Continental establishment. They refused to award a pension to David John because he had declared that he was a member of the Pennsylvania line at the battle of Bunker Hill where, as a department clerk wrote, "no troops from that state were present." In another instance, clerks rejected an applicant because records showed that the claimant's Continental regiment did not exist on the date cited in the application. Clerks also became more strict. They disqualified claimants for the slightest inconsistencies in their application testimonies. The department rejected Felix Mcllany's claim because it contained "a contradiction. . . . he states that he enlisted for a year and afterward says he cannot recollect the term of his enlistment." Veterans with poor memories and no records were kept off the rolls along with impostors.[19]

By the fall of 1818, the War Department was partially successful in gaining control of the program. It had specified service eligibility by defining the Continental Army and the minimum service requirement. It had received state documents to verify service. It thoroughly reviewed service eligibility. These measures prevented nearly twelve thousand men from receiving pensions. Probably most of these men were well-intentioned veterans who believed they were entitled to the pension because they perceived themselves as suffering soldiers.

The department, however, failed to administer the law's other major provision for eligibility: "in reduced circumstances" and "in need of assistance from his country." When reports from officials such as Fisher poured into his office, Calhoun became enraged by the "cupidity of many in affluent circumstances" who exploited the "small and even charitable allowance intended by Congress for the indigent soldier of the revolution." Calhoun desperately tried to close this loophole.[20] Much to the secretary's disappointment, Attorney General William Wirt informed him that the War Department could not use its rule-making authority to define the law's poverty provision because the "language of the act is not very explicit on the subject." Instead, Wirt recommended that Calhoun order local judges to administer a means test to applicants. Wirt advised the worried Calhoun that courts could effectively administer such a test because they "have so much better opportunities from their personal knowledge of the situation of the applicant, and of the character and credibility of his witnesses to ascertain this fact [reduced circumstances]." The only other recourse, Wirt told Calhoun, was an amendment to the law that defined indigence.[21] Based on Wirt's advice, the department ordered courts to require applicants to swear an oath of poverty.[22] The department also ordered courts to certify that each applicant was either a pauper or unable "by manual labor, to support himself without the assistance of his country."[23] The department informed judges that it would rely upon their "sound discretion" to prevent "the numerous impositions which are likely to be practiced upon the government" by wealthy soldiers.[24]

The orders were widely attacked as a betrayal of the law's expression of justice and gratitude. "A Countryman," writing to the *Boston Columbian Centinel,* urged a "liberal construction" of the act because the pension was not charity but a "monument of the high sense of justice [which recognized the] patriotic services of the army." Countryman stated that Congress had not intended that soldiers swear "under oath, a public declaration of their poverty and indigence." He might have had in mind the defeat of Talbot's motion to add a means test to the law and the debate over whether the law was an act of charity or an expression of justice conveyed by the symbol of Belisarius. He assailed the oath as "humiliating." Invoking the image of the suffering soldier to support his criticism of the rule, he wrote, "To see the aged veterans of the revolution who by their valour acquired for us the independence and happiness we now enjoy, come forward in their tattered garments, and make public declarations before a court of record, of their poverty and indigence, must afford a melancholy spectacle." Countryman urged the nation to trust the soldier's honor and to let each veteran decide for himself if he needed assistance from his country.[25] The *Richmond Enquirer* and Philadelphia's *Franklin Gazette* assailed the oath because it would deter applications from "many men who stand in need of the pension [whose] honorable minds [and] standing in society, cause them to revolt at the idea of swearing [to] an oath of poverty." From their viewpoint, which was widely shared in Congress and by a public still unaware of the enormity of the approaching scandal, pensions ought to be liberally distributed.[26] In the summer of 1818, Fourth of July orators demanded that Congress remove any hint of charity from the law and its administration. For example, the *Philadelphia Aurora* printed a toast to local veterans that proclaimed, a "pauper's fate awarded for their service by those who live upon the luxuries of their toils; may its foul stain be wiped away from the Congressional record at the next election." These critics viewed the program as an expression of gratitude and justice, not charity. They were angered because the department's rules tarnished worthy veterans with the stigma of pauperism.[27]

Besides public opposition to the oath, courts refused to comply with the department's order to administer a means test, not because of sensibilities but because of constitutional principle. Judges asserted that the rule violated separation of powers. The courts based their position on the precedent of a 1792 Pennsylvania court decision and the 1793 federal law that overturned a 1792 act that had placed federal judges under the War Department's authority when processing claims from invalid veterans. Courts refused to become administrative agencies of the War Department.[28]

Despairing, Calhoun warned Judge Thomas R. Peters of Philadelphia, one of the principal opponents to the department's order, that the program was out of control. The secretary informed him that between fifteen and twenty thousand applications had been received, "and they are coming in without much abatement." Calhoun pleaded with Peters, as well as other judges, to comply with the department's order to stop "imposition [and] the fear of it being extensively practiced . . ." in order to protect the integrity of the program.[29]

Calhoun expressed his own frustration to Peters. Calhoun wrote that he took "no pleasure [in] enforc[ing] that which may be deemed odious" to judges, veterans, and the public. "To prescribe poverty as one of the conditions to attain the pension was no act of mine," Calhoun assured Peters. The secretary regretted that the new rule embarrassed those veterans who were the intended beneficiaries of the act, but he was sure "that the patriotic Revolutionary soldiers would be the last to desire to see fraud and imposition practiced on the government."[30] Hoping to appease their constitutional scruples, the department restated that it would accept whatever construction courts gave to the meaning of "reduced circumstances." Calhoun advised the courts that "the conscience of the applicant and the sound discretion of the judges can best determine [need] in each case." Despite this concession, courts still refused to apply a means test.[31]

Handcuffed by public sentiment opposed to a means test and by the courts' constitutional scruples, the department was powerless to stop the growing scandal. Desperate, the Monroe administration, through the *National Intelligencer*, warned the public of the brewing scandal. The administration predicted that without strict rules and enforcement there could be "50,000 pensioners" who would cost the government $5,000,000 annually in pensions. It calculated that because applicants averaged fifty-six years of age, the program could last fifteen or twenty years, cost a total of $75,000,000, and require a direct tax to pay for it. Despite this warning, the public continued to celebrate its own virtue for paying the debt of gratitude to republican-warriors. Veterans continued to muster by the scores and hundreds to claim pensions.[32]

Beginning in late 1818 through 1819, however, as the public celebration subsided, alarm over the program's cost rose. Citizens began reporting the names of wealthy veterans who were believed to be "improperly or fraudulently" placed on the pension rolls. In these cases the War Department suspended the pensioner pending affidavits or official investigation of the pensioner's need. In addition, the department ordered each suspended pensioner to "submit a schedule of all property he possesses, including all debts that may be due him, under oath by a 'duly qualified officer'" to the pension office. Clerks began revoking pensions where the veteran's "disencumbered property" exceeded $2,000 in value, a generous ceiling that reflected Calhoun's view that the pension was intended for all but the wealthiest veterans. Calhoun hoped that these individual proceedings would "in general be an effectual guard against imposition" by wealthy veterans. They were not. Claims from wealthy veterans continued to pour into the office.

Even worse, wealthy veterans who were removed from the rolls assailed the department's treatment of them. Outraged for being publicly tarnished as frauds and cheats, their angry criticism of the department's administration contributed to the public's growing disenchantment with the program.[33] Peterborough's Hon. John Scott was one of those outspoken critics. Clerks suspended him from the rolls after receiving a letter accusing Scott of imposition. Dismayed, Scott submitted an inventory of his property, which amounted to nearly $4,000, not counting debts. Clerks ruled Scott ineligible for the pension and removed him from the rolls. Scott was infuriated by his country's ingratitude, embittered by his public humiliation, and angered by the treachery of anonymous neighbors who had accused him of fraud. In his own mind, Scott was a suffering soldier who deserved the pension. Writing to Edwards, Scott who had spent six years in the army, protested to no avail that he merited the pension. Scott was among the growing number of veterans disgraced and enraged by allegations of defrauding the government. Because of cases like his, congressmen increased their criticism of the law and the War Department's administration of the program. As the law's ambiguities and conflicting purposes became apparent in its administration, public and political support for the program weakened.[34]

Hezekiah Niles, a leading advocate of the act, lamented the nation's growing disenchantment with the program. He wrote that one congressman, noted for his liberality and beneficence, had vowed never to support another pension bill because costs always exceeded estimates and because pensions caused corruption. The congressman claimed, according to Niles, that the program's principal beneficiaries are "speculators and knaves." Traditional Republicans such as Senator Macon probably felt vindicated by such confessions from former supporters of the program. Macon had warned that sentiment would produce misguided public policy and had predicted that a pension establishment would undermine civic virtue.[35]

In the summer and fall of 1819, the Ebenezer Huntington scandal brought the growing controversy over the pension program to a head.[36] The Huntington scandal became the focal point for public outrage over the program's immense cost. The scandal became the catalyst for sectional conflict over the distribution of benefits. Nearly 80 percent of the recipients lived in the Northeast; 66 percent of the total lived in New York, Massachusetts, and Connecticut. The scandal renewed ideological conflict in Congress over the law's principles. By the end of 1819, the program and its underlying principles were on trial.

Colonel Ebenezer Huntington was a member of a powerful and wealthy Connecticut family.[37] He was a patriot, war hero, and elitist who delighted in aristocratic pretenses. In 1775 at the age of twenty-one, Huntington left Yale prior to graduation to join Washington's army at Boston. In 1778, at the age of twenty-four, he rose from the rank of captain to lieutenant colonel in the Continental Army. He participated in many of the army's major engagements including Cornwallis's surrender at Yorktown. Huntington was "noted for his fine manly form and military deportment." While in the service, however, he had earned the enmity of Revolutionary leaders by bitterly complaining about the Continental Congress's mistreatment of the army and its failure to provide lifetime pensions for its officers. After eight years of service, Huntington returned to his family's merchant trade in Connecticut, where he became active in the Federalist party. In 1810 he was elected to Congress and served one term. In 1817 he returned to Congress and was a supporter of the Revolutionary War Pension Act. In May 1818 Congressman Huntington received a pension under that act. Later that year, still disdainful of the democracy that honored and rewarded him with the pension, he left Congress to return to his business and partisan politics in Federalist-dominated Connecticut.

In the summer of 1819, in a letter to the Republican *Hartford Connecticut Times*, a partisan spokesman with the pen name Lucius accused Huntington of "filching the treasury." Lucius charged that a "member [Ebenezer Huntington] of one of the most wealthy families" in eastern Connecticut had been placed on the pension rolls and that this case was "representative of a "numerous class" abusing the pension law. Lucius made Huntington a symbol of the "festering canker" of cupidity that threatened to destroy the program. Lucius urged taxpayers not to treat such fraud "with indifference" because the cost of supporting wealthy veterans would soon require a direct tax to pay pensions.[38]

Lucius exonerated the War Department and ordinary troops by blaming a wealthy elite—former officers and Federalists like Huntington—for exploiting the law's generous spirit. Lucius made the program's high cost and corruption a partisan and class issue. He accused wealthy and aristocratic Federalists, represented by Huntington, of "fattening upon the public patronage ever since the revolution." He stated that their abuse threatened republican virtues because they put their own wealth and power ahead of the nation's welfare. Lucius charged that this elite would seize any opportunity to enrich itself even if it meant depriving "the poor, the infirm and disabled soldier" of his reputation and bounty. These aristocrats, Lucius charged, would welcome a direct tax on "the pockets of the industrious and laboring classes" to support their "bloated sinecures." Their greed knew no bounds.[39]

Continuing his attack, Lucius wrote that these pretentious men did not have "the same incorruptible blood" of the "republicans of '76 . . . [who] broke the chains which bound us to the throne of Great Britain." These pretenders like Huntington masqueraded as patriots, but the "greatest portion of these men never served their country" except for "wearing a splendid uniform and receiving an officer's pay during some part of the struggle for independence." In truth, Lucius claimed, they were placemen like those in England who made that country "a living monument of the [evil] consequences" of sinecures and pensions. He reminded his readers that "almost every one of these men, who are now iniquitously preying upon the vitals of the government . . . were ready if the Hartford Convention had approved it, to join the banner of disunion."[40]

"Beware, my fellow citizens, beware, how you create a privileged order," Lucius warned readers. He acknowledged that "the genius of our country is opposed to sinecures and pensions" and that the United States was not immune to the corruption from a class of placemen who "pervert" republicanism to satisfy their greed and who wish to turn the nation into "despotism or a monarchy." History showed, Lucius wrote, that placemen began inconspicuously: "At first they were separated from others by a trifling distinction; only an inconsiderable privilege, or a small pension. They gained [power] as they advanced; and at last subverted the liberties of the people, and assumed the prerogatives of kings and emperors."[41] As historian Robert Cray Jr. has ably shown, conflicts over memories of the revolution were "highly politicized" and were "charged with class identity."[42] Lucius hoped readers would conclude that an aristocratic class of placemen, represented by Huntington and his ilk, had corrupted the pension program.

Lucius urged his readers to "rekindle a flame of virtue upon the altar of their country . . ." by excluding the unscrupulous aristocrats from the pension establishment. Lucius warned, "Be careful that your gratitudes are not bestowed upon the rich and influential, but upon the poor and needy." He observed that "it is easy to distinguish that class of soldiers [the republicans of '76], who exposed themselves to danger because they loved liberty" in contrast to aristocrats "who wore an uniform for the sake of its honors and immunities!" Lucius identified worthy pensioners as "the indigent and war worn hero[es] of the Revolution to be cheered and comforted in the close of life by the liberality of a grateful country."[43] Thus Lucius justified pensions for ordinary men whose selfless dedication to liberty had left them poor. The pension program had been debased by a corrupt class of self-proclaimed aristocrats, so Lucius claimed. He argued that by restricting benefits to suffering soldiers, the program could avoid the "ruinous consequences of such a system," as experienced by Great Britain. Expressing an ideal of democracy, Lucius believed that ordinary citizens could transform corrupt Old World organizations into virtuous republican institutions.

The Huntington scandal was potentially damaging to the Monroe administration, in particular to Calhoun, because the department, contrary to its normal procedures, had given special treatment to Huntington's application. The pension office, its hands tied by court prerogatives, was implicated in the scandal because it had ignored the obvious fact of Huntington's high status and known wealth. Furthermore, it had bent its regulations to accommodate Huntington once his ineligibility had been exposed. Although he was immediately suspended from the rolls, he was not required to submit an inventory of property to the War Department. Nor was he investigated for fraud as had happened in cases that were less controversial. Under public pressure to justify itself, the department later explained that Huntington's admission to the rolls had been a "misunderstanding" that had been corrected by the revocation of his pension in late 1819.[44]

The scandal spread. "It is notorious," the *Hartford Connecticut Times* stated, "that the most palpable and scandalous frauds have been practiced." The *Hartford Connecticut Times* called for an investigation of the program. Similarly, the *Trenton True American* stated that New Jersey had numerous pension cheaters and observed that the "act holds out strong temptations to avarice and this is a vice which fear of exposure and dread of punishment are often too feeble to restrain." It urged revision of the law and expressed confidence that Calhoun "would not shrink from [his] duty."[45] Such allegations of fraud increased criticism of the law and weakened public support of the program.

Supporters of the pension, such as William Coleman, editor of the *New York Evening Post,* beseeched Congress, "in its wisdom and philanthropy," not to repeal the program. Coleman stated that the law "may have been abused in some instances," but he pleaded that the old soldiers not "be deprived of that mite they have so justly earned . . . just as they were sinking into the grave." He praised the program for "granting a small pension to those survivors of the revolutionary war whose pecuniary circumstances render them proper objects of relief." Coleman argued that the veterans had long been neglected, that they deserved much more than the "scanty pittance" granted them and that the "great body of the gallant band" ought to be neither tarnished nor punished because a few men abused the law. Appealing directly to sentimentality, he wrote, "The last pension act has caused many a heart to leap for joy and many an eye to glisten with tears of gladness. Let not this joy and gladness be turned to sorrow." With the program stained by scandal, its supporters depended upon the image of the suffering soldier to defend the law against its critics.[46]

Nevertheless, even the most ardent advocates of the program called for its reform in order to save it from repeal. One writer, whose claim to credibility was his pseudonym "Honestus," recommended to readers of the *Hartford Connecticut Times* that the pension roll be published so taxpayers will know who they are supporting. Honestus stated that his proposal was intended to end corruption and that it was not motivated by the "spirit of detraction, party virulence, or personal animosity." He believed that the list would expose ineligible recipients to "public contempt." Hezekiah Niles urged Congress to "divide the *loaf*" among poor veterans and exclude the "*speculators* among them [who] are just as disgusting as any other breed."[47]

In December 1819, Calhoun gave Congress an account of the program in anticipation of proposals either to repeal or reform the pension act. He reported that since the law's enactment the department had received 28,555 claims, awarded 16,270 pensions, rejected 11,881 applications, and was currently reviewing 404 applications. He admitted that some "errors" had been made identifying Continental Army units, yet "they have been corrected and those improperly admitted have been dropped from the list of pensioners." He reported, however, that his administration had not succeeded in confining benefits to those in reduced circumstances and that the department had received "a very great number of communications . . . from respectable sources" claiming that wealthy veterans had received the pension. He admitted that department rules to deter imposition by wealthy veterans had proved ineffective because the department lacked authority "to give specific instructions" to judges on what constituted reduced circumstances. In less than two years after the act's passage, the program enrolled nearly six times more than Congress had estimated. It was nearly seven times more costly than projected and was nearly ruined by scandal.[48]

On 15 December 1819 the House instructed the Committee on Revolutionary Pensions to propose amendments that would end "fraudulent practices" and "insure . . . that the class or classes of cases which it [the law] has been construed to embrace," including those now "excluded from its provisions," receive benefits. The committee was also instructed to "inquire into the expediency of its repeal" should the law's defects lack remedies. The next month Joseph Bloomfield, reporting for the House Committee on Revolutionary Pensions, told fellow representatives "that it is not expedient, neither will it comport with the honor and dignity of the American nation," to repeal the 1818 Pension Act.[49] That report triggered a new round of intense conflict over the law.

Republican Newton Cannon of Tennessee opened the House debate on the pension program with an attack on the law's principles. Cannon was outraged by the award of higher benefits to officers than to enlisted men. Cannon said that the law suited an aristocratic society, not a democratic-republic, because it retained artificial distinctions created by military rank. He explained that in a democratic-republic, unlike an aristocracy, soldiers returned to the equal "grade of citizen" after fulfilling their "public service" in the army. Cannon also attacked the law's two-tier benefits for being inconsistent with the act's benevolent spirit. He insisted that impoverished veterans were "entitled . . . to an equal quantum of relief." Demanding that the taints of aristocracy be purged from the law, Cannon proposed that officers and men be placed on "equal footing" by paying both eight dollars a month.[50]

Cannon's motion ignited a conflict over social class and egalitarianism. John Culpepper, a former soldier and representative from North Carolina, ridiculed the principle of equal footing. He claimed that officers possessed superior character, "habits," and "talents" and that officers were of "more value to the country" in war than were enlisted men. Richard Anderson of Kentucky, who sided with Culpepper, warned that Cannon's proposal was fraught with radicalism because it would introduce the "levelling principle," into public policy.[51] The appeal of Cannon's motion, despite its radicalism, was not to be underestimated: it lost by a mere four votes, seventy-four to seventy. The battle over benefits was a sectional conflict and clash between traditional social hierarchy and new democratic ideals (see appendix B, table 11).[52]

Following the defeat of his motion, Cannon supported a motion to repeal the law. He told the House that the law was "unjust and inequitable in its operation" for not incorporating the democratic principle of equal benefits. He was also angered, as were many congressmen from the South and West, by the exclusion of militia from the program. Once more Congress debated the memory of the Revolutionary War. Cannon proclaimed that the "service of the militia had been of as much importance, and their sacrifices as great at least as those of the Continental soldiers." He asserted that the militia was "of equal or greater merit . . . as the continental soldier" and therefore deserved a pension. At this early stage in the House debate, congressmen who wanted to equalize benefits joined with some southern and western congressmen angered by the exclusion of militia from the program, a scattering of representatives outraged by the program's exorbitant cost and its corruption, and traditional Republicans to form a fragile coalition that attempted to repeal the law.[53]

Sensing growing danger to the law's survival, Josiah Cushman, Republican from Massachusetts, defended the program with an appeal to the moral sentiment of gratitude and nationalism by evoking the image of the suffering soldier. The rhetoric expressing the image was more coherent and eloquent than it had been during the debate on the pension bill. Possibly the language had become more fluid and evocative because it had penetrated deeply into the political culture. The rhetoric's heightened sentimentality may also have been a reflection of the program's peril.

Cushman movingly recited the well-known miseries endured by patriotic soldiers: "In the first years of the war the soldiers enlisted with little or no bounty; served with little or no pay; frequently subsisted on scanty rations; and, hungry, thirsty and without convenient clothing, endured the severest fatigue. They took the field in the lowest ebb of their country's fortune, with no prospect before them but victory or death." Cushman recounted popular, compassionate portrayals of winter campaigns: the snow was "discolored . . . with

the blood issuing from their lacerated feet"; and in camp soldiers slept un-
covered on the frozen ground. He continued, "under every discouragement
they persevered, and in every scene of action or distress displayed a patience
and fortitude, a patriotism and valor, which no obstacles could overcome, no
dangers appall. They suffered, they fought, and bled, not to swell the triumphs
of a proud conqueror, not to enslave any portion of mankind, but in the cause of
justice and humanity, to ameliorate the condition of their fellowmen and their
achievements were such as to astonish and delight the world. They broke the
rod of the oppressor, and procured for an aggrieved people freedom, sovereignty and independence." Cushman reminded the House of the nation's
debt of gratitude owed to its veterans. To repeal the program, he lamented,
would "snatch from the veteran soldier the only prop on which he can lean now
in the decline of life" and leave a pain in his heart that only death would end.
Cushman continued, "I conjure you, sir, by those almost divine sympathies
which are cherished by the patriotic and the brave to continue your bounty.
Impart to the drooping soldier some gleam of comfort, some ray of consolation, hastening as he is to that undiscovered country from whose bourne [*sic*]
no travellers return." He pleaded to his generation to continue to grant the
"rewards due to patriotism and valor, to moral virtues and generous deeds."
Cushman asserted those suffering soldiers, who have nothing to show for their
"prowess and toils but poverty, wretchedness and scars . . . invoke our justice
as well as our gratitude." He said that no one ought to feel an "unpleasant
sensation . . . [at the] small boon" these men received because they had "devoted the bloom and vigor of life to save his country from oppression." Cushman's expressive articulation of the image rallied opposition to repeal by evoking feelings of gratitude toward the old soldiers and guilt for proposing to deny
them pensions.[54]

Cushman tried to shame congressmen who called for repeal by contrasting
their privileges with the poverty of their benefactors: "does it become those
who, by the courtesy of the people, are clothed with the robes of office and by
their bounty fare sumptuously every day; does it sir, become such to grudge the
plain morsel, the homely meal, to the warworn soldiers, by whose sufferings
and blood they are enabled to participate in those elevated enjoyments? Honor
and every ennobling sensation of the generous mind must recoil from the
attempt."[55] Cushman tarnished the motives of the program's critics by suggest-
ing that they were unsympathetic, greedy, and self—indulgent.

Cushman also defended the program with the notion that Fourth of July

orators and nationalists had made popular. He stated that by rewarding the
nation's benefactors, Congress nurtured "manly virtue, . . . cherish[ed] exalted
merit, [and] uncommon excellence" in his and future generations. He urged
Congress to foster those virtuous "motives calculated to operate on liberal
minds [by generously rewarding] the patriotic and brave who for the public
safety expose their own lives." Cushman stated that revoking the law would
discredit the nation's "honor and dignity," and denigrate the republic as "un-
stable, . . . fluctuating [and] ungrateful." He asserted that by retaining its
"magnanimous [pension] policy" the nation will help "to wipe away this vile
reproach [and] prevent this foul stain."[56] Cushman used the image of the suffering soldier to remind congressmen that the destiny of the nation as a virtuous republic was in their hands. By arousing the powerful sentiment of
gratitude expressed in that image he deflected debate from the divisive issues of
class and privilege to the unifying ideals of national honor, patriotism, and
America's mission.

Possibly concerned that appeals to moral sentiment might not be sufficient
to thwart repeal, Cushman added a legal argument. He asserted that the pension was a vested right guaranteed by contract between his generation and
Revolutionary veterans. In doing so, his colleagues were probably reminded of
the 1819 *Dartmouth College* decision that upheld the sanctity of contracts and
the principle embedded in that case that honoring contracts was essential if
America was to expand as a commercial nation. Cushman made the connection directly between upholding the pension as a contract and honoring
commercial agreements. Cushman warned that to repeal the program would
breach a contract between the government and veterans, and that to do so
would undermine the integrity of the republic. He explained that in passing the
law, the government had placed its full faith and credit behind the program. He
warned that by arbitrarily revoking that contract, the House would "shake a
confidence in the promises of Government and excite suspicion injurious to its
reputation for wisdom or rectitude." Cushman asked, ". . . who hereafter will
have any reliance on your plighted faith?" He stated that the government's
deficit was not a sufficient reason to repeal the act, especially because the nation
was wealthy and could afford more taxes to support the program. This new
argument represented the pension program as an intergenerational contract
that the government was obliged to honor. Moreover, its continuation was
portrayed as upholding a larger principle of contract that was vital to the
country's future growth and prosperity.[57]

WAS THERE ANY STATE SPONSOR TO THE
VETERANS?

Appeals to the moral sentiment of gratitude, nationalism, and the principle of contract overwhelmed opponents who sought to repeal the act. A motion to repeal the law was crushed, 122 opposed and 32 in favor of repeal. By 1820, despite continued criticism of its principles and a nationwide pension scandal, the program remained politically and culturally entrenched and was now considered legally binding by its supporters. It had also become too large, too lucrative, and too popular, particularly in the Northeast, to kill (see appendix B, table 12).

Unable to repeal the act, opponents, led by Philip Barbour, tried to discredit, if not ruin, the program.[58] Barbour proposed that pensions be restricted to men who had served three or more years in the Continental Army, that officers and men be paid eight dollars a month, that benefits be restricted to impoverished veterans who passed a means test administered by the War Department. He proposed that Congress establish a poverty line based on the value of an applicant's estate, "wearing apparel excepted." Barbour claimed that his plan would substantially reduce the costs of the program by trimming 80 percent of the recipients from the rolls.

Barbour cleverly exploited the principles stated in Cushman's defense of the program to justify these radical reforms. Using the image of the suffering soldier for his own purposes, Barbour claimed that his amendment would reward those who suffered most. He stated that his amendment was true to the law's spirit because it "singled out those . . . who bore the heat and brunt of the war," rather than rewarding men who served shorter enlistments. He portrayed the latter as no better than mercenaries who were motivated by self-interest rather than by patriotism. Barbour rejected Cushman's claim that the act had bestowed recipients with a vested right to the pension for life. Barbour asserted that the pension was not a contract. Rather, it was a "gratuitous bounty," a gift from a grateful people. Under these terms, Barbour concluded, the nation was free to withdraw or alter that gift without reproach, particularly if taxpayers were harmed in giving it. Barbour advised the House that "voting for this modification . . . did no violence to the benevolence which dictated the first act, because a man was not bound to extend charity to the injury of his own family." Barbour's proposal retained the act's principle of rewarding those with the greatest merit, as measured by the degree of suffering, by restricting benefits to men with three or more years of service. Moreover, the proposal reaffirmed the intergenerational bonds, but as an act of charity. Thus Barbour assured worried congressmen that his proposal neither breached national honor nor violated the law's benevolent spirit. He also portrayed his proposal as a cost-cutting, crime-prevention measure. Ironically, Barbour's proposal exploited the image of the suffering soldier to decimate the program.[59]

Alarmed by Barbour's proposal, program defenders insisted that the pension program could not be radically changed because it was both an expression of moral sentiment and a vested right. Clifton Clagett, Republican from New Hampshire, stated that the law vested veterans with "a right of which Congress has not now a moral power to divest them." Justifying his assertion, he said that the nation, "actuated by the noblest feelings," had contracted with these veterans to pay them a lifetime pension in "consideration" for their sufferings and sacrifices. Blending the principle of contract with moral sentiment, Clagett stated that veterans had accepted the pension "with tears of gratitude in their eyes, and with benedictions upon their country. . . ." Clagett concluded, "whether you consider this law as founded on a debt due by contract or mere gratitude to the Revolutionary soldier, he has a vested right in his pension for life; and you are bound, morally bound, to perform your engagement." To unilaterally break that pledge, Clagett stated, will produce great hardship— "their joy will be changed to grief, and many of them will have received an injury instead of a benefit." Clagett further justified the pension as a binding contract because pensioners had altered their lives in good faith that their government would honor its promise to pay benefits. The principle of vested rights buttressed moral sentiment to protect the program against ruin.[60] While Clagett's arguments effectively stalemated the ideological conflict over the act, sectional politics blocked radical changes. Congressmen from New England and the Middle Atlantic states, the two sections where 80 percent of the pensioners resided, prevented passage of unwanted reforms.

Nevertheless, some supporters of the act realized that the program had to be reformed so as to lower cost and end the scandal. Various proposals were offered to reduce costs. One proposal cut individual benefits 25 percent.[61] Another proposal called for a means test of one hundred dollars in income and two hundred dollars in property. Disputes arose over whether local authorities or the federal government should administer a means test. Some congressmen wanted grand juries to determine eligibility based on local standards of poverty and "common knowledge" of the applicant's wealth. Others urged that the secretary of war be given discretionary authority to create and administer a means test. Congress could not agree as to whether an applicant could deduct his debts from the value of his estate, or whether to require an applicant to include clothing and bedding in his inventory of property.[62]

These proposals produced a legislative logjam. Southern and western congressmen, aided by a few representatives from the Northeast, broke the impasse. By a narrow margin of eight votes, eighty to seventy-two, the House passed an amendment to the 1818 act that required pension applicants to pass a means test (see appendix B, table 13). It empowered the War Department to administer the test, including setting the poverty line.[63] In the Senate, on 25 April 1820, a coalition of southern and western senators, joined by a handful of senators from the Northeast, passed without debate the House bill (see appendix B, table 14). Senator Josiah Butler of New Hampshire, who voted for the amendment despite objections to the means test, believed that it would end the pension scandal while upholding the honored status of veterans.[64] On 1 May 1820 President Monroe signed the amendment into law.

The amendment wiped the pension rolls clean. All former recipients had to pass a means test to continue on the rolls. The recipient had to submit before a court "a schedule subscribed by him containing his whole estate and income (his necessary clothing and bedding excepted)." Under this amendment, courts retained their independence from the executive branch by limiting their role to taking testimony and certifying documents sent to the pension office. The amendment required each claimant to swear that he was poor and had not "disposed" or put into a trust any property, including income, with the intent to deceive the government in order to receive the pension. The law instructed courts to submit the property schedule, an assessment of the value of the applicant's estate, and a sworn oath of poverty to the War Department. The amendment authorized the War Department to reject any applicant who was not in the secretary's "opinion in such indigent circumstances as to be unable to support himself without the assistance of his country." Claimants not yet on the rolls had to provide proof of service as well as pass the means test.[65]

Detractors charged that the new law tainted innocent pensioners with suspicion of fraud. They feared that it would deter veterans, who were too proud to declare poverty, from seeking the benefit. Critics of the law stated that it stained the nation's honor by limiting the pension to paupers when the law should reward all meritorious veterans regardless of their wealth. The *New York Daily Advertiser* complained that the amendment treated "the high minded patriots of that most interesting period of our history as if they were all rouges. . . ." The *New Hampshire Patriot,* a republican newspaper, attacked the law for not allowing applicants to deduct their debts from the value of their estates. The paper stated that some veterans, who had gone into debt using their pensions as sureties, were removed from the rolls. The paper asserted that the law was "degrading to the character of the nation [and] a disgrace" to the country. "Alas! had no law been passed, much better had it been for them. . . . This is really worse than taking the pound of flesh."[66]

Hezekiah Niles, who favored the amendment, answered these charges by recalling that the scandal and the pension's unexpectedly high cost required reform to save the program from repeal. Niles urged the secretary of war to administer the law "on the side of justice and mercy." He stated, ". . . let us not 'bend the bruised reed,' or break down, by too much rigidity in the law, that sense of honor and honest pride, which the law meant to reward. . . ." To assure readers that the veterans who were reapplying for the pension were truly poor and needy, Niles reported that one old soldier had an estate worth $1.92, including $500 in worthless Continental dollars, and that he possessed engraved prints of the war's heroes—Washington, Putnam, and Lee. Niles also praised the pension for aiding a friend who had served as an ensign in the Continental Army. Niles recalled that after his friend had left the army he worked as a "ditcher, a humble profession." Niles remembered him as "a powerful man," six-foot-two-inches tall, and possessing a "noble countenance and proud spirit." Niles told readers that in recent years old age had broken his friend's body and then his spirit, "and by some unknown neglect, or from unknown cause, he was compelled to seek a refuge in the common poor house. . . ." Niles recounted how the pension had rescued his friend from the "cheerless and misery" of the poor house and had enabled him to live in a "private home and society . . . [where he now lives] contented and happy." Such men, Niles concluded, deserved the pension. Thus Niles consoled readers that the means test was intended only to curb abuse. He assured them it was not a poor law. Niles was sure it would not deny benefits to heroic and deprived suffering soldiers.[67]

PRAISED AT ITS beginning the program came under fire after thousands of veterans and hundreds of impostors received pensions. By July 1818, the War Department had received nearly 15,000 claims rather than the 3,000 claims at most that some pension advocates had anticipated. By December 1819 the department had processed more than 25,000 claims.

The program nearly bankrupted the government. Between 1818 and 1820 the portion of the federal budget allocated to veterans' benefits increased more than ten times, from 1.5 percent to 16 percent of the budget. Appropriations for the new program rose from $300,000 to nearly $2 million and were projected to rise as high as $5 million annually. The total cost of the program was predicted to be more than $75 million, a figure higher than the cost of fighting the Revolutionary War. A depression beginning in 1819 compounded the fiscal strain caused by skyrocketing pension costs. The decline in federal revenues when coupled with increased spending for pensions erased the $12 million federal surplus, forced retrenchment, and required borrowing to cover budget deficits. The pension program became a target for cutting federal expenditures.[68]

The sensational exposé of Ebenezer Huntington, a wealthy and influential veteran who had received a pension, created a nationwide scandal that reopened debate on the law. The pension scandal made a mockery of the law's sentiments, ideals, and principles. Intended as an expression of gratitude, nationalism, democratic-republican virtue, and justice, it had produced a "festering canker" of corruption and avarice. The wholesale rounding up of veterans to generate application fees—pension farming—tarnished the law's liberal and nationalistic purposes. The program was discredited by reports of claimants misrepresenting their service and need, by accounts of impostors forging applications, by stories of crooks counterfeiting pension certificates, and by warnings that judges conspired with their neighbors to get them pensions. Even the War Department fell prey to corruption.

Desperate, Calhoun and Edwards exercised the War Department's rule-making authority to reduce costs and to deter fraud by reducing the number of eligible veterans. They narrowly defined the Continental Army and tightened the minimum service required for a pension. The department, however, was unsuccessful in keeping wealthy veterans off the rolls. The department lacked the authority to effectively administer the law's ambiguous provision defining need.

The program became a source of conflict and public outrage. Citizens were angered by pension rolls swollen with frauds and by the program's enormous cost. Veterans who were denied pensions were infuriated. Pensioners purged from the rolls were embittered. Many veterans had applied for the pension believing that it was their just reward, only to be publicly denigrated, as Peterborough's Scott learned to his sorrow, as greedy frauds. Accusations of injustice, and tensions between neighbors and veterans over alleged cheating, further discredited the program.

The Monroe administration seized the high ground as defenders of the virtue and valor of the ordinary soldier. The administration tried to turn the pension scandal to their own advantage by blaming it on an elite, mainly Federalists. Republicans charged that the program had been corrupted by wealthy aristocrats. Besides deflecting criticism from the administration, more important, such attacks reinforced the democratic ideals embedded in the image of the suffering soldier.

In Congress, the pension scandal touched off a sectional conflict over benefits and renewed attacks on the law's principles. Critics portrayed the law as charity to justify suspension or reduction of its benefits. They exploited the law's moral sentiment to undermine it. Other critics sought to democratize it fully by including all veterans and to make it an expression of egalitarianism. Under fire from a variety of critics, the program was at risk of repeal or ruin.

The program's defenders appealed to moral sentiment, revisionist memories of the Revolution, and the nationalism expressed in the image of the suffering soldier. They reiterated that the Revolution had been won by regular troops motivated by the spirit of '76. Their valor had overcome the severest hardships. The country was reminded that it owed a debt of gratitude to those soldiers because they were the nation's benefactors. They had bestowed liberty, independence, and prosperity to their heirs. Program defenders warned that repealing the program would tarnish their generation's virtue and contribute to the nation's moral declension.

In addition, they portrayed the pension law as a contract that had vested veterans with a right to its benefits. Program supporters reasoned that veterans had given consideration for lifetime pensions by their meritorious service, by their sacrifices and suffering during the war, and later by disadvantages that were associated with their military service. Pension advocates warned fellow congressmen not to abrogate that contract. They asserted that the repercussions would extend far beyond the pension act. Public confidence in the government's word, essential to maintain fiscal integrity and to promote commercial growth, would be undermined. The appeal to moral sentiment, nationalism, social justice, civic virtue, vested rights, and contract thwarted repeal of the program. The passage of the means test was intended to preserve the program by lowering its cost and by ending the scandal.

As a result of the second debate over the program, the image of the suffering soldier became even more firmly rooted in the political culture. Throughout the conflict over the law, supporters relied on that image to protect the program. The image continued to evoke moral sentiment, nationalism, and democratic-republican principles. Although individual veterans found their reputations stained by the scandal, the image of the suffering soldier remained unblemished. The public's desire to pay the nation's debt of gratitude and to aid its suffering soldiers had withstood the scandal. Nevertheless, the law would continue to be attacked because of its means test.

CHAPTER 6

Pension Administration, 1820–1823

Bureaucracy, Moral Sentiment, and Public Policy

THE 1820 PENSION Act ended the legislative crisis over the program and the national scandal over its administration. In the summer of 1820 the public once more celebrated its suffering soldiers. Veterans by the scores and hundreds marched to courts to prove their poverty. As in 1818, their appearance personified the accounts of the Continental Army's heroism and sacrifices that had been told by political orators, written of in revisionist histories and nationalist publications, and recounted in Congressional debates. The new law further embedded the Continental Army in the concept of the Revolution as a people's war. The law reinforced the idealization of regular troops as republican-warriors. It strengthened the image of the suffering soldier by affirming that the pension was both reward for service and assistance for those in need of support. In addition the law was buttressed by making the pension a vested right that veterans earned by military service and by deprivation, the latter viewed as a kind of disability associated with the hardships of service. The 1820 law attested to the increased power of the sentiment of gratitude to shape political culture and public policy.

Nevertheless, the law had detractors. They objected to the requirement that veterans prove their poverty in a court of law. The law invited criticism from veterans who were purged from the rolls and those who failed the means test. Moreover, the administration of the law was vulnerable to attack because the law's provisions were either incomplete or ambiguous. The law did not contain a standardized means test. The law specified that disposing of property to pass the means test was a crime, but only if there was an intent to commit fraud. The War Department and local courts would have to assess motives of veterans who fell under this provision. The provision could produce conflict between the department and veterans over their state of mind, and cause clashes between veterans and neighbors who questioned the reasons why veterans disposed of their property.

The possibility of conflict was increased because the law's means test accentuated the program's ambivalent, if not contradictory, purposes. The pension memorialized heroic soldiers. It succored poor veterans. The law's combination of accolade and aid was contrary to the conventions of poor relief, thereby complicating the War Department's administration of the program. Customarily, poor relief was the last resort for individuals who threw themselves upon the community after exhausting all of their property and after establishing that kin could not support them. Each year communities, such as Peterborough, taxed residents to support their poor. In 1816 Peterborough voted to spend one hundred dollars on poor relief, some to support veteran Benjamin Alld. To recall, probably with the hope of lowering expenses, Peterborough's selectmen had auctioned to the lowest bidder the town's subsidy for Alld.[1]

"To be needy," historian James Leiby has written, "was not to lack the means of decent life but to face a threat to survival." Public aid was initiated when infirmity or illness threatened to undermine an individual's or a household's self-sufficiency. Relief could take the form of financial support, or more likely in-kind aid such as food, fuel, and medical care. This relief was generally short-term until the household could restore itself to self-support. By contrast, paupers were people who were completely dependent upon public aid or private charity. Most paupers were placed in private families at public expense. Some communities, however, had established poor farms or almshouses as refuges for its paupers. They were intended to lower cost as well as end the humiliating vendue of paupers, which were sometimes spectacles animated by alcohol.[2] In general, local poor relief had earned a reputation for parsimony and for grudging charity. Selectmen or overseers of the poor monitored recipients to see if their condition improved to either reduce or remove public support. Officials also kept a watchful eye for kin who could take their wards off the public's hands. The dependent poor lived under constant scrutiny on the periphery of society.

Within this context, the War Department had to dissociate the administration of its means test from conventional poor relief. Yet, the department also had to ensure that each recipient met the law's requirement that he was "in such indigent circumstances as to be unable to support himself without the assistance of this country." Thus, the department was charged with resolving the law's conflicting features and ambiguities, and with administering a novel program that was a hybrid of an honorific pension and alms. Its success further embedded the image of the suffering soldier, its revisionist memory of the Revolution, its representation of American character, and its principle of vested right in the nation's political culture and public policy.

IN THE SUMMER of 1820, to the delight of curious and admiring onlookers, veterans marched to specially convened courts to apply for their pensions. On July Fourth, in Keene, New Hampshire, 116 old veterans assembled under a scorching afternoon sun to select officers, exchange toasts, tell stories, and parade near Wadley's tavern before marching to court. Similarly, in Hartford, Connecticut, 150 colorful veterans, many in tattered uniforms, marched down its main street in a "pensioners muster" to patriotic tunes played on a fife and drum. Elsewhere, Fourth of July celebrants in Plymouth, Massachusetts, were enchanted by 208 veterans who "marched rank and file through the streets, animated by their well accustomed martial music."[3]

The appearance of the old warriors filled citizens with nostalgia and gratitude. "There was something deeply affecting and calculated to force the tear of gratitude," the *Keene New Hampshire Sentinel* reported, "in beholding the congregation of 'silver beards and reverend heads' bleached by the storms of many a winter—some with staves—and some with crutches—some active and energetic—some presenting the appearance of 'toothless, bald decrepitude'— the old man bending under the weight of years, mimicking the scenes of youth and war, striving to obtain an erect posture, while he should[ered] his crutch and show'd how fields were won." The paper reported that the Independence Day celebration in Keene would have been "dull" had these veterans not paraded to the "Pensioners' court in this town *to prove their poverty.*"[4] Elsewhere, one eyewitness to a pensioners' muster in Dedham, Massachusetts, reported that the "very novel and grotesque appearance of these frosted veterans and heroes of the Revolution could not fail to awaken the most lively sensibility of all who beheld them. Some with the entire loss of the use of all their limbs, bowed down with age and worn out with the labors of life, their claims to national gratitude seemed indelibly stamped on their countenances."[5]

Hartford's citizens celebrating the Fourth of July were awestruck by the veterans who mustered for their pensions. It "was affecting beyond description," the *Hartford Connecticut Mirror* reported, to "see so many of the heroes of the Revolution bending beneath the weight of age, endeavoring to step to the sound of music, which for a moment seemed to strengthen their feeble joints, and kindle up in their countenances the remembrances of the deeds of other days; [it] was enough to excite in the cold bosoms the stronger emotion of admiration and gratitude." Nostalgic and thankful townspeople served them a "frugal and substantial dinner" before the old soldiers marched to court to apply for their pensions.[6]

Similarly, in Plymouth, Massachusetts, marching veterans stirred homage and national pride among onlookers. One observer reported that "[t]he scene was calculated to awaken emotion capable of warming even the chill bosom of age and of exciting the veneration of all who are acquainted with the history of our revolution. Ah! children could they have said, 'see the relics of our country's strength. These silvered heads can boast of having encountered the perils of warfare, and contributed to the rescue of our country from the thraldom of political slavery to the establishment of an honorable independence, which you now enjoy—cherish this mighty boon, prize highly the rich inheritance. . . .'" The observer continued, "it was gratifying to observe, that not withstanding their decrepitude and rigidity of limbs they were yet capable of measuring the martial step by which they were so often led to splendid achievements on the field." Following the muster, citizens treated veterans to a "temperate repast" at a local tavern.[7] In Plymouth and elsewhere, aged and infirm veterans' patriotic spirit and vitality produced nostalgia and public celebration. The public took pride in paying the nation's debt of gratitude to its suffering soldiers.

To many citizens, however, the means test tarnished the program. Offended by the test, the *Boston Columbian Centinel* moralized on the veterans' behalf: "It is deemed a grievance that these aged and infirm men should be compelled to travel[,] some of them distances of 25 miles, and subjected to considerable expense to exhibit their humble evidences of indigence, and upon fallacious grounds of success. It is earnestly hoped that these grey hairs will not again be molested, but suffered to descend in peace and comfort" to their graves.[8] Similarly, the *Dedham Village Register* reported that the law operated with "cruel and oppressive weight on many individuals." Many had traveled great distances, "labouring under so many infirmities of age and disease," to take a "disgraceful oath of poverty." For those who embraced the law as an expression of justice and gratitude the test's stigma of pauperism shamed both suffering soldiers and the nation. The shameful test was another burden for the old soldiers to bear.[9]

Ironically, that shame increased the public's sympathy toward veterans. Citizens of New Haven, Connecticut, outraged by the test, took the law into their own hands to stop a local court from further denigrating veterans by charging them $4.75 to apply for the pension. Enraged, citizens closed the court and "immediately raised" donations "for a public dinner, to cheer the needy and desponding pensioners until the indignant voice of the people should make itself heard by the Court." Capitulating to public pressure, the judge waved the court's application fee. Townspeople also persuaded lawyers to donate their services to claimants. When the court reopened, triumphant citizens observed that the "eyes of the worn out soldiers now glistened with joy, on finding no longer, an insurmountable impediment between them and the bounty of their country."[10] An infuriated community forced an unfeeling court to treat claimants as honored citizens, not as paupers who were ordinarily regarded as burdens by a stingy public.

By submitting to the means test with humility, dignity, and even humor, veterans further enhanced their status in the eyes of the public. Not only did the old soldiers parade to courts to submit their applications for pensions, they celebrated their impoverishment and infirmities as badges of patriotism and honor. On July 4, in Salem, Massachusetts, veterans preceded their pension muster with a toast proclaiming that in war they had never yielded to the British, but in their old age they "surrender to the enemies none can resist—palsy, rheumatism, asthma, poverty, lameness, blindness, and a host of ills." Turning the test's shame to their advantage, they jovially acclaimed that as youths "we made our mark with bayonets [but today] we handle goose-quills to prove our poverty." To an admiring public, proud veterans held their heads high when bowing before the law's means test.[11]

In the summer of 1820, Continental Army veterans aroused nostalgia, compassion, and nationalism. A new generation celebrated its payment of the nation's debt of gratitude to suffering soldiers. In 1820 Connecticut newspapers increasingly added the epitaph "Revolutionary Pensioner" or "Revolutionary Soldier, Pensioner," to soldiers' death notices.[12] The title of pensioner, which to the Revolutionary generation signified aristocratic privilege and vice, had come to symbolize veterans' esteemed cultural status and the virtues of a democratic-republic. Awed by their appearance, Americans celebrated aged warriors as symbols of their epochal revolution and the nation's renewed virtue. In an out-pouring of emotion, Americans once again embraced their suffering soldiers.

Yet, as shown in the 1819 scandal, public euphoria over the law could be fickle, and political support could waver if corruption again discredited the program. Despite criticisms of the means test, Congress expected the depart-ment to use the test to reduce the cost of the program and to prevent another scandal. Congress did not want the test to blemish the veterans' honored status, however. To fulfill Congress's wishes, the department used its rule-making and discretionary authority to express the law's spirit of compassion, gratitude, and justice. To thwart fraud the department adopted bureaucratic practices to ad-minister the program efficiently and impartially.[13]

Calhoun and Edwards began to restore confidence in the department's administration of the program by making public examples of swindlers. For example, John Burns tried to defraud the government by falsifying his claim. His was a bungling fraud because he was an inept forger. He penned, in his own handwriting, the names of the four witnesses who allegedly attested to his claim. Calhoun wrote to John Wright, federal attorney for Ohio, that pros-ecuting Burns was "very desirable, not only as an example to deter others from like crimes, but to guard the Treasury more effectually against the numerous attempts at fraud."[14] To deter impostors, the department encouraged the pub-lic to report charlatans to the pension office. In the case of Jacob Grove who resided in Maine, four neighbors reported that the town had recently assessed Grove's estate at $1,458 for tax purposes, a figure substantially higher than the $52.25 in assets the veteran had recorded in his pension application. Further-more, neighbors asserted that the market value of Grove's property was twice the amount assessed by the town. The neighbors explained that their com-plaint against Grove arose "from public motives, alone . . . because our moral feelings, in common with those of the community, have been shocked by the conduct of said Grove on this occasion; and because we fear that the case of Jacob Grove is far from being a solitary one, even under the last pension act [1820]." The department dropped Grove from the rolls and ordered Maine's federal attorney to prosecute him for fraud.[15] Moreover, Edwards tolerated no shady characters or appearances of impropriety in the pension office. Edwards dismissed agent Stephen Cantrell after Tennessee newspapers charged Can-trell with swindling the government. According to the papers, Cantrell allegedly paid pensioners with depreciated bank notes that he had purchased with federal money. Cantrell was accused of skimming the difference between the state and federal notes for himself.[16]

Calhoun and Edwards adopted bureaucratic practices to ensure due process in assessing veterans' claims for pensions. The pension office standardized the application form. Calhoun observed that "experience has proved the necessity of rigid adherence to forms." The department established uniform application procedures and made them known to the public through local newspapers. Each veteran, under an oath in open court, reported his service record, age, occupation, marital status, and capacity to work.[17] Veterans were instructed to submit in court an inventory of "every article of real and personal estate," to declare their indigence, and to swear that no property had been divested with the intent of defrauding the government. Courts assessed the inventories at market value, as if probating an estate. To deter impostors, courts posted veterans' claims for public scrutiny before sending them to the War Department. The veteran also provided the ages, occupations, marital status, and capacity to work for each person in his household. Some claimants, hoping to strengthen their claims, reported personal debts, even though there was no provision in the law for doing so. Although testimony was not solicited, about one-third of the veterans described special circumstances, such as receiving charity or caring for infirm kin, that they believed entitled them to pass the means test.[18]

The department added six clerks to ensure thorough and timely processing of the claims, and established guidelines for them to administer the means test.[19] They were to award pensions to veterans who were paupers, men who were receiving local poor relief. For all other claimants, Calhoun ordered the clerks to weigh "all the circumstances connected with the condition of the applicant such as his age, health, the number of his family residing with him, their ability to contribute to his support and the nature of his property . . ." as well as the veteran's "nature and length of service" when deciding whether the claimant passed the means test.[20] Consistent with the spirit of the law as an honor, the pension office expanded eligibility by permitting claimants to deduct first mortgages and adjudicated debts from the value of their estates.[21] This rule allowed some veterans to reduce the value of their estates and thereby increase the probability of passing the means test. Joseph Spalding's was one of the many cases benefiting from this rule. Spalding appealed the decision to suspend him from the pension rolls because he had failed the means test.

Spalding, a sixty-seven-year-old farmer with a "worn out constitution," who supported his fifty-nine-year-old wife, and ninety-one-year-old mother, explained that he owned $141.48 in personal property, and that rather than owning his farm he had a "right to redeem in equity 21 acres of land mortgaged for its full value." The department reinstated Spalding to the rolls.[22] The rule was especially valuable to veterans who had used the pension received in 1818 as a down payment for a farm. It allowed veterans such as Spalding to retain their modest holdings and to pass the means test. Thus Calhoun rejected Attorney General Wirt's narrow view that the law restricted the pension to paupers.

Chastened by the Huntington scandal, Calhoun and Edwards refused to accommodate influential claimants by giving them preference over ordinary veterans. For example, powerful supporters of Lt. Francis Duclos, whose application Edwards had denied, appealed to President Monroe to intercede on the officer's behalf. Calhoun stood firm. He stated that Duclos would not be admitted to the rolls until he satisfied the department's eligibility criteria. In a similar case, Calhoun told Congressman Thomas J. Rogers, a Pennsylvania Republican, that Gen. Charles Craig was obligated to appear in open court "to render a schedule of his property" and to take the prescribed oath. Calhoun tactfully soothed Rogers's and Craig's disappointment by adding, "it would afford me great pleasure to comply with his [Craig's] request, were not the laws peremptory on the subject."[23] Similarly, disappointed veteran Thomas Grosvenor from Pomfret, Connecticut, appealed to Calhoun to waive the requirement that he disclose his "destitute state before a community in which I have ever been ranked as a respectable citizen." Grosvenor explained, "Although poverty is *no* crime, still among many people it stigmatizes as much as if it were. . . ." Calhoun, still smarting from the Huntington scandal, refused Grosvenor's request. All applicants would be treated equally.[24]

By the end of the decade, about twenty thousand veterans, most of them from the Northeast, had applied for the pension (for information on applicants' residency and migration patterns see appendix B, tables 15, 16, and 17). Nearly 80 percent of the claims were made in 1820 and most of the remainder by 1824. Nine out of ten claimants received a pension. To increase eligibility, the department established a two-tiered means test. The department awarded pensions to claimants who reported less than two hundred dollars in assets. It used its discretion to award pensions to applicants who fell in the second tier, those with assets valued between two and four hundred dollars. Veterans who reported more than four hundred dollars in property did not receive pensions.[25]

Peterborough's David Smiley was one of the more than two thousand veterans who failed the means test. Smiley, like some other rejected applicants, invoked the image of the suffering soldier in his appeal to be restored to the rolls. In 1820 Smiley pleaded that "god [had] moved the mind of the President to grant a favour to wornout soldiers and His beloved government manifested . . . beneficence in adopting a law to grant them a pension." Smiley stated that his health was broken, that he could only work half-time, that he had been "living on credit and charity for a number of years." He claimed that the means test had increased his suffering because "my schedule has brought my state of poverty to light so that my creditors are fearful of loosing their debts. . . ." Smiley reported that he had to sell some of his livestock to pay the creditors who had begun to hound him and that he feared he would lose his farm because he had depended on his pension to pay his second mortgage. The veteran prayed that he would "find grace" in Calhoun's "sight" and be restored to the rolls. Not relying fully on divine will or compassion, Smiley asked Congressman Clifton Clagett, to intervene on his behalf. Smiley's estate, which was valued at well over $500 kept Calhoun from answering Smiley's prayer or yielding to Clagett's pressure.[26]

Hon. John Scott, who had been dropped from the rolls in 1818 because of excessive wealth, failed the means test. In 1820 Scott reported nearly $2,300 in assets and more than $1,300 in debts. Scott, however, viewed himself as a Revolutionary War hero who deserved the pension because of merit. The indignant Scott also demanded justice. Scott wrote Sen. David Morril that "If merit have any weight in this case," Scott wrote, "I think I have additional claims [to the pension]." Scott stated that he had spent eight years in the Continental Army and that he had been among the troops that had defeated Cornwallis at Yorktown. Scott added that his merit was all the greater because of the suffering he and his family had endured because of his father's military service. Scott explained to Senator Morril that Long Bill Scott, John's father, had sold much of his property during the war to pay his expenses as an officer in the army. As a result the younger Scott had lost most of his inheritance.[27]

Scott wrote that his suffering had continued after the war. When Long Bill's wife died in 1784, the veteran deserted his family. Long Bill left his nine children in John's care. He refused to send John money, despite his son's pleas for aid. Tired of his son's appeals, the hardened, alienated, cold-hearted veteran wrote John that if he couldn't provide for his brothers and sisters he should turn them over to Peterborough's selectmen as wards of the town. John's hope for

John Scott's application for a pension in 1818. He stated that "I have . . . a very large and expensive family, four of [which] from sickness & infirmities are unable to support themselves; possess a small property but of an income by no means equal to my necessary expenses . . . and considering all my circumstances, need assistance from my country for support." Scott received a pension in 1818. *Courtesy, National Archives.*

I John Scott of Peterborough in the County of
Hillsborough & State of New Hampshire depose & say
that the following is a true statement of all the Property I possess. My Farm consists of about 110 acres, including a small appendage — it will not rent for more
than 100 Dollars, — — estimated at, — — — $1666.67

My Stock & farming untensils, — — — — — 300 —
Note of hand due from Dan.l Robbe, — — — 100 —
Note of hand due from Sam.l Gates, — — — 220 —
2286.67

My Debts are as follows —
Note due to John Scott, jun — — $500.
Due to the heirs of Lieut. Wm Robbe, — 568.88
Note to Ahiraaz Jewett, — — — 300. —
1368.88

Ballance, — 917.79

My Wife, being infirm & dropsical, has been constantly
under the Physician's hands for more than 16 years —
I have one Daughter, now, 28 years old, who from the nature of her infirmities never has been & it is presumed
never will be able to maintain herself — I have two
children not of sufficient age & strength to earn their support. Owing to age & infirmities I am unable to support my family by labour — I have no other means
but the ballance of the property stated above — and I
do need the assistance of my country for my support.

State of New Hampshire   Peterborough   May 22, 1820
Hillsborough Ss   John Scott

Then personally appeared the above named John Scott &
made solemn oath that the above statement by him subscribed is true
before me John Smith Justice peace

John Scott's application for a pension in 1820 listed his assets at $2286.67 and debts at
$1368.88. Scott pleaded that he needed the pension because he was not able to support
his family because of his age and ill health. Scott was not continued on the pension rolls.
Courtesy, National Archives.

Letter from James Edwards to the Honorable Levi Woodbury, 22 December 1829. Edwards explained that Scott's assets exceeded the means test. Edwards encouraged Woodbury by replying that if Scott's assets were ". . . so reduced as to permit his resoration to the Pension List, he can no doubt get his pension renewed on complying with the instructions contained in the enclosed printed sheet." *Courtesy, National Archives.*

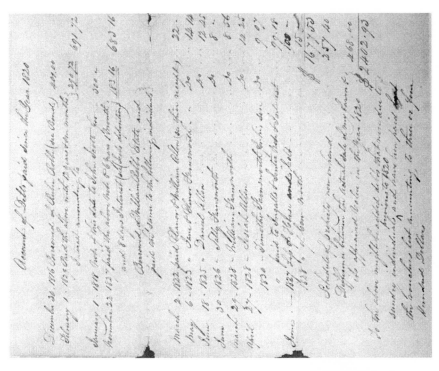

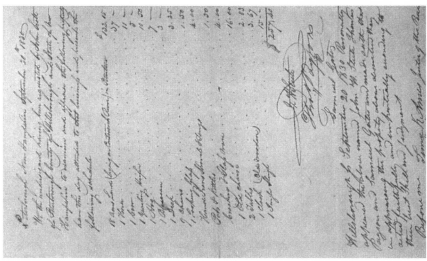

John Scott's application for a pension, 1830. The application listed his assets as of September 1830 and his disposal of his property between 1820 and 1830. Scott, however, was not admitted to the rolls because he had not properly documented his divestiture. In 1831, after he had submitted the documents, his pension was restored. *Courtesy, National Archives.*

aid from his father ended in 1796 when Long Bill died of "lake fever" while stationed in western New York. John Scott concluded, "Thus, in my youth, instead of providing for my own family & for the wants of that season of life to which I have now arrived, I was maintaining my father's children. . . ." Moreover, John Scott claimed to be disadvantaged because he was now experiencing infirmities that he credited to hardships during the siege of Yorktown. He reported that at Yorktown his tent had been lost and after being exposed to the elements "I was taken violently sick of a fever." That illness, he claimed, as well as other service hardships, had made him lame. The veteran wrote that he had "been afflicted most of [my] life with rheumatism—frequently I have been unable to labour for weeks at a time. . . ." Scott appealed for compassion. He added that family hardships had increased his woes: his wife had been chronically ill with "dropsy." His daughter was "infirm." His two young children could not render support to their parents. He had "no son on whom I can call for assistance."[28] Despite these appeals and Morril's influence, Scott was not restored to the rolls. Appeals to merit, justice, compassion, and the image of the suffering soldier did not exempt Scott from the standards set for the means test. Scott was too wealthy to receive the pension.

Scott, however, was persistent. He appeared determined to receive the pension for its honor as well as for its financial benefit. In 1829 Scott reapplied for the benefit. He reported an estate valued at $604.75. He was denied the pension because his assets exceeded the line set by the means test. Scott lobbied his senator, Levi Woodbury, to intervene on his behalf. Despite pressure, Edwards refused to bend the rules to appease Woodbury and Scott. Edwards wrote a bureaucratic-sounding letter to Woodbury to explain his decision: "Mr. Scott is under an erroneous impression in relation to me. I have no opinion, favorable or unfavorable, in regard to him. My business is simply to act according to the prescribed regulations." The following year, Scott applied a third time for the pension. His estate had been reduced to $257.40 after paying debts, including one to his son for supporting his father and mother. Nevertheless, Edwards denied Scott the pension because this time Scott had not documented those payments in accordance with the department's rules. Scott appealed to his congressman, Henry Hubbard, to lobby Edwards to reverse his decision. As before, Edwards refused to bend the rules. He wrote Congressman Hubbard that "Scott is an honest, worthy man and deserving the bounty of his country . . . [but there can be] no departure from the established rules of evidence." In 1831 Scott documented his divestiture of property. He was then admitted to the rolls.[29]

As the Duclos, Craig, Smiley, and Scott cases show, the War Department refused to give preferential treatment to influential and persistent applicants. It did not knuckle under to congressmen who lobbied for their constituents. The department treated applicants impersonally. It was not swayed by appeals to compassion and justice to exempt claimants from its rules. Applicants completed standard forms and followed identical application procedures. They were judged by the same criteria to determine their eligibility for the pension. The department meticulously adhered to its regulations and due process by not making exceptions. In doing so the department prevented scandal, thereby protecting the veterans' honored status and the integrity of the program.[30]

The department's administration expressed the law's spirit of gratitude and justice by using its discretionary authority to expand eligibility to veterans who had disposed of their property in exchange for lifetime support through so-called retirement contracts. A retirement contract was typically a deed of sale, generally between a father and a son, that required the son to support his parents in exchange for the father's property. These agreements were widely employed to provide security and care for parents and dependent kin. Although deeds were generally made when the parties were in good health, often the deeds were not executed until the owner became debilitated, or was near death, or after he had died. The unexecuted deed provided the father leverage to ensure compliance with its terms by retaining the power to name a new grantee. The unexecuted deed was also an insurance policy in case the grantee died before the owner. In such cases the father could transfer the property to another person in exchange for support and care.[31]

No decision made by the department was more perilous to the program than the one to grant pensions to veterans who subsisted under a retirement contract. Citizens who viewed the pension as aid to impoverished veterans objected to awarding it to veterans who had already made provisions for their support in old age, even if their living conditions were sparse as they probably were in many cases. In the minds of those citizens, men who had transferred their property to children or others in return for their support were only technically poor as defined by the department's means test. The assets, while no longer owned by the veteran, were still being used to support him. In some instances, outraged neighbors accused retired pensioners of abusing the law, or, worse, defrauding the government.

The case of Amasa Mills of Canton, Connecticut, illustrated the risk of scandal over awarding pensions to retired veterans. Mills's pension application embroiled Canton in a heated controversy made bitter by personal hostility and possibly political conflict. Mills's case had the potential of eclipsing the Huntington scandal. Mills was a former captain in the Continental Army and a former colonel in the local militia. On 5 August 1820, he testified in court that he was eighty-five years old and a blacksmith, but that he had not worked for the past fifteen years because of disabilities. He reported that in 1814 he had become totally blind and that he could walk only with the aid of crutches. The old veteran stated, "I have no family (meaning no one dependent on him) & I am entirely dependent on my friends for support & have two sons . . . Amasa Mills aged 55 years, Gardner Mills aged 47 years & three daughters . . . one in Canton and two in the state of New York." Mills presented himself to the court as a solitary veteran whose children rendered him no aid. The veteran's inventory reported only a bed and bedstead worth nine dollars, a blanket priced at two dollars, and a kettle appraised at seventy-five cents. In the eyes of the department, Mills was poor. He owned only $11.75 in property.

The day following Mills's testimony, two neighbors, Giles Barber and Elan Gayle, appeared before the justice of the peace, Jared Mills—no relation to Amasa—to file an affidavit disputing Amasa Mills's testimony. Barber (1769–1826) owned a farm adjoining the veteran's land. He was related to Mills by marriage and was considered an upright citizen. Barber, like Mills, was well established in town. Barber could count town founders among his ancestors. He was well-to-do and well educated. Barber's library contained works by Voltaire, Condorcet, and a bound volume of Whig political pamphlets. One suspects that Barber was an avid Jeffersonian who embraced democratic-republican ideals. His neighbor, Amasa Mills, on the other hand, was probably a Federalist, as were many former Continental Army officers. Mills may have espoused an aristocratic ideal and been part of Connecticut's bitter conflict between Federalists and Republicans. Political hostility would have made the feud between Barber and Mills more intense. Nothing is known about the other complainant, Gayle, other than that he lived near Mills and Barber.

Barber and Gayle's affidavit stated that although Mills "had no family and was old and helpless," he was not sick and he did not live alone. They swore that he lived with his son Gardner Mills and Gardner's family. Barber and Gayle attested that "Gardner Mills is in flourishing circumstances abundantly able to maintain his father, and that he has received more property from his father than is sufficient for his support." Barber and Gayle strengthened their accusations with a copy of the deed of sale for four hundred dollars that transferred Amasa's land to Gardner Mills. Following established procedures, upon receipt of Barber and Gayle's testimony, the department refused to place Amasa Mills on the pension rolls. Because the deed was executed after the passage of the 1818 Pension Act, the department informed Mills, under threat of prosecution for fraud, that he must show "by all the proof by which the case is susceptible, that you [Mills] had, in making the conveyance [to his son] no intention of evading the oath."[32] In November 1820, Mills answered the charges made against him by Barber and Gayle. Mills explained that in 1799 he had become infirm. His son Gardner Mills had agreed to care for his father and mother, and to pay his father's debts, which amounted to two hundred dollars. In exchange the veteran agreed to deed the sixteen-acre farm and "a very poor house and barn" to Gardner. The deed was not executed, however.

In 1816, according to Amasa Mills's testimony, the veteran's wife died after an illness lasting four years. During those years the household had suffered because "she was not able to cook a meal of victuals." Mills explained that, being crippled, blind, and aged, he had been unable to help his son run the farm. Moreover, the veteran swore that he had become indebted to his son Gardner and was totally dependent on him. Mills testified that on 23 April 1818, a few weeks after passage of the pension act, he executed the deed to his farm, without "intention of evading" the pension law, to pay Gardner for the support "rendered to me and my wife and the aforesaid debt paid for me." Mills's testimony portrayed the decline of the veteran's household and his increasing dependency and his son's role in providing support for which he would be paid eventually by receiving title to his father's property.

Mills's case divided his family and the community. It produced an acrimonious family conflict apparently made worse by a political feud and by a cultural clash over awarding a pension to a retired veteran who was supported by a well-to-do child. Some aligned with Barber and Gayle. Others rallied to the veteran's defense. Mills's supporters swore that "Col. Mills is a gentleman of fair character [and] his son Gardner Mills . . . is highly esteemed by his acquaintances." They told the department that Gardner could have obtained ownership of his father's property by taking him to court to recover the cost of support incurred over the years. They swore that "Col. Mills has voluntarily done to his son what the law would have compelled." These townsmen also cast doubt on the character of Mills's accusers. They swore that Jared Mills, who had certified Barber and Gayle's affidavit, was not a justice of the peace as the complainants had led the department to believe.[33]

The conflict became more heated when Giles Barber, in response to Mills's defenders, increased his attack on the veteran and his family. Barber alleged that Amasa's land was worth at least one thousand dollars. He charged the veteran with misrepresenting his assets because he did not report money owed him. To support his claim, Barber testified that he had heard Gardner Mills's wife say that her husband, Gardner, and his father had agreed not to transfer the property unless the veteran received a pension. These new charges gained credence when Simeon Mills (1787–1867), another neighbor of Amasa Mills, affirmed Barber's testimony. Simeon was Amasa's nephew but he was also related to Giles Barber by marriage. Simeon's affidavit stated that Gardner Mills had told him that Amasa "would never agree to deed his place to him until after the [1818] pension law was passed." Their testimony implicated Mills's son and daughter-in-law in a conspiracy to defraud the government.[34] The department turned to the district's congressman, Elisha Phelps, to assess the conflicting claims made by Amasa Mills, Giles Barber, Elan Gayle, Simeon Mills, and townsmen involved in this heated controversy. In March 1821, Phelps wrote to James L. Edwards in support of Amasa Mills's version of the dispute. Phelps stated that Mills was among the "respected poor, and has been helpless for years." Phelps assured Edwards that "no imposition is attempted." Phelps added that Simeon Mills's accusations, and by implication Gayle's and Barber's charges, were not to be believed because Simeon "has acknowledged" that he made them with "hostile motives." Although exonerated by Congressman Phelps, Mills died before receiving a pension. As subsequent cases showed, there is little doubt that had Mills lived he would have continued on the pension rolls.[35]

THE INTENSITY OF the Mills case revealed the explosive potential of conflict over awarding pensions to veterans who were supported through retirement contracts. Receipt of the pension had triggered conflict between family members and neighbors. Political division within the family heightened the feud. Mills's enemies used the pension to embarrass him by alleging he had committed fraud. The pension was a new weapon in an ongoing class and political war involving the Mills family. Apart from political and personal antagonisms, the Mills case represented a cultural conflict over care of elderly parents. By law and by custom, children were responsible for maintaining their parents. Capt. Mills had adhered to them when he made a retirement contract with this son. By local standards he was neither poor nor a pauper. Amasa was only poor in the technical sense because by transferring his assets to his son, he appeared propertyless thereby passing the department's means test. Pension records suggest that many veterans such as Mills were vulnerable to accusations of fraud because they had retirement contracts. Four of five Peterborough pensioners—William Blair, William Diamond, John Scott (executed in 1831), and Samuel Spear—had retirement contracts. If Peterborough's pensioners were typical, perhaps as high as 70 to 80 percent of the recipients had such agreements.

Retirement contracts created an administrative dilemma. The department could exclude retirees at the risk of public outrage for subverting the law's sentiments of gratitude and justice. On the other hand the department could include retirees and risk another scandal should more cases like Mills's occur. The department resolved this dilemma by ruling that transferring property under a retirement contract, which included disposing of property to pay debts owed for past support, was not prima facie evidence of intent to defraud the government. Thus the department reconciled the law's conflicting features of honor and alms. The department could both rigorously apply its means test and implement the law's liberal spirit by extending benefits to thousands of veterans who otherwise would have been excluded.

The cases of John Vandeburgh and Robert Hanscom illustrate the department's ruling and its effects. In 1820 Vandeburgh reported that he was sixty-eight years old, that his lame wife was sixty-four years old, that he had no trade, and that he possessed only $14.38 worth of property. After being placed on the rolls, neighbors accused Vandeburgh of fraud for concealing his wealth. Testimony, which resulted from the department's investigation, showed that in 1816 Vandeburgh had divided his $4,600 estate among his sons with the agreement that they would assume his debts and support the veteran and his wife. When Vandeburgh received his pension in 1818, he canceled the agreement that his sons support him. Vandeburgh claimed that he lived only on the income from his pension. Despite the capacity of sons to support their mother and father, and the probability that they rendered some aid, the department viewed Vandeburgh as virtually penniless. Vandeburgh continued on the pension rolls.[36]

Similarly, when Robert Hanscom applied for his pension in 1820, he reported that he was fifty-eight years old, lived alone, and owned property of little value: "an acre of land, half of a small unfurnished house, 1 cow and 2 sheep" all of which the court assessed at $42.50. In October the U.S. attorney for Maine, Ethan Shepley, received information from a "respectable" citizen that Hanscom owned a 150-acre farm worth $1,500 and that he had concealed his wealth by transferring the farm to his sisters. Upon receiving Shepley's report, Edwards ordered Shepley to investigate Hanscom's alleged effort "to defraud the government" and to prosecute him immediately if true. Three months later Shepley reported that the allegations were "groundless" because Hanscom, a "lame and poor husbandman," had transferred the farm's title to his sisters to pay the nine hundred dollars he owed them. The terms of the transfer also allowed Hanscom to retire under his sisters' roof. The department honored this retirement contract. Hanscom remained on the rolls.[37] Through such cases the department made known to pension agents and claimants that veterans would not be disqualified because of retirement contracts. The public, enthralled with its suffering soldiers and sympathetic to expanding eligibility, quickly accepted the department's liberal policy.

Exploitation of a loophole in the department's procedures threatened to weaken public support of the program, however. The loophole appeared inadvertently in the department's administration of the program. Attorney General Wirt had ruled that claimants who failed the means test could not alter their original list of property when appealing the War Department's decision. Believing the attorney general's opinion too restrictive and, in some cases, unjust, the War Department allowed appellants to append a "clarification" to their original property schedule to explain errors. Besides correcting mistakes, the practice invited corruption.[38]

The case of Benjamin Frye illustrates the appeal process as it was intended to work. In 1820 Benjamin Frye of Salem, Massachusetts, a former lieutenant who had served two years in the Continental Army, reported that he was sixty-eight years old, "disabled and crippled." His original claim stated that he worked as a blacksmith and that his household consisted of his sixty-four-year-old wife and twenty-six-year-old deranged son. Frye's estate, which included a house and eight acres, was assessed by the court at $415. He was denied a pension because he failed the means test. Frye appealed to the department to reverse its decision. His appeal included affidavits from neighbors and town overseers of the poor who testified that Frye's application contained errors. They stated that Frye, whom they described as "decayed with rheumatism," had erroneously reported that he was the owner of the house. The house, they testified, actually belonged to his daughter, who "has ceased to be able to do anything toward the support of her father." A local physician affirmed Fry's poverty and dependency: "he has long received pecuniary aid from his charitable neighbors."[39] The veteran had, with the aid of local officials, used the department's appeal process to explain errors in the original claim and to show that he was truly needy. As a result of this appeal, Frye's status changed from a crippled, yet apparently self-sufficient, property holder and household head to a near propertyless invalid who was aided by his daughter and by the charity of his neighbors. The pension office placed Frye on the rolls.

Clever veterans and their congressional allies, however, exploited the department's process of appeal. John Atkins from Virginia exploited the loophole in the appeal process. In 1820 Atkins stated in his original claim that he was sixty-nine years old and infirm and that he lived on his farm with his eighty-year-old wife and with three other persons—Betsey Green, age forty-nine, and her two children, Solomon, age twenty, and Betty, age sixteen. Atkins reported an estate valued at $323.50 which included forty-six acres of land, farm animals, a house, and household goods. The department denied Atkins the pension, probably because of the relatively high value of his estate and because he appeared to be self-supporting.

Atkins appealed twice to the department to reverse its decision. The first appeal was aided by his congressman, Philip Pendelton Barbour, one of the program's most outspoken opponents. Through Barbour, Atkins submitted affidavits testifying that he was in poor health and too weak to work, that the farm was run by the Green family, and that Betsey Green "is a good nurse for the old people." The petition appealed to feelings of benevolence and compassion to gain admission to the pension rolls: "If [the] pension is taken from him he must become an expense to his county in a short time." The War Department denied Atkins's appeal.

In August 1822, Atkins, apparently with the help of Philip Barbour's brother, Sen. James Barbour, submitted a second appeal. This time he claimed that there were errors in his original schedule of property. Atkins resubmitted his original schedule with an addendum that listed each item on the schedule, but at lower values than were reported in his 1820 claim. According to the addendum, the total value of his assets diminished from $323.50 to $126.50. The reason given was declining property values. The two-thirds reduction of the value of assets far exceeded the effects of the deflationary cycle that gripped the nation's economy, however. Nevertheless, the court certified the appended reassessment of Atkins's property, making it the binding document used by the department to assess eligibility. The department pondered this appeal for four months, much longer than normal, before notifying Senator Barbour that

Atkins had been awarded a pension. Although the department had successfully resisted congressmen lobbying for special treatment for their constituents, in this shady case, Atkins and Senator Barbour manipulated the rules to compel Edwards to enroll Atkins. The precedent also opened the door to hundreds, even thousands, of veterans who had failed the means test. By deflating the value of their property they could comply with the rule not to alter inventories and pass the test.[40]

Wirt's ruling, which required that inventories not be altered in any way, not only produced a dangerous loophole, it also became a source of conflict over the program. Intended to deter fraud, the ruling disqualified appellants whose property had been whittled away by debt or sold to sustain their households. Wirt's ruling caused anger in Congress over administration of the law, as occurred in the case of Solomon Ames of Piermont, New Hampshire. In 1820 Ames reported that he was a sixty-five-year-old laborer who headed a household composed of his wife, age fifty-one, two daughters, ages twenty-two and nineteen, and a sixteen-year-old son. Ames possessed no real property and a personal estate worth $240. He was denied the pension probably because he appeared to have a viable household coupled with assets valued at more than two hundred dollars. Ames appealed the decision. Rather than explaining errors in his original claim as Frye and Atkins had done, Ames submitted a new property schedule. It listed fewer possessions, which were assessed at $77.84. Ames also provided new evidence that indicated that his household was on the verge of collapse because most of his property had been disposed to support his family. He also stated that his son had been the household's sole source of support but "comes of age soon and is resolved to leave us for his own benefit . . . [and] unless my pension is received to me I must shortly look for help from the town." Ames explained that he had not given this information previously "being enfeebled in mind by reason of great trials and being unacquainted with this business." Town selectmen supported Ames's claim. Nevertheless, Ames was disqualified because he had revised his inventory of property. Enraged, Ames insisted that his congressman sponsor a special bill to place him on the rolls.[41] Such cases increased Congress's criticism of the program.[42]

Between 1820 and 1823, congressmen, responding to complaints from rejected applicants, introduced hundreds of private bills to reverse department rulings.[43] In addition congressmen made numerous proposals to expand eligibility to the approximately 2,300 veterans, such as Ames, who had failed the means test and who subsequently disposed of their property to support themselves. In 1822, after a brief debate, the House approved, by the overwhelming margin of 128 to 23, an amendment to permit rejected claimants to resubmit pension applications that contained revised inventories and documents verifying the reduction of their estates.[44] As the vote showed, the program and its underlying ideals and principles were thoroughly entrenched in the House.[45]

In the Senate, however, the House's bill caused a heated ideological conflict over the law. This debate proved to be the last major conflict over the program, its sentiment of gratitude, and its liberal administration. William Kelly of Alabama, who wished to repeal the program, asserted that the country was not obliged to continue the pension program because it was neither a contract between generations nor a vested right. He rejected the claim that veterans had given "consideration" through their service to the country in exchange for the pension. Kelly concluded, like critics in prior congresses, that the pension was a "gratuity," a free gift, and not an obligation enforceable by law. He explained that the Fifteenth Congress had acted like "a generous spendthrift" because the "Treasury was full." Congress "sought objects of munificence" and settled upon the veterans because Congress anticipated that the costs would be low, only about $400,000 a year to aid the "few remaining heroes of the Revolution." He stated that the "clear mistake as to the number of pensioners destroys the fairness of the promise, and strips the transaction of that sacred character which had been given to it in argument."[46]

As had others before him, Kelly criticized the pension law for undermining civic virtue. He claimed that the pension fostered cupidity and social declension. He told the Senate, "I entertain the fullest conviction, that . . . human vices have been cultivated, and human misery extended by the law in question; and the same consequences will follow every visionary attempt of the kind— that the retailer and tapster have enjoyed the benefits of the law, and the immediate objects of its bounty have become more vicious and miserable than they were at its passage." Kelly believed that further liberalization of the law, as proposed by the House's bill, would spread vice and corruption by inviting fraud. Kelly observed, "The nature of man forbids the idea of their idleness in *worming* themselves into the Treasury. The temptation of receiving several hundred dollars at one time is too strong to be resisted. Property will disappear in a thousand *honest* ways, and poverty will be achieved when so great a reward awaits it." He thought that nearly all of the 2,300 veterans who had failed to pass the means test plus some fifteen thousand other claimants who had not reapplied under the 1820 act would divest their property to become eligible for the pension. In Kelly's mind, the pension invited greed and assaulted traditional values. The proposed expansion of the program, he charged, would further erode Revolutionary ideals and corrupt public morality.[47]

Republican David Morril of New Hampshire invoked the image of the suffering soldier and the legal claim of vested rights to answer Kelly's charges. Morril said he spoke on behalf of the "poor, honest, disheartened Revolutionary *warrior*—the poor man who fought your battles, defended your rights, sustained your character, and achieved your privileges." Morril reaffirmed that the pension "vest[s] in them a right which is not to be alienated without the consent of both parties." The soldiers, he said, have upheld their part of the bargain and the nation was compelled to uphold its part.[48]

Tired of controversy over the program, the Senate refused to engage in lengthy debate over charges that the law corrupted republican virtues, that it encouraged veterans to worm their way into the treasury, and that the House bill would substantially raise program costs. Nevertheless, sectional resentments toward the program continued to boil. Southern and western senators narrowly failed to reduce benefits and to prevent expansion of the program as proposed by the House (see appendix B, Tables 18 and 19). The opposition defeated, passage of the House's bill opened the pension rolls to the more than 2,300 veterans who had failed the means test. It encouraged another 3,000 former recipients (far fewer than Kelly's prediction), who had chosen not to reapply under the 1820 amendment, to seek a pension. Veterans, such as John Scott, above, and Rufus Burnham, below, resubmitted claims until they were enrolled. By the end of the decade nearly every applicant received a pension. By the end of 1823 the public's spirit of gratitude and justice was fully expressed in the law and in the department's liberal administration of the program. The full scope of that spirit, the growing inclusiveness of the program, and the department's bureaucratic administration can be illustrated in part through the life of Rufus Burnham.

Burnham was born in 1748 in Boxford, Massachusetts, the first of three siblings, all of whom survived to adulthood.[49] In 1763, Burnham's father was declared insane, and his estate of nearly £300 was put into trust by the court to support the Burnham family. Young Burnham was placed under a court-appointed guardianship. By 1777 the cost of supporting the Burnham children had exhausted estate funds. Rufus Burnham, the son of a once prosperous yeoman farmer, faced a bleak future as a landless laborer. When the war began in 1775, Burnham marched with the militia to Boston and fought at Bunker

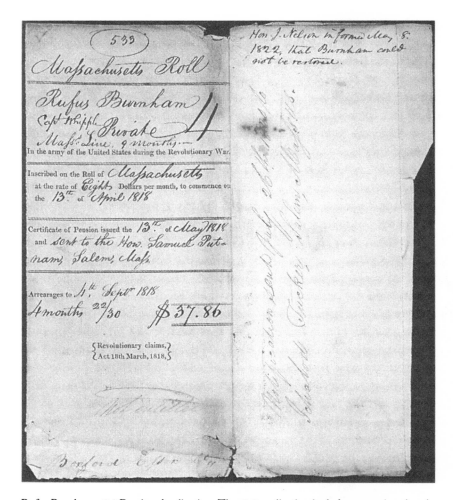

Rufus Burnham, 1818 Pension Application. The 1818 application includes a notation that the Hon. J. Nelson was informed on 8 May 1822 that the War Department had denied Burnham's appeal to be restored to the rolls. *Courtesy, National Archives.*

Hill. He remained with Washington's army near Boston until he was discharged in December 1775. Like many of Peterborough's soldiers, Burnham served in the militia, state regiments, and as a regular. Between 1776 and 1778, Rufus fought on several occasions as a member of Boxford's militia. In June 1778, Burnham enlisted for nine months in a Massachusetts regiment of the Continental Army. The combination of patriotism, politicization during the early days of the war, peer pressure, poverty, and the lure of a bounty probably motivated him to enlist. Congress had appealed for more troops and had offered additional bonuses to men who would enlist for nine months to fill Washington's depleted ranks. Poor and propertyless at that time, Burnham left his wife, whom he had married in November 1777, to fight the British. His tour was uneventful. Burnham saw no more war except as a host for a captured Hessian soldier and the soldier's family. Burnham received a subsidy for supporting these prisoners of war.

Perhaps by saving his enlistment bounties and subsidies, Burnham accumulated enough money during the war to purchase land. Between 1784 and 1785 Burnham paid £210 for forty-three acres of land that included a house and barn. In these same years he also sold most of that land for a slight gain. He may have been speculating in land or have accrued debts that forced the sale of some of his property. For five years, Burnham, his wife, and their children— Sarah (b. 1780), Seth (b. 1782) and Hannah (b. 1789)—lived on their fourteen-acre farm. In 1790 Burnham sold his property and moved to rented quarters. The reasons for the sale can only be surmised. Boxford's population dropped by 8 percent between 1790 and 1800, possibly indicating an economic decline that adversely affected the Burnhams. Whether Burnham's change in fortune was connected to wartime trauma, as seemed to be the case for some of Peterborough's Continental soldiers, can only be surmised.

At the turn of the century, Burnham dropped out of historical sight. His life, like that of thousands of other veterans, was apparently destined to anonymity. By 1818, however, Rufus Burnham and his fellow Revolutionary War veterans were elevated from relative obscurity to an esteemed cultural status. Burnham and his fellow veterans became objects of the nation's moral sentiment. He joined the ranks of apotheosized suffering soldiers who represented American character in the country's quest for national identity. In 1818 he joined the ranks of pensioners. His application showed that he was still living in the quarters he had rented in 1790. He resided there with his wife and two of his children, Seth and Sarah. Hannah, his third child, had married in 1804 and was no longer in the community.

Between 1818 and 1820, the pension made a significant impact on the Burnham household as it had on Peterborough's Blair and Diamond families. Within a few months of its receipt, Seth, age thirty-six, established his own household. He bought a farm two miles down the road from his father's house and married Caroline Herrick, age twenty-two, the daughter of a wealthy neighbor. Most likely, Seth had remained in his father's household to assist his

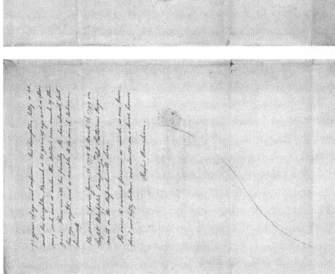
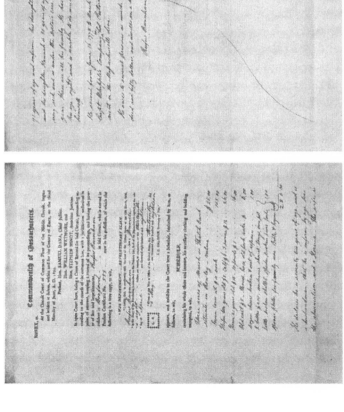

Rufus Burnham, 1820 Pension Application. His application illustrates the standardized form used by courts. Not only does it list his property, but it also contains a description of Burnham's household and the medical condition of people in his household. Burnham did not pass the means test. He was restored to the rolls under the 1823 law that permitted him to submit a new inventory of property and documentation of the disposal of his assets. *Courtesy, National Archives.*

parents while saving money to buy property and waiting for the day when he could marry. The pension released Seth from the obligation to contribute to his parents' support and enabled him to establish his own household.[50]

In 1820 Rufus Burnham reapplied for the pension as required by law. His claim showed that Seth had moved out of the Burnham home and that the veteran's daughter Hannah had returned to Rufus's household in a "sickly" condition. Burnham had used his pension to make his household a refuge for needy kin. Burnham's pension fostered and strengthened interdependence between him and his offspring. The pension ensured the veteran's self-sufficiency and increased his ability to contribute to the well-being of the household. Burnham told the court that he was seventy-two years old, infirm, suffering from a hernia, and nearly blind in his right eye. His wife, age seventy-one, was also reported to be in poor health. Only their daughter Sarah, age forty, who cared for her parents and infirm sister Hannah, was reported to be healthy. Burnham possessed few assets. He had three acres of marshlands worth $25, livestock valued at $147, household goods worth $106. His property amounted to $278. He also reported debts totaling $150, but department rules did not allow him to deduct those debts from the value of his estate. The War Department dropped Burnham from the pension rolls because "his property amounted to more than any other person whose name has been continued on the list and who served so short a time." The value of Burnham's estate fell within the second tier of the means test, property valued between two and four hundred dollars. Clerks had to apply other criteria, such as type and length of service, in deciding whether to admit Burnham to the rolls. His brief service in the Continental Army did not favor Burnham.[51]

For two years Burnham appealed the decision. Meanwhile, the veteran and his wife were aided by friends, his daughter Sarah, and probably Seth. Sometime between 1820 and 1822, neighbors lent Burnham money to build a house next to his rented quarters. The loan was probably made with the expectation that Burnham would be restored to the rolls and would use the pension to repay neighbors. In 1822 Burnham, who had become a widower and totally blind, moved to this new house where he lived with his two daughters. As his neighbors' help demonstrated, Burnham "was much esteemed" by the community and considered "an honest, upright and industrious citizen" deserving assistance. His respected status was no doubt enhanced by his honored place as a Revolutionary War veteran and as a person who fit the popular image of a suffering soldier.

Despite receiving aid from neighbors and kin, the loss of Burnham's pension jeopardized the household. Desperate, Burnham reapplied for the pension after the law was amended in 1823. Burnham claimed to be penniless and was officially reported as such. His application recounted the personal and financial decline that had beset his household. He reported that in 1821 his three acres of marshlands had been conveyed to Sarah to pay a $50 debt owed her for supporting her parents. Burnham stated that his livestock had been either consumed or "sold for expenses for family." He sold six cows and a heifer for $105 to pay rent and taxes. In addition, townsmen testified that without the pension Burnham could not support himself "except by public or private charity." The household appeared to be on the verge of collapse. Impoverishment and infirmity had transformed Burnham's household status. In 1820 he was the head of the household, but in 1823 he was a ward of his children, or as Burnham put it, "two daughters live with me, or rather I live with them." According to Burnham, Sarah and Hannah were too "infirm" and "indigent" to continue to support him. The department did not hold Seth accountable to aid his father and sisters.[52]

In 1823 Burnham was restored to the pension rolls and awarded back payments to 1820. Thus, local taxpayers and Seth were spared the cost of supporting the veteran's household. Between 1818 and 1836, when Burnham died at age eighty-seven, he received more than $1,700 from his pension. The pension sustained the Burnham household, which contained the old soldier and his two daughters, one of them being infirm. Following the veterans' death in 1836, his surviving daughter Sarah (her sister Hannah had died in 1834) inherited the house and the remainder of his estate, which had increased in value to more than $500. In 1842 Sarah, age sixty-two, announced her intention to marry a resident of Middleton, Massachusetts. The marriage never occurred. In 1844 she married a neighbor and widower, Joseph Tyler, who then moved to her house. He apparently had little wealth, but the pension had allowed the Burnhams to accumulate property, enabling Sarah to accrue a small dowry. When she died in 1858, her estate was put in trust for her husband's support, with her brother Seth and his family as heirs. When Tyler died in 1864, the estate was liquidated by Seth, with the small balance going to Tyler's creditors. Burnham's pension in the form of equity had continued to benefit his descendants long after his death.

As illustrated in Burnham's case, the department's administration of the law reinforced the veteran's honored cultural status. The pension sustained the veteran, bolstered his household, and strengthened the bonds tying him to his children and them to the community. Indirectly, the pension had even continued to aid the Burnham family after the veteran's death because it had allowed the Burnhams to build a modest estate that helped to support Sarah (and her husband following Sarah's death).

BETWEEN 1820 AND 1823 the department used its rule-making authority to deter crime and to cut costs. It did so by treating like cases alike and by upholding clerks' decisions to reject unqualified claimants despite strong lobbying to enroll them. Resembling a modern bureaucracy, the department administered a set of consistent, explicit, and well-publicized rules to proficiently administer the program. More important perhaps, the department created a novel program. Despite the taint of the means test, the department's administration removed the stigma of pauperism from the program. Its practices assumed that every Continental soldier who passed the test was worthy of the benefit. Distinguishing its program from local poor relief, pensioned veterans, unlike paupers, retained their autonomy and could increase their assets; kin and community were not required to support pensioners. Furthermore, once judged in need of aid, the pensioner was not granted relief rated according to need, as would be done under poor laws, but rather awarded a lifetime pension based on military rank. Through its administration, the department ensured that the means test would neither blemish veterans' honored status nor discredit the nation's feelings of gratitude. The department's extension of benefits to retired veterans, expanded by the 1823 amendment, strengthened support for the program and its underlying imagery, ideals, and principles. The department treated recipients as venerated symbols of patriotism and national character who deserved payment of the country's debt of gratitude and compensation for their disadvantages.

By 1823, the department's administration of the program virtually insulated the law from partisan and sectional criticism. Local communities welcomed the removal of paupers from poor rolls to pension rolls. Pensioners and their families benefited by completing agreements to transfer wealth between generations while ensuring the security of veterans' households through receipt of a guaranteed annual income in the form of pensions. For veterans, such as pauper Benjamin Alld, proud John Scott, and esteemed Rufus Burnham, pensions were not only public badges of honor, but also sources of household cohesion and personal dignity.[53] Thus the department's efficient, fair, firm, scrupulous, and liberal administration succeeded in ending the threat of further scandal and in expressing the public's moral sentiments of compassion and justice. By strengthening support for the pension program, the department further legitimized the image of the suffering soldier and all that it had come to represent. Between 1820 and 1824, applicants for the pension completed the validation of the image and the transformation of political culture and public policy.

CHAPTER 7

Veterans, Political Culture, and Public Policy

VETERANS WERE BOTH objects of the public's gratitude and contributors to their own apotheosis as suffering soldiers. Ironically, the means test, passed to curb corruption and reduce cost, had enhanced the image of the suffering soldier. The lives of nearly twenty thousand veterans exposed to public scrutiny validated the image of them and the ideals embedded in the law. Claimants marching to pensioners' courts to pass the means test appeared as the heroic, humble, cheerful, impoverished, infirm icons romanticized by political orators and by revisionist histories and nationalist journals. Veterans' demeanor confirmed the public's belief that these men had been citizen-soldiers imbued with the spirit of '76. They personified the new memory of the Revolutionary War that transformed the Continental Army into a republican institution and made regular troops dominant in the concept of the Revolution as a people's war. By displaying their infirmities and deprivations as badges of patriotism under public scrutiny of the means test, veterans affirmed the notion that years of service and attendant hardships had disadvantaged them. Thus veterans contributed to the revised memory of the Revolution, the image of the suffering soldier, and public policy expressing the sentiment of gratitude.

Beyond appearances claimants' service records confirmed the public's belief that these men had dedicated years of their lives to secure the nation's independence. The typical claimant had enlisted in his late teens or early twenties. About half of the twenty thousand claimants had enlisted in 1775 during the *rage militaire* and had continued or resumed their military service after 1775 when the Revolution became a "long and dirty" war. Approximately 75 percent of all applicants enlisted between 1775 and 1777. On average, claimants spent slightly less than three years under arms. A quarter of them, however, served more than three years in the army. Less than 5 percent of the veterans had served the minimum of a nine-month enlistment (for information on applicants' service see appendix B, tables 20, 21, 22, and 23). Generally, the claimants' enlistment patterns resembled those found for Peterborough's Continental Army veterans. For the most part, applicants were hard-core soldiers who formed the backbone of the Continental Army.

If the profile of Peterborough's soldiers reflected claimants as a whole, thousands of pension applicants who enlisted early in the war represented a cross section of their communities' social structures. Their motivations for enlistment may have resembled those of Peterborough's soldiers who joined the army in the first years of the war. Probably thousands of applicants were inspired to fight by the conflict's ideals. They may have been urged by family and friends, as had many of Peterborough's recruits, to enlist as a civic duty. It is likely that many remained in service because they were politicized by the war. It is also likely that they were tightly bound to their regiments by the presence of relatives, friends, and other townsmen in their units as was the case for Peterborough's soldiers. If the insights into the backgrounds of regulars gained from studying Peterborough's soldiers held true generally, then claimants as a whole would have readily fit the public's romantic image of them as heroic patriots, from all social ranks, who dedicated years of their lives in a common cause.

Claimants confirmed the public's belief that veterans were feeble and unwell. The image of the suffering soldier attributed these conditions not just to age but to deprivations resulting from their service in the army. More than 80 percent of the applicants reported they were in poor health (see appendix B, table 24). Silas Russell reported that he was "very infirm," Daniel Rider swore that he was "in bad health," Henry Hallowell said he was "weak in body," Henry Buzzell claimed to be "feeble," Joseph Stevens stated that his health was "broken," and Reuben Clark complained of "afflictions."[1] Richard Hallstead said he had a "weak heart." Philo Philips, "a man of color," suffered from "rheumatism," the most commonly reported medical complaint. Israel Manning reported "afflictions of the kidneys," and Icabod Beckwith said he had "palsy and fits." A few applicants were physically disabled. Samuel Mitchell testified that he was blind. Although these conditions may have been typical of men in this age group, the public regarded these afflictions as a form of military disability. Displayed proudly by veterans and noted in their pension applications, infirmities drew attention to the heroic sacrifices of their youth. They also served to confirm that these men deserved the nation's gratitude and had earned their pensions.[2]

Most claimants were poor, as officially measured by the War Department's means test. Nearly one veteran in eight (13.4 percent) was penniless. About half of the other claimants reported assets valued at less than fifty dollars. Only one applicant in five reported owning real estate. Taken as a whole, the average value of claimants' property was $129 (see appendix B, tables 25 and 26). Generally, claimants' inventories contained a few household items, some farm implements or artisan tools, and possibly one or two animals such as a cow or pig. Hardly any of the veterans reported an income. Using a crude measure derived from veterans' claims and aggregate wealth reported for New York residents, applicants were well below the average per capita wealth. In 1819 the state of New York reported a per capita average of $204 in real and personal property.[3] By comparison, in 1820 the per capita wealth of pension applicants in New York was twenty-eight dollars, or nearly nine times lower than the per capita average of residents in the state.[4] Regardless of state or region, applicants reported owning a meager portion of the nation's wealth (see appendix B, table 27). If these data are extrapolated for the population as a whole, claimants were at the bottom of the economic ladder. To emphasize their destitution, 22 percent of the claimants stated that they had once received, were receiving, or were about to receive private charity or public relief (see appendix B, tables 28 and 29). As seen in chapter 6, however, the official record of veterans' assets produced by the department's mean test was not a complete measure of veterans' wealth in those cases involving retirement contracts. Nevertheless, taken at face value pension applications revealed a stratification of assets and deprivation among the claimants that reflected the interplay of age and household structure. At the bottom were solitary veterans, followed by couples, then by nuclear households, and finally by complex households. The analysis of these strata suggests that aging veterans and those whose households had collapsed, or were near collapse, faced an increasingly dire future of growing dependency and diminishing assets. While similar conditions could no doubt be found among members of their age cohort who had not served in the Continental Army, the study of Peterborough's Revolutionary generation suggests that these conditions may have been more acute among men who had served in the

WHY IS THAT MORE IMPORTANT

Continental Army. More important, the public had come to believe that was so.

Solitary veterans, those who reported no one else in their households, were among the oldest and most desperate men, according to their claims. Comprising slightly less than 15 percent of the applicants, this group contained nearly half of all veterans above the age of seventy-four. On average, these veterans owned only twenty dollars in assets, an average six times less than the value of assets reported by applicants as a whole (see appendix B, table 30). Nearly half of the solitary veterans, more than any other category of claimants, was penniless. One veteran out of twenty reported owning real estate, far fewer than claimants as a whole. Moreover, the relative absence of reported debt by this group (only 10 percent listed liabilities) suggests that these veterans had depleted their assets and were incapable of securing credit. Not surprisingly, this group also had the highest rate of dependency. Nearly 40 percent of the solitary veterans reported having received charity from neighbors, or poor relief from their communities. While some may have been like Amasa Mills, others may have been like pauper Benjamin Alld who had hit rock bottom before being restored to self-sufficiency by the pension. Those with broken lives most closely conformed to the sentimental image of the impoverished, forsaken, hoary-headed, feeble relics of the Revolutionary War romanticized by Fourth of July orators, politicians, and writers in stories like the "Old Soldier." Besides arousing the public's compassion and gratitude, such lives evoked pathos. Their pleas for pensions eloquently revealed the dire effects of advanced age, declining health, grinding poverty, frayed kin networks, and diminished autonomy.

Abraham Taylor and Elijah Caswell were solitary veterans who desperately pleaded for pensions to mend their broken households. In 1820 Taylor told the court that in 1816 his household had disbanded because he could no longer support his wife and their twelve-year-old child. His wife and child had subsequently moved to Vermont to live with friends while he remained in Montgomery County, New York, to earn a living. Taylor never rose above bare subsistence, however, and his household remained splintered. An unemployed laborer, nearly crippled by rheumatism, and owner of paltry seventeen dollars in personal property, Taylor's life itself was an eloquent appeal for the pension to ensure self-sufficiency and to unite his household.[5] Similarly, poverty and illness had dissolved Elijah Caswell's household. In 1820, Caswell, age sixty-eight, wrote in his pension application that he was unemployed and possessed only seven dollars in assets. Caswell told the court in Massachusetts that prior

HOW MANY CONTINENTAL VETERANS WERE COMPARATIVELY ABOVE THE MEANS TEST? IF THERE WERE MANY HOW IS IT THEY WERE VIEWED AS "SUFFERING SOLDIERS" AND WHAT SEPARATED THEM FROM STATE MILITIA?

to receiving a pension in 1818, his invalid wife had been living in the local poorhouse. He reported, "when I got my pension, I took her out." He apparently placed her with another family, possibly to nurse her afflictions, because she did not reside with him when he reapplied for his pension. He swore that if he were not continued on the rolls, he could no longer aid her, and she would have to return to the poorhouse. Although they lived apart, Caswell pleaded for the pension to support his helpless wife.[6] Taylor and Caswell, like most solitary veterans, occupied the bottom rung of the economic ladder. Their pension claims revealed the miseries of unemployment, declining health, poverty, and shattered households. They pleaded for the pension to restore self-sufficiency, to repair fractured households, and to fulfill their patriarchal duties by aiding spouses and children. Both veterans received pensions.

Other solitary veterans who were dependent on alms pleaded for the pension so as to be restored to self-sufficiency.[7] Towns supported their claims not only in order to secure an honor for the veteran in the form of the pension but also to reduce the cost of local poor relief. For example, overseers of the poor in Ludlow, Massachusetts, told the court that Icabod Beckwith, age sixty-nine, was "a pauper disabled in body and mind" with no family to aid him. Without the pension he would remain a ward of the town, a fate he no doubt abhorred and taxpayers resented.[8] If Beckwith had kin living near him, they may have been too poor to help him. Possibly he outlived them. Possibly they had moved away. Perhaps, like the wealthy Alld family who withheld support from Benjamin, Beckwith's family refused to aid him. Regardless, dependent veterans like Beckwith were desperate to become independent and self-supporting, free of the stigma of pauperism. Town selectmen and overseers of the poor gladly lent their support to such applicants.

Reuben Clark of Connecticut, likely with the urging of townsmen, pleaded for the pension so as to keep him from returning to pauperism. Clark was a widower, age sixty-five, and an unemployed seaman who suffered from what he called "afflictions." The veteran reported that prior to receiving his pension in 1818 he had been supported by the town. Clark stated that with the aid of the pension he had once again become self-supporting. After receiving his pension in 1818 he had moved into his brother's home where he occupied his own quarters and enjoyed living independently. Veterans such as Clark, who were once dependent upon alms, anguished over loosing their autonomy and self-esteem should the department deny their claims. Clark received a pension.[9]

Henry Buzzell's plea left a record of rare detail, which illuminates conditions that were only implied in hundreds of terse supplications from other claimants such as Reuben Clark. Buzzell's claim describes his failed struggle to remain a self-sufficient head of household. His application contains a desperate plea for the pension to prevent his fall into pauperism. In 1825 Buzzell, age sixty-five, appearing before court in Strafford County, New Hampshire, claimed to be a penniless, disabled farmer who was unable to support himself because of advancing age and deteriorating health. In addition, Buzzell told the court that his son Jacob had become poor and could no longer aid him. Buzzell told the court that in 1812 he had become "feeble" and had deeded his farm to son Jacob in return for Jacob's agreement to support his father for the remainder of his life. Father and son had completed a typical retirement contract. Buzzell swore that Jacob had lived up to this agreement until 1824 when an unexplained catastrophe impoverished Jacob. Buzzell testified, "Jacob has become poor and wholly unable to support me [or] to contribute to my relief and I am now entirely left destitute." He claimed, "I have no family [to aid me]." Buzzell had become wholly "dependent on charity" from friends. Infirmity and the failed retirement contract threatened to reduce Buzzell to pauperism. The old veteran hoped to regain his independence with the income from his pension. He probably hoped to aid son Jacob as well.[10]

A similar situation faced widower Joseph Stevens, age sixty-eight, from Portsmouth, New Hampshire. At the time of his application in 1822, Stevens was a carpenter who was penniless, infirm, and unable to work. That year he had moved into a dwelling occupied by his widowed daughter and her two children. Her husband had died in Dartmoor prison after being taken a prisoner in the War of 1812. She apparently provided her father with his own quarters and likely cared for him. Based on his testimony, he contributed little to her support. Although Stevens had four other children, a son, age forty-three, and three daughters living nearby, none of them, he reported, were able "to give me any support." They were propertyless and subsisted on "day work and [by] living out." Stevens lived on the brink of pauperism and his growing dependency threatened to bring ruin to his daughter's household. The pension would ensure his independence, reduce his daughter's burden of support, and possibly allow him to aid his struggling children.[11] If the War Department had adhered to Attorney General Wirt's narrow view of the law, only men like Taylor, Caswell, Beckwith, and Stevens—the most needy—would have received pensions.

More than 80 percent of the claimants' households contained wives, children, and in some cases kin (see appendix B, table 31). Most applicants reported that their spouses, like themselves, suffered from infirmities, afflictions, or disabilities. More than half of the veterans still supported large families. Those who submitted pleas reported that this compounded their plight by depleting their health and meager assets (see appendix B, tables 32 and 33). In some instances, the presence of disabled children added to the veteran's distress. Many claimants reported that young children were heavy burdens. Neal McGerry, an eighty-year-old veteran with a twenty-year-old wife and infant child, made this plea.[12] In the face of such woes, veterans pleaded to restore or to sustain patriarchal households. (For information on veterans' marriage patterns see appendix B, tables 34, 35, 36, and 37.) In addition, their appeals portrayed their families as the principal source of comfort, welfare, self-respect, and social status. No doubt the approximately 47,000 kin who resided with claimants anxiously awaited the pension to ensure their subsistence. Most veterans, so it seems, viewed the pension as a form of family assistance to strengthen or restore their households. Their pension applications produced a spectrum of need unimagined in the oratory that invoked the image of the suffering soldier. The department's liberal administration and the 1823 amendment extended benefits to such claimants.

A little more than a quarter of all applicants headed households that only contained a spouse. As a group they were but a step above conditions reported by solitary veterans. Nearly 10 percent of these couples reported themselves penniless and another 52 percent reported property worth less than fifty dollars. These veterans anguished over declining kin support and the grim prospect of the breakup of their households and of becoming paupers.[13] In some instances their households appeared on the brink of becoming like Elijah Caswell's circumstance. Caswell's wife had been removed to a poorhouse after he could no longer support her.[14] These claimants submitted heartrending appeals not only to support themselves, but also to provide for their spouses. Job Hamblin, facing this dire future, desperately pleaded for the pension. Much is known about Hamblin's life because of his extensive testimony and because of information in his wife's application for a widow's pension completed years later. Thus the Hamblin case revealed additional insights into the lives of thousands of veterans and their wives, who struggled to maintain households weakened by growing dependence, by deteriorating health, and by the shattering of kin networks that accompanied aging.

Hamblin was born in Virginia in July 1762. He enlisted at age seventeen in a

Virginia regiment of the Continental Army and was present at the British surrender at Yorktown. In March 1782, he was discharged from the army and seven months later married Eleanor Mullings, age seventeen. In September 1783, the first of their eight children was born. They had five boys and three girls; their last child, Polly, was probably born about 1805. About that time, Hamblin, a carpenter and farmer, moved his family from Virginia to Indiana to start a new life on the frontier. The family struggled and suffered. During the War of 1812 his son George was killed in the Battle of Mackinaw. For a short time, money received from his son's death benefit helped support Hamblin's large family. Hamblin reported that his family lived "in the woods" trying to scratch out a living. Illness plagued their hardscrabble life. Hamblin reported in his application for a pension: "my family was [in] much distress" and all had been "very sickly for one year." Hamblin went deeper into debt to purchase food. In 1818 Hamblin received his pension, which he used to pay physician bills, to pay his creditors, and to buy food. For unexplained reasons, Hamblin did not reapply for the pension in 1820 possibly because he still held title to his farm, whose value probably exceeded the department's poverty line. In the years that followed, the Hamblin household experienced more misfortune. He explained that in "1823 or 4," their mare had died leaving them without a "beast" to plow their fields.

In 1827 when Hamblin applied for the pension, he reported owning thirty dollars in personal property. Only the veteran, age sixty-six, and his wife, age sixty-four, who was "helpless and can do but little," remained in his household. He was too old and too sick to support himself and his wife: "I am very badly ruptured and otherwise disabled from laboring at my trade or working at any other business to secure a living." He swore that six of his children were married and "all were gone," meaning not only that they had left the household but also that they were no longer under his control. Those children, like their parents, struggled to subsist. He reported that none of them "owned any land and are all poor otherwise." Still, Hamblin's children, "indigent as they are," toiled to aid their parents. Hamblin also stated that one of his sons, William, possibly a tenant farmer, had "40 or 50 acres" of "very poor" land, but that William's farm was inadequate to support both William's family and his father and mother. The veteran and his wife appeared to be on the verge of pauperism as a result of misfortune, age, infirmity, and their children's indigency.[15]

Similarly Bartholomew Stevens and his wife, each age seventy-two, from

Somerset County, Maine reported, "I was supported by the town as a pauper before I received the bounty of Government. . . ." Stevens claimed that upon receiving the pension, he and his wife had moved in with their son, "a man of small property," who could not maintain them without income from the pension. Stevens warned that if the pension were discontinued, he and his wife would have to leave their son's household and again become paupers.[16] Many veterans, such as Hamblin and Stevens, claimed that their assets were depleted, their health was failing, and that they were becoming increasingly burdensome to their children. According to such testimony, filial aid had only slowed parents' slide toward greater dependency. As they became more dependent, veterans like Hamblin and Stevens tried not to burden their children with additional sacrifices. The pension assured these veterans that they would remain or become self-sufficient. Moreover, in many cases the pension probably reduced anxieties, if not conflicts, by reducing the burden of filial support.

Many veterans confronted bankruptcy along with ill health and frayed networks of kin support. They wrote that debt added the threat of financial collapse and pauperism.[17] The fear of bankruptcy was particularly acute among claimants who headed nuclear households. These veterans revealed, possibly unintentionally, the effects of excessive debt on their households. Creditors' demands for payment could force parents to liquidate assets and cause them to become destitute and dependent. In Josiah Gary's case, his children, who felt exploited by their father, threatened to take him to court for debt if he didn't pay them for their years of labor on his farm. Gary claimed that if he received the pension he could pay his debt to his children by giving them his farm. An intergenerational revolt caused by debt and hard feelings triggered Gary's application for a pension. Gary's receipt of the pension ensured his independence as head of household apart from his estranged children.[18]

In other instances the threat of bankruptcy helped to retain older children in the household to assist their parents (see appendix B, table 38). Heavy debts endangered parental assets, threatened household viability, and endangered the legacies children had earned or expected to receive through inheritance. In these cases, indebtedness tied older children more closely to their parents' households. Thus self-interest reinforced cultural norms that prescribed that older children, especially females, remain at home to support their parents. Such was the case for Peterborough's William Blair.

Blair was one of ten Continental Army veterans residing in Peterborough when the pension act passed. Eight of them received the pension in 1818. He was among the town's five pensioners who later passed the means test. Prior to receiving the pension in 1818, Blair and his wife, along with their son, William Jr., and his wife, struggled to maintain the farm they shared. By 1818 the farm had been mortgaged to pay debts. The household's taxable assets were reduced to a single ox. In 1818, William Jr. paid $1.70 in taxes, which included his poll tax of $1.30. The veteran's poll tax was abated and the veteran paid no property tax because he had assigned his farm to creditors. The family's fortunes were near collapse. By 1820, having received his pension for two years, the veteran paid off his creditors and resumed full ownership of his farm. The household, composed of the veteran and his wife, and their son and his wife, recovered its former rank just below the midpoint of Peterborough's taxpayers.

In 1820 William Blair reapplied for his pension and accurately reported his circumstances. He told the court that he was seventy years old and lived with his wife, age sixty-four. He owned no real estate. His assets were a cow worth sixteen dollars and a hog worth eight dollars. Blair said that he was a farmer who owed "more than the above property" was worth. His son, William Jr., owned the farm, which he shared with his father who had a life-lease to half of it. Blair passed the means test. The two households—father and son—remained independent and interdependent. They even prospered. In 1825 the veteran was taxed on his leased half-share of the farm, which consisted of one half-acre of mowing land, two horses, one cow, and twenty acres of wild land. With the aid of the pension between 1818 and 1825, by the time the elder Blair died, he had fulfilled his patriarchal and parental obligations to his wife and son. Moreover, the pension had enabled the family to retain the homestead where William Jr. remained to raise his thirteen children and to care for his mother, who died in 1842 at age eighty-six.[19]

Infirmity, liquidation of assets, children struggling to support themselves, and heavy debts created an uncertain and precarious future for Zachariah Cook and his wife. Cook, anxiously facing the threat of bankruptcy, pleaded for the pension. In 1830 Cook, a seventy-nine-year-old farmer in Greenbrier County, Virginia, reported that he owned property valued by a local court at $274. Cook also claimed debts amounting to $342. He stated that he had already sold part of his land and some livestock to pay creditors. He had also sold assets to support himself and his fifty-two-year-old wife, as well as to assist their children who were struggling to maintain their own households. He had given a colt to his son and a cow to each of his two daughters. Cook pleaded for the

William Blair's tombstone, Peterborough, New Hampshire. Its inscription reads, "A Revolutionary Soldier." Blair was a pensioner and proud veteran. Like those of other veterans, his tombstone was a memorial to his patriotism and sacrifices as a suffering soldier. *Courtesy, Peterborough Historical Society.*

pension to support his own household, to continue to aid his children, and to halt his slide toward bankruptcy and the dissolution of his household that would surely follow.[20]

The possibility of household dissolution and pauperism was especially troubling to claimants who headed nuclear families.[21] They amounted to 46 percent of all applicants. Typically, this group of veterans was in their early sixties. Their wives were in their mid-fifties. Generally, they had two or three children in their households. On average these claimants reported estates valued at $141, which, in one out of four cases, included real property. Despite possessing relatively more wealth than other groups of veterans, 40 percent of these claimants (twice the proportion reported by couples) were burdened with debts that nearly equaled their assets. Only a few of these veterans received charity from family and friends or more rarely public relief (see Appendix B, tables 39 and 40).

In 1820 Jonathan Stevens, age fifty-eight, pleaded for the pension to maintain his fragile household. Stevens, his wife, age fifty, and three children, daughters ages eighteen, twenty, and twenty-five, lived on his farm in Caledonia County, Vermont. He had purchased the farm with a down payment from his pension that he had received in 1818. By 1820 his assets totaled $553. In accordance with War Department rules, the court deducted the $230 Stevens owed on his first mortgage, leaving him an estate valued at $323.[22] Stevens reported another $150 in personal debts. Possibly knowing that the department would not deduct these debts from his estate when applying the means test, Stevens pleaded that he was at "half strength," that his oldest daughter was infirm, and that if the pension were not continued, he would lose his farm. Furthermore, he stated that he had purchased the farm "on the faith of my pension that I should thereby be able to pay for it." Stevens had used the pension to change his status from a landless farmer to farm owner and to strengthen his household, which included a debilitated child under his care. The department continued Stevens on the pension rolls and presumably the household remained viable while the veteran lived.[23]

George Ewing, age sixty-seven, and his seventy-year-old wife expressed alarm that without the pension their children might depart their household, which would then surely collapse because the old veteran and his wife could not manage it without their help. Ewing reported that he suffered from a "painful illness," and that his wife was also unwell. Their two unmarried daughters, Abigail, age thirty-nine, and Rachael, age thirty-five, who lived at home, cared for their parents. The relationship between daughters and parents appeared, however, to be fragile and strained. Ewing pleaded for the pension because he and his wife had "no person on whom I can claim for assistance save that of parental affections" which, he implied, were wearing thin. Love and filial duty were not sufficient, in Ewing's mind, to guarantee a viable household. He hoped to strengthen his household by using the pension to reduce his daughters' burden of parental support. In addition, Ewing implied that the pension would also be an insurance policy to maintain the veteran and his wife, should their daughters leave home or become infirm.[24] Similarly Peter Crapo stated that he could not count on his son's aid in the future because "he is now of age" and would soon leave his parents' home to establish his own household. In 1820 Crapo, a seventy-year-old farmer living in Rensselaer, New York, told the court that rheumatism and infirmity made it impossible for him to work. His wife, age sixty-seven, was also "out of health." Crapo hoped that the pension would diminish the burden on their son and possibly encourage him to remain longer at home with his parents.[25]

Veterans such as Ewing and Crapo portrayed their households on the verge of collapse because of poverty and because their children's aid was uncertain. Filial affection and duty had sustained some households, but veterans feared that these sentiments would not be strong enough to prevent children from pursuing their own lives. Normally, as shown in the pension claims, veterans' children left home after reaching adulthood. Only one household in ten among the twenty thousand applicants contained an adult child over age thirty. Parents could anticipate the departure of older sons rather than daughters. Nearly twice as many veterans whose households contained children over the age of fifteen reported daughters rather than sons living with them. Households, such as those headed by Crapo and Ewing, were vulnerable to sudden collapse should the children depart.

Some veterans appealed for pensions to fulfill their paternal obligations to dependents within their households. Solomon Cook claimed that poor health and advancing age made support of his young family increasingly difficult. Cook, age sixty-six, had married either late in life or he had remarried and was raising a young family, perhaps his second. In 1820 he was living in Genesee County, New York, with his wife, age thirty-three. The household contained seven children, three sons, ages three, eleven, and twelve, and four daughters, ages one, five, nine, and thirteen. Cook reported that he had to support his oldest daughter even though she was employed outside of his home. His estate consisted of some livestock and personal property, which totaled $41 in value. He swore that his debts exceeded the value of his assets, and he told the department that he was "dependent upon the Bounty of the Government for [the] support" of his family. Cook portrayed his household to be near collapse, especially under the strain of his failing health, indebtedness, and many young mouths to feed.[26]

A large portion (26 percent) of the veterans who headed nuclear households pleaded for pensions to support their infirm and disabled children. Applications from veterans John Wellman, Dan Weller, and Jeremiah Purdy described fragile family networks of mutual care that were on the verge of collapse. John Wellman, age sixty-five, reported that he nursed his twenty-three-year-old helpless son and "feeble" wife. In turn his three sons, ages thirteen, seventeen, and nineteen, who resided at home, aided their father. Dan Weller, age sixty-one, provided for his wife, age fifty-eight, and cared for his "idiot" daughter, age twenty-eight. They were assisted by their two young daughters, ages ten and thirteen. Jeremiah Purdy, age sixty, headed a household composed of his wife, age fifty-nine, his three daughters, ages eighteen, twenty-five, and twenty-six, and a son, age fifteen. Purdy reported that his son was a cripple. Purdy's twenty-five-year-old daughter suffered from consumption. The other children helped to sustain the household and to care for their ill sister and disabled brother. Without pensions the Wellman, Weller, and Purdy households were less likely to survive as refuges for disabled and helpless kin. According to their claims, structures of mutual support were on the brink of failure.[27]

Joel Atherton's claim more fully illustrates the conditions that led veterans like Wellman, Weller, and Purdy to make special appeals to preserve their households. In 1820 Atherton, age fifty-six, lived on his farm in Portland, Maine, with his wife, age fifty-four, and eight daughters who ranged in age from eight years to twenty-four years. He reported that he could not work full-time "on account of rheumatism," and he claimed that his two oldest daughters, Nancy, age twenty-four, and Harriet, age twenty-two, were "very feeble" and required parental care. Atherton stated that his other daughters, except the youngest, "are able in part to support themselves," and that his wife was in "comfortable health and able to do part of the housework." Atherton's estate consisted of forty acres of land, a barn and attached half-house, a cow, a yearling, five sheep, farm tools, and household items valued at $210. He also claimed $275 in debts, which he said could not be paid "without disposing of the little property I possess." Atherton faced the compound problems of contributing to the support of his young children and assisting his infirm older daughters at a time when rheumatism made him less able to work. In such cases, veterans cited their care for dependent members of their households as a special circumstance that entitled them to a pension. In Atherton's case, despite an estate that exceeded the means test's first tier of two hundred dollars, the department concurred by keeping him on the rolls.[28]

Joseph Craven received a pension in part because his household had become a refuge for his son who suffered a tragic illness. In 1820 Craven, age sixty-one, his wife (he couldn't remember her age), and his son, age twelve, lived in New Jersey. Craven was a baker who had accumulated a modest estate valued at $205. He also reported $102 in debts. Although his health had declined, Craven stated that he had supported his family until his son suddenly became blind. Public officials submitted an affidavit to support Craven's claim. They stated that his son's illness had "contributed not a little to add to the pressure of poverty . . . and is now about to bear upon him more hard than ever." The affidavit explained the woe that befell Craven. After a few months at the hospital, doctors declared the boy's illness incurable. Officials reported that "the father is now required to take him away, and take care of him, that he may no longer be a burden on that institution." The sight of his blind son "has [not only] produced very great despondency, but seems to have rendered him [Craven] incapable of that exertion, which contributed somewhat to keep him above absolute poverty." Craven was depressed as well as despondent. Local officials appealed on the veteran's behalf for the pension to sustain and succor the tragic Craven family.[29]

Other veterans appealed for the pension so as to maintain households that had become refuges for grandchildren and ailing kin.[30] So wrote Phineas Hamblett in his appeal for a pension. In 1820 Phineas Hamblett, age sixty-five, was living on his farm in Cheshire County, New Hampshire. His estate was assessed at $777 and he claimed debts totaling $253. The value of his property was well above the top of the department's discretionary tier of two to four hundred dollars in assets. Hamblett's appeal focused on the role of his household as a refuge. He reported that he cared for his ninety-two-year-old mother-in-law, for his sixty-two-year-old deaf and blind wife, and for their feeble thirty-nine-year-old daughter. Hamblett testified that although he was fairly well off and still in good health, he needed the pension's income because his ability to support the household and to care for his dependents was diminishing. Hamblett had probably hoped to persuade the department to make him an exception to the rule. The department rejected Hamblett's claim because he failed the means test. Despite being denied, he was welcomed to reapply for the pension if his assets fell within the department's means test. The pension was Hamblett's safety net.[31]

The pension saved William Diamond's household. Peterborough's Diamond used the pension to sustain his household and to fulfill his patriarchal duties. As we have seen, Diamond was a war hero who had fought at Lexington, Trenton, and Princeton and had served various enlistments that totaled just more than two years. After the war, he moved to Peterborough where he acquired a farm. He held a precarious place just above the bottom third of the town's taxpayers. In 1817, at age sixty-two, Diamond had divided his farm equally between his two unmarried sons, William Jr., age thirty-three, and John, age twenty-seven.[32] As part of the retirement contract, the sons agreed to support their father and mother in exchange for deeds to the properties. Titles to the farms, however, were not formally registered in William Jr. and John's names for another four and eleven years, respectively, possibly as a precaution to ensure compliance. Nevertheless, the town recognized the legality of these retirement contracts by taxing the father and sons on their respective portions of the divided estate.

In 1818 Diamond applied for the pension. He reported that he was "very destitute of property." Although this claim was exaggerated, Diamond was among the lowest third of the town's taxpayers, and his sons, as would be expected because of the equal division of his farm, occupied an even lower rank. The pension bolstered the family's fortunes. Soon after their father received his pension, Diamond's sons expanded their farms by buying land next to them. In 1820, when Diamond reapplied for the pension, he claimed that he owned no real estate, possessed $42 worth of livestock, and paid $6 annually for a life lease he held to thirty-two acres of land. Diamond reported that his household consisted of his wife, age fifty-eight, and his daughter, Lydia, age twenty-three, and Lydia's two children. Lydia had apparently been abandoned by her husband and had returned home sometime between 1818 and 1820. Diamond also told the court that "he was unable to work" and owed "$50.00" in debts. He did not report that the town had taxed him on one acre of plowed land, one acre of mowing land, four acres of pasture, and a horse. Diamond acted as if the retirement contracts had been executed, and the town looked the other way when he omitted this taxable property from the inventory he submitted to the court. Though he was not impoverished, townsmen may have considered the veteran deserving because Diamond's family hovered between the bottom third and lower half of the town's taxpayers. More important, perhaps, Diamond was a hero because he had fought at Lexington, Bunker Hill, and under Washington at Trenton and Princeton.

Continued on the rolls and guaranteed an income for life, Diamond executed the retirement contracts with his sons. On 16 March 1821, the veteran deeded part of his farm to his older son, William Jr., who soon established his own household. In 1824, at age thirty-nine, he married Lucinda Haggett, age twenty-eight, of Peterborough. William Jr., his wife, and later their three daughters remained on his share of the homestead farm for most of their lives. The pension had helped Diamond's older son gain independence as head of his own household. In October 1822, the veteran bequeathed the remaining share of his farm to his other son, John, who had married in 1821. The veteran retained a life lease to a small portion of John's farm. The old soldier, his wife, and possibly their daughter and grandchildren continued to share the farm with son John, his wife, and their young family, which consisted of a son born in 1821 and a daughter born in 1825. Father and son appeared to maintain their own households by dividing the farmhouse they shared into separate quarters. Both continued to be taxed separately for their shares of the farm. The veteran paid for his lease and likely contributed income from his pension to sustain this compound household.

Following the veteran's death in 1828, Diamond's estate of $163 was reduced to $4.00 after his debts were paid. As he had claimed in 1820, the veteran owed as much as he owned. Nevertheless, he left John with clear title to the farm. John and his brother William Jr. remained below the midpoint of Peterborough's taxpayers for the rest of their lives. Neither brother exceeded the economic status of their father. John continued to support his mother until her death in 1855 at age ninety-three, but the fortunes of John's sister Lydia and her daughters are unknown. The pension had helped to sustain the Diamond's intergenerational household well into the nineteenth century.

SCRUTINIZED UNDER THE means test, veterans conformed to the popular image of them as heroic, virtuous, and patriotic warriors. Once they were Washington's young recruits, mostly teenagers and men in their early twenties who had enlisted early in the war. Most had become hard-core soldiers in the

Continental Army serving three or more years. Likely, as shown by Peter-borough's army enlistees, many also served in militia and state units. These hard-core troops were the heart and soul of the war effort.

Besides being presumed worthy because of their service, applicants affirmed that they needed aid. By 1820 most claimants were laborers, artisans, or farmers in their mid-sixties (see appendix B, tables 41 and 42). Most no longer owned real property and they were unable to work at full capacity. Age and infirmity had reduced their ability to be self-supporting. Based on the means test, they were either destitute, poor, or propertyless. Eight of ten had less than $100 in property. Four of five reported no real property. More than a fifth of the claimants relied either on charity or public relief, or were about to seek aid. Many were strapped with debts, which threatened to deplete their meager assets. Almost half were still responsible for young families, aged parents, or sick, insane, or invalid children who drained veterans' meager resources and health.

Solitary veterans were the most desperate lot. They were the oldest, most debilitated, and poorest of applicants. Those who had once been married witnessed the dissolution of their households because of grinding poverty, illness, death of a spouse, and the departure or death of their children. Advanced age made their meager lives even more miserable. Almost half of them had become paupers, or were on the verge of pauperism. For some, such as Henry Buzzell, dependency was imminent because a son's sudden poverty threatened an otherwise previously successful planned retirement. Solitary veterans pleaded to restore or to conserve their places as heads of households. In some cases these veterans anguished to fulfill their obligation to spouses and children who had been forced out of their households because of poverty.

Many, such as Peterborough's Alld, Blair, and Diamond, had lived subsistence if not hardscrabble lives following the war. While Alld had fallen to pauperism, Blair and Diamond had climbed to an economic level that hovered between the lower quarter and lower half of Peterborough's taxpayers. Although not impoverished, Blair and Diamond had not achieved the higher economic levels generally reached by other townsmen in their generation who had served briefly or not at all. Rather, both occupied a modest economic rank that was typical of the town's Continental Army veterans. Blair and Diamond achieved a small, yet precarious, measure of independence as husbandmen and craftsmen.

In 1815 both Blair and Diamond, ages sixty-five and sixty, respectively, entered the period of greatest risk to their households. Advancing age, increasing infirmity, and uncertain support from their children threatened to ruin their modest estates. Careful to fulfill their patriarchal roles, Blair and Diamond provided for their retirement and their wives' care and assisted their sons in establishing their own households on the homestead. Nevertheless, at this critical juncture, their intergenerational networks were near collapse.

Similarly, based on inventories and pleas, thousands of veterans' households appeared to be in jeopardy of collapse. Alarmed and fearful, veterans pleaded for pensions to stop their relentless slide toward dependence and loss of status, power, and self-respect as heads of household. Aging veterans reported that their households were collapsing due to infirmity, disability, age, diminished assets, and debts. Anxiety was especially great among veterans with young families and those whose households contained infirm wives, sick and disabled children, or grandchildren and elderly kin. Veterans dreaded the forces of age, poverty, illness, and economic misfortune that were grinding down their households and their status as patriarchal heads. One suspects that kin who aided them felt similar anxieties. Kin probably witnessed that their own households were weakened economically as their parents became more dependent. Besides worry, possibly resentment grew between children struggling to be self-sufficient and parents sinking toward greater dependency.

Viewed broadly, in many cases the program prompted the transfer of wealth from fathers to their children. More important, the pension liberated children from the traditional duty of supporting parents. It allowed children to take control of their own lives and it freed pensioners from dependence upon their children. Each generation gained greater independence, which could weaken family bonds. Yet, it seemed, in cases like Rufus Burnham and Peterborough's pensioners, that the program nurtured stronger family relationships rather than weakening them. With receipt of the pension, the veteran's children were no longer burdened with the shame or guilt of abandoning him and their mother to the woes of poverty and charity. Pensioners like Blair and Diamond remained independent. They sustained their traditional patriarchal household. They strengthened intergenerational networks that were bulwarks against the grinding forces of age, poverty, illness, and economic misfortune. Parents were delivered from the dread of dependency and the fear of pauperism. The pension appeared to temper the sense of obligation for children and the patriarchal demand for support—which could produce grudging compliance and resentment—with feelings of security and stronger bonds of affection.

Beyond momentary public fetes where veterans aroused nostalgia, pension claimants helped to instill the image of the suffering soldier in American hearts by revealing their distress and destitution to a sympathetic public. Veterans' plight and deportment aroused pathos, which deepened the public's feelings of compassion, gratitude, and justice toward the old soldiers. Heroes of the Revolution, pensioners were spared the denigrating epithets of pauper or placeman. Veterans, such as Peterborough's Alld, Blair, Diamond, and men such as Caswell, Crapo, and Stevens, appeared as suffering soldiers to friends and neighbors. Veterans' lives, through their appearances in public and as revealed by their claims, reified the image of the suffering soldier. Claimants validated the moral sentiment of gratitude and revisionist memories of the Revolution. Thus veterans secured the transformation of political culture and public policy represented by pensions for Revolutionary War veterans.

Conclusion

WHEN JEFFERSON BEGAN his presidency, Revolutionary veterans enjoyed an honored, but not privileged, place in society. Their status reflected the popular perception of the Revolution as a people's war, and of soldiers as a band of the people. The Continental Army was not included in that concept, however. The army was perceived as a necessary evil, its ranks filled with rabble and men ambitious for power and preferment. Exceptional leaders had kept the army in check. This prevailing view of the war supported the republican creed that regular armies, including the Continental Army, threatened liberty. Americans celebrated their people's war to inspire unity and to express their republican ideals.

Within the first decade of the nineteenth century, discord over Jefferson's commercial and foreign policies divided the nation. Partisan conflict became virulent. Orators sought a symbol to charge opponents with subverting the Revolution and to portray their party as its guardian. Glorifying and honoring soldiers of the Revolution became the rhetorical device, adopted by both parties, to proclaim patriotism, to deliver a jeremiad, and to condemn opponents. Revolutionary War veterans became political fodder in the increasingly bitter partisan conflict in the years leading to the War of 1812. Used for party ends, factional rhetoric modified American memory of the Revolution. It elevated soldiers above the body of the people; it made soldiers models for the people rather than symbols of the people. Although factional rhetoric diminished by 1818, that legacy remained.

New histories revised the memory of the Revolution by including regular troops within the concept of a people's war. Heroic suffering, as portrayed in battles and in encampments like Valley Forge, magnified the bravery and virtue of the Continental Army to mythic proportions. These histories of the Revolution transformed the story of the Newburgh Conspiracy into a parable of virtue. The War of 1812 added credibility to revisionist histories. Defeats in that war disproved the effectiveness of amateur soldiers and disputed the exclusion of regular troops from the memory of the Revolution as a people's war.

During the War of 1812, nationalist publications apotheosized the American soldier and exalted soldiers' devotion to liberty to awaken the spirit of '76 in the people. They made soldiers exemplars of American character. Nationalists implored that sites of heroic suffering, like Valley Forge, be preserved as hallowed monuments to honor venerable soldiers and to inspire patriotism in future generations. Thus, nationalists idealized the soldier of the Revolution, in particular regular troops. They used that ideal as a rhetorical tool to promote unity, civic duty, and the idea that American character and institutions were unique; soldiers were symbols of national greatness.

By 1818 the combination of partisan and nationalist rhetoric, revisionist histories, and the lessons of the War of 1812 had transformed the memory of the Revolutionary War in two ways. First, the role of the people and soldiers was transposed. No longer was the Revolution imagined as a conflict waged by a virtuous and patriotic citizenry and its band of amateur soldiers. While still considered a people's war, soldiers, rather than the populace as whole, became the symbol of the spirit of '76. Second, regulars emerged in the memory of the war from the recessed ranks of the distrusted to the front lines of esteemed patriots. No longer was the Continental Army presumed to be corrupt, vice-ridden, and a necessary evil created to secure the nation's independence and liberty. No longer was it perceived as an army composed of riffraff, greedy misfits, and pretentious officers. Americans embraced the Continental Army as a righteous defender of liberty. They apotheosized regular troops as republican-warriors and as models of American character. Americans adopted the view that regular soldiers had won the Revolutionary War. Suffering in war testified to their bravery and patriotism. The public immortalized the army by consecrating battlefields and bloody encampments. The Continental Army became an icon representing the new concept of the Revolution as a people's war. More important, partisan rhetoric, revisionist histories, and nationalist publications helped to create the image of the suffering soldier. It emerged, with the aid of Monroe's persona and the nostalgia cultivated by Niles, as a powerful metaphor representing the new memory of the Revolution.

The image transcended partisanship, class, and ideology because it evoked widespread feelings of compassion and gratitude toward veterans of the Revolution. It portrayed them as "hoary-headed" and "war-worn" heroes and as deprived, infirm victims of an ungrateful nation. Moreover, ordinary soldiers, as romanticized by American orators and writers, contributed to that image by remaining humble and quiescent, unlike Continental Army officers. Officers demanded and lobbied for pensions, thereby tainting themselves with self-interest and diminishing their moral claim to the nation's gratitude. By contrast, ordinary soldiers waited patiently for the nation's reward, thereby deepening the public's sentiment of gratitude and justice toward them. Appeals from disabled veterans who attributed their infirmities and poverty to hardships while in military service, increased the public's guilt for years of neglect as well as its demand to honor and aid soldiers. Pathos fortified heroism in the image of the suffering soldier.

By 1818 the Revolution's heirs resembled the impartial spectators theorized by Adam Smith. Aging veterans had become objects of compassion, gratitude, and justice. A new generation viewed Revolutionary War veterans as an exemplary, virtuous, and meritorious class. The nation concluded that it had a moral obligation to pay its debt of gratitude to them. Between 1816 and 1818 a substantial surplus increased feelings of shame for not paying that debt. Americans demanded that veterans be rewarded for their merit, compensated for disadvantages, and elevated to a privileged rank. To this generation, civic virtue was best preserved, not by slavishly adhering to their forefathers' ideal that public service is its own reward, but by selectively awarding preferment to worthy citizens. Americans apotheosized ordinary soldiers, elevated them to a privileged rank, conferred honors upon them, and awarded them pensions. Besides assuaging sentiments of gratitude and justice, ennobled veterans became models of a national character. They were icons of a memory of self-sacrifice for the cause of liberty in an emerging democratic society and market economy that placed a premium on self-interest in the pursuit of gain.

The image's power to transform political culture and to overturn the Founders' rejection of a pension establishment was evident in the debate over the bill to award pensions to veterans. In the Senate, opponents realized that passing the bill would legitimize revisionist histories of the Revolutionary War. For three months opponents and supporters of the bill fought over the nature of the

Revolutionary War and the character of a democratic-republic. They also fought over using appeals to the sentiment of gratitude, rather than applying traditional creeds, to define public policy. Sectional and partisan conflicts erupted over eligibility. The image of the suffering soldier overwhelmed these ideological and political fissures to produce a new public policy in the 1818 Pension Act. Tested by scandal, defenders of the law relied on the image of the suffering soldier, braced by the principle of vested rights, to protect the program from repeal. By reforming the program in 1820 and 1823, they protected their sectional interests, served constituents, and satisfied the public's feelings of compassion and justice. By 1823 the federal legislation had officially institutionalized the new memory of the Revolution and the image of the suffering soldier.

Reflecting the public's compassion, the War Department created a liberal and novel program to award pensions not just to paupers, but to retired veterans such as Blair and Diamond who struggled to remain self-sufficient. The department's bureaucratic practices upheld the integrity of the program thereby protecting pensioners' esteemed status both as recipients and as independent heads of households. Pension bills passed in 1823 through the act of 1832, which extended benefits to men who served in the militia and state regiments, expressed emerging democratic ideals that celebrated the virtues of the ordinary citizen in contrast to the traditional practice of bestowing honors on a few great leaders. Guided by moral sentiment, the public and Congress conferred approbation and reward. They created honored Revolutionary War veterans and granted them preferment in the form of lifetime pensions. In contrast to a monarchy where preferment was gained through the patronage of an elite, the people and their representatives had willingly paid the nation's debt of gratitude.

Veterans not only played a crucial role in creating the image of the suffering soldier, but also in entrenching it in the political culture. The appearance of thousands of veterans, in 1818 and especially in 1820, submitting to the means test validated the public's view of them as worthy recipients of gratitude and reward. Claimants, who appeared before a grateful, admiring, yet scrutinizing public, personified the romantic notions of them as once being Washington's young, patriotic recruits, citizen-soldiers. They proudly exhibited their infirmities and poverty as badges of honor, patriotism, merit, and virtue earned as young warriors. Thousands of poor, aged, and infirm army veterans, as revealed in their claims, aroused powerful feelings of moral sentiment in the public because they reified the image of the suffering soldier. At least among Peterborough's veterans, historical reality resonated with the public's image of them. The war had disrupted and diminished the lives of many of Peterborough's Continental Army veterans. Military service weakened ties to their communities. Long Bill Scott deserted his family. Benjamin Alld became alienated from kin and society. Many did not achieve the same levels of wealth and social involvement as did their peers who served only briefly or not at all. Multiplied by the thousands, claimants as suffering soldiers eloquently testified to their merit and evoked the public's sentiments of empathy, gratitude, and justice.

By the mid 1820s the image of the suffering soldier had transformed political culture and public policy. The revised memory of the Revolution, the new status of the Continental Army, and a novel program with its democratic ideals had been codified into law, incorporated in bureaucratic administration, and memorialized in pensions. The glorified image of the suffering soldier had become an integral part of the nation's celebratory rites of self-affirmation and renewal. In civic and political discourse, the image expressed another way Americans viewed their past and themselves. Thus, the first generation after the Revolution believed they had set a higher standard of civic virtue and justice for themselves and future generations, and had established a new way to bind generations. In doing so they trusted their hearts as well as their heads to guide the nation's destiny.

Appendix A

Text

To further assist the reader, this appendix contains information
that elaborates selected topics in the text.

REVOLUTIONARY WAR PENSION FILES

Revolutionary War veterans' pension files are part of Record Group 15 of the Veterans Administration, National Archives. Record Group 15 contains about 88,000 applications for pensions and bounty lands. The records in that group fall under four categories: a few thousand individual claims and applications from invalid soldiers, most made prior to 1818; approximately 30,000 applications submitted under the 1818 act and its amendments of 1820 and 1823 (20,000 claims were submitted under the latter two amendments); over 33,000 claims submitted under the 1832 pension law granting a benefit rated to time of service to any soldier who served at least six months; and nearly 23,000 widows' applications submitted under laws passed in 1834 and later.

The analysis of claimants under the 1820 and 1823 amendments is based on quantitative and qualitative evidence gathered from 877 randomly selected pension applications. I used a "structured random sample," a technique suggested by Richard Jensen and Daniel Scott Smith, to obtain the 877 cases. I included every case from a random selection of microfilmed rolls chosen by the staff of the Clements Library, University of Michigan. I would like to thank John Dann and John Shy for their help and cooperation in obtaining these sources. Just over 900 cases were collected, but were reduced to 877 cases after the elimination of ambiguous claims. Claims from invalid soldiers transferring to the 1818 program to increase benefits were included because these veterans had to pass the means test. The numerical data were analyzed using the *Statistical Package for the Social Sciences* (SPSS).

Applicant pleas and affidavits found in the pension files supplemented the data from the claims. In addition I gathered information from pension applications from 247 widows of the veterans in my sample group. For a study using the widows' pensions see the work by Connie Schulz.[1]

To some degree, the pension claims unveil circumstances among survivors of the Revolutionary generation as a whole. I estimated that in the early 1820s one white male in ten over the age of fifty-nine applied for the pension. That estimate is based on historical statistics that estimate that in 1820 there were 211,000 white males above the age of fifty-nine.[2] The proportion of African Americans applying for the pension is difficult to determine since race was not systematically recorded in pension applications. Only a handful of cases in my sample could be positively identified as African American veterans.

PETERBOROUGH SOURCES

I wish to thank Jim Oeppen of the Cambridge Group for the History of Population and Social Structure for his contributions and help in analyzing the biases and historical usefulness of Albert Smith's genealogy.

Albert Smith's genealogy, found in his *History of the Town of Peterborough*, Part 2, 1–365, provides the only view of Peterborough population structure during the Revolution. Smith compiled the genealogy to create a record of its early families, including his own. Smith gathered vital statistics from extant public records, tombstones, family Bibles, printed genealogies, and family histories sent to him at his request by descendants of early settlers. Many, he wrote, had "come in an imperfect state, which I had to correct from other sources of information." Other genealogies had been "prepared in such a confused manner that it was like deciphering hieroglyphics to read them." Smith took "much trouble and inconvenience" to correct descendants' faulty memories by checking vital dates against public records and other sources.[3]

Despite Smith's efforts to assure an accurate reconstruction of town inhabitants, a demographic analysis of his genealogy reveals three biases that qualify its use as a proxy for town birth, death, and marriage records lost in a 1791 fire, or as a census.[4]

First, his genealogy underrepresents infant mortality. Few infant deaths appear in this source. The number reported is far less than expected when the town population is compared to a standard life table.

Second, the age of death of males tends to cluster or heap at intervals ending in zero and five, for example 1810 or 1815, especially for residents who were not early settlers, 1750–80. This suggests that some vital statistics were rounded off in those instances where the actual year of death was unknown. Age heaping was far less evident for birth years, however. The overall effect of rounding off older resident ages added years to the person's life as indicated by the higher than normal life expectancy of the town's older residents when compared to standard life tables. Nevertheless, Smith's data produced an accurate demographic record for inhabitants who survived infancy through age fifty-five. An unusually high death rate occurred for men and women between ages twenty and thirty, however. Although some women died during or shortly after childbirth and a few men were killed in accidents, no one cause such as military deaths or disease accounted for the high death rate. We can only speculate that it may suggest another bias in Smith's genealogy, either toward underrecording the number of men and women in this age category in town or including deaths of family members who had moved from Peterborough.

The third bias in Smith's genealogy is its underrepresentation of transients and families that stayed only a few years in town or left but continued a connection with Peterborough. Smith admitted as much: "I could not, of course, embrace all the families in town in my genealogy."[5] For example, he omitted John Butler, a Revolutionary war soldier who lived in Peterborough until his death around 1790. According to probate records, Butler was a "yeoman" resident of the town who left a small estate that was liquidated to support his widow and four children.[6] Demographic analysis of the genealogy further reveal that Smith concentrated on family histories whose heads were born prior to 1800.

These biases appear to be intrinsic in genealogical sources but do not invalidate their use for historical research.[7] Chinese historical demographers, for example, rely largely upon clan genealogies.[8] Despite its biases, Smith's town genealogy is particularly accurate and useful in studying Peterborough's core population, which settled in town prior to 1800, and their descendants who remained. The town's youthful character is consistent with what one would expect in a recently settled frontier community. The genealogy provides individual data on births, deaths, marriage dates, dates entering and exiting the community, and kin networks. In addition Smith's genealogy can be supplemented from other sources such as lists of town officers beginning in 1760, a 1776 militia muster roll, probate records, signers of petitions and the 1776 Association Test, tax lists starting in 1792, and federal censuses initiated in 1790.

Jonathan Smith's study of Peterborough's Revolutionary soldiers supplements Albert Smith's genealogy. Jonathan Smith compiled the service records, biographical sketches, and some genealogical information for every Revolutionary soldier credited to Peterborough or who claimed residence in the town and those soldiers who moved to Peterborough after the war. Smith's study includes transients omitted in the town genealogy and provides vital statistics for some cases missing in Albert Smith's genealogy. Jonathan Smith also distinguished between town residents and nonresidents who credited their military service to Peterborough. By including soldiers who later resided in Peterborough, Smith's study helps to illuminate that most elusive group of veterans, those who resettled to new areas after the war.

Albert and Jonathan Smiths' histories provide birth, death, and residence data for 156 men who were, or who came of, military age—sixteen to fifty—during the Revolutionary conflict, 1775–1782, and those under sixteen and over fifty who served. Only men positively identified as town residents during part or all of the conflict were included on the list of men at risk of service. Lists of town officers, a 1776 militia list, deeds, and service records help to identify and confirm town residency for specific years. Sons of town residents who came of military age were counted as town residents on the assumption that they were as yet too young to set up households in other communities.

Using these sources, the composition of the list of men at risk of service changed each year, 1775–82, by adding men who came of military age, by deleting names of militarily eligible residents who died or who moved from town, and by including newcomers who were eligible for military service. For example, Joseph Taylor, who was killed at Bunker Hill, was counted as "exited" from the population as of 17 June 1775. The members of the Miller family who returned in 1776 to Londonderry, New Hampshire, were counted as "exited" from Peterborough's population at risk of service as of 1 January 1776. On the other hand, Samuel Robbe, who was fifteen years old when the war began was added to the list of "at risk" residents in 1776, the year he turned sixteen years of age; in 1777 he mustered for service during the Saratoga campaign. Lacking the birth days and exact date of exit for most cases, an individual was treated as part of Peterborough at-risk group for military service for the entire year he came of military age. If an individual exited the town sometime during the year, he was removed from the at-risk group for the entire year. Also, unless exempted or if data indicated otherwise, all men of military age were assumed physically fit for service.

Confidence in the capacity of these sources to accurately recreate the town's age structure was strengthened by figures reported in a September 1775 census of Peterborough. Using the methodology above, the combination of Albert and Jonathan Smith sources reported 100 men of military age, including a total of 42 men under arms in 1775. The census reported 102 males of military age, between ages sixteen and fifty, and that twenty-five of them were "gone [to] the army." The 1775 census of all New Hampshire towns ordered by the Fourth Provincial Congress provided the following account of Peterborough:

Males under 16 years of age 139
Males between ages 16 and 50 not in the army 77
Males over 50 years of age 23
"Persons gone to the army" 25
All females 277
"Negroes and slaves for life"   8
Total 549

The 1775 census figure, 102 men of military age and 25 in service, varies from my figure of 100 men at risk of service and 42 in service that same year because my figures represent the period from April to December 1775, not just the fall of 1775 as is the case for the census.[9]

JEFFERSONIAN VIEWS TOWARD THE REGULAR ARMY

Between 1800 and 1812, Jeffersonians upheld their party's Rule of 1798—the policy opposed to establishing a large regular army and navy. Historians Theodore Crackel and Richard Kohn have shown that anti-army sentiment diminished throughout the Jefferson and Madison administrations. Indeed, Crackel argued that Jefferson's opposition to a regular army was primarily rhetoric. The reality was otherwise, according to Crackel. Jefferson strengthened the regular army by turning West Point into a military school. He tried to make the army a Republican establishment through partisan appointments to the school and to the officer corps, especially following the army's expansion in 1808. To quote Crackel: "On the surface the construct is simple: Jefferson, out of fear of a standing army and with a republican regard for economy, reduced the regular force, and then consigned it to a distant frontier while trusting the defense of the nation to the militia he had always preferred. . . . But beneath the surface lay paradox and contradiction [of] his creation of a military school at West Point [and] . . . his dramatic expansion of the army in 1808. . . ." Crackel's work, reflecting recent scholarship such as Lawrence Cress's studies, questioned the view that Republicans "uniformly and faithfully" subscribed to "anti-army sentiments." Crackel asserted that Jeffersonians were much more pragmatic about the army than originally believed and that only a small portion of Republicans, led by John Randolph, stubbornly clung to anti-army ideology. Crackel observed, "President Jefferson, far from ignoring or shunning the regular military establishment, undertook a social and political reformation of it in an effort to insure its loyalty to the new regime." Crackel wrote, "The expansion Congress authorized in 1808 allowed the administration to make wholesale appointments of the faithful at every level from ensign to brigadier general. The outcome was indeed a Republican army. . . ." Crackel concluded that as a result of Jefferson's partisanship, "Mr. Jefferson's army was no longer the object of suspicion and fear that the Federalist force had been only a decade earlier. For most Republicans, fears that a standing army would subvert civil liberties dissipated as reforms took effect and as the army became more Republican."[10] Crackel's account reinforces the view in this book that Republican opposition to a regular army was diminishing in the early years of the nineteenth century.

RAMSAY'S *HISTORIES*

Ramsay's *History of the American Revolution* also contrasts the patriotism and virtue of regular troops with self-seeking citizens. His *History* criticizes civic leaders for believing that the "citizen should be lost in the soldier of our army." By 1778, he wrote, although the army had been "reduced in number and badly clothed" it continued to fight while the citizenry's "military enthusiasm" cooled. Citizen-soldiers returned to "their former habits of lucrative business. This made the distinction between the army and the citizen. . . ." even greater. Thus Ramsay contrasted the virtuous self-sacrifice of regular soldiers with the vice-ridden self-interest of citizens.[11]

Ramsay's biography of Washington reproduces the officers' appeal in 1783 to the army at Newburgh to join them in demanding pensions from Congress. The appeal stated that the officers had hoped "the coldness and severity of government would relax and that more than justice, that *gratitude* would blaze forth upon those hands which had upheld her in the darkest stages of their passage from impending servitude to acknowledged independence." The officers wrote to their fellow soldiers that once disbanded "no remaining mark of military [sacrifices will be] left, but your wants, infirmities and scars! Can you consent to be the only sufferers by this revolution, and returning from the field grow old in poverty, wretchedness and contempt!" Ramsay wrote that among the troops at Newburgh this address found "favourable reception. It operated like a torch on combustible material." Ramsay used the mutiny of the Pennsylvania troops in June 1783 to further emphasize the virtue of the republican, patriot army. Those mutinous troops, he wrote in *Life of Washington* in 1807, were new recruits who had not "borne the heat and burden of the war." By contrast, Ramsay described the army's veterans as men "who have patiently endured hunger, nakedness, and cold; who have suffered and bled without a murmur . . . retiring peacefully to their homes. We shall be as much astonished at the virtue of the latter, as we are struck with detestation at the proceedings of the former."[12]

PORT FOLIO

Port Folio began in 1801 and quickly became "the most respected literary journal in American."[13] In its early years *Port Folio* was deeply involved in politics under its editor Joseph Dennie. In 1805 Dennie was acquitted of the charge of seditious libel against Thomas Jefferson. Dennie remained *Port Folio*'s editor until his death in January 1812. However, after 1809 the journal became less partisan and more nationalist under the influence of a group of young men who formed a "confederacy of letters" known as the Tuesday Club.[14] Nicholas Biddle; Robert Walsh, who founded the *American Review* in 1811; and Dennie were among club members. While sympathizing with Federalists, they identified themselves as men of letters with a mission to promote American nationalism.[15] In 1811 Dennie's health declined and Biddle assumed more editorial responsibilities. Biddle gathered sketches of the "Chief American worthies," which included figures from the Revolutionary War, to foster unity through a common national identity.[16] After Biddle left *Port Folio* to join Madison's cabinet as secretary of state, later secretary of war during the War of 1812, Dr. Charles Caldwell, another staunch nationalist, became *Port Folio*'s editor. Caldwell had served as a medical officer in Washington's army that suppressed the 1794 Whiskey Rebellion in western Pennsylvania and had become a noted medical writer and lecturer. Caldwell continued *Port Folio*'s commitment to advance American arts, sciences, and national identity.[17]

OFFICERS' CLAIMS

Veterans' claims of mistreatment originated during the Revolution. In 1777 officers demanded lifetime pensions at half pay for officers who remained in service until the war's end (a practice borrowed from the British army). Until 1780 Congress resisted this demand because of the high cost of pensions, because service pensions were incompatible with the concept of a people's war fought by amateur citizen-soldiers, and because of the republican creed that pensioners were "placemen" who corrupted government and public virtue. Nevertheless, in 1780, threatened with the army's collapse, Congress accepted the officers' demand for half-pay pensions. In March 1783, Congress withdrew that promise because of New England's insistence that Congress abide by the republican principle opposed to service pensions and because the government was bankrupt. In place of half-pay pensions, Congress awarded officers commutation certificates valued at five years at full pay, earning 6 percent interest annually until redeemed. The certificates, with an original value of $11 million, became nearly worthless after the war, and speculators purchased most of them at a small fraction of their face value from officers desperate for cash. In 1790 the federal government redeemed the certificates at their full value. In 1790 the federal government paid cash on two-thirds of their value, paid back interest, and awarded new government securities to cover the balance, thereby redeeming the debt incurred by the certificates. Officers claimed that they had been cheated twice: the government had reneged on its promised half-pay pensions and speculators had duped them. Congressional committees felt bound by legal principles to deny officers' petitions for half-pay pensions. Congress ruled that commutation certificates, issued to officers in lieu of half-pay pensions, concluded the government's contract with the officers.

Appendix B

Tables

TABLE I

PETERBOROUGH COHORT AVERAGE TAX PER YEAR

Year	Continentals N=17 (n each year)	Militia N=44 (n each year)	Nonservice N=64 (n each year)
1792	$4.93*(n=13)	$7.04 (n=36)	$7.70 (n=41)
1796	7.02*(n=10)	8.09 (n=31)	7.84 (n=46)
1797	6.79*(n=10)	9.28 (n=30)	9.09 (n=41)
1798	7.76*(n=10)	8.90 (n=31)	8.23 (n=42)
1799	7.74*(n=9)	9.63 (n=29)	7.96 (n=42)
1800	7.55*(n=9)	9.23 (n=30)	7.81 (n=47)
1801	7.47*(n=9)	9.00 (n=28)	8.21 (n=42)
1802	7.67*(n=9)	9.43 (n=29)	8.01 (n=45)
1803	6.35*(n=11)	9.34 (n=28)	8.44 (n=43)
1804	5.09 (n=9)	9.05 (n=28)	8.64 (n=43)
1805	4.74 (n=10)	9.50 (n=29)	8.81 (n=41)
1806	4.88 (n=11)	9.48 (n=28)	9.03 (n=38)
1807	5.42 (n=9)	8.85 (n=27)	7.52 (n=41)
1808	5.10 (n=9)	8.03 (n=26)	7.67 (n=37)
1809	6.17 (n=8)	8.30 (n=24)	7.41 (n=36)
1810	6.18 (n=8)	8.14 (n=24)	7.54 (n=29)
1811	6.00 (n=8)	7.65 (n=26)	7.61 (n=29)
1812	7.01 (n=7)	7.91 (n=23)	8.12 (n=28)
1813	6.49 (n=8)	8.35 (n=21)	7.91 (n=28)
1814	5.18 (n=8)	8.66 (n=21)	8.66 (n=25)
1815	4.05 (n=8)	8.01 (n=18)	7.83 (n=25)
1816	4.42 (n=8)	8.24 (n=20)	7.81 (n=25)
1817	4.32 (n=7)	7.34 (n=19)	7.55 (n=22)
1818	3.88 (n=7)	7.65 (n=16)	7.47 (n=23)
1819	3.89 (n=7)	8.24 (n=14)	7.57 (n=22)
1820	3.63 (n=7)	7.50 (n=16)	7.70 (n=23)
1821	3.46 (n=8)	7.44 (n=14)	7.65 (n=23)
1822	3.44 (n=6)	7.53 (n=14)	8.01 (n=23)
1823	3.84 (n=5)	6.84 (n=14)	8.05 (n=22)

Peterborough Tax records exist for 1792, and 1796 to the present. These records through 1850, were computerized to obtain individual taxes paid and annual tax distribution. The average annual tax varied little over this period, generally about $5.50 per taxpayer. Table 1 was created by linking the tax records to members of the cohort. For Peterborough tax records in 1792, the first extant list, see *Peterborough Town Book*, vol. 1. For tax lists for 1796–1820, see *Peterborough Tax Lists*.

* For each of these years there was one outlier among the Continental veteran taxpayers. For example, in 1796 that individual paid $24 in taxes, almost three times higher than the next Continental veteran who paid $9.42 that year. Without that $24 tax figure the average tax for the remaining nine ratepayers would have been $5.13 rather than $7.02 shown in the above table.

TABLE 2

PETERBOROUGH COHORT

TOWN OFFICES HELD IN 1801

Office	Continentals	Militia*	Nonservice
Minor Offices	2	7	10
Major Offices	0	2	2
N	2 (8.7%)	9 (39.1%)	12 (52.2%)

* Category of soldiers who marched from Peterborough under arms in militia units or in state regiments only.

The distribution of office-holding shown in table 2 remained fairly constant except for a few years when former militiamen held more town offices than their nonservice cohort.

TABLE 3

PETERBOROUGH REVOLUTIONARY WAR COHORT

LIFELONG RESIDENTS: MARRIAGE AGES

	Continental N=7	Militia N=15	Nonservice N=43
Average Age of Marriage	25	27	28

The data for births and marriages for lifelong male residents was obtained from genealogical records in A. Smith, *History of Peterborough*, pt. 2, and supplemented by biographical information in Jonathan Smith, *Peterborough New Hampshire in the American Revolution.*

TABLE 4

PETERBOROUGH COHORT

EVER MARRIED

Number of Children per Household	Continental Households N=17	Militia Households N=42	Nonservice Households N=49
1	1	1	1
2	2	1	5
3	0	0	2
4	0	4	0
5	0	4	3
6	4	4	9
7	4	8	4
8	1	9	7
9	3	4	4
10	2	4	3
11	0	3	6
12	0	0	4
13	0	0	1

Nearly two-thirds (65 percent) of the army veterans had seven or fewer children compared with just over half (52 percent) of the other veterans and just under half (49 percent) of nonveterans in their cohort.

TABLE 5

AMENDMENT TO REDUCE SERVICE ELIGIBILITY
FROM THREE YEARS TO TWO YEARS

	POLITICAL AFFILIATION		
	Republican	Federalist Coalition	
Ayes	14	4	N=18
Nays	3	10	N=13

Rice Index of Cohesion
Republican = .64
Federalist Coalition = .42

(*Annals of Congress*, 15th Cong., 1st sess., 220.)
Federalists such as Robert Goldsborough deserted party ranks because they thought that the three-year limitation was a "great injustice to many who have nobly signalized themselves in the cause of the Revolution, and are justly entitled to our grateful remembrance" (*Annals of Congress*, 15th Cong., 1st sess., 197).

The Rice Index of Cohesion is derived from the equation:

$$C = \frac{\text{ayes} - \text{nays}}{\text{n partisan vote}}$$

A .50 coefficient represents a breaking point between strong and weak association. A score of .50 indicates that 66 percent of the group was united on an issue. The .50 break point, although somewhat arbitrary, appears to be a standard cutoff line in gauging party cohesiveness. Dollar and Jensen also suggest a break point of .40 to indicate strong cohesion (107–8). See also Hatzenbuehler, 50–55.

TABLE 6

AMENDMENT TO REDUCE ELIGIBILITY
FROM TWO YEARS TO NINE MONTHS

	REGIONAL AFFILIATION				
	NE	MA	South	West	
Ayes	5	2	7	2	N=16
Nays	1	5	3	6	N=15

Rice Index of Cohesion

NE = .66   MA = .42   South = .40   West = .50

(*Annals of Congress*, 15th Cong., 1st sess., 221.)
Key:
New England (NE): Connecticut, Rhode Island, Massachusetts (including Maine), Vermont, and New Hampshire.
Middle Atlantic (MA): New York, New Jersey, Pennsylvania, Delaware, Maryland.
South: Virginia, North Carolina, South Carolina, Georgia, Mississippi, Alabama.
West: Tennessee, Kentucky, Ohio, Indiana, Illinois, Michigan.

TABLE 7

AMENDMENT TO REDUCE ELIGIBILITY
FROM TWO YEARS TO NINE MONTHS

	Vote	Rice Coefficient
Ayes	6	.50
Nays	2	

Vote of states requested by the Continental Congress to provide four-fifths of the troops for the Continental Army.

Ayes: Massachusetts (1), Virginia (2), Maryland (1), North Carolina (2)
Nays: Pennsylvania (2)
No Vote: Connecticut

TABLE 8
AMENDMENT TO REDUCE ELIGIBILITY
FROM TWO YEARS TO NINE MONTHS

	Republican	Federalist Coalition	
Ayes	7	9	N=16
Nays	10	5	N=15

Rice Index of Cohesion
Republican = .17
Federalist Coalition = .35

TABLE 9
AMENDMENT TO ADD A MEANS TEST

	POLITICAL AFFILIATION		
	Republican	Federalist Coalition	
Ayes	2	12	N=14
Nays	16	2	N=18

Rice Index of Cohesion
Republican = .77
Federalist Coalition = .77

(*Annals of Congress*, 15th Cong., 1st sess., 211.)

TABLE 10
HOUSE VOTE TO RESTORE MILITIA AND
STATE TROOPS TO THE PENSION BILL

	NE	MA	South	West	
Ayes	8	5	36	10	N=59
Nays	30	43	12	7	N=92

(*Annals of Congress*, 15th Cong., 1st sess., 1109.)

TABLE 11

VOTE ON WILLIAMS'S AMENDMENT TO EQUALIZE
AND INCREASE BENEFITS

	REGION				
	NE	MA	South	West	
Ayes	8	8	33	13	N=62
Nays	27	44	11	7	N=89

Rice Index of Cohesion
NE = .42   MA = .79   South = .47   West = .30

Although there was no roll call recorded for Cannon's proposal to equalize the pension, a subsequent motion by Lewis Williams from North Carolina to pay all recipients, regardless of rank, ten dollars a month was decided by a roll call. Analysis of that roll call revealed a regional division over the issue of equalized payments. To analyze Congressional voting patterns, information was gathered on party affiliation, military service, Washington residence, and terms served in Congress. The data were converted into a file for analysis using the *Statistical Package for the Social Sciences* (SPSS). Half of the House members were serving their first term, and a quarter of them reported military service. Thirteen had served in the Revolutionary War, ten of them as officers. Revolutionary War veterans were nearly evenly split over Williams's measure. Six of them, including three former officers, voted in favor of the amendment. Party affiliation proved to be a slippery factor to test because of the loose structure of parties caused by factions within them. Over half, 56 percent, were identified as Republican or by the affiliation used later, Democrat. Only 17 percent had been or were affiliated with the Federalist party, which was rapidly dissolving at this time. The remainder, 27 percent, lacked party identification. Regression analysis revealed no strong correlations, except for region, between any of the factors and the vote on Williams's measure (*Annals of Congress,* 16th Cong., 1st sess., 1705–6).

TABLE 12

MOTION TO REPEAL THE 1818 REVOLUTIONARY WAR PENSION ACT

	REGION				
	NE	MA	South	West	
Ayes	3	3	22	4	N=32
Nays	31	52	22	17	N=122

Rice Index of Cohesion
NE = .82   MA = .88   South = .00   West = .62

Representatives from New England and the Middle Atlantic states were nearly unanimous in opposing repeal. Most support for repeal came from the South, which was also the center for ideological opposition to the program. For example, Virginia, which recorded the largest number of pensioners—693 men—outside of the New England and Middle Atlantic States, split its vote on repeal. Eight of its seventeen representatives voted in favor of repeal, including Philip Barbour, the "Old" Jeffersonian. Western states divided on repeal. For example, Ohio's congressmen, who represented 647 pensioners, opposed repeal. Kentucky's congressmen who represented 474 pensioners split their vote: three favored repeal and four opposed repeal (*Annals of Congress,* 16 Cong., 1st sess., 1709–10; Am. St. P.: Military Affairs 2: 703).

TABLE 13
VOTE ON AMENDMENT TO ASSESS APPLICANT ASSETS

	REGION				
	NE	MA	South	West	
Ayes	9	19	37	15	N=80
Nays	27	35	5	5	N=72

Rice Index of Cohesion
NE = .50   MA = .30   South = .76   West = .50

(The vote was taken on 1 April 1820. *Annals of Congress*, 16th Cong., 1st sess., 1715–16.)

TABLE 14
SENATE VOTE ON HOUSE PENSION BILL AS AMENDED

	REGION		
	NE/MA	South/West	
Ayes	2	22	N=24
Nays	15	2	N=17

Rice Index of Cohesion
NE/MA = .76   S/W = .84

There were several differences between the House and Senate. In the House, representatives from the Northeast formed a majority. In the Senate, senators from the South and West formed a majority. There was more continuity of service in the Senate than in the House. A majority of senators (60 percent) had served in the Fifteenth Congress; most representatives entering the Sixteenth Congress were serving their first term. Over 35 percent of the senators had served in the military compared to 26 percent in the House. Republicans (or Democratic-Republicans), composed 61 percent of the Senate. Only a few Federalists appeared in the Sixteenth Congress's Senate—21 percent. The remainder were not classified with a party affiliation. Regression tests showed that only region explained the voting pattern in the Senate, although there was some confluence with party (*Annals of Congress*, 16th Cong., 1st sess., 640).

TABLE 15
REGIONAL DISTRIBUTION OF APPLICANTS

	REGION			
	NE	MA	South	West
% Applicants	49.8	31.5	10.6	8.1

Two states, New York and Massachusetts (including Maine), accounted for 42 percent of all applicants.

TABLE 16

STATE DISTRIBUTION OF APPLICANTS

	Mass.	N.Y.	Others
% of Applicants	22.3	19.8	57.9

Veterans were highly mobile geographically. During the thirty years following the war, approximately half, or 10,000 of the 20,000 claimants, had moved either to a nearby state or to another region of the country. Of these 10,000 claimants, roughly 4,000 of them had moved to another state within their own region, and approximately 6,000 of them had moved to another section of the country.

Intraregional migration patterns varied by section. As table 17 shows, intraregional movement was greatest among New England veterans.

TABLE 17

INTRAREGIONAL MIGRATION

Region	Total Moved	Total Moved Intraregionally	% of Total
New England	270	146	54
Middle Atlantic	82	28	34
South	70	10	14

One out of two New Englanders who changed state residence between enlistment and application remained in their own region. By contrast, one of three veterans from the Middle Atlantic states and only one of seven southern soldiers who changed state residence remained in their own region.

Veterans were probably more mobile than shown in table 17. Pension claims submitted under the 1818 act do not record changed residence within a state. However, claims submitted under the 1832 act do provide detailed descriptions of veteran migration patterns. Claimants who applied under the 1832 program were required to record where they were born, where they lived when enlisting for service, where they lived after leaving the miltary, and where they resided when applying for the pension. Their responses resulted in a detailed record of their movements— county by county and state by state. The results, historian Theodore Crackel wrote, were "the most comprehensive individual records dealing with mobility . . . [which] allow us to study the geographic mobility of this generation at a level of detail never before possible." He reported that "[h]alf the population ultimately made state to state moves." Crackel's migration figures are similar to those I found using cruder data discussed above (Theodore J. Crackel, "Revolutionary War Pension Records and Patterns of American Mobility, 1780–1830," *Prologue* 16 [Fall 1984], 156, 166).

TABLE 18
VOTE TO REDUCE PENSION BENEFITS 20 PERCENT

	REGION				
	NE	MA	South	West	
Ayes	0	1	11	9	N=21
Nays	12	7	1	2	N=22

Rice Index of Cohesion
NE = 1.0   MA = .75   South = .83   West = .64

The coalition also succeeded, by the narrow margin of three votes, to defeat a motion to kill the House bill.

TABLE 19
VOTE TO KILL HOUSE BILL EXTENDING ELIGIBILITY

	REGION				
	NE	MA	South	West	
Ayes	0	2	10	8	N=20
Nays	12	6	2	3	N=23

Rice Index of Cohesion
NE = 1.0   MA = .50   South = .66   West = .45

The last-ditch efforts to amend or kill the bill having failed, it passed the Senate on 1 March 1823 (*Annals of Congress*, 17th Cong., 2nd sess., 313–15).

TABLE 20
ENLISTMENT AGE
N=877

Ages:	8–15	16–17	18–26	23–27	28+
% of Applicants	7.8	14.7	38.2	22.5	17.8

Mean Age: 22.3   Median Age: 21   Modal Age: 18
Youngest Enlistee: Age 8   Oldest Enlistee: Age 55

TABLE 21

FIRST ENLISTMENT

N=877

Year	1775–1776	1777	1778+
% of Applicants	47.6	28.2	24.2

TABLE 22

LENGTH OF SERVICE

N=877

# of Months	9	12	13–36	37+
% of Applicants	4.7	21.4	46.0	27.8

Mean Number of Months Served: 34
Median Number of Months Served: 33
Modal Number of Months Served: 36

The proportion of officers and enlisted men who applied for the pension was the same as the proportion of rank and file found in a typical company in the Continental Army. Fears that officers would not subject themselves to the humiliation of a means test proved to be unfounded (Wright, *The Continental Army*, 127).

TABLE 23

MILITARY RANK

N=877

	Officer	Noncom Officer	Private
% of Applicants	4.8	6.6	88.6

TABLE 24

HEALTH REPORTED BY APPLICANTS

N=877

	Not Stated	"Healthy"	Medical Ailment	Claimed to Be Infirm
% of Applicants	17.4	0.5	20.1	62.0

TABLE 25
COURT-ASSESSED WEALTH DISTRIBUTION

Value in Dollars	N	%
0	118	13.4
1–50	406	46.3
51–100	138	15.7
101–200	99	11.3
201–500	62	7.1
501 or more	54	6.2
Total	877	100

Overall, about three out of four applicants owned less than $100 in personal and real property.

TABLE 26
APPLICANT ASSETS LESS ALL REPORTED DEBTS

Value in Dollars	N	%
Zero or less	232	26.4
1–50	362	41.3
51–100	118	13.5
101–200	84	9.6
201–500	44	5.0
501 or more	37	4.2
Total	877	100

Personal debt was probably underreported because applicants were not allowed to deduct debts, except for first mortgages, from their assets. About one in three applicants reported personal debts. Had those debts been deducted, the number of veterans whose assets were zero (or less) would have nearly doubled. (Compare table 25 and table 26.) In addition, the number of veterans with assets worth more than $200 would have shrunk by nearly a third. Moreover, had all debts been deducted, the average household wealth would have declined from $129 to $70.

TABLE 27

Per Capita Wealth*

Region	Average per Capita ($)
New England	47
Middle Atlantic	30
South	35
West	27

* Based upon court-assessed wealth divided by the total number of people in veteran's households (including the veteran).

TABLE 28

Private Charity and Public Poor Relief

	N	%
Assisted by Family, Friends, or Public Relief	147	16.8
Not Reporting Assistance	730	83.2
Total	877	100

The Department viewed reports of family assistance of the veteran as evidence of need. Therefore, it was to the applicant's advantage to report it. Despite the temptation to fabricate charitable dependance, few probably did so because declarations were made under oath and because public watchfulness, as a result of the 1819 pension scandal, discouraged falsehoods.

TABLE 29
VETERANS RECEIVING ASSISTANCE
N=147

Sources	
Family	74
Friends	62
Public	45
	181*

* The larger number, 181, appearing in this table represents sources of aid. It should be read as follows: a total of 147 veterans received assistance, but some received aid from more than one source.

At the time of their application, one of six veterans (16.8 percent) reported receiving charity mainly from family and friends, with some receiving supplemental support from public relief. One in twenty (5.4 percent) of the applicants stated that they were on the verge of seeking charity or poor relief. Paupers amounted to less than 5 percent of the 20,000 applicants or only about 1,000 claimants. Most veterans received outdoor relief rather than being placed in poorhouses. Although the number of institutions for the poor increased in this period, particularly in or near urban areas, few pauper veterans were living in them at the time of their application.

TABLE 30

WEALTH DISTRIBUTION BY HOUSEHOLD TYPE
(COURT-ASSESSED AVERAGE)

Type of Household	Court Assesed Wealth ($)	N
Solitary	20	131
Couple	105	232
Nuclear	141	402
Complex Nuclear		
Veterans living with kin	64	21
Kin living with veteran	279	78
Nonrelative with veteran	500	13
Total		877

The distribution of applicants in table 30 is based upon a modification of Peter Laslett's classification scheme—solitary, couple, nuclear, and complex. Only a small proportion (6.8 percent) of all applicants who reported being married also reported that they were either widowed, divorced, or separated from their wives.

From a broader perspective, the prevalence of nuclear households reflects the Anglo-American cultural preference for that form of family organization. Barbara Hanawalt's work on fourteenth- and fifteenth-century English peasants, Jeremy Boulton's analysis of seventeenth-century London suburbanites, and Richard Wall's comparison of several eighteenth- and nineteenth-century English villagers found that between 70 and 80 percent of the population lived in couple or nuclear households. The consistency of these figures across time within Anglo-American culture, including this subgroup of elderly veterans, suggests a persistent norm favoring marriage over living on one's own and a preference for nuclear households over complex nuclear households (Hanawalt, 90–104; Boulton, 120–37; Wall, 89–113).

TABLE 31

DISTRIBUTION OF HOUSEHOLD TYPES
N=877

Type of Household	N	Percent
Solitary	131	14.9
Couple	232	26.5
Nuclear	402	45.8
Complex Nuclear		
Kin living with applicant	78	8.9
Applicant living with kin	21	2.4
Nonrelatives living with applicant	13	1.5
Total	877	100.0

TABLE 32
ALL CASES
NUMBER OF PEOPLE IN APPLICANT'S HOUSEHOLD
(APPLICANT INCLUDED)

People	N Households	% Households
1	139	15.8
2	250	28.5
3	142	16.2
4	123	14.0
5	102	11.6
6	54	6.2
7	26	3.0
8	21	2.4
9	13	1.5
10+	7	.7
Total	877	99.9

Mean Household Size: 3.35   Modal Household Size: 2.85

As would be expected given claimants' advanced ages, veteran households in the 1820s contained fewer people than other American households in that period. Veterans' households, including claimants, contained an average of 3.4 persons compared with an average of more than 5 persons per household for the population as a whole.

TABLE 33

NUMBER OF PEOPLE IN APPLICANT'S HOUSEHOLD

(APPLICANT INCLUDED)

People	N Households	N People
3	142	426
4	123	492
5	102	510
6	54	324
7	26	192
8	21	168
9	13	117
10+	7	70
Total	488	2,299

Mean Household Size: 4.7

Counting only the smaller number of claimants heading nuclear households, household size rose to an average of 4.7 persons. A quarter of their households contained more than 5 people.

Nuclear households varied greatly in size. About a third of the households contained only the veteran, his wife, and a child, or on occasion a single parent (the veteran) and his child. On the other hand, a quarter of the households contained both parents and four or more children.

Nuclear households varied greatly in composition. Three-quarters of them had children over the age of fifteen, mostly between the ages of sixteen and twenty-four years. A quarter of the nuclear households had children under the age of fifteen. Another group of households had two age sets of children, one composed of young children and the other composed of children nearing their majority.

Households containing infants and young children occured for various reasons. Some veterans had married late in life, or remarried younger women, or fathered children just prior to their wives' entering menopause. Possibly as many as a third of the claimants had delayed marriage into their late twenties and early thirties, rather than marrying in their early or mid-twenties, as was normally the case.

Comparative figures for household size are approximations based on a variety of community studies. Historian Philip Greven shows a decline in household size from an average of 7.2 prior to 1700 to 5.2 in families constituted between 1725 and 1744 (Greven Jr., 202). The trend toward smaller families was also found in England. (Wall, 89–113) Boulton found that in Boroughside, mean household size was 3.8, slightly lower than the bench mark, 4.2 persons per household. More important, perhaps, he showed that household size varied according to wealth. Those households receiving poor relief were relatively small, a mean size of 3.2, compared to a mean size of 5.2 for households not receiving poor relief (Boulton, 120–23).

TABLE 34
AVERAGE AGE AT MARRIAGE AND AT ENLISTMENT

Married between Years	Age of Wife at Marriage	Age of Veteran at Marriage	Age of Veteran at Enlistment	N of Cases	%
1740–1775	20	23	27	8	3.2
1776–1783	21	24	21	56	22.7
1784–1789	24	27	19	79	32.0
1790–1799	25	35	19	57	23.1
1800–1820	38	54	21	26	10.5
1821–1830	65	72	20	21	8.5
Total				247	100.0

Additional information on veterans' marriages found in their widows' pension applications produced a subset of 247 claims, which supplemented their husbands' claims. Widows' applications
provide a rough measure of veteran marital patterns. The 1834 law authorizing pensions for
widows of Revolutionary War veterans required that the widow verify her marriage date to the
soldier. Some widows listed the births of their children to support their claims of marriage.
Widows' applications proved to be useful in supplementing veterans' accounts of marriage and
household composition. A widow's application, however, did not explicitly indicate whether she
was the veteran's first wife or his wife from a later marriage, although it is possible to deduce this
by comparing veterans' and widows' reports on the number and ages of their children. Based on
the 247 claims of veterans and their widows, some rough estimates of marriage and or remarriage
ages can be made (tables 34 and 35).

In the late eighteenth century, men generally married in their mid-twenties to women in their
early twenties. For example, at least twice the proportion of pension applicants married after the
age of thirty than did men of comparable age living in Andover, Massachusetts, just prior to the
Revolution. In particular, see Greven's table of marriage ages for four generations of men (Greven,
34–35, 205–11). Greven's study reveals that marriage ages of men and women varied by generation:
fourth-generation sons tended to marry at a younger age than first-generation sons. The average
age of marriage ranged from twenty-five to twenty-seven for the fourth- and first-generation
sons, respectively. Other factors, particularly birth order and availability of land, affected sons'
ages of marriage. Historian Robert Gross's study of Concord reported that prior to the Revolution
women generally married at age 21 or 22 and that men generally married at ages 25, 26, or 27
(Gross, 77). The pattern is observed in table 35 for the small number of cases, 8 of 247, of soldiers
who married before the war.

TABLE 35

SOLDIERS AND WIVES MARRIED PRIOR TO 1775

N=8

Period Married	AVERAGE AGE OF MARRIAGE AND ENLISTMENT		
	Age of Wife at Marriage	Age of Veteran at Marriage	Age of Veteran at Enlistment
Before 1775	20	23	27

Tables 35 and 36 show that few applicants, because of their youth, married prior to the war. At least 75 percent of the 192 veterans who married between 1775 and 1799 postponed marriage until after the war. Consequently, many were well above the normal age of marriage.

TABLE 36

SOLDIERS AND WIVES MARRIED BETWEEN 1775 AND 1799

N=192

Period Married	AVERAGE AGE OF MARRIAGE AND ENLISTMENT			N of Cases
	Age of Wife at Marriage	Age of Veteran at Marriage	Age of Veteran at Enlistment	
1775–1783	21	24	21	56
1784–1789	24	27	19	79
1790–1799	25	35	19	57
Total				192

Average age of marriage increased slightly for men married during the war and increased among veterans who married after the war ended in 1783. Men who married shortly after the war were in their late twenties and their wives in their mid-twenties. Their ages suggest first marriages rather than remarriage, although this cannot be verified from widows' pensions because they do not record husbands' successive marriages.

TABLE 37

SOLDIERS AND WIVES MARRIED BETWEEN 1800 AND 1820

N=47

Period Married	AVERAGE AGE OF MARRIAGE AND ENLISTMENT			N of Cases
	Age of Wife at Marriage	Age of Veteran at Marriage	Age of Veteran at Enlistment	
1800–1820	38	54	21	26
After 1820	65	72	20	21
Total				47

TABLE 38

NUCLEAR HOUSEHOLD COMPOSITION DEBTORS AND NONDEBTORS

N=402

	Average Size	AGE DISTRIBUTION				N
		% Males < 15	% Females < 15	% Males >=15	% Females >=15	
Debtors	4.8	41.6	45.4	47.4	60.4	154
Nondebtors	4.4	40.8	43.7	36.0	44.7	248

Nearly 40 percent of the veterans who headed nuclear households reported personal debts. Generally, these veterans differed from those not reporting their debts in several ways: debtors reported more assets; debtors were twice as likely to own real estate; debtors tended to be younger than other applicants. Furthermore, debtor households contained more children, particularly older sons and daughters, than were found in nuclear households of claimants not reporting debts. Nearly half of the debtor households contained at least one son, and many of those sons were nearing or had reached adulthood. Three out of five debtor households had daughters who were fifteen years of age or older.

By contrast, veterans who did not report debts had fewer older children living under their roof: just over a third of these claimants had older sons in their household; and well under half had older daughters living in their homes.

TABLE 39
DEPENDENT VETERANS
N=142

Type of Household	Reported Being Dependent N	Total Number of Households n	Percent N/n
Solitary	28	132	28.8
Couple	36	232	15.5
Nuclear	52	402	13.0
Complex			
Veterans living with kin	19	21	90.5
Kin living with veteran	5	78	6.4
Nonrelative with veteran	2	13	15.3
Totals	142	877	16.2

Few veterans heading nuclear households claimed that they received either charity or poor relief.

TABLE 40
DEPENDENT VETERANS
N=142

Type of Household	SOURCES OF ASSISTANCE RENDERED						
	Family		Friends		Town		Total
	N	%	N	%	N	%	N
Solitary	6	12.5	15	31.2	27	56.3	48
Couple	11	23.9	17	37.0	18	39.1	46
Nuclear	39	60.9	11	17.2	14	21.9	64
Complex							
Veteran living with kin	19	90.5	1	4.3	1	4.3	21
Kin living with veteran	5	100.0	0	0.0	0	0.0	5
Non relatives with veteran	1	50.0	0	0.0	1	50.0	2
Totals	81		44		61		186*

* The total 186 is greater than the number of cases (N=142) because a few applicants reported more than one source of assistance.

TABLE 41
AGE DISTRIBUTION AT TIME OF APPLICATION
N=877

Ages:	51–59	60–64	65–69	70–74	75+
% of Applicants	14.4	32.1	30.0	12.6	11.9

Mean Age: 65　　Median Age: 65　　Modal Age: 62

TABLE 42
OCCUPATIONAL CATEGORIES REPORTED IN APPLICATIONS
N=877

	Farm Owner, Business, or Profession *	Trade	Nonlandowning Farmer or Laborer+
% of Applicants	12.5	21.4	61

*Includes land-owning farmers.
+Includes farmers who reported not owning land.

Notes

Works frequently cited have been identified by the following abbreviations:

Am. St. P.	*American State Papers*
BDAC	*U.S. Biographical Directory of the American Congress*
DAB	*Dictionary of American Biography*
CPRC	*Records of the United States House of Representatives: Records of the Committee on Pensions and Revolutionary Claims*
GCCP	*General Correspondence of the Commissioner of Pensions*
HCDR	*Hillsborough County Deed Records*
HCPCR	*Hillsborough County Probate Court Records*
NA	*National Archives*
NHPPDR	*New Hampshire Provincial Probate and Deed Records, 1623–1772*
NHSP	*Documents and Records Relating to New Hampshire, 1623–1800.* This collection is known as the New Hampshire State Papers and therefore is cited as NHSP
RG	*Record Group*
ROSW	*Records of the Office of the Secretary of War, Registered Letters*

PREFACE

1. *Annals of Congress*, 15th Cong., appendix, 2518–19.
2. *Annals of Congress*, 16th Cong., appendix, 2582–83.
3. See Appendix A, *Revolutionary War Pension Files*, for a detailed description of these files and their use in this study.
4. Richard Kohn has urged historians to do community studies of soldiers to study the "interaction between the military and the rest of society." Kohn, "The Social History of the American Soldier," 566.

INTRODUCTION

1. William Alld, Pension File W23824, RG15, NA.
2. *Peterborough Town Book*, 1:79–80; J. Smith, *Peterborough New Hampshire in the American Revolution*, 142–52.
3. Otis, *An Oration July 4, 1788*, 9.
4. Livingston, *An Oration July 4, 1787*, 20.

5. Carp, 72, 172–73.

6. Moves like Scott's were common among veterans of Peterborough, N.H. By 1800, fifty-one men, 53 percent of Peterborough's ninety-six soldiers who survived the war, had moved from town. For a detailed study of veterans' migration, see Crackel, "Revolutionary War Pension Records and Patterns of American Mobility, 1780–1830," 156, 166. Crackel's migration figures are similar to those I found for Continental Army veterans who applied for pensions in 1818 and in 1820 and the years following.

7. J. Smith, *Peterborough New Hampshire in the American Revolution*, 323.

8. Ibid., 316–33. Smith stated that Short Bill Scott did not receive a pension until 1807. Smith overlooked benefits paid by the states, however. It appears that Scott received an invalid pension, beginning in 1792 or 1793, from the state of New York. In 1807 the states relinquished the invalid pension program to the federal government. See William Scott, Pension File W23824, RG15, NA. Note this file does not have a number and includes materials on Short Bill and Long Bill Scott.

9. Royster, *A Revolutionary People at War*, 39. For an account of Adams's meaning, including his reasons for not enlisting, see Ferling, 258–75.

10. J. Smith, *Peterborough New Hampshire in the American Revolution*, 218–19.

11. Len Travers examines the role of July Fourth celebrations—orations, dinners, processions—in forming and communicating the nation's culture and national identity. He identifies four functions for the celebration: to reconnect postwar America to its past, especially the Revolution; to stress common origins and values; to redefine the collective past; to be a venue for conflict and for creation of consensus. Until 1815, July Fourth was often a partisan celebration. After the War of 1812 July Fourth became part of a "democratic resurgence." Travers, 4, 6–7, 192, 204. Also see Alexander, 10–13; Hawken, 1–3; Bercovitch, 132–75. My examination of selected Fourth of July orations given between 1787 and 1799 revealed that orators focused their remarks on the Constitution, the value of the federal union, and the controversy over Jay's Treaty, 1798, not the Revolutionary War and its soldiers.

12. Davis, *An Oration, July 4, 1800*, 8–10; Fowle, *An Oration July 4, 1800*, 5; Russell, *An Oration July 4, 1800*, 4–6; D'Ogley, *An Oration July 4, 1803*, 7–8, 16–18.

   On 4 July 1800 Daniel Webster's oration before the Federal Club in Hanover, New Hampshire, honored the "people" as Revolutionary patriots. Hawken, 11. Orators paid homage to the people's leaders—Washington, Warren, Mercer, Montgomery, and Franklin—as "the ghosts of departed worthies."

   Federalist Noah Webster (1758–1843) referred to those leaders as "venerable sages." Webster, *An Oration July 4, 1802*, 23.

   For an expression of these images later see E. D. Smith, *An Oration July 4, 1812*, 3–4.

13. Sarah Purcell describes how the public memorialized leaders of the Revolution. She argues that two forms of commemoration emerged after the war: ". . . gratitude for the aristocratic heroic sacrifice . . ." of selected military leaders, and a democratic form of commemoration that expressed gratitude for the contributions of ordinary soldiers. By the 1820s, she says, these two forms merged to help shape both the memory of the Revolution and national identity. See Purcell, iii, 7–13, 117–29, 171–75.

14. Denny, *An Oration July 4, 1818*, 8–10. Dexter, 5:638–39.

   Denny stated that the nation and its political leaders shared honor and virtue with

these veterans for paying that debt. Denny treated the act as a sign of emerging greatness in national character and observed that the nation would enjoy "more honour . . .
were the justice complete" by increasing the amount of the pension and removing any
reference to need ("in reduced circumstances").

15. Senator Robert Goldsborough noted in his defense of the army that when it sought
pensions the public denigrated it with the reproachful epithets, "hireling, mercenary
and pensioner." His speech capsulized the still popular anti-army rhetoric that diminished the valor and role of the Continental Army in winning the Revolutionary War.
Annals of Congress, 15th Cong., 1st sess., 192.

16. Sarah Purcell points out that the image of the suffering soldier, including expressions of
gratitude, was used immediately after the Revolutionary War ended, during the constitutional crisis of 1787–88, following the publication of soldiers' memoirs and upon the
dedication of a monument in Lexington in the late 1790s. Its use diminished until
the early nineteenth century. Purcell, 81–85, 135–45, 163, 176–81. As Purcell shows,
the aristocratic form, honoring leaders, prevailed through the first decade of the nineteenth century.

17. David Waldstreicher's important book complements these themes. He describes nationalism not as a fixed belief but as a product of political conflict and a "political
strategy" to create and promote a vision of the nation. Waldstreicher, 6. The process
involves ". . . the everyday interplay of rhetoric, ritual, and political action, . . ." which
make nationalist abstractions "real, effective, practical. . . ." Waldstreicher, 3. The
conflicts occur in celebratory events, festivals, public holidays like the Fourth of July.
The "conflict produced 'the nation' as contestants tried to claim true American nationality and the legacy of the Revolution." Waldstreicher, 9.

18. Waldstreicher, 207, 226; Purcell, 242.

19. The sentiment of gratitude has a deep foundation in Western philosophy and religion.
In her discussion of the meaning, Purcell cites Plato, Cicero, and Samuel Mather to
define gratitude as a virtue that arises from a feeling of "debt." Purcell, 55–57.

20. I wish to thank my colleague Terry Savage for his comments and suggestions, which
helped to clarify my understanding of moral philosophy and the views of Hume and
Smith. David Hume, Section 2, Part 2; Section 5, Part 2. Also see Rawls, 22–33. See also
Miller, 187–205.

21. Smith's *Theory of Moral Sentiment* contained the term "invisible hand," which expressed
his belief in human governance by "appetite, passion or instinct" rather than by reason.
Cropsey, *Polity and Economy,* 5, 27.
   Unlike Hume's collectivism, Smith thought that an individual's "ordinary moral
sentiments" could advance social ethics. T. D. Campbell, 76. Cropsey, *Polity and Economy,* 24.

22. Cropsey, "Adam Smith and Political Philosophy," in Skinner and Wilson, *Essays on
Adam Smith,* 133–35, 148.

23. Ibid., 148.

24. D. D. Raphael, "The Impartial Spectator," in Skinner and Wilson, *Essays on Adam
Smith,* 87, 90, 95.

25. A. Smith, 2:63–64; 1:1.

26. Campbell, 79–81.

27. A. Smith, 1:53–53, 55, 59.

28. Ibid., 1:64.

29. Ibid., 1:65.

30. Cropsey, *Polity and Economy*, 31, 67.

31. John Bodnar makes a distinction between vernacular and official memories. The vernacular memory tends to be more populist and to enshrine the feelings of participants, such as their grief, loss, pride. The official memory tends to embody abstract ideals such as patriotism and nationalism; official memories represent the "nation-state" and are defenders of "national power" and the "official culture." The two forms of memory are not exclusive. They intersect in the public realm of debate and are mediated in a political process. Bodnar wrote, "Public memory emerges from the intersection of official and vernacular cultural expressions." "Public memory," he stated, "is produced from a political discussion that involves not so much specific economic or moral problems but rather fundamental issues about the entire existence of a society; its organization, structure of power, and the very meaning of its past and present. This is not simple class or status politics, although those concerns are involved in the discussions, but it is an argument about the interpretation of reality; this is an aspect of the politics of culture." Bodnar, 9, 13–14. For opposing views on the construction of national identity see Gillis, 3–24, and Handler, 27–40.

32. J. Smith, *Peterborough New Hampshire in the American Revolution*, 168.

33. Shy, "Hearts and Minds in the American Revolution: The Case of 'Long Bill' Scott and Peterborough, New Hampshire" in Shy, *A People Numerous and Armed*, 172–73; Papenfuse and Stiverson, 117–32; Gross, 146–52; Lender and Martin, *A Respectable Army: the Military Origins of the Republic, 1763–1789*, 65–97; Cress, passim; Lender, "The Social Structure of the New Jersey Brigade: The Continental Line as an American Standing Army," in Peter Karsten, ed., *The Military in America: From the Colonial Era to the Present*, 65–78; Rosswurm, *Arms, Country, and Class: The Philadelphia Militia and "Lower Sort" During the American Revolution, 1775–1783*, passim. A few historians argue that the soldiers came from a cross section of society. See Jensen, 32–33; Royster, *A Revolutionary People at War*, passim. For a detailed study of the view given by an ordinary soldier see Alfred F. Young, 561–623.

34. Neimeyer, 25. Neimeyer claims that "[t]he myth of the classless, independence minded farmer or hard-working artisan-turned-soldier has been a longstanding legend. . . . the well-to-do and 'yeoman farmers,' seemed to prefer staying at home rather than rushing to the front lines. . . ." after 1775; Ibid., xiii.

35. Ibid., xiii–26, 17; Neimeyer quotes John Shy, *A People Numerous and Armed*, 171–72, and cites J. Smith, *Peterborough New Hampshire in the American Revolution*, 165–395; Neimeyer, chap. 1, n. 29.

I. PETERBOROUGH IN THE REVOLUTIONARY WAR

1. I wish to thank Richard Herr and my colleagues attending his summer seminar on preindustrial communities sponsored by the National Endowment for the Humanities for their contributions to the following account of Peterborough's history. For a more detailed account of Peterborough's early history see Resch, "The Transformation of a Frontier Community: Peterborough, New Hampshire," 227–48.

2. S. E. Morison, 7–9. Gross, 80.

3. S. E. Morison, 7–9.

4. Parker, 148; 1–66, 274, 277–78; *Londonderry N.H., West Parish Records, 1736–1821*, Presbyterian Historical Society, MSS; *Londonderry N.H., East Parish Records, 1742–1827*, Presbyterian Historical Society, MSS; A. Smith, *History of Peterborough*, pt. 1:58–68, 73–74, 98–101, 115, 175. Despite the dominance of conservatives a slight undercurrent of religious conflict remained. It became prominent in the 1790s but appeared to have little effect upon the town during the Revolution.

5. A. Smith, *History of Peterborough*, pt. 2:73–74, 144–61; *NHPPDR*, 98:53. J. Smith, *Peterborough New Hampshire in the American Revolution*, 333–34; 241–43.

6. J. Smith, *Peterborough New Hampshire in the American Revolution*, 24–25. *NHSP*, 7:762.

7. Demographic data are based on Albert Smith's genealogy. A. Smith, *History of Peterborough*, pt. 2:1–365. For a chart of the town's age structure see Resch, "The Transformation of a Frontier Community: Peterborough, New Hampshire," 228.

8. J. Smith, *Peterborough New Hampshire in the American Revolution*, 23.

9. Ibid., 1–23; A. Smith, *History of Peterborough*, pt. 1:144–46.

10. The settlers from nearby Londonderry were probably skilled weavers. Londonderry's weavers had a reputation for making fine linen, which they protected with their own trademark to prevent other weavers from profiting from Londonderry's reputation. Parker, 63–64.

11. A. Smith, *History of Peterborough*, pt. 1:69–77. See also, John Hopkins Morison, "An Address Delivered at the Centennial Celebration in Peterborough, N.H.," in Ibid., pt. 1:254–69. Mrs. Wilson's red cloak can be seen on display at the Peterborough Historical Society.

12. *NHSP*, 13:174; 9:666–67, 669–71.

13. A. Smith, *History of Peterborough*, pt. 1:83–102. Most of the following account is based on Smith's chapter on the ecclesiastical history of Peterborough.

14. Ibid., pt. 1:88–89, 272; pt. 2:73–73, 86–87, 202–05; J. Smith, *Peterborough New Hampshire in the American Revolution*, 264–70; J. Smith, "Annals of Peterborough," 207–12.

15. J. Smith, *Peterborough New Hampshire in the American Revolution*, 24–25.

16. I wish to thank Mrs. Roland Hemmett of Southbury, Connecticut, for genealogical information on the Scott, Robbe, and Loomis families. Mrs. Hemmett is a direct descendant of Capt. Long Bill Scott and Peterborough's Robbe family.

    For an account of the Scott family's contributions to the French and Indian, and Revolutionary Wars see J. Smith, *Peterborough New Hampshire in the American Revolution*, 1:23; 299–335; Shy, "Hearts and Minds in the American Revolution: The Case of 'Long Bill' Scott and Peterborough, New Hampshire," 163–79. Rallying around men who fought in the French and Indian War appeared common in the militia units formed in the war's early days. See Gross, 133–70.

17. J. Smith, *Peterborough New Hampshire in the American Revolution*, 25.

18. *NHSP*, 14:558. In May 1775, the New Hampshire Provincial Assembly established three regiments and called for two thousand men to fill them. In June 1775, Congress established the Continental Army under Washington's command and ordered each state to reorganize its militia to make them effective manpower pools and fighting units. Upton, 89, 93. New Hampshire's Assembly implemented that order by requiring town censuses of able-bodied men and military stores; *NHSP*, 7:724.

    By January 1776, Peterborough's militia captain Alexander Robbe had formed a company of 116 men divided between a "training band" and "alarm list." His training band consisting of eighty-five men, generally youths and young men (ages were found for sixty-one cases). Most of the band, thirty-six in all, were under age twenty-five; twenty-two others ranged from their mid-twenties to late thirties; and only three were over forty years of age. Altogether they averaged twenty-six years of age. Members of the alarm list were, by contrast, much older (ages were found for twenty-five of thirty-one men). Only one was in his twenties, eleven were in their thirties and forties, and the remaining thirteen ranged in age from age fifty to age seventy-four. The average age of Robbe's alarm list was fifty-two years of age J. Smith, *Peterborough New Hampshire in the American Revolution*, 27-28. The original militia list can be found in the Peterborough Historical Society.

19. Short Bill Scott's company contained troops from northern Massachusetts, where the Scotts and other Peterborough inhabitants had once resided, and from southern New Hampshire, which included Hillsborough and Cheshire counties. For a printed list of Scott's regiment see J. Smith, *Peterborough New Hampshire in the American Revolution*, 87-89; John Stark's regiment contained men recruited from New Hampshire's Merrimack Valley region, which includes Hillsborough and Rockingham counties. Wright Jr., *The Continental Army*, 15-16, 197-99, 209-10.

20. For a list of town officers see *Peterborough Town Book*, vols. 1 and 2, 1760-1856, located in the Peterborough Town Hall. There is also a list of town officers including ad hoc committee members compiled by Albert Smith in the manuscript collection of the Peterborough Historical Society. *HCDR* 2:433. A. Smith, *History of Peterborough*, pt. 2:161.

21. Shy, "Hearts and Minds in the American Revolution: The Case of 'Long Bill' Scott and Peterborough, New Hampshire," 168. *NHPPDR* 83:238; 90:199; 94:516 for land transactions involving the Taggarts and Samuel Miller's grant to his son, James. Also for James Taggart's transactions in 1762, 1767, 1772, and two in 1773 see *HCDR* 2:436; 6:213; 3:104-05, 534. Capt. Long Bill Scott accompanied his father, Alexander Scott, James Taggart, James's son, William Taggart, and John Alexander to Dublin, New Hampshire, where he had a farm. Long Bill had helped to settle and plan Dublin before moving to Peterborough. Leonard, 4, 5, 142, 143, 148, 179, 648, 956. James McKean, who died early in 1776 after his tour of duty, had been a cordwainer. In 1762 he purchased one hundred acres in Peterborough from James Mathews a local weaver. In 1769 McKean added fifty acres to his holdings with a purchase from William Scott (which of the three William Scotts in town is not clear). *NHPPDR* 83:363; *HCDR* 1:505.

22. Because of the battle's chaos and because units fragmented when moved into action, I used Jonathan Smith's service accounts to determine which men had actually engaged in the battle. Stark's troops defended the rebels' left flank along the Mystic River beach. They stopped the British light infantry's assault and protected the troops retreating from the redoubt. Sargent's troops, including Scott's company, were at Lechmere Point prior to the attack and appeared to be among troops who rushed to Bunker Hill to meet the British assault. For accounts of the battle describing Stark's and Sargent's units see Richard Ketchum, 113-26, Higginbotham, *The War of American Independence*, 74, and Martyn, 130. J. Smith, *Peterborough New Hampshire in the American Revolution*, 202-03, 370, 239-40, 176-78, 287, 264-70.

23. J. Smith, *Peterborough New Hampshire in the American Revolution*, 325.

24. A. Smith, *History of Peterborough*, pt. 1:292–93.

25. The account of the troops' hardships during Arnold's march to Quebec was given by Richard Vining in his 1832 pension application. See Dann, 17–18.

26. J. Smith, *Peterborough New Hampshire in the American Revolution*, 177, 239–40, 287. Howard Peckham estimated that 10,000 of the 25,000 military deaths occurred in camp. Peckham, 131–33.

27. John Shy argued that the war politicized troops. See Shy, "The American Revolution: The Military Conflict Considered as a Revolutionary War," in Stephen G. Kurtz and James H. Hutson, eds., 124–25, 145–56. For a recent study of the war's politicizing effects on a divided and apathetic local community see Tiedemann, 417–44, especially 443.

28. Thomas Little and Alexander Robbe were both age fifty. In 1776 Little served for a month at Cambridge. From July to December 1776, Robbe, a militia captain, rendezvoused at Haverhill, New Hampshire, with forces gathered to reinforce the American army in Canada. J. Smith, *Peterborough New Hampshire in the American Revolution*, 226–27, 288.

29. Wright Jr., *The Continental Army*, 67–90; Washington expected the regular army to be reinforced by state troops composed of short-term enlistees—three to six months—and masses of militia called out for a few days during critical engagements.

30. Only seven out of the sixty-two nonresident soldiers (11 percent) who credited their service to Peterborough appeared to have no tie to the town except to credit their service to it. Most others, while not residents, lived in contiguous towns such as Sharon, Dublin, Hancock, and Jaffrey. Short Bill Scott and Long Bill Scott recruited some of these men from their Continental Army companies to fill the town's quota. For example, in 1776 Short Bill Scott recruited John Wallace to serve for Peterborough, in 1777 Scott persuaded Wallace to reenlist for three years for Peterborough, and in 1782 convinced him to reenlist a third time to fill the town's quota. The Scotts also enlisted John Barlow and Michael Silk to meet the quota; J. Smith, *Peterborough New Hampshire in the American Revolution*, 175, 335–36, 374–75; Titus Wilson and Samuel Wier, both black men, claimed to be Peterborough residents but their residency cannot be confirmed. Neither Wier's nor Wilson's names appear in Peterborough records. They may have been, however, among the slaves listed in the town's census. Another recruit, Samuel Lee, seems to have been a transient; Peterborough drew sparingly on such men to meet its quotas. Ibid., 225, 386, 391.

31. Three of the town residents who credited their service in the Continental Army to other towns also served at least one enlistment to Peterborough's credit.

32. A. Smith, *History of Peterborough*, pt. 2:161–64, 300; J. Smith, *Peterborough New Hampshire in the American Revolution*, 246. Isaac Mitchell, age fifteen, possibly a relative of Samuel and Benjamin, enlisted for the first time in 1776 and served under Short Bill Scott until the end of the war. J. Smith, *Peterborough New Hampshire in the American Revolution*, 247–51; A. Smith, *History of Peterborough*, pt. 2:317–18. William White, age twenty-five, was also part of the town's establishment. His father, Patrick, was reputed to be "a man of education and possessed some wealth." Ibid., pt. 2:335. Another example is Robert Swan, age twenty-three. Young Swan was a member of the town's founding families. He was described as a "man of limited education, but of superior abilities, and

through his long life was one of the most influential men in town." J. Smith, *Peterborough New Hampshire in the American Revolution*, 362.

33. J. Smith, *Peterborough New Hampshire in the American Revolution*, 288.

34. Two of the twelve men who first enlisted in 1776, Ephraim Stevens and Joseph Babb, could have been transients. In 1777 Babb enlisted in Long Bill Scott's company and was later reported "deserted." Stevens enlisted with Short Bill Scott in 1777 and died in service. J. Smith, *Peterborough New Hampshire in the American Revolution*, 352–53, 170–71.

35. Ibid., 167–69, 371–73. Todd's unit was subsequently assigned to a Pennsylvania regiment performing guard duty in the Peekskills. Todd did not reenlist after 1777.

36. Men who first enlisted in 1776 participated in major military engagements. Mitchell, Alld, and Robert Smith answered Washington's appeal for state regiments to reinforce his beleaguered army in New York, which suffered a series of defeats that summer and fall. These men fought in the battle of White Plains. William White answered a second call for more state troops. He caught up with Washington's army, which included a number of townsmen serving under Long Bill and Short Bill Scott, as it retreated through New Jersey and nearly disintegrated before being victorious at Trenton and Princeton. Half of the men who first enlisted in 1776 returned to duty in 1777 as part of the state's militia and many were in battles at Bennington and Stillwater. In 1777 Benjamin Alld, Joseph Babb, Isaac Mitchell Jr., and Ephraim Stevens enlisted in the Continental Army.

37. Furneaux, 49–54.

38. J. Smith, *Peterborough New Hampshire in the American Revolution*, 320, 368–68. Kidder, 25–56; Furneaux, 77–78.

39. Kidder, 25–56; also see Furneaux, 55–78.

40. Higginbotham, *The War of American Independence*, 188–98; Stark, 128–30. J. Smith, *Peterborough New Hampshire in the American Revolution*, 389.

41. J. Smith, *Peterborough New Hampshire in the American Revolution*, 112, 169, 223–24. Kennady was reported "deserted" on 25 August 1779. He may have taken a furlough and returned, because Smith found him on Continental rolls in April 1780 and 1784. Other soldiers in this group included Jacob Baldwin (1760–1844) and Samuel Lewis (?–1790). Ibid., 172–75, 226.

42. J. Smith, *Peterborough New Hampshire in the American Revolution*, 376–78.

43. Ibid., 222.

44. Ibid., 238, 191–92; A. Smith, *History of Peterborough*, 2:140–41, 50–53; in August 1778, Charles McCoy joined Enoch Hale's state regiment reinforcing Continental troops in Rhode Island.

45. J. Smith, *Peterborough in the American Revolution*, 189–91, 240–41, 240; A. Smith, *History of Peterborough*, pt. 2:45–48, 211–13, 142–43; Cunningham was in the battle at Bennington and distinguished himself at Saratoga where he served as a lieutenant assigned to Col. Moses Nichols's Continental regiment; in one action, Cunningham's platoon was ambushed by Tories and Sgt. John Robbe was wounded. As recalled in a nineteenth-century commemoration of the war, "Cunningham's coolness and consummate address supplied the want numbers. With the noise of a lion, he called on an officer to bring up a body of 500 men to flank the enemy. The Tories fled, leaving

behind them their baggage and plunder, and an open, unmolested road to the Army." Cunningham and Nay enlisted a second time the following summer, 1778, to reinforce Continental troops fighting the British in Rhode Island.

Other examples include the Blair, Miller, and Gregg families. In mid-July 1777 new recruit William Blair, age twenty-seven, and his father, John, age sixty—veteran of Bunker Hill, Quebec, and former prisoner of war—enlisted with Stark. William was a hired substitute for a resident of Sharon, New Hampshire, who had been drafted into Stark's regiment. William fought alongside his father, John, at Bennington. In late July 1777, William's brother John Blair 2d., age fourteen, enlisted for the first time "for the war" as a drummer in Long Bill Scott's company. Similarly, Joseph and Samuel Miller, ages twenty-one and eighteen, respectively, mustered for the first time in 1777; they followed in the footsteps of their brother James, a veteran of Bunker Hill. In June 1777 Adam Gregg, age thirty-two, enlisted with his brother Hugh Gregg, a veteran of the siege of Boston, 1775, for five months service in 1776; J. Smith, *Peterborough New Hampshire in the American Revolution,* 176–81, 207–10, 241–43; A. Smith, *History of Peterborough,* pt. 2:18–19, 98–101, 144–47.

46. J. Smith, *Peterborough New Hampshire in the American Revolution,* 240, 293–297, 309–315, 333–344, 340–345, 358–362, 368–370, 382–84, 393–394; A. Smith, *History of Peterborough,* pt. 2:110–16, 164–73, 235–42, 244–50, 258–79, 300–07, 334–39, 361–63. The Moores and their relatives the Morisons and Smiths, who had contributed a total of ten men, enlisted in 1775 and 1777 and may have exerted some pressure on their brother-in-law Daniel Mack, age twenty-seven, to join the army even after he had removed to Ackworth, New Hampshire, early in 1777. Mack had moved to Peterborough before the Revolution when he married Nancy Holmes, thereby becoming a part of the Moore-Morison-Smith-Holmes network. Mack joined his relatives at the battle of Saratoga where he fought alongside of three kin by marriage—Jeremiah, James, and Thomas Smith. J. Smith, *Peterborough New Hampshire in the American Revolution,* 228–29.

47. All four of William Smith's sons of military age served briefly in the Revolutionary army; in late 1775, John, age twenty-one, was one of the soldiers raised by the town's Committee of Safety for a unit replacing the Connecticut troops that returned home, despite Washington's pleas that they remain at Boston, after their enlistments expired in December. After three months' service John returned to Peterborough and remained at home for the rest of the war. In the fall of 1776, his brother Robert, age twenty-two, was mustered into Enoch Hale's regiment raised to reinforce Washington's army in New York. Robert served three months, was probably in the battle of White Plains, and returned home where he remained. In 1777 two more brothers, James, age twenty-one, and Jeremiah, age seventeen, mustered to repel Burgoyne's army; James served a total of five days, marching to Vermont in late June under Alexander Robbe's command and returning upon meeting the retreating American army. That exercise marked the end of James's military service for the war. Jeremiah was wounded at Bennington, his only action in the war. J. Smith, *Peterborough New Hampshire in the American Revolution,* 340–44; for Robbe see Ibid., 289–93.

48. Ibid., 299–335.

49. Ibid., 187–88.

50. Ibid., 191–92, 379–86.

51. Abel Parker, age fifty-four, who held minor town offices in 1777 and 1778, enlisted in 1778 with his son Abiel, age seventeen, for nine months in the Continental Army. Both were new recruits who served together in the Hudson Highlands possibly on garrison duty. William McCoy, age fifty-one, joined his son Charles, a veteran of Bennington, to fight in Rhode Island. Isaiah Taylor, age fifty-three enlisted in 1778 in the state troops reinforcing Continental soldiers fighting the British in Rhode Island. Taylor may have been seeking to even the score for the death of son Joseph at Bunker Hill. Ibid., 278-80, 370-71, 238. Only one townsman, Joseph Covell, was a "hired recruit." Covell was probably hired by a local resident who had been drafted for short service in the Continental Army. Covell spent six months on the western frontier, and then returned to Peterborough where he remained until 1788, apparently impoverished, because he was unable to pay his taxes. By 1790 Covell had moved from town without leaving a trace. Ibid., 187.

52. Ibid., 182.

53. Ibid., 9-11, 299-335.

54. *NHPPDR*, 59:428; 98:250. Alexander mortgaged part of the land in 1758, paid back part of his debt in 1759, and then sold the one-hundred-acre parcel in 1761 possibly to repay the mortgage. *NHPPDR*, 59:431; 98:365, 368.

55. A. Smith, *History of Peterborough*, pt. 1:342, 244-47, 355; Leonard, 4, 5, 142, 143, 148, 179, 648, 956.

56. *HCDR* 1:505; 4:189. Also see *NHPPDR* 98:251.

57. J. Smith, *Peterborough New Hampshire in the American Revolution,* 9-11, 299-335.

58. *Peterborough Town Book.* William Scott was elected hogreeve in 1762 and constable in 1768. John Scott held a town office in 1762, was elected hogreeve in 1768, and held minor town offices in 1774, 1775, 1776, 1779.

59. *NHSP,* 9:666-67, 669-71.

60. Quoted in Shy, *A People Numerous and Armed,* 168.

61. *HCDR,* 10:263; 17:260. There are a number of Peterborough deeds with the name William Scott. I was able to identify Long Bill and Short Bill only in those transactions that included their wives' names, Phoebe and Rose. *HCDR,* 1:505; 4:190.

62. J. Smith, *Peterborough New Hampshire in the American Revolution,* 328, 331. Near the end of the war, Long Bill Scott gambled again, this time possibly for profit. He volunteered for duty on a privateer.

63. In 1777 Hon. John Scott, age thirteen, enlisted to the credit of Attleboro, Massachusetts, in the Massachusetts regiment containing his father, Long Bill Scott's, company. John Scott served through the war as a fifer, rising to Fife Major in 1781. In 1778 a cousin also named John Scott enlisted in First New Hampshire Regiment containing his father, Short Bill Scott's, company. John Scott was also a fifer and served through the war. Ibid., 306-07, 309-10.

64. Ibid., 299-335.

65. The Scotts also recruited nonrelatives who had previously served under their command. They included two residents, James Hockley and Randall McAllister, who had deserted the British army prior to the war and moved to the area and fought at Bunker Hill in Short Bill Scott's company. The Scotts also recruited newcomers to Peterborough into the Continental Army. Their ability to recruit men testified to the Scotts' military leadership. One recruit, Jonathan Wheelock Jr., moved to town in 1775 and in 1777

enlisted to Peterborough's credit for three years in Short Bill's company. In 1780 Wheelock reenlisted for the war to the credit of Townsend, Massachusetts, in Long Bill Scott's company. A total of twenty-five of the town's thirty-four residents who enlisted in the Continental Army served at one time under one or the other Scott captains.

66. *NHPPDR*, 43:415. For some reason the deal was not completed. The following year, 1754, the same lot was sold to Eleazer Green. *HCDR*, 2:5. The sale was not recorded until 1771, which explains why it appeared in the Hillsborough county records.

67. J. Smith, *Peterborough New Hampshire in the American Revolution*, 176–81. A Smith, *History of Peterborough*, pt. 2:18–19. Details in these two biographical accounts differ. Albert Smith was unable to determine when the Blairs moved to Peterborough. Jonathan Smith placed the date of their arrival at 1763, citing John Blair 2d's birth in town. Furthermore, no information was found on the birth dates of John Blair Sr.'s last five children by Mary.

68. *Peterborough Town Book. NHSP*, 9:666–71.

69. J. Smith, *Peterborough New Hampshire in the American Revolution*, 27–28; A. Smith, *History of Peterborough*, pt. 1:148–49. Albert Smith reported that John Blair Sr. signed the Association Test, which is unlikely because he was still a prisoner of war according to Jonathan Smith's account. Possibly William signed for his father.

70. J. Smith, *Peterborough New Hampshire in the American Revolution*, 181. Smith reported the town of Sharon records as follows: "to see if the town will allow Captain John Taggart £10 10s paid by him to William Blair in July last [1777], in order to hire him to go into the war."

71. *HCDR*, 6:130.

72. John Blair, Pension File S45296, RG15, NA. Blair had been promised one hundred acres of bounty land, but as of 1818 he had not received the warrant entitling him to the property. In 1832 his heirs successfully applied for the land. See also J. Smith, *Peterborough New Hampshire in the American Revolution*, 180.

73. Between 1780 and 1791 John Blair 2d., settled in Newburgh, New York. In 1791 widow Mary Blair sold her land and moved from Peterborough. Not until the third and fourth generations did the Blairs become more firmly entrenched in Peterborough's community through their children's and grandchildren's intermarriages with the Little, Field, Swan, Alld, and White families. Members of the family still reside in Peterborough. *HCDR* 11:537, 25:400; A. Smith, *History of Peterborough*, pt. 2:18; J. Smith, *Peterborough New Hampshire in the American Revolution*, 180.

74. This section on Benjamin Alld and his family synthesizes information from a variety of sources. For genealogical information see A. Smith, *History of Peterborough*, pt. 2:7–8; Smith reported Benjamin's marriage to Nancy White, but no marriage record exists; for the Swan and White families see Ibid., 2:300–06, 342–43; for biographical and military service see J. Smith, *Peterborough New Hampshire in the American Revolution*, 167–69; for the Swan and White families military service see Ibid., 357–63, 382–87; for the Alld family history and genealogy in Merrimack, see *The History of Merrimack, New Hampshire*, 189, 195–96; Merrimack, New Hampshire, *Merrimack Town Records*, 96, 381. The town records provide genealogical information not found in Albert Smith's genealogy. Smith only recorded the names of four of William's children and does not include William Jr. or James Alld. Merrimack town records show that two Alld brothers, William and David, and John Alld, who appears to be another brother, had moved from

Dunstable, Massachusetts, to Merrimack; see Peterborough Historical Society, *Peterborough Tax Lists*. For Benjamin Alld's service record, see J. Smith, *Peterborough New Hampshire in the American Revolution*, 167–69, and Pension File S45498, RG15, NA. Alld identified himself as a "day labourer" in his pension application. Affidavits from Samuel Alld, Samuel Spear, and Hon. John Scott testified to Benjamin's service.

75. Shy, *A People Numerous and Armed*, 172.

76. For Capt. William Alld's tax records see *Merrimack New Hampshire Tax Invoices*, 3:97–98, 175. It is likely that Alld speculated in land; for example, in 1773, "Gentleman" Alld sold 103 acres in Bedford, New Hampshire, to William Stinson for £63; he seems to have been holding that parcel of land for a profitable sale; *HCDR*, 3:76. For other transactions involving William Alld as grantor see *HCDR*, 2:300, 382; 4:187, 453; 5:234–35, 258; 6:351; 9:190; 17:364; 18:251; 20:23; 28:89; 29:19; 30:147; 32:507; 38:397; 39:119; 44:426. For transactions involving William Alld as grantee, see *HCDR*, 7:50–51; 14:407, 419; 18:253, 256; 31:99, 438; 38:235, 237–39; 57:249.

77. *HCDR*, 5:258, 234–35; 28:89.

78. *HCDR*, 14:407, 419.

79. For James Alld's transactions as a grantor in this period see *HCDR*, 6:534; 7:51, 391; 9:190, 193–94; 10:243; for his transactions as a grantee see *HCDR*, 6:351; 7:381; 9:190–91. Samuel's transactions began just after the war; for Samuel's transactions as grantor see 29:114; 41:507; 55:218; 86:463, 590; 106:13; 108:640; 126:387, 415; 128:72, 374; 129:327; 130:120, 123–124; 143:466; 151:252, 481; 168:130; 177:480; 210:369, 374; 231:85; for Samuel's transactions as a grantee see *HCDR*, 20:23; 22:171; 38:235, 237–39; 39:426; 48:436; 60:471; 68:357; 81:180; 103:243–44; 126:386; 129:326; 130:121; 135:42; 142:271; 210:368, 370; 211:547.

80. J. Smith, *Peterborough New Hampshire in the American Revolution*, 362. For Gustavus Swan's will see *HCPCR*, 08148.

81. *HCDR*, 44:426.

82. *Peterborough Town Book*; A. Smith, *History of Peterborough*, pt. 2:7; J. Smith, *Peterborough New Hampshire in the American Revolution*, 52–55.

83. Four Allds from Merrimack—Isaac, John, David, and William Jr.—served in the Continental Army; Isaac and John were brothers, sons of John Alld; David was probably the younger brother of William Alld, later of Peterborough. An 1839 affidavit from Samuel Alld, William Jr.'s brother, described his service; the affidavit was part of Hannah Clark's (William Alld Jr.'s widow) 1844 application for a widow's pension. According to Samuel's testimony, William Jr. had enlisted in March 1776 for one year's service; he was taken prisoner in Canada at the "Ceders" and returned to Merrimack sometime during the winter of 1776 and 1777, possibly on parole. In the spring of 1777 he moved to Maine; the town history of Merrimack reported that a William Alld was reported deserted from Valley Forge in 1778, but it is not clear if he was William Alld Jr., who enlisted in 1778. Samuel Alld testified that his brother William Jr. served from 1781 to 1783 in Joseph Cilley's Continental regiment, which contained Short Bill Scott's company. Samuel recalled that William Jr. "was at my father's house (in Peterborough) . . . in November 1783" after leaving the army; William Alld, Pension File W23824, RG15, NA; William Alld Jr. appeared on Merrimack's tax records in 1775 and 1776 and then disappeared from the town records. This disappearance is consistent with removal to Maine; *History of Merrimack, N.H.*, 195–96; *Merrimack New Hampshire Tax Invoices*, 3:200, 205, 210, 220.

84. Wright, *The Continental Army*, 215–16.

85. Benjamin Alld, Pension File S45498, RG15, NA.

86. Seventy percent of Peterborough's Continental soldiers also served at other times, in militia or state units; J. Smith, *Peterborough New Hampshire in the American Revolution,* passim.

87. In 1981 Richard Kohn urged historians to blend social and military history to gain deeper insights into American society; Kohn urged historians to use communities rather than military units to study soldiers in order to reveal the "interaction between the military and the rest of society"; Richard Kohn, "The Social History of the American Soldier: A Review and Prospectus for Research," 553-67.

88. Shy, *A People Numerous and Armed,* 172.

89. In 1775, James Miller (1738-1825), one of four sons of well-to-do Samuel Miller, served for eight months with Gen. John Stark at the siege of Boston and was probably with Stark at Bunker Hill; his brother, John Miller (1742-?), fought with the militia at Saratoga in the fall 1777; in 1779 he enlisted in the Continental Army for the war's duration; Matthew Miller's son, Samuel (1759-1819), served two months during the 1777 Saratoga campaign; John Ferguson's son, Henry (1736-1812), served briefly at Cambridge, Massachusetts, in the winter, 1775-76. In 1777, homesteader William Scott (1713-95), age sixty-four, marched with his son William Scott Jr. (1756-1829) in the state militia to repel Burgoyne's New England invasion. William Scott Jr. had previously served with Washington at the 1775 siege of Boston and later, in 1778, enlisted for nine months as a Continental soldier. Homesteader Scott's other two sons, David (1749-1815) and Thomas (1752-1833), had also served at Boston in 1775. In 1777 Thomas Scott enlisted in the Continental Army and served until war's end in 1783; J. Smith, *Peterborough New Hampshire in the American Revolution,* 241-43, 198-99, 334-35, 303-04, 315-16.

90. Robbe, for example, had combat experience with Rogers's Rangers; in 1758 he was one of two townsmen who survived an ambush in which six Peterborough residents were killed; Ibid., 9-10, 13-23.

91. I wish to thank Walter Sargent for sharing his paper given at the Early American History Workshop at the University of Minnesota; his study of 589 cases from Plymouth, Massachusetts, corroborated my study of Peterborough. Sargent concluded, "In the case of Plymouth, the conduct of the Revolution was not transferred to an impoverished, foreign born, or displaced lower class. Rather, the long war of the Revolution represented a community-wide and persevering commitment." Sargent, 19.

92. For the Peterborough soldiers see Ibid., passim. For accounts of the Scotts' service, see Ibid., 316-33. Also see Wright, *The Continental Army,* 197, 209-210; Lesser, 55-252. Lesser's study was also useful in determining regiments' geographic locations and their brigades.

93. J. Smith, *Peterborough New Hampshire in the American Revolution,* 135-37.

94. Ibid., 135-36.

2. REVOLUTIONARY WAR VETERANS IN PETERBOROUGH

1. A. Smith, *History of Peterborough,* pt. 1:242.

2. For the table on the town's age distribution see Resch, "The Transformation of a Frontier Community," 228. Also see appendix A, *Peterborough Sources,* for a discussion of the use of Albert Smith's genealogy to construct the table cited above.

3. *New Hampshire Census, 1790*, 53–54; Threlfall, *Heads of Families: New Hampshire, 1800*, 105–06; *Peterborough Tax Lists;* A. Smith, *History of Peterborough,* pt. 2:passim. Also see appendix A, *Peterborough Sources.*

4. A. Smith, *History of Peterborough,* pt. 1:87–102.

5. Resch, "Peterborough after the Revolution," 125–28.

6. Rothenberg, 781–808; Mendels, 832–50; Banning, "Jeffersonian Ideology Revisited," 3–19; Appleby, "Republicanism in Old and New Contexts," 20–34; A. Smith, *History of Peterborough,* pt. 1:195–205.

7. J. Smith, *Peterborough New Hampshire in the American Revolution,* 167–69; A. Smith, *History of Peterborough,* pt. 2:342; *HCDR* 17:362. In June 1784 "Husbandman" Benjamin Alld sold fourteen acres to Ezekiel Shattuck for £12.

8. *HCDR* 38:235, 237–39.

9. For William Alld's will see *HCPCR* 057. For wife Lettice Alld's will see *HCPCR* 082. After making a few minor provisions in her will, Lettice Alld stated that the remainder of her estate should be divided equally among her children, including Benjamin.

10. Alld's marriage to Nancy White is uncertain. Although it is recorded by the town's genealogist, there is no marriage record, nor is there any information on the gender or life of that child. It is possible that Alld and White had the child out of wedlock. J. Smith, *Peterborough New Hampshire in the American Revolution,* 167–69; A. Smith, *History of Peterborough,* pt. 1:342. Alld died intestate. For Benjamin Alld's estate administration see *HCPCR* 0134.

11. Forming a close group identity that continued after the war appears to be one behavior that derives from the shared experience of serving in a war zone. Elder and Clipp, 196; Scott, 258–59.

12. William Diamond's life is illustrative of Peterborough's Continentals who, although not impoverished, occupied the lower half of Peterborough's economic strata. He was also one of the twelve veterans who moved to town after the war, thereby providing some insight into the fortunes of soldiers who either migrated or were uprooted from their hometowns.

    The discussion of William Diamond's life is a synthesis of material from a wide range of sources. Military and genealogical information appeared in A. Smith, *History of Peterborough,* pt. 2:53–55, and J. Smith, *Peterborough New Hampshire in the American Revolution,* 405–08. Tax information was found for every year from 1796 to Diamond's death in 1828 in the *Peterborough Tax Lists,* Peterborough Historical Society. William Diamond's land sales, leases, and mortgages, and those of his sons, are recorded in the Hillsborough County Deed Records in Nashua, New Hampshire. See *HCDR* 47:199; 47:288; 48:455; 90:572; 92:478; 133:408; 138:8; 154:485–86. William Diamond died intestate, but the court made an inventory of his estate. *HCPCR* 02641. Diamond's wife's estate and his son's will are also recorded. *HCPCR* 0287, 1756. For information on the Simonds—sometimes spelled Symonds—of Lexington, Massachusetts, see Hudson, 214–19. See also William Diamond, Pension File W22941, RG15, NA; Resch, "The Continental Veterans of Peterborough, New Hampshire," 180–83.

13. The section on the Blair and McAllister families synthesizes a number of sources. Before listing them I would like to express my appreciation to Lucy Blair, one of the Blair descendants, who introduced me to some of her family's material. Her keen interest in local history was infectious. Her sudden death in April 1985 was a loss to the

community, the Peterborough Historical Society, and to me as a researcher. For genealogical information see A. Smith, *History of Peterborough*, pt. 2:18–19, 149. For families
related by marriage to the Blairs and McAllisters see Ibid., 79–83, 133–34, 305–06. Also
see J. Smith, *Peterborough New Hampshire in the American Revolution*, 176–81, 232–35.
See *Peterborough Tax List* and *Peterborough Town Book*. Regarding Randall McAllister's
estate, see *HCPCR* 0381. Also see William Blair, Pension File, W21680, and John Blair,
Pension File, S45296, RG15, NA.

14. *HCDR* 11:537; 27:400.

15. In 1800 one of the Blair households consisted of William, his wife, and their three
children, Agnes, age twelve, William Jr., age six, and John, age four. The other household included William's sister, his invalid brother-in-law Randall McAllister, and
McAllister's only child, Mary Blair McAllister, age fifteen.

16. Previously, veterans had applied to their state legislatures for invalid pensions. The
federal government had reimbursed states for pension payments. Under the new federal
law passed in 1807, veterans unable to fully support themselves because of war injuries
applied directly to the War Department for a disability pension. Applicants had to
submit affidavits from two physicians testifying as to the nature and degree of disability,
and the veteran was required under oath to prove that the disability was service related.
Unfortunately the extent of McAllister's disability is unknown because his pension
application was lost in 1814 when British troops burned the War Department during
their raid on Washington, D.C.

17. A. Smith, *History of Peterborough*, pt. 2:310–12; J. Smith, *Peterborough New Hampshire in
the American Revolution*, 412. Christopher Thayer, Pension File, S43994, RG15, NA.

18. *HCDR* 111:554; 124:467. For Blair's transactions as a grantor see *HCDR* 47:292; 64:349;
87:125; 100:24; 105:9. For his transactions as a grantee see *HCDR* 6:130; 29:120. The
transactions cited are only for land bought and sold in Peterborough because there were
a number of John and William Blairs in the area, particularly in New Boston and New
Ipswich, involved in land sales in those communities.

19. *HCDR* 103:424.

20. Thayer purchased his land in 1789 and 1791. Ibid., 24:255; 29:46. Between 1814 and 1820
he made six transactions selling small parcels. Ibid., 103:244, 424; 116:316; 122:105; 128:541;
133:110. His last sale occurred in 1823. Ibid., 141:69.

21. The discussion of the Smith and Morison families is based upon the following sources.
J. Smith, *The Home of the Smith Family*, 1749–1842, 5–9, 27, 28, 37, 44, 52, 62, 59, 74, 98,
100, 107–08, 116–28, 138, 163–74; A. Smith, *History of Peterborough*, pt. 2:174–204, 258–
87; *NHPPDR* 32:222–24, 328; 38:434; 42:434; 56:384; 57:334; 67:545; 74:512; 78:237; 80:254;
89:516; 90:283; 97:28. *HCDR* 1:346; 7:4; 9:89; 12:523; 13:15–17, 75; 16:2; 18:242–47; 21:370;
24:365; 26:446; 28:431; 29:546; 30:77; 34:469; 35:512; 41:278; 55:178, 232; 63:186; *Peterborough
Tax Lists*. The original tax lists for 1796 onward are located in the Peterborough Historical Society. There are forty-three boxes of Smith family papers at the Peterborough
Historical Society. *Smith Family Papers*, Peterborough Historical Society, MSS 103.
The Historical Society also has the stock transactions and board meeting records of the
Bell Mill, one of the first in Peterborough. The Smiths were involved in the Bell Mill
and then established their own, the Phoenix Mill. Jeremiah and Samuel Smith served
in Congress. *BDAC*, 1618, 1623.

22. A. Smith, *History of Peterborough*, pt. 2:265.

23. Smith later recalled that during his tenure in Congress, 1790–1797, he helped secure an invalid pension for Robbe. J. Smith, *Peterborough New Hampshire in the American Revolution*, 342–43. For Robbe see Ibid., 289–93.

24. J. Smith, *Peterborough New Hampshire in the American Revolution*, 270–77.

25. A. Smith, *History of Peterborough*, pt. 2:275; 2:258–83.

26. Ibid., pt. 2:174–86.

27. Ibid., pt. 2:174–204, 281, 295–97; *HCDR* 47:339–40.

28. The second-generation Smiths were deeply involved in the town church, as was their father, William. They embraced liberal convictions and greater toleration, however, in contrast to Peterborough's Old Side Calvinists. For example, in 1791 Representative Jeremiah Smith voted to remove the state constitution's clause prohibiting non-Protestants from being elected "senator or representative." Jonathan Smith became a deacon in Elijah Dunbar's Congregational church. Jonathan was a "leader of the choir," which had been a source of conflict between traditional Calvinists and liberals. In the 1820s he became "a strong Unitarian." The Smiths were recalled as "in favor of a liberal policy of education and in what ever might elevate the standards of morals." A. Smith, *History of Peterborough*, pt. 2:264.

29. Reginald Ellery, a psychiatrist relying upon medical records, described the personal and social damage World War I inflicted upon many veterans. Among his findings Ellery reported that warfare "brought about a distortion of emotional values, a slackening of parental control and a loss of parental identification. It has obscured the goals of adulthood," caused economic and political dislocation, and weakened "moral ties." Ellery, 49–50, 109, 126, 136.
     For other studies of World War I's impact on veterans McCurdy; Culpin; Ward; and Marwick.

30. Brill and Beebe, 34, 38, 53–54, 122, 124, 126–27, 135, 216–17, 222–27, 279, 309.
     For other studies of the World War II veterans see Pratt; Stouffer; Havighurst, 1, 177, 243, 257, 260. For a general psychoanalytic treatment of war's effect, see the study by anthropologist Franco Fornari.

31. Despite evidence of PTSD among many veterans, just over half (56 percent) of the Vietnam veterans in Card's study reported that their military experience was "entirely or mostly positive." Military service did not diminish the lives of these veterans. Card and other researchers found that many soldiers resumed their former lives or sought higher goals following their discharge. These veterans stated that travel had broadened their understanding of different cultures, that military life improved their ability to get along with people and afforded them new responsibilities. Many stated that military service had helped them in "becoming a man," had given them greater self-confidence, and had contributed to their personal growth and maturity. However, many of these men had not experienced combat or field conditions in Vietnam. Thus for these soldiers military service was a period of maturation and discovery of manhood and a source of self-esteem and ambition, especially for those who served short enlistments or behind front lines. Card observed that many of these men aspired to higher social and economic status following their discharge from the service. Card, 71, 76, 87, 100, 103, 107–10, 124–27, 140–41, 146. Also see Starr.

32. For an insightful and moving description of the traumatic effect of combat on troops in Vietnam see Shay, *Achilles in Vietnam*. For the controversy over PTSD see Allan Young,

The Harmony of Illusions: Inventing Post-Traumatic Stress Disorder, 3, 5, 50–62, 84, 117, 287–90; Scott, *The Politics of Readjustment,* passim; Dean Jr., 1–6, 29–45, 114.

33. Kulka, xvii–xix, 130–35.

34. Dean Jr., 1–6, 70–71, 113, 134, 179, 221; Gerald Linderman has shown how war-zone experiences in the Second World War transformed individuals into hardened soldiers thus enabling them to endure the rigors of camp and combat. Linderman 1–47, 345–62.

35. Dean Jr., 100, 179, 134.

3. THE IMAGE OF THE SUFFERING SOLDIER

1. Higginbotham, *War and Society in Revolutionary America,* 174–83.

2. Waldstreicher, 156–73. During this period the militia emerged as a symbol of the "virtuous republican citizen." Standing armies retained their stain of corruption and remained objects of "hostility." Ibid., 156.

3. Clinton Jr., *An Oration July 4, 1798,* 13.

4. "[L]egends created by the militia at Lexington, Concord, and Bunker Hill," Elkins and McKitrick wrote, "served to impart a certain inviolability to the citizen-soldier ideal and—despite repeated bad experience later on—to guarantee its preservation as one of the sacred fictions of the early republic." Elkins and McKitrick, 717. Although the bill for the New Army passed, the army was never created. In May 1800, Congress voted to disband the New Army. Ibid., 719. For a discussion of the controversy over the buildup of the army see Ibid., 714–19. Also see Waldstreicher, 186–95.

5. Eacker, *An Oration on July 4, 1801,* 5–8. Thomas, 114.

6. See appendix A, *Jeffersonian Views toward the Regular Army,* for a discussion of the diminution of Republican anti-army doctrine and policies between 1800 and 1812.

7. For a detailed account of divisions within the Republican party over foreign policy and defense are Stagg, 48–176, 270–386, 419–68, 501–17.

8. *Boston Columbian Centinel,* 3 May 1806.

9. *New York American Citizen,* 28 April 1806; *Boston Columbian Centinel,* 3 May 1806.

10. It was common for orators such as Webster to invoke powerful cultural symbols in July Fourth orations to defend or attack administration policies before party loyalists making these addresses an "ideal source . . . for studying patterns of thought on major issues of the day." Alexander, 11. David Waldstreicher has shown that these celebrations were venues for conflicting views of the political culture. As such they were creative. "In their festive activities and newspaper missives, each party sought to make *its* respective practices epitomize the true national and Revolutionary perspective, to spur citizens to act as self-evidently good Americans would act at election time." Waldstreicher, 196. Also see Travers, 4–7.

11. *Boston Columbian Centinel,* 10 May 1806.

12. Webster, *An Address July 4, 1806,* 11, 13–14, 19–20.

13. Perley, *An Oration July 4, 1807,* 11, 14, 18. For information about Perley, see Chapman, 113–14.

    On 4 July 1807 John Hanson Thomas (n.d.) addressed members of the Washington Society of Alexandria, part of the network of veterans' organizations, such as the Society of the Cincinnati, aligned with the Federalist party. He called on them to revive America's resolve and patriotism in the general's name. Thomas, *An Oration July 4, 1807,* 12–24.

14. Gleason proclaimed that their victories surpassed "Plataea," "Thermopylae," and "Austerlitz." Gleason exclaimed, "It is enough aged fathers to have it said you lived in those momentous times; our hearts instantly feel for you all respect, and we exclaim—*Brave men, your names shall be immortal.*" He credited soldiers with laying the foundation for the "present . . . *Golden Age*" where "equal rights, and equal liberties, with peace, prosperity, and happiness are the rewards of all." Benjamin Gleason, *An Oration July 4, 1807,* 7. For information on Gleason see Brown University, *Historical Catalogue,* 92. Purcell, 199–206.

15. Bacon, *An Oration on July 4, 1807,* 4–5.

16. In 1807 Levi Lincoln (1782–1868) honored Revolutionary War soldiers to convey his party's devotion to patriotism and its capacity to keep the spirit of '76 burning in the hearts of a new generation of Americans. The young Lincoln assured party loyalists in Brookfield, Massachusetts, that the spirit of '76 personified by veterans of the Revolution, filled the hearts of a new generation of Americans. No doubt Lincoln's speech reflected Republican views. His father had served in Jefferson's cabinet from 1801 to 1804, and in 1807 the elder Lincoln was lieutenant governor of Massachusetts. Lincoln, *An Oration July 4, 1807,* 4, 9, 7–8, 14. *BDAC,* 1220.

17. As historian Sarah Purcell explained, "The Tammany Society hoped that the monument would call out not only for national gratitude but for renewed national action against Britain." Purcell, 191–99.

18. S. K. Livermore, *An Oration July 4, 1809,* 7. Palmer, 223–24. Livermore was the fifth son of the Rev. Jonathan Livermore of Wilton, New Hampshire, a town bordering Temple. Solomon was described as partisan Federalist. Abiel Abbot Livermore and Sewell Putnam, 280–81.

19. August Alden's 4 July 1809, oration to Federalists of Augusta, Maine, did not entirely discard the concept of the people's war. He told his listeners, "we behold a *brave* and *virtuous* people struggling for freedom [in 1776] . . . animated by a glorious life of liberty. . . ." Nevertheless, he focused on the role of the Revolution's soldiers to inspire patriotism in Augusta's citizens and the militia gathered before him. Alden, *An Address July 4, 1809,* 3, 11–12; Chapman, 107.

20. This theme is illustrated in Tristan Burges's Fourth of July oration in 1810. Burges (1770–1853), a lawyer and prominent member of the Federalist party, warned the citizens of Providence, Rhode Island, that Republican policies jeopardized American "Sovereignty [and undermined its] Love of Liberty." He observed that when the Republicans took power, "our liberty, honor and union [were] pure and undefiled, a praise and glory in the whole earth. It has since been polluted with ceremonial democracy. . . . The history of these times is a narration of deviation from the great principles of our nation's Independence." Burges closed with a demand to rebuild the navy, to restore the army's strength, and to renew the nation's militant patriotism. Burges, *An Oration July 4, 1810,* 17, 20. *BDAC,* 626–27.

21. Higginbotham, *War and Society in Revolutionary America,* 183–88.

22. Caldwell, *An Oration July 4, 1810,* 9–10, 17, 21, 28; *DAB* 3:406.

23. Osborn, *An Oration July 4, 1810,* 6, 23; *DAB* 14:69–70.

On 4 July 1809 Joseph Bartlett (1762–1827), playwright, poet, and "ardent" Republican, reminded party loyalists in Portsmouth, New Hampshire, that part of the price of independence was "outraged and violated" women. Bartlett venerated patriotic women. He also praised revolutionary soldiers: "their virtues" are "embalm[ed] in our grateful hearts [and] their patriotism we will teach posterity to imitate." His speech represents the efforts by Republicans to celebrate soldiers within the concept of the people's war. Bartlett, *An Oration July 4, 1809*, 5–6; *DAB* 2:8–9.

24. L. Cohen, *The Revolutionary Historians*, 16. In describing these histories, Cohen wrote, "The revolutionary histories are indeed romances, heroic stories of adventure and overcoming, for only romance could simultaneously capture 'the truth' of the Revolution and make it accessible to future generations in an endlessly repeatable story." Ibid., 214.

25. Marshall, *Washington* 3:375–76.

26. Warren, 1:388–89. Also see Hannah Adams, 145–73. Hannah Adams's text was based on her 1799 history of New England, but her 1807 version included new materials from Marshall, *The Life of George Washington*, and oral histories of the Revolutionary War given by veterans.

27. The image of the suffering soldier appeared in various parts of Ramsay's *History*. Ramsay described American troops retreating in December 1776 through New Jersey as a "half naked army." Elsewhere he wrote that in the winter of 1777 soldiers "suffered . . . many without shoes, though marching over frozen ground, which so gashed their naked feet, that each step was marked with blood . . . the country everywhere presented melancholy sight of soldiers suffering poverty and disease . . ." Ramsay, *History* 1:314, 329, 331. For a similar description of troops in 1781 in the south under Greene's command see Ramsay, *History* 2:236. Ramsay described the troops at Valley Forge as "half clothed and more than once on the point of starvation." Ibid., 2:81.

   For more on Ramsay see appendix A, *Ramsay's Histories*.

28. Ramsay, *Washington*, 78–88.

29. Higginbotham, *The War of American Independence*, 405–12, 439.

30. Ramsay, *History* 2:325–26.

31. Ramsay, *Washington*, 163–78. In his *History* (1789), Ramsay wrote that Congress had no choice but to dismiss the troops encamped at Newburgh without pay because the government was bankrupt. It was, he said, "a hard and unavoidable case" that an "anonymous" officer exploited with a "seditious publication to inflame the minds of officers and soldiers." His 1789 account praised Washington for calming the troops and for preventing the "floodgates of civil discord" from opening. Ramsay, *History*, 325–27.

32. Ramsay, *Washington*, 175. For Ramsay's earlier account see Ramsay, *History* 2:325–26.

33. Ramsay, *Washington*, 111–12.

34. Other editions of this work were published in Baltimore by Joseph Cushing in 1814, 1815, and 1818.

35. Marshall excused the Army's near rebellion. Using the image of the suffering soldier, Marshall wrote that the army had been "soured by their past sufferings, their present wants, and their gloomy prospects; and exasperated by the neglect with which they believed themselves to be treated, and by the injustice supposed to be mediated against them, the ill temper of the army was almost universal." Marshall described the "anonymous" letter calling for a march on Congress as "admirably well prepared to work on the passions of the moment." Marshall, *Washington* 4:587–603.

36. In addition, *Monthly Magazine* proposed pantheons filled with the statues of the nation's Founders—"Washington, Franklin, Greene, Gates, Warren, Mercer . . ."—be built in every part of the nation, each to become a "Holy Place" where every citizen came "at least once in his life . . . to worship in the national temple." These monuments would instruct the "mass of the people [who] pass a life of labor" in the patriotism and the virtues of their forefathers. "Valley Forge," *The Monthly Magazine and Literary Journal* 1 (May 1812), 5–8. The Valley Forge article was reprinted from *Freemason's Magazine and General Miscellany* 2 (October 1811), 47–54.

37. Salma Hale's prize winning *History of the United States* (1822) illustrated the convention of that symbolism at its height. Hale wrote that at Valley Forge, "[Washington's] troops were destitute of shoes, and might have been tracked by the blood of their feet. They passed the winter in huts, suffered extreme distress from want of clothing and of food, but endured their privations without a murmur. How strong must have been their love of liberty? With what lively gratitude ought a prosperous country, indebted to them for the most valuable blessings to remember their sufferings and service?" Hale's history reaffirmed that Continental troops ought to be revered as a "republican army" of patriotic soldiers. Salma Hale, 188–89, 205–6, 183. In 1822 Salma Hale won a $400 award and a gold metal from the American Academy of Language and Belles Lettres for his *History of the United States.*

38. Romaine, *An Oration July 4, 1812*, 3–6, 16; McDonnell, 1:51, 64.

   With great hope, William Clagett (1790–1870), a lawyer and son of Republican Congressman Clifton Clagett, announced in his Fourth of July oration to celebrants in Portsmouth, New Hampshire, that "The spirit of '76 has revived in the American soldiery. . . . your country now calls for your services, she looks to you for protection." Clagett, *An Oration July 4, 1812*, 24–27; *BDAC*, 693. For other orations expressing similar views, see Jackson, *An Oration July 4, 1812*, 8; E. D. Smith, *An Oration July 4, 1812*, 21.

   Federalists such as John Anthon, who supported the war with England, also called for renewed patriotic spirit. Anthon (1784–1863), one of New York's leading attorneys, told the New York City Washington Benevolent Society on 4 July 1812 that it was the "sainted spirits of revolutionary heroes . . . which led us to independence." Despite the crisis, Anthon couldn't resist attacking Republican policies. He hoped that after twelve years of Republican rule, when "our national character and prosperity have been retrograde," that the "mantle of patriotism bequeathed by the heroes [of the Revolution] still remains all powerful to save the nation." Anthon, *An Oration July 4, 1812*, 19; *DAB* 1:314–15. Federalist positions, however, quickly divided between the majority who resisted the war as illegal and opposed all war measures, including raising a professional army, and those, especially nationalists like Biddle, who assisted the administration's efforts to build an effective army.

39. Rush, *An Oration July 4, 1812* in Hawken, 45; *DAB* 16:231–34.

40. "To the Public," *The Military Monitor and American Register* 1 (17 August 1812), 1–2.

41. "To the Public," Ibid., 5 (14 September 1812), 32–34. Mrs. Pruitt's valor was juxtaposed to the lack of valor in her faint-hearted husband. He was a Revolutionary War veteran who "gave way to paternal affection" by disapproving his sons' enlistments.

42. Stagg, 262–63, 461–66; "Proclamation by his Excellency, Martin Crittenden," *The Examiner* 1 (22 November 1813), 45–46.

43. Ellis, 208. See also Caldwell, 321–28; Edgar, 39, 189–90; Ellis, 202–08; Govan, 38–43; Lochemes, 57. Robert Walsh also used his journal to promote nationalism. "Prospects," *American Review of History and Politics* 1 (January 1811), i–iii.

44. Caldwell, *Autobiography*, 327.

45. As early as April 1811, *Port Folio* began linking military and civic virtues through biographies of Revolutionary War officers. In April 1812, it announced a new series, "American Gallantry." Two months after the war began, it added a companion series, "American Biography," with an article on General Daniel Morgan, a Revolutionary War hero, to exemplify the image of the republican-warrior and to promote patriotism.

Through both series, "American Gallantry" and "American Biography," Americans became more familiar with a wider range of Revolutionary heroes such as Nathan Hale and William Barton. Barton (1748–1831), the hatter and later a Continental Army sergeant, captured British Gen. Richard Prescott in December 1776. Barton rose to the rank of major. "American Gallantry," *Port Folio*, 3d ser., 1 (January 1813), 86; "American Biography," *Port Folio*, 2d ser., 8 (August 1812), 101–10; "American Gallantry," *Port Folio*, 2d ser., 8 (September 1812), 245–51; *DAB* 2:24–25; "American Gallantry" *Port Folio*, 2d ser., 8 (November 1812), 481–84.

Beginning in 1811, *Port Folio* used biographical sketches of Revolutionary War officers to inspire national unity. It apotheosized Washington (as was common in the period) as "a rallying point for virtue and patriotism and heroism and honour . . . [in these] gloomy times." "Washington," *Port Folio*, 2d ser., 5 (April 1811), 282. A sketch of Maj. Gen. Henry Knox in its August 1811 edition celebrated his character for its "disinterested love of country and a noble zeal in the cause of freedom. . . ." "Biographical Sketch of Major-General Knox," *Port Folio*, 2d ser., 6 (August 1811), 99–100.

46. "History of the American War," *Port Folio*, 2d ser., 8 (November 1812), 481–84; see also the *Monthly Magazine and Literary Journal* 2 (November 1812), 7–9. It reprinted the article from *Port Folio*. Hannah Adams's 1807 history of New England, unlike her 1799 account, contained the story of Nathan Hale. That story was based on an account told to Adams by Gen. William Hall of Newton, Massachusetts. Hannah Adams, 157.

47. "Plan of a National Burial Ground," *Port Folio*, 3d ser., 2 (October 1813), 388. The proposal's author stated that in place of the "unfulfilled" construction of a monument to Washington, the nation ought to establish a national cemetery for "any American preeminently distinguished." Washington's monument had been long delayed. On 20 December 1799, five days after Washington's death, Congress resolved to build a marble monument to mark his grave. Martha Washington's refusal to transfer the general's body to the Capital stopped the project. Emery, 3.

48. "Valley Forge," the *Monthly Magazine and Literary Journal* 1 (May 1812), 8.

For growth of the sentiment, following the War of 1812, to honor and memorialize soldiers see Kammen, *A Season of Youth*, 17–18, 35; and, Kammen, *Reflections*, 237–43.

49. In one edition, it used Comdr. Oliver Hazard Perry's life to illustrate the character of an American serviceman. *Port Folio* described Perry as a "gallant officer . . . adorned with milder virtues" in private life: "as a son he is dutiful, submissive and affectionate; as a

husband kind; as a friend generous and sincere; as a master humane and indulgent."
Perry's character, *Port Folio* claimed, combined "the gentleman, the warrior and the
Christian. This concentrated blaze affords an unanswerable proof that all moral virtues
appear more lovely when they harmonize together. They afford decided evidence that
the True Christian the True gentleman and the True soldier are all but different parts of
the same character; and that they all lead to the same glorious result"—in short, a heroic
American soldier. "Life of Commander Perry," *Port Folio*, 3d ser., 3 (March 1814), 218–
19; *Port Folio*, 3d ser., 3 (April 1814), 298; *Port Folio*, 3d ser., 4 (May 1814), 385, 391.

50. "To Readers and Correspondents," *Port Folio*, 3d ser., 4 (September 1814), 339–40.

51. Throughout the years 1813 and 1814 *Port Folio* published a variety of documents, biographies, letters, and accounts dealing with the Revolutionary War and the War of 1812. In
addition to accounts cited above, see "A Biographical Sketch of Commodore John
Barry," *Port Folio*, 3d ser., 2 (July 1813), 1–10. Barry was a Revolutionary War hero who
was credited with being the "father" of the United States Navy; "Naval History of the
United States," Ibid., 38–51. Also see the following: "Original Letters of General
Greene," Ibid., 69–74; "Original Letter of General Greene," *Port Folio*, 3d ser., 2
(August 1813), 203–09; "Biography of Captain James Lawrence," *Port Folio*, 3d ser., 2
(September 1813), 235–55; "Original Letters of General Greene," Ibid., 290–95; "Origi-
nal Letters of General Greene," *Port Folio*, 3d ser., 2 (October 1813), 390–94; "Life of
Commodore Murray," *Port Folio*, 3d ser., 5 (May 1814), 399–409. Murray fought in the
Revolutionary War in the Maryland line and in the navy during the Revolution. He also
participated in the War of 1812. "Military and Naval Gallantry," *Port Folio*, 3d ser., 4
(August 1814), 231–33; "American Heroism," *Port Folio*, 3d ser., 4 (September 1814), 326–
31. This is an account of the valor of individual seamen in defense of the "Essex." Poem
to Capt. David Porter, captain of the "Essex," *Port Folio*, 3d ser., 4 (November 1814), 515;
"Life of Captain Jesse Elliot," *Port Folio*, 3d ser. (December 1814), 529–39. Elliot was a
naval hero in the 1813 battle of Sackett's Harbor. "A Biographical Memoir of Jacob
Brown . . . ," *Port Folio*, 3d ser., 5 (February 1815), 105–23. For a poem commemorating
the valor of the "Essex" crew, see "Battle of Valparaiso," Ibid., 200–201.

52. "American Gallantry," *Port Folio*, 3d ser., 1 (January 1813), 86–91; "To Readers and
Correspondents," *Port Folio*, 3d ser., 1 (June 1813), 633–37; and "Published Letters from
General [Christopher] Greene," Ibid., 602–10.

53. "Original Letter of General Washington," *Port Folio*, 2d ser., 8 (November 1812), 459–
65; the *Monthly Magazine and Literary Journal* 2 (December 1812), 96–100.

54. "Printed Extracts from Henry Lee's memoirs of the war in the Southern Department of
the United States," *Port Folio*, 2d ser., 8 (December 1812), 551–52.

55. "Unpublished Letter of General Washington," *Port Folio*, 3d ser., 2 (December 1813),
605–07.

56. "Life and Memoirs of the Late Major General Lee" *Port Folio*, 3d ser., 3 (February 1814),
128.

57. "Civis," the *Military Monitor and American Register* 1 (2 November 1812), 94–95. Civis
proposed an idea long favored by Federalists to build a peacetime standing army using
retired officers to teach citizens the art of war so that in time of war they would form the
core of a regular army "counterbalanced by an armed militia." His pseudonym is not
revealed. See Cushing.

58. Morris, *An Oration July 5, 1813,* 6, 11; *BDAC,* 1359–60.

59. S. H. Smith, *An Oration July 4, 1813,* 20. Fuller, *An Oration July 4, 1814,* 18–19; *BDAC,* 920.

Louis M'Lane (1786–1857), a Federalist and lawyer who served in the War of 1812, speaking before the Artillery Company of Wilmington, Delaware on 5 July 1813 implored the soldiers "to contemplate the example of the Revolutionary heroes." He called those soldiers the "illustrious men of the days of Seventy-Six [whose] virtues [and] actions excite an emulation to equal their elevation of soul . . . to derive an example for the preservation of our . . . liberties and our rights." M'Lane, *An Oration July 5, 1813,* 5, 16; *BDAC,* 1308.

On 4 July 1814 Rollin Mallary (1784–1831), a former Vermont attorney general and future congressman, told Republican citizens in Poultney, "Patriotism alone became powerless against the veterans of Europe. . . ." Mallary, *An Oration July 4, 1814,* 18; *BDAC,* 1257.

Republican John Thompson (1790–1831), a lawyer from Windsor, Vermont, turned to the Revolutionary soldier to inspire perseverance in the war with England. Speaking before an assembly in Windsor, Vermont, 4 July 1814, Thompson acknowledged that American "arms have not been so successful" in the war with England but that this was also true in the first years of the Revolutionary War. He said the "revolutionary patriot . . . was often fatigued, exhausted and discouraged." Appealing to the legacy of the soldier, Thompson said, "We are defending 'liberty in her last retreat' and we will not desert her till every fortress be a Fort Griswold (defended at great cost by American militia and discharged regular troops at Groton, Connecticut, in 1781) and every strait a Thermopylae." Thompson, *An Oration July 4, 1814,* 22–24. For information on Thompson, see Crockett, 5:98–99.

60. July Fourth orations between 1815 and 1817 celebrated American military prowess as an indication of a noble national character. See Bates, *A Discourse July 4, 1815,* 14–16; Berrion, *An Oration July 4, 1815,* 10–15; Carter, *An Oration July 4, 1815,* 5, 7–10, 13; Williams, *An Oration July 4, 1815,* 4–5, 11–15; Woodbury, *An Oration July 4, 1815,* 3, 14–15; J. Davis, *An Oration July 4, 1816,* 18; Allen, *An Oration July 4, 1817,* 9–12, 15; Channing, *An Oration July 4, 1817,* 5; Elliot, *An Oration July 4, 1817,* 3–9; Ware, *An Oration July 4, 1817,* 3–5, 14.

61. Speakers at the dedication, in praise of the men who fought there in 1814, said that the monument marked a "hallowed spot" that people will visit "to be informed at once of virtue and its praise of duty, and its proud reward. Remember what has been done and what has been endured by the men whose *deathless names* this monument records; and go, and endure, and do likewise. Their country has not forgotten *them. Your country* will never forget *you.* " "Monument," *Port Folio,* 4th ser., 1 (January 1816), 1–12.

62. "Oration in Defense of the American Character," *Port Folio,* 3d ser., 6 (July 1815), 18–25. The orator rejected the European claim that the Americans were in "all respects degraded when compared with the old [world]." The speaker referred to charges of cultural inferiority that had received scientific support from the French naturalist Georges Buffon's (1707–88) conclusion that all species degenerated in the New World. Europeans contemptuous of American character could use Buffon's science to support their cultural bias. Fellows and Milliken, 120–21, 146. Also on Buffon see Lyon and

Sloan, 1–32, and Boorstin, 445–48. Thomas Jefferson had gone to great lengths to disprove Buffon's ideas, even going so far as to take a moose carcass to Europe to show the immense size of this animal.

63. "The Old Soldier," the *Juvenile Port Folio and Literary Miscellany* (Philadelphia: John Bioren, 17 October 1812) 1:2.

64. The *Juvenile Port Folio and Literary Miscellany* was not connected to *Port Folio*. Nevertheless, both were Philadelphia publications and "reflected admiration for the urbane style of the later eighteenth century . . . classicism, nationalism and sentimentalism in fiction." Kelly, 262–64; Spencer, 7. Condie's *Juvenile Port Folio* was published between 1812 and 1816.

For other stories about soldiers or related themes of benevolence, sympathy, and compassion, see *Juvenile Port Folio*, "Benevolence in Youth" (28 November 1812) 1:26–27; "The Wounded Soldier" (2 January 1813), 1:45–46; "Gratitude" (13 October 1813), 1:215; "Sympathy" (3 July 1813), 1:151; "The Wandering Mendicant" (5 March 1814), 2:33–34; "Picture of an American Hero" (24 January 1815), 3:7. The *Juvenile Port Folio* also published patriotic pieces and an annual poem to George Washington. I would like to thank Paula Petrick for introducing me to these sources on children's literature.

65. "Petition of Abraham Davis," *CPRC*, RG233, NA. In some instances congressmen successfully obtained an increase in a veteran's pension through private bills. In one case, Rep. William Finley secured passage of a private bill to increase Barnabus McQuire's invalid pension from $4.80 a month, the amount awarded by the War Department, to $8 a month, the maximum award allowed by law. Finley and McQuire submitted medical testimony to the Committee on Claims that stated that McQuire's disability had become worse with age. The physician supporting McQuire's claim described the invalid soldier as "now seventy-two years old, with a large family and forms in my opinion one of the most proper objects for the bounty of Congress." "Petition of Barnabus McQuire," *CPRC*, folder 65, RG233, NA. For other petitions for increased benefits that congressmen sent directly to the War Department for its determination, see "Petition of Thomas Goodrum," *CPRC*, folder 33, RG233, NA; "Petition of John Hayley," *CPRC*, folder 42, RG233, NA; "Petition of Ambrose Lewis," *CPRC*, folder 58, RG233, NA; "Petition of Robert Mitchell," *CPRC*, folder 67, RG233, NA; "Petition of Joseph Patrick," *CPRC*, folder 79, RG233, NA.

66. "Petition of John Montgomery," *CPRC*, folder 71, RG233, NA.

67. "Petition of Henry Martin," *CPRC*, folder 79, RG233, NA. Similarly, Hugh Hofferman's (no residence given) January 1816 petition for a pension claimed that he was "unable to provide for or maintain myself [because of] wounds and other privations I suffered while in the service of my country." "Petition of Hugh Hofferman," *CPRC*, folder 43, RG233, NA. Lambert Robinson also based his appeal for an invalid pension on age, infirmity, and poverty. "Petition of Lambert Robinson," *CPRC*, folder 79, RG233, NA.

68. "Petition of John Montgomery," *CPRC*, folder 71, RG233, NA; "Petition of Henry Martin," *CPRC*, folder 79, RG233, NA.

69. *CPRC*, folder 83, RG233, NA.

In 1810 the House Committee on Claims overturned legal precedents against awarding service pensions when it approved the officers' petition for half-pay pensions. The committee's report asserted that officers had "spent the vigor of their manhood in service" and that many of them returned to civilian life "maimed and scarcely able to halt along . . . the griping hand of poverty bore hard upon them . . . they fell early prey to the wiles of the artful and insidious speculator. . . ." The committee also stated that the certificates at full pay for five years breached a contract because "they [the officers] were compelled from imperious necessity to accept the sum in gross in lieu of half-pay for life. . . ." *Am. St. P.: Military Affairs* 2:372–73. Despite the committee's favorable recommendation to approve the petition for half-pay pensions, Congress rejected the officers' claim. For more discussion of the officers' efforts to secure pensions see appendix A, *Officers' Claims.*

70. Glasson, 23–53; Bodenger, 8–20; *Am. St. P.: Military Affairs* 2:372–73.
71. *Am. St. P.: Military Affairs* 2:372–73.
72. Letter from "Citizen" reprinted in *Philadelphia U.S. Gazette,* 24 February 1816.
73. Congress affirmed earlier decisions that no breach of contract had occurred in 1783 because officers had freely entered into an agreement with the government to accept commutation certificates and that redemption of the certificates in 1790 was part of a general policy of settling the Revolution's public debt. *Am. St. P.: Military Affairs* 2:591. Also see the *Examiner* 5 (11 March 1816), 199; *CPRC,* folder 83, RG233, NA.
74. Eliot and Niles sought to preserve the speeches of Revolutionary statesmen for "posterity for edification and example, . . . to encourage a spirit to seek after and hold on to the principles which appear essential to the preservation of the rights and liberties of the people of the United States," and to create "a literary monument in honour of those who laboured and suffered at the birth of the nation." The "Prefatory" to *Of the Revolution in America* contains the letter, published on 23 November 1816, that urged Niles to begin collecting the speeches made during the Revolution and Niles's brief account of his collecting efforts. Niles, "Prefatory," *Of The Revolution in America. Niles Weekly Register,* 4 January 1817. *DAB,* 94–95.
75. *Niles Weekly Register,* 1 March 1817, 2.
76. *Niles Weekly Register,* 2 February 1817; *American Mercury,* 18 November 1817.
77. Quoted in *Niles Weekly Register,* 8 February 1817.
78. Noah, *An Oration July 4, 1817,* 5–8. *DAB* 13:534–35.
79. *Am. St. P.: Military Affairs* 2:473–74.

The House Committee on Pensions and Revolutionary Claims, in support of the increase, stated that recipients ought to live "plentifully and comfortably" at their "advanced age." The committee assured Congress that the country could afford the additional costs of increased benefits. It reported that there were "185 officers and 1,572 noncommissioned officers and soldiers of the revolution" on the invalid rolls. The increase in benefits would only cost the federal government about $120,90 annually for the first year and then decrease as pensioners died. Besides those pensioned as a result of war injuries sustained during the Revolution, the invalid pension program included "52 officers and 391" soldiers who had "become disabled since the revolution." A total of 2,200 pensioners, mostly Revolutionary War veterans, were on the rolls as of 1816. The Committee's proposed monthly increases follow: Ensigns—$10 to $13; third lieutenants—$11.50 to $14; second lieutenants—$12.50 to $15; first lieutenants—$15 to $17. The maximum amount of the pensions awarded the three highest ranks was unchanged as follows: captains—$20; majors—$25; lieutenant colonels—$30. *Am. St. P.: Military Affairs* 2:473–74. The bill to increase the amount awarded to invalid pensioners passed on 12 April 1816, and was approved on 24 April 1816. *Annals of Congress,* 14th Cong., 1st sess., 1308–09, 1851.

For a description of the invalid pension program, see Bodenger, 22–28; Glasson, 54–65; Wehmann, "Introduction."

80. William Henry Harrison introduced a second bill to create an invalid corps on 6 December 1816. The bill was indefinitely postponed on 24 February 1817. *Annals of Congress,* 14th Cong., 2nd sess., 245, 255, 1035.

81. Writing in *Port Folio* in support of the idea, "Americanus" attacked the "lamentable system of parsimony pursued by Congress towards those illustrious citizens whose talents, bravery, and public spirit have achieved for us the highest ranks we possess among the nations of the earth." He said that Congress's parsimony was a "revolting feature of our national character," which will permanently stain the nation's honor. Americanus wrote that history will record the "heroism which shed a halo of glory around the American name . . . [and] will likewise record the chilling neglect, the base ingratitude which that heroism experienced." He warned that "remote posterity will sigh for the disgrace of their ancestors" for failing to give pensions to these veterans. "Americanus" also urged adoption of the English policy of awarding pensions to those who served the nation—"great service [is assured] of great rewards." Like England, he said, the United States must add "the strong stimulus of self-interest" to "ambition and love of glory" to motivate public service. He concluded that there must be "national gratitude for national services." *Port Folio,* 4th ser., 1 (April 1816), 328–33; 358–59.

82. Objections to the invalid corps arose not over the principle of entitlement but over eligibility. The bill, originally excluding militia, was amended to include them. Opponents of the amendment claimed that rewarding both militia with regular troops would weaken the "martial spirit" in the professional army because revisionist histories of the Revolution had revealed the ineptness of the citizen-soldier. Others objected to the bill because its proposed invalid corps copied European models. "Thucydides," writing to the *Philadelphia Aurora,* asserted that bill was a "wretched imitation of the [British] establishment of pensioners." Rather than rejecting the concept of service pensions, however, Thucydides proposed that the United States devise its own pension program. He advocated that Congress reform existing "pension laws and . . . support the disabled, aged and infirm of every grade." Political sentiment was growing to reward, honor, and aid America's veterans with pensions. Whether to include the militia and how to create a uniquely American program were stumbling blocks to codifying the veterans' new cultural status into a privileged social rank.

Philadelphia Aurora, 1 January 1816; 6 January 1816; 13 January 1816.

83. *Journal of the 28th House of Representatives of the Commonwealth of Pennsylvania,* 128.

84. *Journal of the 27th House of Representatives of the Commonwealth of Pennsylvania,* 527–28.

In 1812 Pennsylvania provided up to $40 annually to veterans of the army who were "unable to earn a living by labor" because of "bodily infirmity" and who were ineligible for a federal disability pension. *Laws of the Commonwealth of Pennsylvania,* 369–70. In 1813 and 1814, Pennsylvania liberalized its relief program for impoverished Continental

Army veterans. Legislation passed in 1813 and 1814 lowered the service requirement from three years to one year and replaced the rigid poverty line—possession of an estate valued at less than $50—with a discretionary guideline, "does not possess property sufficient to maintain him." The law continued to authorize the state orphans courts to appoint guardians to administer the pensions for helpless recipients. Ibid., 523–24.

85. Pennsylvania's legislative committee on veterans' pensions reported that the proposed increase in benefits would cost the state about $18,000 annually because few of the 337 men currently on the rolls were eligible for the maximum payment and because death would soon reduce pension rolls. *Journal of the 27th House of Representatives of the Commonwealth of Pennsylvania*, 527–28.

4. SUFFERING SOLDIERS AND PUBLIC POLICY

1. *Richmond Enquirer*, 13 June 1817.

2. Hamilton, 6:13–14. Radcliffe, 8, 39–40. See also the *Hartford Connecticut Mirror*, 7 July 1817; *Wilmington American Watchman*, 12 July 1817; Ketcham, 126. Monroe, *A Narrative of Observation*.

3. Casualty figures for the battle differed. In *The Battle of Groton Heights* American casualties were given as 84 dead, 35 wounded and paroled, and 30 prisoners of war. Mark Boatner cited the casualties as 85 dead and 60 wounded, "most of them mortally." Boatner, 787–88. Howard Peckham stated that 85 were killed, 60 wounded, and 70 captured at the battles of Fort Griswold and its companion fort, Fort Trumbull. Peckham, 90.

4. The *Boston Gazette*, 17 September 1781.

5. The *New London Connecticut Gazette*, 7, 14 September 1781. The account of the battle published by the *New London Connecticut Gazette* appeared quickly in other newspapers. See the *Boston Gazette*, 17 September 1781; *New Haven Connecticut Journal*, 20 September 1781; the *Worcester Massachusetts Spy*, 13, 26 September 1781. An additional account of the battle appeared in the *Boston Gazette*, 17 September 1781 in a letter from a "militia officer" date 7 September 1781. For later published accounts see the *Battle of Groton Heights: A Story of the Storming of Fort Griswold and the Burning of New London*, 5–12, 20–30. This volume contains the account of the assault given by Rufus Avery, one of the defenders. See also Copp, 9–19; *Story of the Battle of Fort Griswold*, 10–26; Rogers, ed., 14–30.

6. Ibid.

7. Information on the Avery family and their role at the battle at Fort Griswold was compiled from the following sources. Avery, 168–69, 258–59, 264–67. Sweet, 37, 57–60. *Collections of the Connecticut Historical Society*, 8:120, 267–78. *The Pension Roll of 1835*, 1:14. Ebenezer worked as a tailor "in a room of his own dwelling house" near the fort for the rest of his life. Both men became invalid pensioners after the war. Parke used his pension to support an aged aunt, Thankful Avery, in exchange for her farm upon her death. Aunt Thankful lived to be 100, which led Parke to comment to his son that "'it was the poorest speculation I ever made in my life.'" In August 1814, Parke then in his seventies gained notoriety when he volunteered for militia duty to fight the British who were bombarding nearby Stonington Point.

8. *Hartford American Mercury,* 8 July 1817.

9. Hamilton, 6:26–27; Ammon, 373–79; Ketcham, 126. Newspapers reprinted speeches and occasionally commented on the tour, almost entirely with praise and approval. *Hartford Connecticut Mirror,* 7 July 1817; 14 July 1817; 11 August 1817; *Hartford American Mercury,* 17 June 1817; 1 July 1817; 8 July 1817; 15 July 1817; 22 July 1817. Periodicals such as the *National Register* closely followed the tour. See, for example, the *National Register* 3 (7 June 1817), 367–68; (21 June 1817), 398–400; 4 (27 September 1817), 202–04.

10. Radcliffe, 24; 18, 19, 23–24, 32; Risjord, 157–59; Ammon, 345–46; Cress, 173. *Hartford American Mercury,* 8 July 1817.

11. *Hartford American Mercury,* 24 June 1817. John Quincy Adams later described Monroe as one of a "unique race of men . . . in whose bosoms the love of liberty had been implanted from their birth." J. Adams, 7–8, 16.

12. Ammon, 368.

13. Historian Ralph Ketcham wrote that Monroe modeled his presidency after Washington's "patriot king—the image and the reality of the national patriot." Monroe's administration, according to Ketchum, was "the high water mark of the republican intention . . . to blend [a] public-spirited, harmony-loving Augustan world view with the self governing ideals of the New World." Ketcham wrote that Monroe was, next to Washington, "the most nonpartisan chief executive in American history." Ketcham, 4, 124. Monroe had long held nationalist views. In 1788, during Virginia's debate to ratify the federal Constitution, he told delegates that he supported a vigorous national government because of his ideal to "collect the citizens of America . . . [and] lay aside all those jarring interests, arrange them under one government and make them one people. . . ." He called this "an ideal not only elevated and sublime, but equally benevolent and humane." In his March 1817 inaugural address Monroe repeated those ideas. "Discord," he said, "does not belong to our system. . . . [Americans] constitute one great family with a common interest." He pledged to "promote this harmony, in accord with the principles of our Republican Government . . . to advance . . . the best interests of our Union. . . ." In that address he recalled that the nation had experienced "severe trials" in the War of 1812 but he observed that the country enjoyed the "blessings" of "happiness" and "prosperity," and that it had an opportunity to preserve the "virtue and enlightening . . . the minds of the people. . . ." Monroe, *Some Observations on the Constitution,* 7, 11, 19, 23. Risjord, 2–10, 88–95, 116–17. McCoy, *The Last of the Fathers,* 39–83.

14. *Annals of Congress,* 15th Cong., 1st sess., 12, 19.

15. Glasson, 1–3, 20–53; Bodenger, 27–28.

16. *Boston Columbian Centinel,* 10 December 1817. See also, Ibid., 20 December 1817; *Richmond Enquirer,* 27 December 1817; *Federal Republican and Baltimore Telegraph,* 30 December 1817; Myers, 216.

17. James Young, 90.

18. Members of the Military Committee included Bloomfield; Samuel Smith (1753–1839) of Maryland, who was a prominent Republican and who had fought at Long Island and Monmouth and wintered at Valley Forge; James M. Wallace of Pennsylvania; Philip Reed and Philip Stuart from Maryland; Thomas Hall from North Carolina; and John Rhea from Tennessee. *New Jersey American Watchman,* 10 December 1817; *DAB* 1:386; *DAB* 9:341.

19. Mark Lender and James Kirby Martin note that Bloomfield always took "pride in his military service [and] took the lead in framing relief legislation for revolutionary war veterans. . . ." Lender and Martin, 23–28.

20. "HR 8: A Bill to Provide for Surviving Officers and Soldiers of The Revolutionary Army," *Bills and Resolutions of the House of Representatives and the Senate* (Library of Congress, 1964) 15th Cong., 1st sess. 1817–1818. *Annals of Congress,* 15th Cong., 1st sess., 445.

21. Prior to 1904 veterans' disability pensions were directly tied to service-related injuries. In 1904 Theodore Roosevelt changed that principle by ordering any Civil War veteran over the age of sixty-two be considered "disabled one-half in ability," and at sixty-five years old two-thirds disabled, and fully disabled at age seventy. In 1907 this order was written into pension legislation that "gave precise boundaries to age-related dependence." Haber, 112.

22. Howard Peckham used the total number of casualties to arrive at a "tentative guess of 200,000 men in service at one time or another . . ." during the Revolutionary War. Peckham, 133. The figure of 70,000 men alive in 1817 is my estimate based on the number of Peterborough soldiers who survived until 1817. That just over 20,000 men received a pension under the 1818 Pension Act, and another 33,000 men received a pension under the 1832 act, seems to confirm my extrapolation from the Peterborough figures. Glasson, 95.

23. *Vermont Intelligencer,* 30 March 1818.

24. *Boston Columbian Centinel,* 20 December 1817.

25. "Our Revolutionary Patriots," *Federal Republican and Baltimore Telegraph,* 30 December 1817.

26. *Philadelphia Aurora,* 27 December 1817.

27. *Annals of Congress,* 15th Cong., 1st sess., 1817, 491, 492. Bloomfield's estimates and extrapolations indicate the growing desire to change statistics from their use in 1800 as "any sort of descriptive fact about the civil relations of men" into a more quantitative measure that "meant that the benefits of republicanism were most readily demonstrated by appeals to quantitative facts, notably of demographic or economic character." Patricia Cohen, 150–51.

28. *Am. St. P.: Military Affairs* 2:473–74; John Forsyth of Georgia called the "graduation of pay according to rank . . . a work of unnecessary detail." *Annals of Congress,* 15th Cong., 1st sess., 505.

29. Possibly Harrison's motion reflected the general's resentment toward militia, which resulted from his failed campaign in 1812 to recapture Detroit from the British. On the eve of that battle, militia forces whose enlistment terms had expired left camp. Furious and embarrassed, General Harrison called off the attack. Ibid., 492–93; Stagg, 213–26.

30. *Annals of Congress,* 15th Cong., 1st sess., 497–99.

31. Ibid., 497–99.

32. Ibid., 498–99, 511. Another amendment, which Congress defeated, proposed to restrict benefits to soldiers who served at least one year. Another rejected amendment proposed using six months as a minimum service requirement. See ibid., 492–93, 509, 511; "HR 8," *Records of the United States Senate, 15th and 16th Congress, Amendments to HR Bills and Committee Papers for Military Affairs Committee* NA; see also *Boston Columbian Cen-*

tinel, 31 December 1817; *Wilmington American Watchman,* 24 December 1817; 27 December 1817; 31 December 1817. *Annals of Congress,* 15th Cong., 1st sess., 507.

33. *Annals of Congress,* 15th Cong., 1st sess., 492.

34. Ibid., 505–7.

35. Ibid., 511.

36. Ibid., 509–12. The motion to recommit received 57 votes out of possibly 150 votes. The number of votes opposed was not recorded.

37. The amendment specifying troops raised by Congress or the states does not appear in the *Annals of Congress.* The House bill with the change of language appeared in Senate documents on the bill. "H.R. 8" *Records of the U.S. Senate, 15th and 16th Congress: Amendments to H.R. Bills and Committee Papers for the Military Affairs Committee,* NA.

38. The ambiguity and flux in the nation's military structure during the Revolution, compounded by incomplete military service records, made it likely that nearly every surviving male of military age during the war could still lay claim to the pension. Fred Berg, 139–42. Boatner, 262–64.

39. *Federal Republican and Baltimore Telegraph,* 6 February 1818.

40. HR 8 Amendments, 12 January 1818; *Records of the U.S. Senate, 15th and 16th Congresses, Amendments to HR Bills and Committee Papers for Military Affairs Committee,* NA.

41. Lowrey, 87–95; *Annals of Congress,* 15th Cong., 1st sess., 139–40, 141, 153, 158; 148–49. Banning, *The Jeffersonian Persuasion,* 70–90.

42. *Annals of Congress,* 15th Cong., 1st sess., 158; 147–49; 156, 158.

43. Ibid., 148–50.

44. Ibid., 141–42.

45. Ibid., 144–47, 143–47, 155.

46. Ibid., 145–46.

47. Ibid., 154, 147.

48. Ibid., 147, 156–57.

49. Ibid., 141, 148–50, 156–58.

50. Ibid., 151–52.

51. Ibid., 191, 197.

52. Ibid., 200, 159.

53. Following the defeat of Barbour's motion, Rufus King withdrew his amendment to limit the bill to half-pay pensions for Revolutionary officers. Ibid., 192–94. King said he was "almost alone" in supporting his motion to award half-pay pensions to officers "and therefore abandoned the project." King turned his attention to "shutting out the militia" from the bill. Rufus King to Jeremiah Mason, 21 April 1818, and Rufus King to C[hristopher] Gore, 18 November 1818, in King, 6:143, 173.

King's appraisal of the pension bill appeared in a letter to Christopher Gore. King wrote that the pension bill embraced "only those who from their reduced circumstances stand in need of public support—it will relieve the alms & poor houses but the officers who have been able to bear up against adversity and to hold their standing in society, will with much reluctance avail themselves of this provision, and these are the persons who stand in most need of help." King to Christopher Gore, 26 February 1818, *Rufus King Papers,* The New York Historical Society.

54. *Annals of Congress,* 15th Cong., 1st sess., 198.

55. Ibid., 191.

56. Ibid., 140, 197.

57. Ibid., 197.

58. *Annals of Congress,* 15th Cong., 1st sess., 211.

59. Shaw Livermore, 13–14.

60. Belisarius (A.D. 505–565) was a Roman general who was repeatedly called from private life to save Rome from the barbarians. Gibbon described Belisarius, who had risen from being the son of Thracian peasants to being a Roman general, as a selfless, loyal, diligent, brave, daring, sincere soldier whose "spirit . . . animated" his troops. His appearance, Gibbon wrote, "attracted and satisfied the eyes of the people. His lofty stature and majestic countenance fulfilled [Roman] expectations of a hero; the meanest of his fellow citizens were emboldened by his gentle and gracious demeanor. . . ." Despite his victories over the barbarians, Belisarius was disgraced, humiliated, and impoverished by a jealous emperor, Justinian, and his spiteful wife, Theodora. Instead of honor and rewards for saving Rome, Gibbon wrote, Justinian and Theodora "received him with cold ingratitude; the servile crowd, with insolence and contempt. . . ." He was stripped of his wealth and, according to legend, blinded and forced to live as a beggar. Gibbon, 4:117–88, 283–87.

    For the first American editions see Edward Gibbon, *The History of the Decline and Fall of the Roman Empire* (Philadelphia: Robert Carr, 1804–1805) and Edward Gibbon, *The History of the Decline and Fall of the Roman Empire* (Philadelphia: Abraham Small, 1816).

61. The bill providing St. Clair with a pension was introduced in the House on 30 January 1818 and approved in early February after a debate marked with "ardor and unusual eloquence." The bill produced controversy over the amount of the pension. On 5 February 1818, the House rejected annual pensions of $960, $900, $840. By a four-vote margin, 75 to 71, the House approved a pension of $720. Efforts were made in the Senate to kill the House bill and cut the award in half. Nevertheless, on February 20, by a 21 to 10 margin, the Senate approved the House bill. Six of those voting against the St. Clair bill also voted against the final version of the Revolutionary War Pension bill. They included Barbour, Smith, and Macon—the Old Republicans who believed service pensions were inconsistent with Revolutionary republican principles. *Annals of Congress,* 15th Cong., 1st sess., 173, 176, 200, 212, 214, 831, 849, 851–53. Unfortunately there is no record of the House and Senate debates and there are only a few newspaper commentaries on that debate.

62. *New Hampshire Patriot,* 24 February 1818. *Annals of Congress,* 15th Cong., 1st sess., 831, 849, 851–53, 866. *Richmond Enquirer,* 21 February 1818.

63. For newspaper references to Belisarius see the *Philadelphia Weekly Aurora,* 16, 30 March 1818. These editions of the *Aurora* carried articles from other newspapers, such as the *New York Evening Post,* that cited Belisarius.

64. For Goldsborough's comments see *Annals of Congress,* 15th Cong., 1st sess., 195–96. James Barbour said it was impossible to provide for all under the House bill. For comments on economic constraints see Ibid., 140. Also see Macon's comments and Goldsborough's discussion of the expected costs of the program, Ibid., 159, 195–96. Copies of the Senate versions of the bill and hand-written amendments exist. See H.R.

8 *Records of the U.S. Senate,* 15th and 16th Congress NA. For the Senate vote on the bill
   see *Annals of Congress,* 15th Cong., 1st sess., 221. Barbour, Macon, and Smith voted
   against the bill.
65. *Annals of Congress,* 15th Cong., 1st sess., 497–99, 1108–09, 1698.
66. In two related actions the Senate voted not to accept applications under the Invalid
   Pension Program. Invalid pensioners who wanted an increase in benefits were encouraged to transfer to the new pension program. *Annals of Congress,* 15th Cong., 1st Sess.,
   384–85. The petition for half pay for officers was denied and officers were told that their
   demands were covered by the new act. *Am. St. P.: Military Affairs* 2:591. The Society of
   Cincinnati members responded by hiring a lobbyist, William Jackson, an officer and
   Federalist who Jefferson had removed from office. Jackson was offered a percentage of
   the pensions awarded should he be successful. In March 1818 Jackson submitted a new
   petition to Congress laying out the officers' claims. He calculated that the public owed
   the officers $42 million in arrears for unpaid pensions promised in 1783. Jackson's lobby
   failed. Jackson.
67. *Annals of Congress,* 15th Cong., 1st sess., 2518–19.
68. To recall, the War of 1812 had forced the nation to reconsider how it could arouse and
   sustain the spirit of '76 because appeals to patriotism had proved an unreliable means to
   muster troops and mobilize the people. Stagg, 147, 162–67, 193–95, 225–26, 231, 251, 254–
   59, 263, 270–77, 337, 366–68, 437–38, 456, 501–9. One response to this dilemma, expressed in nationalist writings, was a call to the nation to reward its soldiers with honors
   and even pensions. For example, in October 1813, the *Examiner,* a "Federal Republican"
   journal dedicated to protecting "our republican institutions," announced its forthcom-
   ing articles describing the "exploits of AMERICAN HEROISM" with the proposal
   that financial rewards be given to soldiers as an expression of the nation's gratitude. The
   nation must never forget, the *Examiner* told its readers, "that as liberty is essential to the
   internal happiness of a state so in national virtue and valour consists the great security of
   that liberty; and that national gratitude is best displayed in bestowing *substantial rewards* on brace and honorable men." *Examiner* 1 (25 October 1813), 1.

5. THE PENSION SCANDAL, 1818–1820

1. Newspapers reporting Fourth of July celebrations recorded that citizens especially honored veterans and paid tribute to Congress for passing the pension act. In Dracut,
   Massachusetts, celebrants toasted the veterans, the nation, and the pension act: "May
   their declining years be solaced by the gratitude and generosity of their country." In
   Morristown, New Jersey, a Fourth of July toast paid tribute to the pension legislation
   and Congress: "The National Legislature: binding up the wounds of the veteran
   soldier . . ." Similar toasts were given in Port Breeze and Norristown, Pennsylvania, and
   in Madison, Indiana. *New York National Advocate,* 7 July 1818; *Boston Patriot and Daily
   Chronicle,* 14 July 1818; *National Intelligencer,* 17 July 1818, 1, 11 August 1818. See also
   Aurora, 6, 27, 30 July 1818; 11 August 1818 for similar toasts from Beaufort, South
   Carolina; Pittsburgh, Pennsylvania; Stubenville, Ohio; and Mercer County, Kentucky.
   National Intelligencer, 4 July 1818. The *New York National Advocate* (7 July 1818) reported
   that seventy thousand people celebrated the Fourth of July in New York City with
   "uncommon enthusiasm and ardor."

Peter Kean (1788–1828), a banker and leader in civic affairs in Elizabethtown, New Jersey, observed that "America had not degenerated" since the Revolution. He insisted that the nation was on the threshold of a new era in the arts, sciences, politics, prosperity, and civic virtue. He told his listeners gathered in the Presbyterian church in Connecticut Farms, New Jersey, that the "Age of Reason and Philosophy . . . is past and it is our happy lot to witness the commencement of an age of common sense and piety. . . ." He cited the pension for the "virtuous efforts of the 'war-worn veterans' . . . [who] were almost forgotten," as proof of his optimism. Kean, *An Oration July 4, 1818*, 4–8. For information on Kean, see Thayer, 218–19.

Francis Calley Gray (1790–1856), a lawyer and Harvard graduate, told Boston celebrants that the genius of the Revolution and the ancestors' cause was to be found in their "FEELINGS, MANNERS, and PRINCIPLES" and proposed that they guide the creation of a national identity in literature, science, and education. Gray, *An Oration July 4, 1818*, 5–9, 20–22. For information on Gray, see Palmer, *Harvard Alumni*, 120–21.

Sounding a similar theme, Henry Laurens Pinckney (1794–1863), a member of the South Carolina legislature and son of Revolutionary hero Charles Pinckney, celebrated the "propitious" times of prosperity, peace, and emerging national greatness in his Fourth of July oration in Charleston. He said that the "descendants of patriots are not unworthy of their origins . . . [and] the progress of our country has overthrown the theories and ridiculed the ignorance of Europe." The pension act had helped the United States become a nation of superior virtue, "happiness and harmony." Pinckney, *An Oration July 4, 1818*, 3, 6, 21. *BDAC*, 1460.

2. *New York National Advocate*, 8–10 July 1818; Charles Royster, *A Revolutionary People at War*, 124–26. For accounts of Montgomery's burial see *Niles Weekly Register*, 25 July 1818; *New York Columbian*, 9 July 1818; *Aurora*, 9 July 1818. That fall, the *North American Review*, in its review of Benjamin Franklin's *Memoirs*, promised more revelations that showed "the intellectual prowess, high efforts of virtue, and willing and generous sacrifices" of Revolutionary War soldiers. Those soldiers were guided, the *North American Review* continued, with a "real spirit of patriotism, and an ardent and intelligent love of liberty." The soldiers had suffered and had acted without "hope of any personal reward," to fulfill the "cause of their country." The *North American Review* 7 (September 1818), 310–11.

3. One soldier's appearance was compared to that of an Egyptian mummy because he looked so "fresh and lifelike." *Niles Weekly Register*, 18 April 1818, 150; 25 April 1818, 135.

4. *Niles Weekly Register*, 27 June 1818, 312.

5. Fourth of July orator, Benjamin Gleason, speaking before celebrants in Charlestown, Massachusetts, in 1819 credited the nation's happiness with the public's satisfaction for paying its debt of gratitude to revolutionary soldiers. He portrayed the Revolutionary war veteran, "with bleached locks . . . bowed down with the weight of years . . . resting on his staff with one hand, and in the other holding a *Pension Certificate*." Gleason, continuing his romantic image of the pensioner, depicted the veteran's children observing his "smile seated in his fearless brow, [which] indicated much happiness and gratefulness to be remembered and to be rewarded." Gleason imagined the veteran telling the story of the Revolution to his children, and when done he "dropped a tear of gratitude [as he mentioned the name of] St. Clair [and spoke of] . . . national credit and

honor. When speaking of the times, the name of Monroe was uttered with benediction." Gleason, *Anniversary Oration July 1819*, 9–10. See also Sampson, *An Oration 4 July, 1818*.

6. Hemphill, 2:xlvi–liii.

7. Ibid., xlvi–liii, 46–47, 113, 165, 192, 199, 216–17, 219, 266. John C. Calhoun to John J. Crittenden, 18 March 1818, *GCCP*, 5:121, RG 15, NA. For additional discussion of departmental procedures see *GCCP*, 5:10–11, 15, 16, 42–45, 61, 81, 122, RG 15, NA.

8. Bodenger, 27. Pension Office to General Joseph Bloomfield 24 March 1818, *GCCP*, 5:108, RG15, NA. Pension Office to William Allen, 8 April 1818, *GCCP*, 5:147, RG15, NA. Pension Office to William Rich, 8 April 1818, *GCCP*, 5:147, RG15, NA. Pension Office to S. Hall, 20 April 1818, *GCCP*, 5:172, RG15, NA. John C. Calhoun to Thomas R. Peters, 3 July 1818, *GCCP*, 5:296, RG15, NA. James L. Edwards to Jonathan Dayton, 2 April 1819, *GCCP*, 6:383, RG15, NA.

9. William Wirt to John C. Calhoun, 26 March 1818, *GCCP*, 5:109–10, RG15, NA.

10. Heman Allen to John C. Calhoun, 30 April 1818, *ROSW*, RG107, NA. Allen quoted the "gentleman" as saying that the "more rigid this law is constructed and conducted, the more popular it will be, [but] it will be a very unpopular law from the unforeseen effect it will have on the treasury." Heman Allen to John C. Calhoun, 14 May 1818, *ROSW*, RG107, NA.

11. Heman Allen to John C. Calhoun, 14 May 1818, *ROSW*, RG107, NA. *GCCP*, 5:280, RG15, NA.

12. Gardner, 162–63. Information on Edwards is scant. He joined the Marine Corps in June 1811 and was decorated with a silver metal for his part in Decatur's capture of the British ship *Macedonian* in October 1812. Edwards left the service in 1816. In June 1818 he was appointed the principal clerk in the War Department's pension office and essentially became its commissioner. In 1833 he officially became the department's first commissioner of pensions, a position he held until 1850. Bodenger, 39–40.

13. John Fisher to John C. Calhoun 11 May 1818, *ROSW*, RG107, NA. Fisher named the two officers, Capt. Peter Jaquett and Dr. George Monro. An examination of the pension files revealed no application from Monro and that Jaquett did not apply under the 1818 act, but that he did receive a pension under the 1828 act, an entirely different piece of legislation. It could be that Fisher acted on a rumor or that once warned, the department simply returned Jaquett's and Monro's applications. Peter Jaquett, Pension File, S46500, RG15, NA.

14. Pension Office to G. Merrill, 8 April 1818, *GCCP*, 5:148, RG15, NA; John C. Calhoun to Benjamin Tallmadge, 9 April 1818, *GCCP*, 5:153–54, RG15, NA; Pension Office to Titus Hosman, 10 April 1818, *GCCP*, 5:157–58, RG15, NA. For the department's ruling on the service eligibility of state troops see James L. Edwards to John C. Calhoun, 10 January 1820, *GCCP*, 8:112–22, RG15, NA. For the department's interpretation of the nine-month term meaning nine consecutive months of service, see James L. Edwards to John C. Calhoun, 30 January 1819, *GCCP*, 6:205–07, RG15, NA. For the department's ruling on the ineligibility of deserters, see James L. Edwards to John C. Calhoun, 18 February 1819, *GCCP*, 6:273, RG15, NA. For a ruling on militia ineligibility, see George Boyd to Arthur McLane, 4 April 1818, *GCCP*, 5:139, RG15, NA; James L. Edwards to W. Thomas Love, 3 March 1819, *GCCP*, 6:387, RG15, NA; James L. Edwards to Dudley Chase, 3 March 1819, *GCCP*, 6:388, RG15, NA.

15. *Am. St. P.: Military Affairs* 2:683–84. George Boyd to Major Lyon, 22 July 1818, *GCCP,* 5:274–75, RG15, NA.
16. Edwards was forced to defend his narrow interpretation of service eligibility to Calhoun, who was pressured by Congress to loosen those strict rules. Edwards had ruled that men who had enlisted with Washington in June 1775 and were discharged in December 1775 were not eligible for the pension even if they reenlisted and continued in service for two additional months. Edwards had ruled that these men had not served a single term of nine months. In his view Congress's use of the word "term" indicated its intent to include only soldiers who served one enlistment of at least nine consecutive months. In the disputed cases of soldiers who began in Washington's army in June 1775 and continued under arms in January and February 1776, Edwards argued that these men had served two terms, one of seven months and a second of two months, and therefore were ineligible for the pension. James L. Edwards to John C. Calhoun, 30 January 1819, *GCCP,* 6:205–07, RG15, NA; James L. Edwards to John C. Calhoun, 18 February 1819, *GCCP,* 6:273, RG15, NA. In another instance Edwards cited evidence from the *Journals of the Continental Congress* to support his ruling that soldiers in three Rhode Island regiments did not meet the service requirement. "Congress never recognized" these regiments as part of the Continental establishment. James L. Edwards to John C. Calhoun, 10 January 1820, *GCCP,* 8:112–22, RG15, NA.
17. James L. Edwards to David Johnson, 9 October 1818, *GCCP,* 15:397, RG15, NA. James L. Edwards to John C. Calhoun, 18 February 1819, *GCCP,* 6:273, RG15, NA. James L. Edwards to John C. Calhoun, 22 December 1819, *GCCP,* 8:75–76, RG15, NA. George Boyd to Joseph Bloomfield, 6 April 1818, *GCCP,* 5:144, RG15, NA; George Boyd to Benjamin Tallmadge, 9 April 1818, *GCCP,* 5:153–54, RG15, NA. James L. Edwards to Thomas Waties, 22 November 1819, *GCCP,* 8:15, RG15, NA. For additional comments on the nine-month service requirement, see James L. Edwards to John C. Calhoun, 30 January 1819, *GCCP,* 6:205–07, RG15, NA.
18. Although in April Calhoun had ordered states to send these military records, nine states had not complied by the time Edwards became the chief clerk. George Boyd to the governors of New Hampshire, New York, Pennsylvania, Delaware, Massachusetts, Virginia, North Carolina, South Carolina, and Georgia, 21 April 1818, *GCCP,* 5:176, RG15, NA. James L. Edwards to Theodore Fowler, 12 August 1818, *GCCP,* 5:314, RG15, NA. James L. Edwards to Jonathan Branch, 4 September 1818, *GCCP,* 5:347, RG15, NA. Edwards sent a list of sixty-four names to Maryland's auditor, R. Lockerman, to certify that they had served in that state's regiment of the Continental Army. James L. Edwards to R. Lockerman, 11 October 1818, *GCCP,* 5:392–93, RG15, NA.
19. James L. Edwards to Alex Atkins, 14 January 1820, *GCCP,* 8:136, RG15, NA. James L. Edwards to Henry Wilson, 18 January 1818, *GCCP,* 6:168, RG15, NA; James L. Edwards to Thomas Hance, 17 December 1818, *GCCP,* 6:106, RG15, NA. James L. Edwards to R. M. Johnson, 21 November 1818, *GCCP,* 6:18, RG15, NA. James L. Edwards to John C. Calhoun, 22 December 1819, *GCCP,* 8:75–76, RG15, NA.
20. John C. Calhoun to Heman Allen, 24 May 1818, *Confidential and Unofficial Letters Sent by the Secretary of War, 1814–1835,* RG107, NA. John C. Calhoun to John Fisher, 28 May 1818, Ibid. See also Hemphill, 2:312.
21. William Wirt to John C. Calhoun, 26 March 1818, *GCCP,* 5:109–10, RG15, NA.
22. *Am. St. P.: Military Affairs* 2:683–84.

23. George Boyd to Edward Evans, 27 May 1818, *GCCP,* 5:212, RG15, NA.

24. George Boyd to William Brayton, 1 June 1818, *GCCP,* 5:215, RG15, NA.

25. *Boston Columbian Centinel,* 15, 22 April 1818.

26. *Richmond Enquirer,* 24 February 1818 and 10 April 1818. For additional criticisms of the poverty provision as an injustice to veterans see *Philadelphia Weekly Aurora,* 16 March 1818; *Philadelphia Aurora,* 6 January 1818; *Federal Republican and Baltimore Telegraph,* 30 December 1817, 6 February 1818.

27. *Philadelphia Aurora,* 6, 9 July 1818.

28. John C. Calhoun to Thomas R. Peters, 3 July 1818, *GCCP,* 5:292–97, RG15, NA; Pension Office to A. Harris, 8 August 1818, *GCCP,* 5:305, RG15, NA.

29. John C. Calhoun to Thomas R. Peters, 3 July 1818, *GCCP,* 5:292–97, RG15, NA. Glasson, 61–62; Bodenger, 23–24.

30. John C. Calhoun to Thomas R. Peters, 3 July 1818, *GCCP,* 5:292–97, RG15, NA.

31. John C. Calhoun to J. Moore, 8 August 1818, *GCCP,* 5:307–08, RG15, NA. James L. Edwards to David Johnson, 9 October 1818, *GCCP,* 5:397, RG15, NA. George Boyd to A. Harris, 8 August 1818, *GCCP,* 5:305, RG15, NA. James L. Edwards to Taber Clark, 19 November 1818, *GCCP,* 6:6, RG15, NA.

32. *Amherst New Hampshire Farmers' Cabinet,* 18 July 1818. This paper reprinted the story from the *New York National Intelligencer.*

33. *Niles Weekly Register,* 16 October 1819, 99–100. George Boyd to Edward Bangs, 14 July 1818, *GCCP,* 5:267–68, RG15, NA. Daniel Woodward's property was valued at $5,256, and John Scott of Peterborough, New Hampshire, was reported to have an estate valued at $4,000. James L. Edwards to John C. Calhoun, 8 December 1819, *GCCP,* 8:72, RG15, NA; James L. Edwards to Salma Hale, 5 January 1820, *GCCP,* 8:104–05, RG15, NA. James L. Edwards to John C. Calhoun, 11 January 1819, *GCCP,* 6:174, RG15, NA. James L. Edwards to James Enott, 6 January 1820, *GCCP,* 8:106, RG15, NA; James L. Edwards to Abraham Morrison, 7 January 1820, *GCCP,* 8:107, RG15, NA; James L. Edwards to Jesse Ballard, 13 January 1820, *GCCP,* 8:131, RG15, NA. James L. Edwards to Joseph Buffum Jr., 16 December 1818, *GCCP,* 8:61, RG15, NA. James L. Edwards to Stephen Cantrell, 9 December 1819, *GCCP,* 8:47, RG15, NA; James L. Edwards to John Colbey, 8 December 1819, *GCCP,* 8:44, RG15, NA; James L. Edwards to John C. Calhoun, 21 December 1819, *GCCP,* 8:72, RG15, NA.

   The department's liberal view of "reduced circumstances" reflected Calhoun's objection to the law's poverty provision and his inclination to view it as a reward by a grateful nation for meritorious service, and not as poor relief. Nevertheless, he opposed awarding the pension to wealthy veterans.

34. James L. Edwards to John C. Calhoun, 8 December 1819, *GCCP,* 8:72, RG15, NA; James L. Edwards to Salma Hale, 5 January 1820, *GCCP,* 8:104–05, RG15, NA. John Scott, Pension File W24918, RG15, NA.

35. *Niles Weekly Register,* 16 October 1819, 99–100.

36. Elisha Tracy (1766–1842), a Norwich, Connecticut, lawyer, militia colonel, state legislator, and neighbor of Huntington, recalled in a "private and confidential" letter to Calhoun that the Huntington exposé had caused "the great clamour, respecting the operation and practice" of the pension program and had nearly caused Congress to repeal the program. Elisha Tracy to John C. Calhoun, n.d., Ebenezer Huntington,

Pension File S36595, RG15, NA. Tracy claimed that the Huntington scandal was directly responsible for "the subsequent act [1820 amendment] which removed so many from the pension list. . . ."

37. This section on Huntington is a synthesis of the following sources. Ebenezer Huntington, Pension File S36595, RG15, NA. Abbey, 121–22. Ebenezer Huntington to Calvin Goddard (Mayor of Norwich, Connecticut) 10 August 1824, and "Declaration," 14 August 1824, Connecticut State Archives, Ebenezer Huntington MSS.

38. *Hartford Connecticut Times*, 31 August and 7 September 1819.

39. Ibid.

40. Ibid., 31 August, 7, 14 September 1819.

41. Ibid., 14 and 21 September 1819.

42. Cray, "Major Andre," 389. In this award-winning article Gray shows how the controversy, which occurred between 1817 and 1831, over honoring the three captors of Major Andre reflected and added to the rise of the image of the common man in the age of Jackson.

43. *Hartford Connecticut Times*, 31 August 1819; 7, 14, 21 September, 1819.

44. Caulkins, 419–20; Nafie, 151–52; "Letters of Ebenezer Huntington," 702–29. *Who Was Who in America, 1607–1896*, 338–39; *BDAC*, 1100. James L. Edwards to Ebenezer Huntington, 24 December 1818, *GCCP*, 8:82, RG15, NA; James L. Edwards to Ebenezer Huntington, 31 January 1820, *GCCP*, 8:171, RG15, NA. *Hartford Connecticut Times*, 31 August 1819, and 7 September 1819. James L. Edwards to Ebenezer Huntington, 24 December 1819, *GCCP*, 8:72, RG15, NA; James L. Edwards to Ebenezer Huntington, 31 January 1820, *GCCP*, 8:171, RG15, NA. On 5 January 1820 the department stated that it required "proof under oath" from anyone reported to be on the rolls "improperly or fraudulently." James L. Edwards to Salma Hale, 15 January 1820, *GCCP*. 8:104–05, RG15, NA; James L. Edwards to Abraham Morrison, 7 January 1820, *GCCP*, 8:108, RG15, NA; James L. Edwards to John Ellis, 8 January 1820, *GCCP*, 8:110, RG15, NA.

45. *Hartford Connecticut Times*, 21 September 1819. The article from the *Trenton True American* appeared in the *Daily National Intelligencer*, 4 December 1819.

46. *New York Evening Post*, 15 December 1819. Similarly, the *Hartford Connecticut Mirror* stated that nothing in the pension act should "call forth censure of anyone unless [it is] that [the] relief it affords to the remaining few of the band of patriots to whom under providence, we are indebted for the richest blessing ever bestowed upon man, is much too small." It added that no one should "complain" about the pension during "hard times," referring to the depression that caused the federal government to go deeper into debt to pay benefits to its suffering soldiers. The paper concluded: "The cup of life has been bitter enough. Let us not add wormwood to the dregs." *Hartford Connecticut Mirror*, 20 September 1819.

47. *Niles Weekly Register*, 15 January 1820, 321. See also a letter from "Aristide." *Hartford Connecticut Times*, 26 October 1819.

48. *Annals of Congress*, 16th Cong., 1st sess., 851–55.

49. Ibid., 734, 747–48. The report probably reflected Bloomfield's assessment of the program. The report spared Congress or his committee any blame for the scandal. In a later session of the House, Bloomfield spoke about the history of the act, "the different features it assumed, and its ultimate shape, compared with the bill originally reported

by the committee, of which he was chairman, to show that the committee are innocent of having produced the embarrassments which had grown out of that act." His frustration with the scandal was reflected in his statement that he had been willing to give the House an opportunity to repeal the program. Ibid., 1651.

50. Ibid., 892. Philip Barbour of Virginia later included equalized pay as part of a larger reform package that was sent to committee for study. Ibid., 1651.

51. Ibid., 1654.

52. There was no roll call on Cannon's motion. Ibid., 892.

53. Ibid., 1706–07. Cannon offered an amendment to include militia in the pension program as a matter of "equity and justice." He told his colleagues that he was ready to vote for a direct tax to pay for it. Opponents to Cannon's proposal told the House that including the militia would increase program costs by $5,000,000; "only five or six members [rose] in support of it." Cannon's maneuver appeared to be aimed at discrediting the law rather than incorporating the militia into the program. Following the defeat of Cannon's proposal, the debate in the House focused on the law's repeal. Ibid., 1706.

54. Ibid., 1707–09.

55. Ibid., 1708.

56. Ibid., 1707–08.

57. Ibid., 1707–09. Wood, 332.

58. *Annals of Congress,* 16th Cong., 1st sess., 1651–54.

59. Ibid., 1653–54.

60. Ibid., 1713–15.

61. Ibid., 1651. The proposal reduced benefits for officers from $240 to $180 per year and cut benefits for enlisted from $96 to $72 a year. This amendment also prescribed an oath of poverty in which the applicant swore that he had not disposed of his property to become eligible under the act (although he was allowed to pay his just debts) and that he did not have "power to command the means for obtaining for myself (or myself and family, as the case may be,) a comfortable support for the time being. So help me God."

62. The House considered an amendment that made the poverty oath, then only required by a departmental rule, part of the law. Ibid., 1650–52.

Official reports on many of the proposals to amend the law are sketchy. For example, on 21 March 1820 it was reported that the House considered "various amendments . . . proposing all sorts of modifications of the present law; all which were successively rejected." Ibid., 1662. On March 22, Ezekiel Whitman, a Federalist from Massachusetts, proposed that the secretary of war be authorized to investigate the estates of all recipients and ordered to remove any with annual incomes greater than $100 or who had estates valued at more than $200. Ibid., 1669–70. Barbour's motion to add a poverty line was defeated (no roll call). Ibid., 1703. Whitman followed with an amendment to tighten enforcement against fraud by requiring the attorney general in each state, or federal marshals, to submit the list of pensioners before grand juries in their districts at every court session to see if the jurors "had any knowledge . . . of any person" not entitled to a pension. These persons were to be reported to the secretary of war for investigation and possible criminal action for perjury. Whitman also wanted to stop "agents" from exploiting veterans when they applied for pensions. He proposed that any agent who withheld any part of a veteran's pension to collect his fee be liable to criminal charges. He also proposed that anyone who "wittingly and willingly [testified] falsely in relation to any matter and thing required by this act" be charged with a criminal offense. Ibid., 1703–05.

63. On 23 March 1820 the House appointed a special committee composed of Ezekiel Whitman; Philip Barbour; Alney Mclean, Republican from Kentucky; Samuel Foote, Independent from Connecticut; Thomas Forest, Independent from Pennsylvania; and Giden Tomlinson, Republican from Connecticut to draft a compromise of the various proposals to reform the program. Ibid., 1673. For the Committee's report, see Ibid., 1700–1701.

64. Butler observed that "many men of influence were receiving a pension under the law of March 1818 and he could not consent to loan money nor lay a tax upon the people, while such men were enjoying the bounty of the Government, contrary to the true intent of the law under which they received it." Ibid., 2222.

65. Ibid., 2582–83.

66. The *New York Daily Advertiser* stated that the amendment set all pensioners under "severe and suspicious restriction." The paper admitted that some fraud had been committed, but not enough to justify the means test. The paper feared that the require-ment to expose poverty "to the world" would deter many eligible veterans from apply-ing for the benefit to avoid the humiliation of pauperism. The *Daily Advertiser* story was quoted from the *Connecticut Courant*, 30 May 1820. The *New Hampshire Patriot* story cited here was found in the *Exeter Watchman*, 8 August 1820.

67. *Niles Weekly Register,* 15 July 1820, 345.

68. Hemphill, 2:xlvi–liii. U.S. Bureau of the Census, 2:1104.

6. PENSION ADMINISTRATION, 1820–1823

1. *Peterborough Town Book,* 1816.

2. Leiby, 35–47. Also see Cray, "Poverty and Poor Relief," 10, 107, 167–68, 703–18.

3. *Keene New Hampshire Sentinel,* 15 July 1820. *Boston Columbian Centinel,* 26 July 1820.

4. *Keene New Hampshire Sentinel,* 15 July 1820. The *Sentinel* also reported that Fourth of July celebrants in nearby Fitzwilliam, New Hampshire, had toasted the veterans and praised the pension act for honoring them: they deserved "the highest rewards of a free people. May the evening of their days be happy. . . ."

5. *Dedham Village Register,* 21 July 1820.

6. *Boston Columbian Centinel,* 12 August 1820. Reprinted from the *Hartford Connecticut Mirror.*

7. *Boston Columbian Centinel,* 26 July 1820.

8. Ibid. The paper stated, "They cannot long be encumbered upon the government: their number is daily decreasing—their exit is rapid."

9. *Dedham Village Register,* 21 July 1820.

10. The incident in New Haven, Connecticut, was reported in the *Dedham Village Register,* 21 July 1820. The court's charge included fees for the clerk who drafted the forms and for the sheriff for opening the court. The paper reported that opposition to the court's fees was not the result of partisan feelings—it "was confined to no party." Townspeople "burst" with "indignation" when the judge called the public's demand for "gratuitous services" an "insult" to the court.

Other states set fees to prevent greedy lawyers and judges from exploiting veterans. The New Hampshire legislature, which empowered courts of common pleas to hold special sessions to process applications, mandated that judges receive no more than fifty cents per application and clerks be paid one dollar for drafting the application and for assessing veterans' estates. See the *Exeter Watchman*, 4 July 1820.

11. Reported in the *Dedham Weekly Register*, 8 July 1820.

12. Charles R. Hale, *Hale Collection of Connecticut Newspaper Marriage and Death Notices* consists of abstracts of death notices recorded from Connecticut newspapers by WPA project workers. The volumes are arranged by individual newspapers, and obituaries appear in chronological order. My survey of the abstracts from these papers revealed that death notices for officers remained unchanged in this period. In general they were written, "Patriot and Officer." Death notices for enlisted men changed from "Revolutionary War Patriot" or "Revolutionary Soldier" to "Revolutionary Pensioner." Only in one instance prior to 1820, the death notice for Hovey Preston, did I find the epitaph "Pensioner." See *Norwich Currier*, Hovey Preston "Revolutionary War Pensioner," 23 June 1819 in *Hale Collection*, 56:161. See *Hartford Courant* death notices for Capt. Joseph Burgess, 6 June 1820, and for privates George Seymour, Robert Westland, and Thomas Wygatt, 25 July 1820 in *Hale Collection*, 27:461, 464. Also see John Peat, "Rev. Soldier, Pensioner," 13 April 1821 in *Hale Collection*, 35:63. Also see *Norwich Courier* and *Litchfield Democrat* in *Hale Collection*, 56:142–94; 64:226.

13. Max Weber's "ideal type" bureaucracy remains the starting point and framework for understanding bureaucracy. Weber wrote that modern bureaucracies, unlike earlier forms of administration, have a clear division of labor based upon specialized functions and hierarchical authority. A bureaucracy, according to Weber, follows a consistent set of explicit and publicized rules, treats like cases alike, processes cases objectively and impartially, and protects its employees against retribution for decisions unfavorable to powerful individuals or groups. Weber wrote that this "type of rational, legal administrative staff is capable of application in all kinds of situations and contexts. It is the most important mechanism for the administration of every profane affair." Henderson and Parsons, 324–41.

Sociologists have claimed that bureaucracy, so defined, emerged in the late nineteenth century and developed fully in the twentieth century as an underpinning for modern government. Etzioni-Halevy, 10–40; La Palombara, 34–61. For a comprehensive discussion of bureaucracy, see Blau and Meyer, 18–23, 27–29, 163–68.

For a discussion of the principle of justice based on treating like cases alike see Hart, 153–63.

14. John C. Calhoun to John Wright, 10 March 1821, *GCCP*, 10:316, RG15, NA. James Edwards to G. Black, U.S. attorney for Boston, 24 June 1823, *GCCP*, 13:310, RG15, NA.

In another case, Edwards ordered Nathan Hicks prosecuted because "discrepancies" in his claim prompted suspicion of fraud. Hicks was dropped from the rolls but later received a pension under the 1832 act, which awarded pensions to veterans who had served in the militia or in state regiments. For other examples of department prosecutions, see Edwards to Capt. Jonathan Parker, 8 August 1823, *GCCP*, 13:400, RG15, NA, and Jonathan Parker, Pension File S41039, RG15, NA.

15. Jacob Grove, Pension File W23130, RG15, NA. John C. Calhoun to E. Shepley, U.S. attorney in Maine, 10 March 1821, *GCCP*, 10:289, RG15, NA. For other examples of

community watchdogs, see Moses Howe, Pension File S45375, RG15, NA, and John C. Calhoun to E. Elliot, 8 July 1823, *GCCP,* 12:336, RG15, NA. In Howe's case, townsmen later repented and admitted that their charges of fraud against the veteran were in error.

16. James L. Edwards to Stephen Cantrell, 15 March 1823, *GCCP,* 13:114, RG15, NA; Edwards to Cantrell, 29 July 1823, Ibid., 383–84; Edwards to J. Crutcher, 29 July 1823, Ibid., 384–85. Crutcher was the new agent. Edwards explained that pension agents did not receive a salary but "were paid two percent on all sums paid the pensioners together with all expenses necessarily incurred." He told Crutcher that in 1821 Cantrell had managed to steal $1,025 by paying pensioners with discounted notes.

17. Pension claims made under the 1818 act did not require detailed service records. As a result "descriptions of war time action are sketchy or non existent." Dann, xvi. Veterans reapplying under the 1820 act did not have to restate or clarify their service records. They summarized, or referred to, the enlistments, rank, and length of service that had been stated in their original applications for the pension. First-time applicants, however, described their military service in more detail.

18. James L. Edwards to R. V. Vose, 15 July 1820, *GCCP,* 9:246–47, RG15, NA; Edwards to George Comwell, 10 June 1820, *GCCP,* 9:197, RG15, NA; Edwards to Amos Elmaker, 11 August 1820, *GCCP,* 9:300–301, RG15, NA.

19. Calhoun and Edwards declared that all dependent veterans, those unable to "live without [some] aid of public or private charity," were eligible for the pension. Calhoun to Bloomfield, 18 June 1820, in Hemphill, 5:265.

On 9 May 1820 Wirt responded to Calhoun's request for an interpretation of the law's indigent provision, "in such indigent circumstances as to be unable to support himself without the assistance of his country." Wirt thought that "it was the intention of Congress" to define indigence as follows: "the income of the property is inadequate to the support of the applicant." *Am. St. P.: Military Affairs* 2:837. In 1819 Congressman William Burwell of Virginia had asked Calhoun's advice in formulating a bill that would reflect Congress's wish to make the law's indigence requirement more precise by indicating a "degree of poverty [a] little above pauperism." Calhoun to Burwell, 13 February 1819, in Hemphill, 3:572. Edwards to Amos Elmaker, 11 August 1820, *GCCP,* 9:300–301, RG15, NA.

20. James L. Edwards to Judge John Davis, 23 May 1820, *GCCP,* 9:141, RG15, NA. James L. Edwards to Elijah Luce, 31 May 1820, *GCCP,* 9:163, RG15, NA. See Amasa Mills, Pension File S36148, and *GCCP,* 9:394, RG15, NA. James L. Edwards to John Taylor, 4 December 1820, *GCCP,* 10:54, RG15, NA. Also see the following for discussion of the criteria to define indigence: Hemphill, 5:95, 108, 265, 468; *Annals of Congress,* 16th Cong., 1st sess., 854.

21. At first, to deter swindlers, the department ruled that claimants could not deduct any debts from the value of their estates. Calhoun explained to Congressman Bloomfield that because "the law is silent as to debts due from the pensioner," allowing one claimant to deduct his debts would "constitute a general rule, under which the public would be liable to be greatly imposed upon." Calhoun to Bloomfield, 18 June 1820, Hemphill, 5:265. Also see Wirt to Calhoun, 19 February 1821, Ibid., 5:637. Calhoun to John Cocke, Chairman of the House Committee on Revolutionary Pensions, 7 February 1822, Ibid., 5:677.

22. Joseph Spalding, Pension File S43169, RG15, NA.

23. John C. Calhoun to Lt. Francis Duclos, 23 March 1821, *GCCP,* 10:325, RG15, NA. John C. Calhoun to Hon. T. J. Rogers, 1 January 1822, Ibid., 11:423, RG15, NA. *BDAC,* 1682.

24. Hemphill, 5:287–88.

25. Hemphill, 5:xx, 94–95, 108, 273, 468, 565, 637; 6:677. See also *Am. St. P.: Military Affairs* 2:824. James L. Edwards to Congressman John Taylor, 4 December 1820, *GCCP,* 10:54, RG15, NA. Taylor was Speaker of the House. Edwards was responding to the House's inquiry about department eligibility standards. Edwards repeated the criteria and underscored two points. First, besides paupers the program enrolled applicants who were not "maintained by public or private charity" and, second, the two-hundred-dollar estate level was only a guideline and not a poverty line. He told Taylor that ninety-four applicants with estates valued at between two and four hundred were continued on the rolls but that no applicant with an estate more than four hundred was enrolled.

   For departmental procedures for evaluating applicants, see James L. Edwards to Judge John Davis, 23 May 1820, *GCCP,* 9:141, RG15, NA; Edwards to Elijah Luce, 31 May 1820, *GCCP,* 9:163, RG15, NA; Edwards to Thomas Paris, 1 June 1820, *GCCP,* 9:166, RG15, NA. See *New Hampshire Sentinel,* 29 July 1820. The paper stated that based upon the names of accepted and rejected applicants, the department appeared not to accept any applicant with more than two hundred dollars in property. In January 1821 Edwards wrote Congressman William Lowndes that no claim "whatever with property greater than four hundred dollars had been continued on the rolls." Edwards to Lowndes, 15 January 1821, *GCCP,* 10:171, RG15, NA.

26. David Smiley, Pension File S43164, RG15, NA. Smiley was restored under the 1823 law. His 1823 application showed that his estate had been reduced to $55.84. Between 1820 and 1823 he had sold his farm to his son, John, and used the money to pay his debts. By 1824 Smiley was taxed for only his poll, $1.30. *Peterborough Tax Lists.*

   His applications in 1820 and 1823 stretched the truth in order to make Smiley's claim more appealing. He cited his own ill health and that of his wife but both enjoyed longevity. Smiley died in 1855, and his wife died in 1842. He stated that he had supported his daughter and granddaughter. His daughter, Elizabeth Skinner, lived on a farm contiguous with the family farm. However, it is possible that she helped to keep her parents' household. When Smiley died in 1855 his estate was valued at just over $400. He owned no real estate but had issued loans of nearly $400. A. Smith, *History of Peterborough,* part 2:255–58. J. Smith, *Peterborough New Hampshire in the American Revolution,* 337–40. David Smiley, HCPCR, 08944.

27. John Scott, Pension File W24918, RG15, NA.

28. Ibid.

29. Ibid. For other material on this episode, see Jonathan Smith, 311–15. Scott's success at finally getting the pension was noted by family members. His sister, Sally Scott Loomis of Alstead, New Hampshire, wrote to her son, "Uncle Scott has gone onto [*sic*] to the pension list." Letter, Sally Scott Loomis to Anthony Loomis, 30 January 1831, Sally Scott Loomis Papers.

   Neighbors and family cooperated with the veteran's efforts to get on the rolls. He was aided by Jeremiah Smith to divest his property until its value fell below the department's standards. For example, in 1829 Scott was taxed $4.85 for half the farm he shared with his son, William. Having been rejected for the pension, he transferred more property to his son. In 1830 John Scott's tax fell to $2.95. He was taxed on one poll, one horse, and nine cows. William was taxed $9.95 for the farm. After receiving the pension the veteran began to accumulate property. By 1834 John Scott was taxed $10.18 for an estate that included nineteen acres, one horse, two oxen, one carriage, and $500 he had loaned at interest. William's estate had also grown, however, suggesting that the entire family benefited from John Scott's pension. He was taxed $14.64 for the family farm. When John Scott died in 1847 his estate was worth approximately $4,000. It included $1,195.10 in real estate and more than $2,500 in principal and interest on twelve notes. *Peterborough Tax List.* John Scott, *HCPCR* 08785.

30. In 1820 Jeremiah Greenman, a former lieutenant who served eight years in the Continental Army, was sixty-two years old, had no occupation "that he can follow," owned a one-hundred-acre "upland hilly farm," a log cabin and barn, two old horses, and tools— all valued at $294.28. Greenman's wealth was above the conventional property guideline (two hundred dollars) but within discretionary limit (four hundred dollars) for admission to the rolls. His eight years of service as an officer stood him in good favor. Nevertheless, Greenman appealed to compassion. He said he was in poor health, in debt, and living off "the charity of his children." Greenman wrote that his current distress was the direct result of his sacrifices and suffering as a soldier, "having devoted my youthful days to the service of my country I was deprived of the opportunity which young men generally possess, of acquiring any mechanical art or perfecting myself in any profession." He appealed to his congressman, Levi Barber from Ohio, to intervene on his behalf. To no avail, Barber urged the department to keep Greenman on the rolls. Jeremiah Greenman, Pension File W23146, RG15, NA. No explanation was found for discontinuing Greenman. Greenman was restored under the provisions of the 1823 act and later enrolled under the 1828 act, which granted full pay to officers who remained in service until the end of the war.

31. See Greven, 222-68; Ditz, 82-118.

32. Amasa Mills, Pension File S36148, RG15, NA. James L. Edwards to Amasa Mills, 20 October 1820, *GCCP,* 9:394, RG15, NA. Abel Brown, 18-29, 73-85, 91-104. Mills was described as a "good officer and a useful citizen." Ibid., 99. Barber left an estate valued at $4,023.30, which included 140 acres and an extensive library that contained *Life of Voltaire, Condorcet on the Mind, Voltaire's Dictionary, Independent Whig,* and a bound volume recorded as *Political Pamphlets.* Simsbury Probate District, Town of Canton, 1826, *Probate Packets* 224, Connecticut State Archives, Reel 1312. Barber and members of the Mills family were in the upper half of town taxpayers. In 1817, in the only tax record for this period found for Canton, Barber paid a tax of $1.82. Gardner Mills paid $1.92 and Amasa's other son, Amasa Jr., paid $1.87 in taxes. *Canton Tax Records* RG62, Box 20, Connecticut State Archives. Amasa "sold" the farm on 23 April 1818 to Gardner for four hundred dollars but did not legally transfer title until 24 December 1818, well after he received the pension. Town of Canton, Connecticut, *Deeds,* 3 vols. (1809-1843), 2:372. Also see *Connecticut Census, 1820* Connecticut State Archives, 579.

33. Amasa Mills, Pension File S36148, RG15, NA. The affidavits were signed by James Humphrey, justice of the peace; Capt. Moor Humphrey, selectman; Ephraim Mills, a representative to the Connecticut general court; and William H. Hallock, town constable.

34. Amasa Mills, Pension File S36148, RG15, NA. Brown, 92–99. In 1817 Simeon Mills ranked among Canton's lowest taxpayers because he was living on his father's farm. It appears that Simeon and his first cousin, Gardner Mills, cared for their respective fathers. However, because his father received a pension, Gardner gained possession of his legacy prior to his father's death. Simeon had to wait for his father's death in 1818 to inherit his patrimony. In 1819 and 1820 Simeon and Gardner were engaged in minor land transactions to adjust the boundaries of their adjoining farms. See Canton Connecticut *Deeds*, 2:170, 173.

35. Mills's documentation was richer than was found in similar cases and provided deeper insight into controversy over the department's administration of the program. Cases similar to Mills's were resolved in the veterans' favor, which strongly suggests that had Mills lived longer, he would have received his pension.

36. Supporting testimony also discredited Vandeburgh's accusers, whose motives were impugned by charges of political hostility caused by a dispute "at the election." Vandeburgh's accusers were overheard vowing to keep Vandeburgh from receiving his pension. John Vandeburgh, Pension File S42600, RG15, NA. John C. Calhoun to J. Southerland 10 March 1821, *GCCP*, 10:296, RG15, NA. Southerland was the U.S. attorney in the northern district of New York with an office in Albany.

John Williams was also under investigation. He had claimed to be a laborer who couldn't work. Williams reported that he lived with his wife, age sixty, and that he had only $33.31 in personal property. However, townsmen charged that he had "settled his estate upon his sons with an obligation from them to pay him twenty dollars a year and support him and his wife during their lifetime without their being obligated to labor." The accusers stated that Williams's sons "are in affluent circumstances" and that they persuaded their father "to destroy the obligation" to support him to take the "oath that he has no means of support." Williams's allies responded that the veteran had transferred property to his sons for debts owed them and that his sons had no legal obligation to support their father. Williams continued on the rolls. John Williams, Pension File S34542, RG15, NA. John C. Calhoun to George Black, 19 March 1821, *GCCP*, 10:313, RG15, NA. Black was the U.S. attorney located in Boston.

37. James L. Edwards to Ethen Shepley, 3 November 1820, *GCCP*, 10:7, RG15, NA. Robert Hanscom Pension File S35401, RG15, NA.

38. Edwards to Josiah Harris, *GCCP*, 9:398–99, RG15, NA. Also see Edwards to Sen. Walter Lowrie, 18 May 1821, *GCCP*, 11:70, RG15, NA. Calhoun explained the policy to Congressman John Cocke, chairman of House Committee on Revolutionary Pensions as follows: "It is proper to observe that the opinion of the Attorney General has not been constructed to extend to prevent reconsideration where there are any grounds to believe that an error has been committed in dropping a pensioner from the list." Calhoun to Cocke, 17 December 1821, *Am. St. P.: Military Affairs* 2:837.

39. Benjamin Frye, Pension File S33260, RG15, NA; *GCCP*, 10:256, RG15, NA.

40. John Atkins, Pension File S37690, RG15, NA. *GCCP*, 10:267–68, RG15, NA. In a similar case Connecticut Sen. James Lanman helped Kimball Prince get reinstated on the pension rolls. Prince's first petition appealed for compassion to persuade the department to reinstate him. After Prince failed in his first attempt, neighbors submitted a second petition on his behalf. Besides appealing to compassion, the petition averred

that Prince had overvalued the worth of his property in the original schedule. The petitioners claimed that his estate was actually worth "less than 200," instead of its assessed value of $353.67, and that his house was out "of repair and unfinished." Prince was admitted to the rolls. Kimball Prince, Pension File S36245, RG15, NA. *GCCP,* 10:256, RG15, NA.

41. Solomon Ames, Pension File S45503, RG15, NA. *GCCP,* 10:267–68, RG15, NA.

42. Sen. David Morril of New Hampshire said that Calhoun had subverted the intent of the law with "unreasonable and unjust" rules that prevented rejected applicants from obtaining the pension even if they became poor. Rep. Elias Keyes, a Revolutionary veteran from Vermont, accused Calhoun of deleting more men from the rolls than were killed "in any one battle of the Revolution." *Annals of Congress,* 17th Cong., 1st sess., 1362; Ibid., 17th Cong. 2nd sess., 310–11.

43. For example, Connecticut Congressman Gideon Tomlison submitted a special bill to enroll veteran Joseph Bunnell. Tomlison described Bunnell's reduced circumstances and told his colleagues that a special bill was necessary because he had been informed by Calhoun that he lacked power to restore Bunnell to the rolls. Joseph Bunnell, Pension File S36448, RG15, NA. *GCCP,* 10:267–68, RG15, NA.

44. *Annals of Congress,* 17th Cong., 2nd sess., 313, 735, 1409–10. Between 1820 and 1823, Congress continued to debate the pension program. Congressmen introduced numerous proposals ranging from repealing the program to expanding it to include militiamen. For these debates, see *Annals of Congress,* 17th Cong., 1st sess., 409, 710–20, 726, 1133–34, 1362–72. *Annals of Congress,* 17th Cong., 2nd sess., 10–12, 182, 199, 262–64, 367, 278–85, 307–14, 721–23, 726, 734–35, 1141, 1371–72.

45. The Senate had postponed consideration of the House bill until it received Secretary Calhoun's full report on pension enrollment and costs. On 22 April 1822 the Senate, without debate, voted twenty-six to twelve to indefinitely postpone discussion of the House bill. Ibid., 408–09.

Calhoun's 8 February 1823 report to the Senate favored supporters of a more liberal law. That report showed a decline in program enrollment and reductions in costs since the passage of the 1820 pension bill. Calhoun reported that since August 1818, the department had received a total of 27,948 claims, including 2,039 new applications submitted following the passage of the 1820 amendment. He stated that 18,880 veterans had been admitted to the rolls under the 1818 act. Following the passage of the 1820 amendment, 4,221 pensioners had left the rolls either because of death or for failure to submit a schedule of property in compliance with the new law. A second group of veterans, amounting to 2,328 applicants, had submitted schedules of their estates but had been denied the pension because of excess wealth. He reported that as of September 1822 the number of pensioners totaled 12,331. His report showed that program costs had risen from $104,900 in 1818 to $1,811,328 in 1819 but had declined to about $1,500,000 since 1820.

Calhoun reported program costs as follows: 1818—$104,900; 1819—$1,811,328; 1820—$1,373,849; 1821—$1,200,000; 1822—$1,833,936. The 1822 figure was unusually high because it contained a $451,836 expenditure due to delayed payments to veterans who had been enrolled in 1821.

Calhoun recommended that the Pension Committee consider amending the law to begin payments from the date of the applicant's enrollment rather than 4 March 1820. Calhoun believed that eliminating retroactive payment would reduce expenses and diminish the temptation for fraud. He wrote to the Committee's chairman, James Noble, "the prospect of receiving the amount of three years' stipend, at one time, opens a door to attempts at fraud, and is no small inducement for many to dispose of their property with a view of receiving pensions." Letter, John C. Calhoun to James Noble, chairman of the Senate Committee on Pensions. *Annals of Congress* 17th Cong., 2nd sess., 199.

46. Ibid., 279–84.

47. Ibid., 279–84.

48. Ibid., 308, 311.

49. The discussion of Rufus Burnham was composed from a wide range of sources. See *Massachusetts Soldiers and Sailors of the War*, 865–66; *Vital Records of Boxford*, 18, 121; Perley, *The Dwellings of Boxford*, 70–71, 227–28; Perley, *The History of Boxford*, 219–31, 237–38, 283, 384; *An Abstract Valuation of Real and Personal Property in the Town of Boxford for the Year 1855*, 18; Essex, South District Court, *Grantee Deeds*, Docket 142, 169; Docket 143, 188; Essex, South District Court, *Grantor Deeds*, Docket 141, 215; Docket 142, 20; Docket 151, 146; Essex, South District Court, *Probate Court Records*, Documents 4155, 4163, 55942; and Pension File S34125, RG15, NA. Burnham's claim resembled that made by many of the twenty thousand veterans who applied for the pension. He was the head of a nuclear household (45 percent of the cases), infirm, and a landless farmer who had few possessions and was burdened with debts.

50. Within two years of the marriage, Seth and Caroline had their only child, Charlotte. In 1821 he was elected a selectman for Boxford and served in that capacity for one year. By 1855, the year he left Boxford, Seth had acquired a taxable estate valued at $2,400.

51. J. L. Edwards to Jeremiah Nelson, U.S. representative from Massachusetts, 7 May 1822, in Rufus Burnham, Pension File S34125, RG15, NA. Sixteen percent of the applicants in 1820 were rejected, most because of excessive wealth. One third of these applicants were restored to the rolls under the 1823 amendment. Resch, "Federal Welfare for Revolutionary War Veterans," 171–95.

52. Rufus Burnham, Pension File S34125, RG15, NA.

53. As a measure of the program's success, Congress passed new laws awarding pensions, regardless of wealth, to nearly all Revolutionary veterans and also to their widows.

In 1828 Congress granted full-pay pensions to officers and men entitled to pensions under Congress's resolution of 15 May 1778. In 1832 full-pay benefits without regard to applicant wealth were extended to any veteran who had served a total of two or more years. Veterans who accumulated between six months and two years of service were eligible for partial benefits. In 1834 Congress awarded pensions to veterans' widows. In 1836 and 1838 it expanded coverage to widows by easing eligibility requirements.

Debate on the 1832 veterans pension bill also raised sectional and ideological issues that resembled those debated from 1818 through 1823. The debate lacked the intensity surrounding the 1818 act and its 1820 amendment, however. The new pension programs contributed to the growth of the department's pension bureaucracy. The unexpected flood of applicants, charges of "imposition," and high costs led to the creation of a separate Bureau of Pensions out of the War Department's pension office. James L. Edwards, head of the Office, became commissioner of pensions. Glasson, 73–93.

7. VETERANS, POLITICAL CULTURE, AND PUBLIC POLICY

1. Silas Russell, Pension File S45128, RG15, NA; Daniel Rider, Pension File W5705, RG15, NA; Henry Hallowell, Pension File S32800, RG15, NA; Henry Buzzell, Pension File S45529, RG15, NA; Joseph Stevens, Pension File S43175, RG15, NA; and, Reuben Clark, Pension File S12506, RG15, NA. Also see Christian Hubbert, Pension File S39754, RG15, NA. Hubbert said he was in "poor health."

2. Richard Hallstead, Pension File S44909, RG15, NA; Philo Phillips, Pension File S39013, RG15, NA; Israel Manning, Pension File S33043, RG15, NA; Icabod Beckwith, Pension File S34023, RG15, NA.

3. *Niles Weekly Register,* 26 February 1820.

4. To arrive at this figure, I divided total court-assessed wealth for applicants from New York by the number of people reported in the households of applicants from New York.

5. Abraham Taylor, Pension File W26508, RG15, NA.

6. Elijah Caswell, Pension File S34155, RG15, NA. See also the claim made by Daniel Stevens. Stevens had suffered from "chronic illness" and was placed in the Essex County, Massachusetts, poorhouse after exhausting his savings. The court reported that Stevens "still remains there and must until he again receives his pension." Poorhouse walls had separated Stevens from his wife, Sarah, whom Stevens married in 1784 and who lived to enjoy a widow's pension. Daniel Stevens, Pension File W4823, RG15, NA.

7. One such case was John Shearwin, age seventy-five, a penniless laborer from New Jersey who suffered from rheumatism. He reported that he was supported by a neighbor's charity. John Shearwin, Pension File S42290, RG15, NA.

8. Icabod Beckwith, Pension File S34023, RG15, NA.

9. Reuben Clark, Pension File S12506, RG15, NA. Also see the following:

Asher Russell was beset with infirmity and destitution. For ten years prior to receiving his pension in 1818, Russell, age sixty-six, had been supported by the town of Wethersfield, Connecticut. He claimed that if his pension was not continued, he would once again become a pauper. Asher Russell, Pension File S40368, RG15, NA.

The overseers of Hartford, New York, described James Graton, age seventy-three, as an insane pauper. The town also supported Graton's wife who lived apart from him. James Graton, Pension File R21885, RG15, NA.

Joshua Bedel, age seventy-nine, from Grafton County, New Hampshire, reported that he was penniless and suffered from poor health. Before receiving his pension, he had been a pauper and he would be one again if the pension was not continued. He reported that his children lived near him, but he claimed that they were too poor to assist him. Joshua Bedel, Pension File S45523, RG15, NA.

John Needham served as a private for almost the entire war in a Massachusetts regiment of the Continental Army. At the time of his application, he was penniless, blind, and infirm. His only means of subsistence was his pension. The court reported that "if it were not for the assistance he received from his country, he would become a charge upon the town. . . ." Needham was sharing living quarters with another person at the time of his application. John Needham, Pension File S43070, RG15, NA.

Ephrain Hiscox, a seventy-two-year-old shoemaker from Rhode Island, claimed to be disabled since 1805 and that he "cannot support himself if his pension is taken away." Ephrain Hiscox, Pension File S38827, RG15, NA.

10. Henry Buzzell, Pension File S45529, RG15, NA. For other examples see the following:
    Some solitary veterans anxiously reported being on the verge of pauperism and pleaded for the pension to prevent dependency. John Waid, a seventy-two-year-old laborer, told the department that he was penniless, in poor health, and unable to work. Without the pension the "town would be obliged to support me." John Waid, Pension File S35378, RG15, NA.
    Isaac Dicks, a widower and a penniless laborer, was still supporting himself. Dicks lived in Baltimore, Maryland, near his three daughters, one of them a widow, and his only son, an apprentice in a cotton factory. Although he had family nearby, he claimed, "I have no reason to expect or depend upon [them] for any aid[,] support or relief." He swore that his children were too poor to help him. Dicks stated that his advanced age and declining health had reduced his capacity to support himself. Isaac Dicks, Pension File S34748, RG15, NA.
    Richard Worsham, from Wilks County, Georgia, was a penniless, sixty-five-year-old former lieutenant in the Virginia Line. Worsham lived alone and was too old to work. He depended on aid from his six children who lived near him. Richard Worsham, Pension File S38478, RG15, NA.

11. Joseph Stevens, Pension File S43175, RG15, NA. Also see James Worren, Pension File S45452, RG15, NA; Thomas Abbe, Pension File S38105, RG15, NA.

12. In 1822 McGerry appeared before the court in Allegheny County, Pennsylvania, to apply for his pension. He told the court that in 1777 he had enlisted as a private and served throughout the war in a Pennsylvania regiment of the Continental Army. He reported that he was a laborer but could no longer work. McGerry was living with a twenty-year-old woman whom he claimed as his wife and their infant daughter who was three weeks old. McGerry testified that his young wife could no longer provide for the family. He also said that his son by another marriage could no longer aid them because he was poor and had seven children of his own to support. The court assessed the value of the veteran's property at twelve dollars. Once on the rolls, McGerry married (May 1823) the woman he claimed as his wife. Neal McGerry, Pension File, W8276, RG15, NA.

13. Silas Russell's circumstances resembled those of other veterans and their wives who claimed to be nearing dependency. Russell, age seventy-six, and his wife lived in Hillsborough County, New Hampshire. They had been cared for by their son. The veteran claimed to be "very infirm" and unable to work. He reported that his wife was "bed ridden." The old couple was penniless, and the court reported that their "son is now unable to render him a comfortable support." Silas Russell, Pension File S45128, RG15, NA.
    Much is known about Samuel Mitchell, whose appeal for the pension resembled Silas Russell's. Mitchell served two months in the militia, spent three years in the Massachusetts Line as a sergeant, enlisting in the fall of 1777 at age fifteen. A little more than a year after his discharge in 1780, Mitchell married a woman who was about four years younger than himself. In 1820 Mitchell, age 68, and his wife, "about 64," were disabled by rheumatism. He reported $35 in property, $158 in debts, and that he was unable to support his household because of blindness. Although Mitchell's children had assisted the couple since 1813, the court concluded that the children could no longer

be expected to aid their parents because they "are farm laboring people in debt," and they had all they could "do to get a living for themselves and families without aiding" their parents. Samuel Mitchell, Pension File W26262, RG15, NA.

Prior to its receipt, Reuben Crane, age seventy-six, a lame farmer living in Addison County, Vermont, and his wife, age sixty-six, were wards of their son. After receiving the pension under the 1818 act, Reuben once again became self-sufficient. Crane appealed for the pension to remain head of his household, which included his wife. Reuben Crane, Pension File, S38643, RG15, NA.

14. Judah Stevens, age sixty-six, a former private in the Massachusetts Line, who served from 1781 to 1783, reported assets worth eight dollars. For five years prior to receiving his pension in 1818 his wife, age sixty-two, had been supported by the town because he could not provide for her. Without the pension, she would again become a pauper. Judah Stevens, Pension File W22353, RG15, NA.

In August 1776, at age thirty-four, Samuel McGuin enlisted in the Continental Army and served as a private for just over three years. When he applied in 1822, McGuin was eighty years old and unable to work. His wife was much younger, age fifty-nine, but "very infirm." Between them they had no real property and an estate valued at thirty dollars. McGuin and his wife had lived on public relief since 1817. When the War Department made its Census of Pensions in 1834, Samuel McGuin was still alive. He had collected nearly $1,400 in the twelve years he had been a pensioner. Samuel McGuin, Pension File S45001, RG15, NA. Also see John Hubbell, Pension File, W9484, RG15, NA.

15. Job Hamblin, Pension File W10085, RG15, NA. Hamblin reported thirty dollars in personal property. For other examples, see the following:

Philip Travis, age sixty-two, a laborer from Greene County, New York, told the court that he and his wife, age fifty-six, suffered from rheumatism, owned property valued at twelve dollars, and that their eight children could not aid them. Travis stated that they were "gone from me," and "all [were] very poor," struggling to support their own families and "not one able to help me one cent to live." Philip Travis, Pension File S42525, RG15, NA.

John Smith had enlisted in a Maryland unit as a private at the age of thirty-four and served from 1777 until the end of the war. When he applied for his pension in 1825, Smith was eighty-two years old, living in Anne Arundel County, Maryland, with his wife, age sixty-five. He declared himself to be "in reduced circumstances." His total estate was valued at forty dollars and he received forty dollars annually from a military pension provided by the state of Maryland. He declared that his eight children were "in indigent circumstances" and unable to aid their parents. John Smith, Pension File W4060, RG15, NA.

Robert Hawes joined the Massachusetts Line of the Continental Army when he was twenty-two years old and served five years as a private. The war left him a partial invalid. He had received payments as an invalid veteran but surrendered that pension to receive increased benefits under the 1818 act. When he applied in 1820, Hawes was living in Worcester, Massachusetts. He worked as a farm laborer and blacksmith but claimed that he could no longer support himself and his wife, age sixty-nine. Hawes and his wife had three married children "and none able to assist" them. He owned a few tools and household items valued at twenty-five dollars. Robert Hawes, Pension File, S33290, RG15, NA. Also see Peter Wormwood, Pension File W22680, RG15, NA; and Jonah Garrison, Pension File W108, RG15, NA.

16. Bartholomew Stevens, Pension File W25074, RG15, NA. Despite their hardships, Bartholomew Stevens and his wife were probably more fortunate than many of their peers because, with the aid of the pension, one of their children had given them refuge and succor, and the veteran had retained his household and remained its head. For other examples see the following:

Nathaniel Pardee had served for seven years in the Continental Army. Infirm and penniless, Pardee, age sixty-one, his wife, age fifty-eight, and their daughter, age twenty-three, had moved into his son's home where each of them had their own room but took their board from their son. Nathaniel Pardee, Pension File S43795, RG15, NA.

Nathan Mann's household shared a house owned by his son and partially occupied by his son's family. Mann reported that for his part he had to support his wife, age sixty-five, and their unmarried son as well as provide aid to his "feeble" daughter-in-law and an infirm grandchild who were part of his household. Mann claimed that he was a farmer who suffered from rheumatism. He reported $30 in assets and $119 in debts. Nathan Mann, Pension File W9908, RG15, NA.

When Ephraim Stevens applied for his pension in 1820, he was a laborer living in Rutland, Vermont. He was in poor health. He and his wife, age fifty-two, lived with their son, age twenty-three, who was their principal source of support. Stevens claimed no real property, and assets worth only twenty-seven dollars. Ephraim Stevens, Pension File S41198, RG15, NA.

Jedidiath Russell was a sixty-seven-year-old widower living in Hillsborough County, New Hampshire, when he applied for his pension in 1820. He reported that he was infirm and no longer able to work as a farmer. Russell was living with his son, age twenty-six, who "maintained" him as well as supporting his own family. Jedidiath Russell, Pension File S45127, RG15, NA.

George Buyers had served about twenty months as a sergeant in a Pennsylvania regiment of the Continental Army. He had enlisted in the fall of 1776 at the age of nineteen. In 1820 Buyers, a widower, was living in Armstrong County, Pennsylvania, where he made a living as a blacksmith. Buyers claimed that declining health had diminished his capacity to be self-supporting. Previously, he had received a forty-dollar military pension annually from the state of Pennsylvania because of his poverty. His assets consisted of tools and household items amounting to ninety-six dollars in value. Buyers reported that he alternately roomed and boarded with his daughter's and son's families. George Buyers, Pension File S40768, RG15, NA.

In May 1778 Daniel Condit enlisted as a private in a New Jersey Line of the Continental Army. He had served as a "replacement" for nine months and had fought in the Battle of Monmouth. He did not reenlist in the army. At the time of his application, Condit was nearly blind and living with his son. Nevertheless, he continued to head a household composed of his wife and a daughter, age twenty. The old couple received help from their son and probably from their daughter. He reported that friends also assisted his family. More is known about Condit because of his wife's application for a pension following the death of her husband in September 1839. From her application we learn that in May 1785 he had married Mary Dodd, who was two years younger than himself. Their first child was born the following April. Mary had a child every two or three years—usually in the spring or fall—until 1801 when their last child was born. Seven of the nine children (seven boys and two girls) were alive in 1843, when their mother received her widow's pension. Daniel Condit, Pension File W449, RG15, NA.

William Worster was a seventy-five-year old blacksmith from York, Maine. Worster described himself as suffering from old age, "decrepitude and poverty," and unable to support himself. He reported that his wife, age seventy-seven, was in "tolerable" shape. He owned twenty dollars in personal property. He and his wife were "wholly dependent on the charity and benevolence of my son Samuel Worster with whom I live." William Worster, Pension File S35148, RG15, NA.

Similarly, Thomas Gratton reported that he and his wife, age sixty-seven, were living with their son who "is now unable [to support his parents] without assistance" of the pension. Thomas Gratton, Pension File S21773, RG15, NA.

17. Couples were far more likely to be burdened by debts than were solitary veterans. One couple in five reported debts compared to one out of ten solitary veterans. If all of their reported debts were deducted from their assets, the average value of their estates would decrease from $179 to $74.

18. Josiah Gary, Pension File S37003, RG15, NA. Gary joined the Continental Army in December 1775. He served as a private for one year and then returned to civilian life for the remainder of the war. In 1820 Gary, age sixty-four, who suffered from "palsy," lived in Windham County, Connecticut, with his wife, age sixty, and two children. His assets amounted to $1,900, including farmland, barn, house, tools, livestock, and household goods. He owed various people $140 and indicated that he owed about $2,000 to his son, age thirty, and his daughter, age thirty-three, for their "hard work for 10 years past" on the farm. He swore that both children wanted to be paid for their labor and that he was required either to give them the farm or sell it to raise cash to pay them. They had invested their labor to secure those assets; now they wanted to be paid off. In this case Gary's independence was threatened by his own children's demands to collect what was owed them.

Also see Joseph Hinshaw, Pension File W24425, RG15, NA. After enlisting in December 1776 at age fourteen or fifteen, Joseph Hinshaw served five years as a sergeant in the Massachusetts Line. In 1794 Hinshaw married a woman five years younger than himself. By the time of his application in 1820, he was living in Worcester, Massachusetts, and working as a tailor. He accumulated a sizable estate worth $2,943, but also managed to fall into even larger debt, which totaled $3,100. He had worked himself into a tighter financial bind through an arrangement with his son. Since 1812, when his son had turned twenty-one, he had worked for his father. They had agreed that should the son pay off the debts encumbered by his father, all the father's real estate would be transferred to the son. The transfer did not seem to be imminent, and the son appeared to pressure his father for payment. To make matters worse, Hinshaw and his wife had to continue to care for an "infirm" thirty-five-year-old daughter who lived with him, and two grandchildren, ages four and seven, who had been sent to live with them by a daughter whose husband had deserted her.

19. William Blair, Pension File S45296, RG15, NA. *Peterborough Tax List.*
20. Zachariah Cook, Pension File S42555, RG15, NA. He had served two and a half years in the Virginia Line as a private until the end of the war. The War Department refused to grant Cook a pension, probably because clerks deemed his assets adequate.

    Henry Hallowell, a fisherman, age sixty-five, from Lynn, Massachusetts, shared Cook's torment over impending bankruptcy and the breakup of his household. His carefully built financial structure, which had previously supported his household and aided his sons who lived apart from him, was near collapse. In 1820 Hallowell testified that he owned property valued at $448.50, a figure just above the means test's ceiling for eligibility. To support his claim that he was not wealthy, Hallowell tried to show the pension office that he was in imminent danger of becoming impoverished.

    Hallowell reported that he owned three-quarters of an acre of land, "part of a dwelling house . . . consisting of two back chambers," an "old shop," an "old barn, part of a cellar," and "one-half pew in a Methodist Meeting House." Hallowell stated that he had acquired some of this property through his first marriage. A second marriage added to his assets. Hallowell gained his second wife's part interest in a dwelling house, her four-fifths of an acre of land, her wood lot, and her salt marsh, which Hallowell leased for twenty-eight dollars a year. He also received twelve dollars annually by renting rooms and part of the cellar in his house.

    Hallowell claimed that he used his income from rents and fishing to support himself and his wife, and to aid his two married sons. He stated that both sons were poor and that one of them received alms from the town. Hallowell swore that his recent poor health undermined this intricate network of property, income, and aid to kin. He told the court that he had become "weak in body" and unable to earn as much money as usual from fishing. Furthermore, his wife's health had deteriorated and as a result, he implied, had diminished the household's viability. He forecast pauperism for himself and sons because he had to go deeper into debt to make ends meet. The pension office refused to award him a pension because he failed to pass the means test. In such cases, veterans would reapply for the pension after they fell below that line. Henry Hallowell, Pension File S32800, RG15, NA. Also see Michael Waggoner, Pension File S40636, RG15, NA.
21. Nearly two-thirds of the veterans heading nuclear household were under the age of sixty-five, the average of age of all claimants; only 5 percent of them were over the age of seventy-five. By contrast, a majority of solitary veterans were in their seventies; and, 15 percent of the veterans heading couple households were over the age of seventy.

    In general, veterans heading nuclear households reported seven times more wealth than solitary veterans and they reported 50 percent more wealth than couples. Nearly 25 percent of these veterans owned real property. By contrast, only 5 percent of solitary veterans and 20 percent of couple households reported owning real estate.
22. This amount was midway between the means test's cutoff point of $200 in assets and the department's discretionary ceiling of $400 for exceptional cases.
23. Jonathan Stevens, Pension File W2456, RG15, NA.
24. George Ewing, Pension File S35916, RG15, NA.
25. Peter Crapo, Pension File S43414, RG15, NA.
26. Solomon Cook, Pension File S43375, RG15, NA. In October 1775, when he was nineteen years old Cook enlisted as a private in a Massachusetts regiment of the Continental

Line. He had previously served seven months in a state regiment that laid siege to Boston. For other examples see the following: Ichabod Phillips had fought for about three years, 1781–1783, in a Massachusetts regiment of the Continental Army. At age fifty-five, Phillips headed a household that had two cycles of child rearing. His older children by an earlier marriage had left home, and his young wife was bearing more children. In 1820 Phillips was living in Kennebec County, Maine, with his wife, age thirty, an infant daughter, and two sons, ages eight and eleven. He told the court that he suffered from a rupture and could no longer work at full capacity. Although well off, by applicant standards, with $855 in assets—a house, land, livestock, tools, and household goods—Phillips claimed $300 in debts. He stated that trying to support his young family had further weakened his health. Ichabod Phillips, Pension File S36733, RG15, NA.

John Wellman had first enlisted as a private in a Connecticut regiment of the Continental Army in January 1777. He served various enlistments that totaled forty-four months of service. In 1820 Wellman reported that he had six dollars in assets and sixty-one dollars in debts. He told the court in Genesee County, New York, that he was a farmer but could not support his household because of "ague." Wellman lived with wife, age fifty-three, and six children, ages seven to twenty. Wellman had married in May 1787 and nine months later the first of their eleven children was born. After John Jr. came Ira, March 1790; Sally, April 1793; Lydia, July 1795; Barnabus, April 1798; Stephen, April 1800; Polly, June 1802; Samantha, May 1805; Barnibas, October 1807; Philemon, April 1810; and Philinda, November 1812. The last six of his children were living at home at the time Wellman applied for his pension. His son Ira had married twice, first to Philinda Perry in 1811 and then to Debrah Bradshaw sometime before the end of the decade. Wellman referred to Ira in his application. He said that the family resided in a "small, poor log house" on Ira's farm of 113 acres of rough land and ten acres of improved land. It was valued at over $850. Ira assisted his father and his household. In 1845 the family was still living in Genesee County. John Wellman had been dead four years, but his widow resided on Ira's farm until her death in 1854. Another son, Stephen, was living in Chatauqua County along with John Wellman's brother Barnabus. John Wellman, Pension File W18324, RG15, NA.

In 1820 William Kelly, age sixty, a cooper, told the court in Genesee County, New York, that infirmities had reduced his capacity to work and to support his young family. Kelly testified that his household was composed of his wife, age fifty, and four daughters, ages six, ten, twelve, and seventeen. He swore that he still provided for the eldest child and that the twelve-year-old daughter was ill and required medical care. The Kellys had few assets—a log cabin on their son's land and twenty dollars in personal property. William Kelly, Pension File S45443, RG15, NA.

William Russell, age sixty-four, an infirm farmer, and his wife, lived in Ostego, New York. Russell testified that their two resident daughters, ages nineteen and twenty-seven, cared for them. William Russell, Pension File S42221, RG15, NA.

27. John Wellman, Pension File S42317, RG15, NA; Jeremiah Purdy, Pension File W10937, RG15, NA. Also see the following:

In January 1776, at the age of seventeen, Dan Weller enlisted in a Massachusetts regiment of the Continental Army. He served at least two tours of duty totaling seventeen months and achieved the rank of corporal. In 1820 Weller, age sixty-one, was living in Washington County, New York. He was a landless farmer who suffered from infirmities. His assets amounted to sixty-eight dollars.

His wife's application for a pension revealed more about the couple and their family. Weller and his wife, Lucynda Treat, had been raised in Lenox, Massachusetts. She was born in December 1762 and at the age of seventeen married Weller, then age twenty. Between 1780 and 1807, Lucynda had eleven children, five boys and six girls. Ten of their children were married, the exception being their idiot daughter, Lucynda. Their daughters married just after turning twenty to men who were on the average six years older. Their brothers married at about the age of twenty-five to younger women whose average age was twenty-two years. By 1837 when Lucynda applied for her widow's pension, all of her children and their spouses were alive except for her daughter Marian, who died at the age of thirty, ten years after her marriage in 1816, and her son Henry, who died in 1836 at the age of thirty-eight. Dan Weller, Pension File W16466, RG15, NA.

28. Joel Atherton, Pension File W23472, RG15, NA. Atherton was seventeen years old in 1781 when he enlisted as a private in a Massachusetts regiment of the Continental Army.
29. Joseph Craven, Pension File S34612, RG15, NA. Craven had served through the entire war as a private in a New Jersey regiment of the Continental Army.
30. Claimants heading complex households were among the least poor veterans who applied for the pension. They averaged $280 in assets, and a large proportion (40 percent) owned real estate. Most (85 percent) of these veterans headed households that contained their own older children and young grandchildren, generally under ten years of age. Specifically, less than one out of three of these households contained children under the age of fifteen. Approximately 80 percent of these households reported children over the age of fifteen. As would be expected, these complex households contained more people than nuclear households. They averaged 5.1 people compared to an average of 4.6 people in nuclear households.

There were exceptions to the general profile. For example, Joseph Mann of Massachusetts reported that he was a sixty-year-old cordwainer who owned eighty-one dollars in assets. He headed a household that contained some of his own children, his son-in-law, and a grandchild. Joseph Mann, Pension File S33034, RG15, NA.

Only 1 percent of the claimants heading complex households reported nonkin living with them. As a group, they were the wealthiest applicants. Their assets averaged $500 in value and over half of them owned real estate. Typically, their households contained the veteran and his wife and one or two people living with them as hired help and caregivers. Rarely was one of their children living with them. For example, Joseph Hawes, age sixty-five, and his wife, age seventy-two, were poor, "weak," and in debt. They had hired their ten-year-old granddaughter "to live with [them]" and care for them. Joseph Hawes, Pension File S353596, RG15, NA. On the other hand, some who were quite poor had taken in lodgers or children to earn money. In 1820 Abner Mitchell, age seventy-two, and his wife, age seventy, a black couple living in Lunenburg, Massachusetts, were subsidized by the town to provide a room and board for two pauper children. The Mitchells reported six dollars in assets. Abner Mitchell, Pension File W15084, RG15, NA. Also see James Mitchell, Pension File S41877, RG15, NA.

31. Phineas Hamblett, Pension File S44407, RG15, NA.

Similarly, Job Manning claimed that he needed the pension to support his two orphaned grandchildren, both under the age of ten. Manning, age sixty-eight, and his "infirm" wife, age fifty-five, were a relatively prosperous couple living in Hillsborough County, New Hampshire. Manning was a cabinetmaker who owned his own lot and house. His total assets amounted to $434, but he reported $109 in debts. Job Manning, Pension File S44537, RG15, NA.

Other examples of veterans who received the pension are summarized below. In 1820 Joseph Mann, age sixty, lived in Norfolk County, Massachusetts. He reported that he was in "tolerable" health but that he was in precarious financial circumstances. He owned no real property, possessed personal property worth eighty-one dollars, and owed creditors ninety-nine dollars. He lived with his wife, age forty-eight, and four children. One of them was a young child and the others were daughters, ages fifteen, sixteen, and nineteen. The oldest daughter was "diseased" and the sixteen-year-old child was married. She and her husband and young child—an infant or toddler—had moved in with Mann and his family. Mann appealed for the pension because he believed that he could no longer support this complex household. Joseph Mann, Pension File S33034, RG15, NA.

Daniel Davis was twenty-five years old when, in April 1777, he enlisted in a New York regiment of the Continental Army. Three years later private Davis left military service. In 1820 he was living in Hamilton, Ohio, sixty-eight years old, a laborer, and unable to work because of rheumatism. He owned seventeen dollars in property. He was part of a complex nuclear household. His daughter and her husband had taken Davis and his family into their household. Four other children who lived nearby contributed to the support of their father and his family. Nevertheless, this network of aid had become inadequate. Davis reported that he was no longer able to support his wife, age forty-seven (married in September 1796), and three sons, ages seven, eight, and ten, one of whom was an "idiot." Daniel Davis, Pension File W3519, RG15, NA.

Nathaniel Hubbard, age fifty-six, and his wife, age fifty-one, maintained their household with the help of an older son, age twenty-three, who lived with them. In addition to that son, they also shared the household with another son, age fourteen, and a five-year-old granddaughter. Hubbard reported that he had worked as a common laborer in Plymouth, Massachusetts, but claimed to be debilitated and no longer able to work. His estate totaled $136 in real and personal property. Nathaniel Hubbard, Pension File S19350, RG15, NA.

Christian Hubbert was eighteen years old when he enlisted as a private in a Pennsylvania regiment of the Continental Army. He served for nearly four years. When he applied for his pension in 1820, Hubbert owned fifty-one dollars in personal property. He reported making one dollar a week as a laborer and receiving forty dollars a year from Pennsylvania under its program pensioning impoverished Continental Army veterans who had served in the state's regiments. He and his wife claimed to be in "poor health." Their household consisted of a daughter and her three young children. His daughter's husband was living in Virginia and although he sent some money to support his family it was not enough to meet their needs. Hubbert stated that he had to assist his daughter and her family. In addition to family circumstances, Hubbert stated that he had been disadvantaged by serving in the army. He wrote that he had lived his life in relative poverty since he had been unable to acquire property because he had left his apprenticeship as a carpenter to join the army. His application stated that his failure to learn a trade "has proved a principal cause of preventing him from acquiring property." Christian Hubbert, Pension File S39754, RG15, NA.

James Nedson, age sixty-three, was an invalid veteran who lived with his wife, age sixty-six, two daughters, and two granddaughters in New London, Connecticut. He made his living as a laborer but his ability to work had declined because of rheumatism. He stated that everyone in his household was "dependent" on him for support, but that he was no longer able to provide fully for them. Nedson owned no real property and possessed only thirty-five dollars in personal property. James Nedson, Pension File S36188, RG15, NA.

In 1820 Steven Russell was a fifty-five-year-old farmer who lived in Chrittenden County, Vermont. Forty years earlier, in June 1780, he had enlisted at age fifteen. He served as a private until the end of the war. Although he owned neither land nor a home, Russell owned $240 in personal goods and chattel property. He also reported $250 in debts. Russell and his forty-five-year-old wife had five young children at home, three of them under eight years of age. He also provided for his eighty-five-year-old infirm mother. Steven Russell, Pension File S18583, RG15, NA.

In 1820 William Willey was a sixty-five-year-old tenant farmer living in Rockingham County, New Hampshire. He had served in the militia for eight months. In the winter of 1775, he had enlisted as a private in a New Hampshire regiment of the Continental Army and served until the end of the war. In the winter of 1783, shortly after being mustered out, Willey, age twenty-seven, married a woman age twenty-three. At the time of his application, the court recorded that Willey had only thirty-nine dollars in personal property. Willey claimed that he was unable to work full time. Nevertheless, he reported that he was still responsible for young children. His own son, age fourteen, lived with them and probably rendered some help. His household also included an eight-year-old grandson whose father had been killed in the War of 1812. William Willey, Pension File W16162, RG15, NA.

Thomas Grant's household in Kennebec County, Maine, contained his "idiot" twenty-four-year-old son and an eight-year-old granddaughter. Grant, age sixty-eight, made his living as a seaman but claimed he could no longer work because of age and ill health. Grant owned a lot, a house, and a few personal possessions valued at sixty-seven dollars. Thomas Grant, Pension File W24304, RG15, NA.

Jonathan Jennings, age sixty-two, reported that he was a farmer living in Vermont and suffering from a rupture and rheumatism. Jennings was part of an intricate network of kin support. He provided for the kin in his household, and his household received assistance from other kin not living with him. Jennings's household consisted of his sixty-three-year-old wife, a thirty-year-old widowed daughter, and her six-year-old daughter. Jennings reported an estate valued at thirty-five dollars. They got "charity" from their thirty-five-year-old son, who had a family of his own to support. Jonathan Jennings, Pension File S38871, RG15, NA.

Also see William Jennings, Pension File S36622, RG15, NA; Joseph Hallock, Pension File W19682, RG15, NA; James Harmar, Pension File S41618, RG15, NA; Nathan

Barker, Pension File W25206, RG15, NA; John Grant, Pension File W23143, RG15, NA; Paul Shearmas, Pension File S42290, RG15, NA; Jacob Mitchell, Pension File S38217, RG15, NA; Charles Phillips, Pension File S43848, RG15, NA.

32. Resch, "The Continentals of Peterborough, New Hampshire," 180–83.

APPENDIX A

1. Schulz, 139–53.
2. *Historical Statistics*, 10. Andrew Achenbaum estimates that "at least 1.7 percent of the total population was over sixty by the Revolution [and] it is very unlikely that the proportion of older Americans nation wide increased any more than 1 percent between 1790 and 1830." Achenbaum, 59.
3. A. Smith, *History of Peterborough*, pt. 2:1–3.
4. Ibid., 1:83.
5. Ibid., 2:2.
6. *HCPCR*, 385.
7. Morrill and Dyke, xi–xii, 1–9. Also see Vinovskis, 1–25.
8. Liu, 13–16.
9. The census also reported twenty-three firearms in stock. J. Smith, *Peterborough New Hampshire in the American Revolution*, 25.
10. Crackel, *Mr. Jefferson's Army*, 1–3, 7, 10, 15, 179, 181. Kohn stated that Republican anti-army sentiment had diminished by the turn of the nineteenth century except among most southern Republicans. Kohn, *Eagle and Sword*, 301–03.
11. Ramsay, *History*, 2:124. Also see Ibid., 1:332.
12. Ramsay, *Washington*, 163–66, 180–81.
13. Mott, 207.
14. Ellis, 202–03.
15. *Port Folio* 1 (January 1813), 41.
16. Ellis, 206.
17. Caldwell, 321–28.

Selected Bibliography

T<small>HE FOLLOWING BIBLIOGRAPHY</small> contains sources cited in this book and a few selected sources.

MANUSCRIPT COLLECTIONS

Barbour Family Papers. University of Virginia. MSS 38–144.
Coles Collection. University of Virginia. MSS 3029.
Collections of the Connecticut Historical Society. 8 vols. Hartford, Conn.: Historical Society, 1901.
Londonderry N.H., East Parish Records, 1742–1837. Presbyterian Historical Society.
Londonderry N.H., West Parish Records, 1736–1821. Presbyterian Historical Society.
Rufus King Papers. The New York Historical Society.
Sally Scott Loomis Papers. Peterborough Public Library.
Smith Family Papers. Peterborough Historical Society, MSS 103.

GOVERNMENT DOCUMENTS

Annals of the Congress of the United States, 1789–1824. 42 vols. Washington, D.C.
Connecticut State Archives, *Canton Tax Records*, RG62, Box 20.
——. *Connecticut Census, 1820.*
——. *Simsbury Probate District, Town of Canton*, Probate Packets 224, 1826.
Documents and Records Relating to New Hampshire, 1623–1800, in Bouton, Nathaniel et. al., eds., 40 vols. Concord and Manchester, 1867–1954. Also referenced as *The New Hampshire State Papers.*
Essex, South District Court, *Grantee Deeds.*

——. *Grantor Deeds.*

——. *Probate Court Records.*

Library of Congress, *Bills and Resolutions of the House of Representatives and the Senate,* 1964.

Merrimack, New Hampshire, *Merrimack New Hampshire Tax Invoices.*

——. *Merrimack Town Records.*

Nashua, New Hampshire, *Hillsborough County Deed Records.*

——. *Hillsborough County Probate Court Records.*

National Archives. *Confidential and Unofficial Letters Sent by the Secretary of War, 1814–1835,* RG107.

——. *General Correspondence of the Commissioner of Pensions, Military Reference Branch (formerly Navy and Old Army Records Division).* RG 15.

——. *Records of the Office of the Secretary of War, Registered Letters.* RG 107.

——. *Records of the United States House of Representatives: Records of the Committee on Pensions and Revolutionary Claims.* RG 233.

——. *Records of the United States Senate, 15th and 16th Congress, Amendments to HR Bills and Committee Papers for Military Affairs Committee.*

——. *Revolutionary War Pension Files.* RG 15.

New Hampshire State Archives. *New Hampshire Provincial Probate and Deed Records, 1623–1722.* 100 vols.

Pennsylvania. *Journal of the 27th House of Representatives of the Commonwealth of Pennsylvania.* Harrisburg: James Peacock, 1816–1817.

——. *Journal of the 28th House of Representatives of the Commonwealth of Pennsylvania.* Harrisburg: James Peacock, 1816–1817.

——. *Laws of the General Assembly of the Commonwealth of Pennsylvania.* 2 vols. Harrisburg, 1959.

Peterborough, New Hampshire. *Peterborough Town Book,* 2 vols. 1760–1856.

Peterborough Historical Society. *Peterborough Tax Lists.*

Salem, Massachusetts. *An Abstract Valuation of Real and Personal Property in the Town of Boxford for the Year 1855,* 1856.

Topsfield, Massachusetts. *Vital Records of Boxford,* 1905.

Town of Canton, Connecticut. *Deeds.* 3 vols., 1809–1843.

U.S. Congress. *American State Papers: Military Affairs.*

Washington: Government Printing Office. *New Hampshire Census, 1790.* 1907.

FOURTH OF JULY ORATIONS

Fourth of July orators were generally young men who wished to display their rhetorical skills and erudition. They recounted the inception, birth, and growth of the nation. They continued the Puritan tradition of the jeremiad, which proclaimed declension and used powerful cultural symbols to inspire spiritual renewal to achieve the nation's destiny. The partisan character of Fourth of July orations intensified after Jefferson's election and particularly during his second administration, 1804–08. Administration supporters and critics used Fourth of July orations to support their positions, thus providing an important historical source for understanding the imagery contributing to the veterans' new cultural status.

Alden, August. *An Address Delivered at Augusta [Maine] . . . July 4, 1809.* Augusta, Maine: Peter Edes, 1809.

Allen, Benjamin Franklin. *An Oration Pronounced before the Students at Brown University, July 4, 1817.* Providence R.I.: James & Wheeler, 1817.

Anthon, John. *An Oration Delivered before the Washington Benevolent Society and Hamilton Society of New York, July 4, 1812.* New York: Largin & Thompson, 1812.

Bacon, Ezekiel. *An Oration Delivered at Pittsfield on the Thirty First Anniversary of American Independence.* Pittsfield, Mass.: Phineas Allen, 1807.

Bartlett, Joseph. *An Oration Delivered at the Request of the Republican Citizens of Portsmouth, New Hampshire, July 4, 1809.* Portsmouth, N.H.: N. Weeks, 1809.

Bates, Barnabas. *A Discourse Delivered to the Inhabitants of Bristol (RI) . . . July 4, 1815.* Warren, R.I.: Samuel Randall, 1815.

Berrion, Samuel. *An Oration Delivered Before the Tammany Society . . . in the City of New York, July 4, 1815.* New York: John Low, 1815.

Burges, Tristan. *Liberty, Glory and Union or American Independence: An Oration Pronounced before the People of Providence, July 4, 1810.* Providence, R.I.: Dunham and Hawkins, 1810.

Caldwell, Charles. *An Oration Commemorative of American Independence Delivered before the American Republican Society of Philadelphia, July 4, 1810.* Philadelphia: Bradford and Inskeep, 1810.

Carter, Nathaniel Hazeltine. *An Oration Delivered before the Republicans of Portland.* Portland, Maine: F. Douglas, 1815.

Channing, Edward Tyrell. *An Oration Delivered July 4, 1817 at the Request of the Selectmen of Boston.* Boston: Joseph T. Buckingham, 1817.

Clagett, William. *An Oration of Pronounced at Portsmouth, New Hampshire on the Fourth Day of July 1812.* Portsmouth, N.H.: N. Weeks, 1812.

Clinton, George Jr. *An Oration Delivered on the Fourth of July, 1798 Before . . . The Tammany Society.* New York: W. A. Davis, 1798.

Davis, John. *An Oration Pronounced at Worcester.* Worcester, Mass.: William Manning, 1816.

Davis, Matthew Livingston. *An Oration Delivered in St. Paul's Church on the Fourth of July, 1800 before the General Society of Mechanics and Tradesmen, Tammany Society . . . and Other Associations and Citizens.* New York: W. A. Davis, 1800.

Denny, Austin. *An Oration Delivered at Worcester July 4, 1818.* Worcester, Mass.: William Manning, 1818.

D'Ogley, Daniel. *An Oration Delivered in St. Michael's Church before the Inhabitants of Charlestown, South Carolina, on This Fourth of July, 1803.* Charlestown, S.C.: T. B. Bower, 1803.

Eacker, George. *An Oration Delivered at the Request of the Officers of the Brigade of the City and County of New York and the Mechanics, Tammany, and Coopers' Societies on the Fourth of July, 1801.* New York: William Durell, 1801.

Elliot, Benjamin. *An Oration Delivered in St. Philip's Church before the Inhabitants of Charlestown, South Carolina, July 4, 1817.* Charlestown, S.C.: W. P. Young, 1817.

Fowle, Robert. *An Oration Delivered at Plymouth, New Hampshire, July 4, 1800.* Concord, N.H.: George Hough, 1800.

Fuller, Timothy. *An Oration Pronounced at Lexington, Massachusetts on the Fourth of July by Request of the Republican Citizens of Middlesex County.* Boston: Rowe & Hooper, 1814.

Gleason, Benjamin. *Anniversary Oration in Commemoration of American Independence Pronounced before the Republican Citizens of Charlestown, July 1819.* Charlestown, Mass.: T. Green, 1819.

——. *An Oration Pronounced before the Republican Citizens of the Town of Hingham, July 4, 1807.* Boston: Hosea Sprague, 1807.

Gray, Francis Calley. *An Oration Pronounced July 4, 1818 at the Request of the Inhabitants of the Town of Boston in Commemoration of the Anniversary of American Independence.* Boston: Charles Callender, 1818.

Jackson, John George. *An Oration Pronounced in Clarksburg [Virginia] on the Fourth Day of July, 1812.* Clarksburg, Va.: F. & A. Britten, 1812.

Kean, Peter. *An Oration Pronounced in the Presbyterian Church at Connecticut Farms, New Jersey before the Citizens of the Township of Union, July 4, 1818.* Elizabethtown, N.J.: n.p., 1818.

Lincoln, Levi. *An Oration Pronounced at Brookfield . . . July 4, 1807.* Worcester, Mass.: Henry Rogers, 1807.

Livermore, Solomon Kidder. *An Oration Pronounced at Temple [New Hampshire] . . . July 4, 1809.* Amherst, N.H.: Joseph Cushing, 1809.

Livingston, Robert. *An Oration Before the Society of the Cincinnati . . . July 4, 1787.* New York: Francis Childe, 1787.

Mallary, Rollin Carolus. *An Oration Address to Republicans Assembled at Poultney, Vermont, July 4, 1814.* Rutland, Vt.: Fay & Davidson, 1814.

M'Lane, Louis. *An Oration Delivered before the Artillery Company of Wilmington, July 5, 1813.* Wilmington, Del.: Porter, 1813.

Morris, Gouverneur. *An Oration Delivered July 5, 1813 before the Washington Benevolent Society in the City of New York.* New York: Washington Benevolent Society, 1813.

Noah, Mordecai Manuel. *An Oration Delivered by Appointment before the Tammany Society.* New York: J. H. Sherman, 1817.

Osborn, Selleck. *An Oration Commemorative of American Independence Delivered to a Republican Audience at New Bedford, Massachusetts, July 4, 1810.* New Bedford, Mass.: Lemuel Child Jr., 1810.

Otis, Harrison Gray. *An Oration Delivered July 4, 1788 at the Request of the Inhabitants of the Town of Boston.* Boston: Benjamin Russell, 1788.

Perley, Jeremiah. *An Anniversary Oration Delivered before the Federal Republicans of Hallowell . . . July 4, 1807.* Augusta, Maine: Peter Edes, 1807.

Pinckney, Henry Laurens. *Oration Delivered in St. Michael's Church before an Assemblage of the Inhabitants of Charleston, South Carolina, July 4, 1818.* Charleston, S.C.: W. P. Young, 1818.

Romaine, Samuel Brower. *An Oration Delivered before the Tammany Society or Columbian Order . . . in the City of New York, July 4, 1812.* New York: John Low, 1812.

Rush, Richard. *An Oration Delivered on the Fourth of July, 1812 in the Hall of the House of Representatives.* Found in Hawken, 45.

Russell, Jonathan. *An Oration Pronounced in the Baptist Meeting House in Providence, July 4, 1800.* Providence, R.I.: Bennett Wheeler, 1800.

Sampson, John Philpot Curran. *An Oration Delivered before the Members of the Law Institution at Litchfield, July 4, 1818.* New York: E. Conrad, 1818.

Smith, Edward Darrell. *An Oration Delivered on the Fourth Day of July, 1812 to the Citizens of the Pendleton District [South Carolina].* Augusta, Ga.: The Herald Office, 1812.

Smith, Samuel Harrison. *An Oration Pronounced . . . in the City of Washington . . . The Fourth of July, 1813.* Washington: Roger C. Weightman, 1813.

Thomas, John Hanson. *An Oration Delivered in the Presbyterian Meeting House, July 4, 1807, at the Request of the Washington Society of Alexandria.* Alexandria, Va.: S. Snowden, 1807.

Thompson, John Champlin. *An Oration Pronounced at Windsor before a Numerous Collection of Republicans.* Windsor, Vt.: Jesse Cochran, 1814.

Ware, Asher. *An Oration Delivered before the Republicans of Portland, July 4, 1817.* Portland, Maine: Francis Douglas, 1817.

Webster, Daniel. *An Anniversary Address Delivered before Federal Gentlemen of Concord . . . July 4, 1806.* Concord, N.H.: George Mason, 1806.

Webster, Noah. *An Oration before the Citizens of New Haven on the Anniversary of the Declaration of Independence, July 1802.* New Haven: William Morse, 1802.

Williams, Melanchton Brown. *An Oration Delivered at Springfield, New Jersey.* Newark: John Tuttle, 1815.

Woodbury, Levi. *An Oration Pronounced at Lyndeborough, New Hampshire . . . July 4, 1815.* Amherst, N.H.: R. Boylston, 1815.

NEWSPAPERS AND PERIODICALS

American Mercury
American Review of History and Politics
Amherst New Hampshire Farmers' Cabinet
Boston Columbian Centinel
Boston Gazette
Boston Patriot and Daily Chronicle
Connecticut Courant
Daily National Intelligencer
Dedham Village Register
Dedham Weekly Register
Examiner
Exeter Watchman
Federal Republican and Baltimore Telegraph
Freemason's Magazine and General Miscellany

Juvenile Port Folio and Literary Miscellany
Hartford American Mercury
Hartford Connecticut Mirror
Hartford Connecticut Times
Keene New Hampshire Sentinel
Military Monitor and American Register
Monthly Magazine and Literary Journal
National Intelligencer
National Register
New Hampshire Patriot
New Hampshire Sentinel
New Haven Connecticut Journal
New Jersey American Watchman
New London Connecticut Gazette
New York American Citizen
New York Columbian
New York Evening Post
New York National Advocate
Niles Weekly Register
North American Review
Philadelphia Aurora
Philadelphia True American
Philadelphia U.S. Gazette
Philadelphia Weekly Aurora
Polyanthus
Port Folio
Richmond Enquirer
Vermont Intelligencer
Wilmington American Watchman
Worcester Massachusetts Spy

BOOKS, ARTICLES, THESES

Abbey, Matilda A. *Genealogy of the Family of Lt. Thomas Tracy of Norwich, Connecticut.* Milwaukee: D.S. Harkness & Co., 1889.

Achenbaum, Andrew. *Old Age in the New Land.* Baltimore: Johns Hopkins University Press, 1978.

Adams, Hannah. *Abridgment of the History of New England for the Use of Young Persons.* Boston: Belcher and Armstrong, 1807.

Adams, John Quincy. *A Eulogy on the Life and Character of James Monroe.* Boston: J. H. Eastburn, 1931.

Alexander, Carol R. "Changing Attitudes toward Political Parties Reflected in Massachusetts Fourth of July Orations, 1800–1840." Master's thesis, Clark University, 1981.

Alpers, Benjamin L. "This Is the Army: Imagining a Democratic Military in World War II." *The Journal of American History.* 85 (June 1998): 129–63.

Ammon, Harry. *James Monroe: The Quest for National Identity.* New York: McGraw Hill, 1971.

Anderson, Fred. *A People's Army: Massachusetts Soldiers and Society in the Seven Years' War.* New York: W. W. Norton, 1985.

Appleby, Joyce. *Capitalism and the New Social Order: The Republican Vision of the 1790s.* New York: New York University Press, 1984.

——. "Republicanism in Old and New Contexts." *William and Mary Quarterly.* 43 (1986): 20–34.

Avery, Elroy. *The Groton Avery Clan.* Cleveland: n.p., 1912.

Banner, James M. *To the Hartford Convention: The Federalist and the Origins of Party Politics in Massachusetts, 1789–1815.* New York: Alfred A. Knopf, 1970.

Banning, Lance. "Jeffersonian Ideology Revisited: Liberal and Classical Ideas in the New American Republic." *William and Mary Quarterly.* 43 (1986): 3–19.

——. *The Jeffersonian Persuasion: Evolution of a Party Ideology.* Ithaca, N.Y.: Cornell University Press, 1978.

Battle of Groton Heights: A Story of the Storming of Fort Griswold and the Burning of New London. New London, Conn.: E. E. Darrow, 1931.

Bercovitch, Sacvan. *The American Jeremiad.* Madison: The University of Wisconsin Press, 1978.

Berg, Anderson. *Encyclopedia of Continental Army Units.* Harrisburg: The Stackpole Co., 1972.

Blau, Peter M., and Meyer, Marshall W. *Bureaucracy in Modern Society.* New York: Random House, 1971.

Boatner, Mark M., III. *Encyclopedia of the American Revolution.* New York: David McKay Co., 1966.

Bodenger, David. "Soldiers' Bonuses: A History of Veterans' Benefits in the United States, 1776–1967." Ph.D. diss., Pennsylvania State University, 1972.

Bodnar, John. *Remaking America: Public Memory, Commemoration, and Patriotism in the Twentieth Century.* Princeton: Princeton University Press, 1991.

Boorstin, Daniel J. *The Discoverers.* New York: Random House, 1983.

Boulton, Jeremy. *Neighborhood and Society: A London Suburb in the Seventeenth Century.* Cambridge: Cambridge University Press, 1987.

Brill, Norman, and Beebe, Gilbert. *A Follow-up Study of War Neuroses.* Washington, D.C.: Veterans Administration, 1955.

Brooke, John L. *The Heart of the Commonwealth: Society and Political Culture in Worcester County, Massachusetts, 1713–1861.* Cambridge: Cambridge University Press, 1989.

Brown, Abel. *Genealogical History with Short Sketches and Family Records of the Early Settlers of West Simsbury, Now Canton, Connecticut.* Hartford: Case, Tiffany and Co., 1856.

Brown University. *Historical Catalogue.* Providence, R.I.: Brown University, 1905.

Buel, Richard, Jr. "Samson Shorn: The Impact of the Revolutionary War on Estimates of the Republic's Strength." In Ronald Hoffman and Peter J. Albert, eds. *Arms and Independence: The Military Character of the American Revolution.* Charlottesville: University Press of Virginia, 1984.

——. *Securing the Revolution: Ideology in American Politics, 1789–1815.* Ithaca, N.Y.: Cornell University Press, 1972.

Caldwell, Charles. *Autobiography.* Philadelphia: Lippincott, Grambo and Co., 1855.

Calhoun, Craig, ed. *Habermas and the Public Sphere.* Cambridge: MIT Press, 1992.

Campbell, T. D. "Scientific Explanation and Ethical Justification in the *Moral Sentiments.*" In Andrew S. Skinner and Thomas Wilson, eds. *Essays on Adam Smith.* Oxford: Clarendon Press, 1975.

Card, Josefina J. *Lives After Vietnam: The Personal Impact of Military Service.* Lexington, Mass.: D. C. Heath, 1983.

Carp, E. Wayne. *To Starve the Army at Pleasure: Continental Army Administration and American Political Culture.* Chapel Hill: University of North Carolina Press, 1984.

Cassell, Frank A. *Merchant Congressman in the Young Republic: Samuel Smith of Maryland, 1752–1839.* Madison: University of Wisconsin Press, 1971.

Caulkins, Francis M. *History of Norwich, Connecticut.* Hartford: Case, Lockwood & Brainard, 1873.

Chapman, George. *Sketches of the Alumni of Dartmouth.* Cambridge: Riverside Press, 1867.

Cohen, Lester H. *The Revolutionary Historians: Contemporary Narratives of the American Revolution.* Ithaca, N.Y.: Cornell University Press, 1980.

Cohen, Patricia Cline. *A Calculating People.* Chicago: University of Chicago Press, 1982.

Copp, John J. *The Battle of Groton Heights: The Massacre of Fort Griswold and the Burning of New London.* The Groton Heights, Centennial Committee, 1879.

Crackel, Theodore J. *Mr. Jefferson's Army: Political and Social Reform of the Military Establishment, 1801–1809.* New York: New York University Press, 1987.

——. "Revolutionary War Pension Records and Patterns of American Mobility, 1780–1830." *Prologue* 16 (Fall 1984): 155–67.

Cray, Robert. "Major Andre and the Three Captors: Class Dynamics and Revolutionary Memory Wars in the Early Republic, 1780–1831." *Journal of the Early Republic.* 17 (Fall 1997): 371–97.

——. "Poverty and Poor Relief: New York City and Its Rural Environs, 1700–1830." Ph.D. diss., SUNY, Stony Brook, 1984.

Cress, Lawrence. *Citizens in Arms: The Army and Militia in American Society to the War of 1812.* Chapel Hill: The University of North Carolina Press, 1982.

Crockett, Walter Hill. *Vermont: The Green Mountain State.* 5 vols. New York: Century History Co., Inc., 1921.

Cropsey, Joseph. "Adam Smith and Political Philosophy." In Andrew S. Skinner and Thomas Wilson, eds. *Essays on Adam Smith.* Oxford: Clarendon Press, 1975.

——. *Polity and Economy: An Interpretation of the Principles of Adam Smith.* Westport, Conn.: Greenwood Press, 1977.

Culpin, Millais. *Psychoneuroses of War and Peace*. Cambridge: Cambridge University Press, 1920.

Cunningham, Noble E., Jr. *The Jeffersonian Republicans in Power: Party Operations, 1801–1809*. Chapel Hill: University of North Carolina Press, 1963.

Cunningham, Noble E., Jr., ed. *Circular Letters of Congressmen to Their Constituents, 1789–1829*. 3 vols. Chapel Hill: University of North Carolina Press, 1978.

Cushing, William. *Initials and Pseudonyms*. Waltham, Mass.: Mark Press, 1963.

Dangerfield, George. *The Awakening of American Nationalism 1815–1828*. New York: Harper & Row, 1965.

Dann, John. *The Revolution Remembered*. Chicago: The University of Chicago Press, 1977.

Dean, Eric T., Jr. *Shook Over Hell: Post-Traumatic Stress, Vietnam, and the Civil War*. Cambridge: Harvard University Press, 1997.

Dexter, Franklin Bowditch. *Biographical Notices of Graduates of Yale College*. 6 vols. New York: Henry Holt and Co., 1885.

Ditz, Toby L. *Property and Kinship: Inheritance in Early Connecticut, 1750–1820*. Princeton: Princeton University Press, 1986.

Dollar, Charles, and Jensen, Richard. *Historian's Guide to Statistics*. New York: Holt, Rinehart, and Winston, 1971.

Edgar, Neal Z. *A History and Bibliography of American Magazines, 1810–1820*. Metuchen, N.J.: The Scarecrow Press, Inc., 1975.

Elder, Glen H., Jr., and Clipp, Elizabeth. "Wartime Losses and Social Bonding: Influences Across Forty Years in Men's Lives." *Psychiatry*. 51 (May 1988): 177–98.

Elkins, Stanley, and McKitrick, Eric. *The Age of Federalism: The Early American Republic, 1788–1800*. New York: Oxford University Press, 1993.

Ellery, Reginald S. *Psychiatric Aspects of Modern Warfare*. Melbourne: Reed and Harris, 1945.

Ellis, Harold Milton. "Joseph Dennie and His Circle." *Bulletin of the University of Texas* (15 July 1915): 174–214.

Emery, Ina Capitola. *The Washington Monument*. n.p., 1907.

Etzioni-Halevy, Eva. *Bureaucracy and Democracy: A Political Dilemma*. London: Routledge & Kegan Paul, 1983.

Fellows, Otis E., and Milliken, Stephen F. *Buffon*. New York: Twayne Publishers, 1972.

Ferling, John. "Oh That I Was a Soldier: John Adams and the Anguish of War." *American Quarterly* (Fall 1984): 258–75.

Fischer, David Hackett. *The Revolution in American Conservatism: The Federalist Party in the Era of Jeffersonian Democracy*. New York: Harper and Row, 1965.

Formisano, Ronald P. *The Transformation of Political Culture: Massachusetts Parties, 1790s–1840s*. New York: Oxford University Press, 1983.

Fornari, Franco. *The Psychoanalysis of War*. Bloomington: Indiana University Press, 1977.

Furneaux, Robert. *Saratoga: The Decisive Battle*. London: George Allen & Unwin, Ltd., 1971.

Gardner, Charles K., ed. *A Dictionary of the Army of the United States.* New York: Van Nostrand, 1860.

Gibbon, Edward. *The History of the Decline and Fall of the Roman Empire.* 6 vols. Boston: Phillips, Sampson and Co., 1850.

Gillis, John R. "Memory and Identity: The History of a Relationship." In John R. Gillis. *Commemorations: The Politics of National Identity.* Princeton: Princeton University Press, 1994.

Glasson, William. *Federal and Military Pensions in the United States.* New York: Oxford University Press, 1918.

Govan, Thomas Payne. *Nicholas Biddle: Nationalist and Public Banker.* Chicago: University of Chicago Press, 1959.

Greven, Philip, Jr. *Four Generations: Population, Land and Family in Colonial Andover.* Ithaca: Cornell University Press, 1970.

Gross, Robert. *The Minutemen and Their World.* New York: Hill and Wang, 1976.

Gullickson, Guy L. "Agriculture and Cottage Industry: Redefining the Causes of Proto-Industrialization." *Journal of Economic History.* 43 (1983): 832–50.

Haber, Carole. *Beyond Sixty-Five: The Dilemma of Old Age in America's Past.* New York: Cambridge University Press, 1983.

Hale, Charles R. *Hale Collection of Connecticut Newspaper Marriage and Death Notices.* 68 vols. Hartford: Connecticut State Archives, 1937–1941.

Hale, Salma. *History of the United States.* Keene, N.H.: J. Prentiss, 1835.

Hamilton, Stanislaus Murray. *The Writings of James Monroe.* 6 vols. New York: Ames Press, 1969.

Hanawalt, Barbara A. *The Ties That Bound: Peasant Families in Medieval England.* New York: Oxford University Press, 1986.

Handler, Richard. "Is 'Identity' a Useful Cross-Cultural Concept?" In John R. Gillis. *Commemorations: The Politics of National Identity.* Princeton: Princeton University Press, 1994.

Hart, H. L. A. *The Concept of Law.* New York: Oxford University Press, 1961.

Haskell, Thomas. "Capitalism and the Origins of the Humanitarian Sensibility." *American Historical Review.* 90 (April and June 1985): 339–61, 547–67.

Hatzenbuehler, Ronald L. "Foreign Policy Voting in the U.S. Congress, 1808–1812." Ph.D. diss., Kent State University, 1972.

Havighurst, Robert, et. al., *The American Veteran Back Home: A Study of Veteran Readjustment.* New York: Longmans, Green and Co., 1951.

Hawken, Henry A. *Trumpets of Glory: Fourth of July Orations, 1786–1861.* Granby, Conn.: The Salmon Brook Historical Society, 1976.

Hemphill, Edwin H., ed. *The Papers of John C. Calhoun.* 17 vols. Columbia: University of South Carolina Press, 1963.

Henretta, James A. "Families and Farms: Mentalite in Pre-Industrial America." *William and Mary Quarterly* 35 (January 1978): 3–32.

Higginbotham, Don. *War and Society in Revolutionary America: The Wider Dimensions of Conflict.* Columbia: University of South Carolina Press, 1988.

——. *The War of American Independence: Military Attitudes, Policies, and Practice, 1763–1789.* Boston: Northeastern University Press, 1983.

History of Merrimack, New Hampshire. Merrimack, N.H.: Merrimack Historical Society, 1976.

Hudson, Charles. *History of the Town of Lexington.* n.p., 1868.

Hume, David. *An Enquiry Concerning the Principles of Morals.* London: T. Cadell, 1777.

Jackson, William. *Documents Relative to the Claim of the Surviving Officers of the Revolutionary Army of the United States for an Equitable Settlement of the Half Pay for Life as Stipulated in the Resolves of Congress.* n.p.: The American Antiquarian Society.

Jensen, Merrill. *The New Nation: A History of the United States during the Confederation, 1781–1787.* New York: Alfred A. Knopf, 1950.

Johnson, Allen, and Malone, Dumas, eds., *Dictionary of American Biography.* 22 vols. New York: Charles Scribner's Sons, 1934.

Journal of the 27th House of Representatives of the Commonwealth of Pennsylvania. Harrisburg: James Peacock, 1816–1817.

Journal of the 28th House of Representatives of the Commonwealth of Pennsylvania. Harrisburg: James Peacock, 1817–1818.

Kammen, Michael. *From Liberty to Prosperity: Reflections upon the Role of Revolutionary Iconography in Nation Tradition.* Worcester: American Antiquarian Society, 1977. It is reprinted from *The Proceedings.* Worcester: The American Antiquarian Society 86 Part 2 (October 1976).

——. *A Season of Youth.* New York: Alfred A. Knopf, 1978.

Kelly, R. Gordon, ed. *Children's Periodicals of the United States.* Westport, Conn.: Greenwood Press, 1984.

Ketcham, Ralph. *James Madison: A Biography.* New York: The Macmillan Co., 1971.

——. *Presidents above Party.* Chapel Hill: University of North Carolina Press, 1984.

Ketchum, Richard. *The Battle for Bunker Hill.* London: the Cresset Press, 1962.

Kidder, Frederick. *History of the First New Hampshire Regiment in the War of the Revolution.* Albany, N.Y.: Joel Munsell, 1868.

King, Charles R., ed. *The Life and Correspondence of Rufus King.* 6 vols. New York: G.P. Putnam's Sons, 1900.

Kloppenberg, James T. "The Virtues of Liberalism: Christianity, Republicanism, and Ethics in Early American Political Discourse." *Journal of American History* 74 (1987): 9–33.

Kohn, Richard. *Eagle and Sword: The Federalists and the Creation of the Military Establishment, 1783–1802.* New York: The Free Press, 1975.

——. "The Inside History of the Newburgh Conspiracy." *William and Mary Quarterly.* 3rd ser. 27 (1970): 187–220.

——. "The Social History of the American Soldier: A Review and Prospectus for Research." *The American Historical Review* (1981): 553–67.

Koschnik, Albrecht. "Political Conflict and Public Contest: Rituals of National Celebration in Philadelphia, 1788–1815." *The Pennsylvania Magazine of History and Biography* 118 (January/April 1994): 209–48.

Kulka, Richard A., et. al. *The National Vietnam Veterans Readjustment Study.* New York: Brunner/Mazel, Inc., 1990.

La Palombara, Joseph. "Bureaucracy and Political Development: Notes, Queries and Dilemmas." In Joseph La Palombara, ed. *Bureaucracy and Political Development.* Princeton: Princeton University Press, 1963.

Laws of the Commonwealth of Pennsylvania. Philadelphia: John Bioren, 1822.

Leiby, James. *A History of Social Welfare and Social Work in the United States.* New York: Columbia University Press, 1978.

Lender, Mark Edward. "The Social Structure of the New Jersey Brigade: The Continental Line as an American Standing Army." In Peter Karsten, ed. *The Military in America: From the Colonial Era to the Present.* New York: Macmillan, 1980, 65–78.

Lender, Mark E., and Martin, James Kirby. *Citizen Soldier: The Revolutionary War Journal of Joseph Bloomfield.* Newark: New Jersey Historical Society, 1982.

———. *A Respectable Army: The Military Origins of the Republic, 1763–1789.* Arlington Heights, Ill.: Harlan Davidson, Inc., 1982.

Leonard, Levi W. *The History of Dublin, N.H.* Dublin: Town of Dublin, 1919.

Lesser, Charles H. ed. *The Sinews of Independence: Monthly Strength Reports of the Continental Army.* Chicago: University of Chicago Press, 1976.

"Letters of Ebenezer Huntington." *American Historical Review* 5 (July 1900): 702–29.

Linderman, Gerald. *The World Within War: America's Combat Experience in World War II.* New York: The Free Press, 1997.

Liu, Ts'ui-jung. "The Demography of Two Chinese Clans in Hsiaso-Shan, Chekiang, 1650–1850." In Susan B. Hanley and Arthur P. Wolf, eds. *Family and Population in East Asian History.* California: Stanford University Press, 1985.

Livermore, Abiel Abbot, and Putnam, Sewall. *History of the Town of Wilton.* Lowell: Marden & Rowell, 1888.

Livermore, Shaw. *The Twilight of Federalism.* Princeton: Princeton University Press, 1962.

Lochemes, M. Frederick, Sr. *Robert Walsh: His Story.* New York: Irish American Historical Society, 1941.

Lowrey, Charles D. *James Barbour, A Jeffersonian Republican.* Tuscaloosa: The University of Alabama Press, 1984.

Lyon, John, and Sloan, Phillip R. *From Natural History to the History of Nature: Readings from Buffon and His Critics.* Notre Dame: University of Notre Dame Press, 1981.

McCoy, Drew R. *The Elusive Republic: Political Economy in Jeffersonian America.* Chapel Hill: University of North Carolina Press, 1980.

———. *The Last of the Fathers.* New York: Cambridge University Press, 1989.

McCurdy, J. T. *War Neurosis.* Cambridge: Cambridge University Press, 1918.

McDonnell, Mildred D. *The Romaine Family Book.* n.p., n.d.

Marshall, John. *The Life of George Washington.* 5 vols. Philadelphia: C. P. Wayne, 1804.

Martin, James Kirby. *Citizen Soldier: The Revolutionary War Journal of Joseph Bloomfield.* Newark: New Jersey Historical Society, 1982.

——. "A 'Most Undisciplined, Profligate Crew': Protest and Defiance in the Continental Ranks, 1776–1783." In Ronald Hoffman and Peter J. Albert, eds. *Arms and Independence: The Military Character of the American Revolution.* Charlottesville: University Press of Virginia, 1984.

Martyn, Charles. *The Life of Artimas Ward.* Port Washington, N.Y.: Kennikat Press, 1921.

Marwick, Arthur. "The Impact of the First World War on British Society." *Journal of Contemporary History* 3 (1968): 51–63.

Massachusetts Soldiers and Sailors of the Revolutionary War: A Compilation from the State Archives. 17 Vols. Boston: Wright and Potter Printing Co., 1896.

Mendels, Franklin. "Proto-Industrialization: The First Phase of the Industrialization Process." *Journal of Economic History* 32 (1972): 241–61.

Miller, David. *Philosophy and Ideology in Hume's Political Thought.* Oxford: Clarendon Press, 1981.

Monroe, James. *A Narrative of Observation Made during the Summer of 1817.* Philadelphia: S. A. Mitchell & H. Ames, 1818.

——. *Some Observations on the Constitution.* Petersburg, Va.: Hunter and Prentis, 1788.

Moore, George W. *The Moore Family.* Peterborough, N.H.: Peterborough Transcript Printers Co., 1925.

Morison, George Abbot. *Nathaniel Morison and His Descendants.* Peterborough, N.H.: Peterborough Historical Society, 1951.

Morison, John Hopkins. *A Memoir.* Boston: Houghton, Mifflin & Co., 1898.

Morison, Samuel Eliot. "The Proprietors of Peterborough, New Hampshire." Peterborough: Peterborough Historical Society, 1930.

Morrill, Warrant, and Dyke, Bennett, "Ethnographic and Documentary Demography." In Morrill and Dyke, eds. *Genealogical Demography.* New York: Academic Press, 1980.

Mott, Frank Luther. *American Journalism: A History, 1690–1960.* New York: The Macmillan Co., 1962.

Myers, Minor, Jr. *Liberty without Anarchy: A History of the Society of the Cincinnati.* Charlottesville: The University of Virginia Press, 1983.

Nafie, Joan. *To the Beat of a Drum: A History of Norwich, Connecticut during the American Revolution.* Norwich: Old Town Press, 1975.

Neimeyer, Charles Patrick. *American Goes to War: A Social History of the Continental Army.* New York: New York University Press, 1996.

Niles, Hezekiah, ed. *Of the Revolution in America.* Baltimore: William Ogden Niles, 1822.

Pamer, Joseph. *Necrology of Alumni of Harvard College, 1851–1852 to 1862–1863.* Boston: J. Wilson and Son, 1864.

Papenfuse, Edward D., and Stiverson, Gregory A. "General Smallwood's Recruits: The Peacetime Career of the Revolutionary War Private." *William and Mary Quarterly.* 3rd Series 30 (January 1973): 117–32.

Parker, Edward L. *The History of Londonderry.* Boston: Perkins and Whipple, 1851.

Peckham, Howard. *The Toll of Independence: Engagements and Battle Casualties of the American Revolution.* Chicago: University of Chicago Press, 1974.

Pension Roll of 1835. 4 vols. Baltimore: Genealogical Publishing Co., 1968.

Perley, Sidney. *The Dwellings of Boxford.* Salem, Mass.: n.p., 1893.

——. *The History of Boxford.* Boxford, Mass.: n.p., 1880.

Pratt, George K. *Soldier to Civilian: Problems of Readjustment.* New York: McGraw-Hill, 1944.

Purcell, Sarah J. "Sealed with Blood: National Identity and Public Memory of the Revolutionary War, 1775–1825." Ph.D. diss., Brown University, 1997.

Radcliffe, Richard, ed. *The President's Tour: A Collection of Addresses Made to James Monroe, Esq. on His Tour through the Northern and Middle States, A.D. 1817.* New Ipswich, N.H.: Salmon Wilder, 1822.

Ramsay, David. *History of the American Revolution.* 2 vols. Philadelphia: R. Aitken and Son, 1789.

——. *The Life of George Washington.* New York: Hopkins and Seymour, 1807.

Raphael, D. D. "The Impartial Spectator." In Andrew S. Skinner and Thomas Wilson, eds. *Essays on Adam Smith.* Oxford: Clarendon Press, 1975.

Rawls, John. *A Theory of Justice.* Cambridge: Harvard University Press, 1971.

Resch, John P. "The Continental Veterans of Peterborough, New Hampshire." *Prologue* 16 (1984): 169–83.

——. "Federal Welfare for Revolutionary War Veterans." *The Social Service Review* 56 (June 1982): 171–95.

——. "Peterborough after the Revolution." In William Gardner, Frank Mevers, Richard Upton, eds. *New Hampshire: The State That Made Us a Nation.* Portsmouth, N.H.: Peter Randall, 1989.

——. "Politics and Public Culture: The Revolutionary War Pension Act of 1818." *Journal of the Early Republic* 8 (Summer 1988): 139–58.

——. "The Transformation of a Frontier Community: Peterborough, New Hampshire." In Richard Herr, ed. *Themes in Rural History of the Western World.* Ames: Iowa State University Press, 1993.

Risjord, Norman K. *The Old Republicans: Southern Conservatism in the Age of Jefferson.* New York: Columbia University Press, 1965.

Rogers, Ernest E., ed. *Sesquicentennial of the Battle of Groton Heights and the Burning of New London, Connecticut.* New London: Fort Griswold & Groton Monument Commission, 1931.

Rosswurm, Steven. "The Philadelphia Militia, 1775–1783: Active Duty and Active Radicalism." In Ronald Hoffman and Peter J. Albert, eds. *Arms and Independence: The Military Character of the American Revolution.* Charlottesville: University Press of Virginia, 1984.

——. *Arms, Country, and Class: The Philadelphia Militia and "Lower Sort" during the American Revolution, 1775–1783.* New Brunswick, N.J.: Rutgers University Press, 1987.

Rothenberg, Winifred B. "The Emergence of a Capital Market in Rural Massachusetts, 1730–1838." *Journal of Economic History* 65 (1985): 781–808.

Royster, Charles. *A Revolutionary People At War.* New York: W. W. Norton & Co., 1979.

———. "Founding a Nation in Blood: Military Conflict and American Nationality." In Ronald Hoffman and Peter J. Albert, eds. *Arms and Independence: The Military Character of the American Revolution.* Charlottesville: University Press of Virginia, 1984.

Sargent, Walter. "The Soldiers of Plymouth: Citizen Soldiers or Sunshine Patriots." Unpublished Paper, Early American History Workshop, University of Minnesota, 1998, 19.

Schoenbachler, Matthew. "Republicanism in the Age of Democratic Revolution: The Democratic-Republican Societies of the 1790s." *Journal of the Early Republic* 18 (Spring 1998): 237–61.

Schulz, Constance. "Daughters of Liberty: The History of Women in the Revolutionary War Pension Records." *Prologue* 16 (1984): 139–53.

Scott, Wilbur J. *The Politics of Readjustment: Vietnam Veterans since the War.* New York: Aldine De Gruyter, 1993.

Selesky, Harold E. *War and Society in Colonial Connecticut.* New Haven: Yale University Press, 1990.

Sellers, John R. "The Common Soldier in the American Revolution." In Stanley J. Underdal, ed. *The Proceedings of the 6th Military History Symposium.* Washington: Office of Air Force History, 1976.

Severo, Richard, and Milford, Lewis. *The Wages of War: When America's Soldiers Came Home—From Valley Forge to Vietnam.* New York: Simon and Schuster, 1989.

Shalhope, Robert. "Toward a Republican Synthesis: The Emergence of an Understanding of Republicanism in American Historiography." *William and Mary Quarterly* 29 (1972): 49–80.

Shay, Jonathan. *Achilles in Vietnam: Combat Trauma and the Undoing of Character.* New York: Atheneum, 1994.

Shy, John. "The American Revolution: The Military Conflict Considered as a Revolutionary War." In Stephen G. Kurtz and James H. Hutson, eds. *Essays on the American Revolution.* Chapel Hill: University of North Carolina Press, 1973.

———. "Hearts and Minds in the American Revolution: The Case of 'Long Bill' Scott and Peterborough, New Hampshire." In John Shy. *A People Numerous and Armed.* New York: Oxford University Press, 1976.

Skinner, Andrew S., and Wilson, Thomas eds. *Essays on Adam Smith.* Oxford: Clarendon Press, 1975.

Smith, Adam. *The Theory of Moral Sentiment.* 2 vols. New York: Evert Duyckinck, 1822.

Smith, Albert. *History of the Town of Peterborough.* 2 Parts. Boston: George Ellis, 1876.

Smith, Jonathan. "Annals of Peterborough." In *Historical Sketches of Peterborough, New Hampshire.* Peterborough: Peterborough Historical Society, 1938.

———. *The Home of the Smith Family in Peterborough, New Hampshire*. Clinton, Mass.: W. J. Coulter, 1900.

———. *Peterborough New Hampshire in the American Revolution*. Peterborough: Peterborough Historical Society, 1913.

Spencer, Truman J. *The History of Amateur Journalism*. New York: The Fossils, Inc., 1957.

Stagg, J. C. A. *Mr. Madison's War: Politics, Diplomacy and Warfare in the Early American Republic, 1783–1830*. Princeton: Princeton University Press, 1983.

Stark, Caleb. *Memoir and Official Correspondence of Gen. John Stark*. Boston: Gregg Press, 1972.

Starr, Paul. *The Discarded Army: Veterans after Vietnam*. New York: Charterhouse, 1973.

Stiverson, Gregory A. "General Smallwood's Recruits: The Peacetime Career of the Revolutionary War Private." *William and Mary Quarterly*. 3rd ser. 30 (1973): 117–32.

Story of the Battle of Fort Griswold. Groton, Conn.: James M. Bacon, 1892.

Stouffer, Samuel. *The American Soldier*. 2 vols. Princeton: Princeton University Press, 1949.

Sweet, Homer DeLois. *The Averys of Groton*. Syracuse, N.Y.: Rice-Taylor Co., 1894.

Thayer, Theodore. *As We Were . . . Elizabeth, New Jersey*, n.p., 1964.

Thomas, Milton H. *Columbia University Officers and Alumni, 1754–1857*. New York: Columbia University Press, 1936.

Threlfall, John B. *Heads of Families: New Hampshire, 1800*. Chicago: Adams Press, 1973.

Tiedemann, Joseph S. "A Revolution Foiled: Queens County, New York, 1775–1776." *Journal of American History* 75 (September 1988): 417–44.

Travers, Len. *Celebrating the Fourth: Independence Day and the Rites of Nationalism in the Early Republic*. Amherst: University of Massachusetts Press, 1997.

Upton, Richard. *Revolutionary New Hampshire*. New York: Octagon Books, 1971.

U.S. Biographical Directory of the American Congress. Washington, D.C.: Government Printing Office, 1961.

U.S. Bureau of the Census. *Historical Statistics of the United States*. 2 vols. Washington, D.C.: U.S. Government Printing Office, 1975.

Vinovskis, Maris. "Recent Trends in American Historical Demography." In Maris Vinovskis. *Studies in American Historical Demography*. New York: Academic Press, 1979.

Waldstreicher, David. *In the Midst of Perpetual Fetes: The Making of American Nationalism, 1776–1820*. Chapel Hill: University of North Carolina Press, 1997.

Wall, Richard. "Regional and Temporal Variations in English Household Structure from 1650." In John Hobcraft and Philip Rees, eds. *Regional Demographic Development*. London: Croom Helm, 1979.

Ward, Stephen R., ed. *The War Generation: Veterans of the First World War*. Port Washington, N.Y.: Kennikat Press, 1975.

Warren, Mercy Otis. *History of the Rise, Progress and Termination of the American Revolution*. 3 vols. Boston: Manning and Loring, 1805.

Watts, Steven. *The Republic Reborn*. Baltimore: The Johns Hopkins University Press, 1987.

Weber, Max. *Max Weber: The Theory of Social and Economic Organization.* Henderson, A. M., and Parsons, Talcott, trans. New York: The Free Press, 1974.

Wehmann, Howard H. "Introduction." *Records of the Veterans Administration.* RG15, NA.

Who Was Who in America, 1607–1896. Chicago: A. R. Majors, 1967.

Wood, Gordon. *The Radicalism of the American Revolution.* New York: Alfred A. Knopf, 1991.

Wright, Robert K., Jr. *The Continental Army.* Washington, D.C.: Center of Military History, 1983.

——. "'Nor Is Their Standing Army to Be Despised'": The Emergence of the Continental Army as a Military Institution." In Ronald Hoffman and Peter J. Albert, eds. *Arms and Independence: The Military Character of the American Revolution.* Charlottesville: University Press of Virginia, 1984.

Young, Alfred F. "George Robert Twelve Hewes (1742–1840): A Boston Shoemaker and the Memory of the American Revolution." *William and Mary Quarterly.* 3rd ser. 37 (1981): 561–623.

Young, Allan. *The Harmony of Illusions: Inventing Post-Traumatic Stress Disorder.* Princeton: Princeton University Press, 1995.

Young, James Sterling. *The Washington Community, 1800–1820.* New York: Columbia University Press, 1966.

Index

CPSIA information can be obtained at www.ICGtesting.com
Printed in the USA
BVOW071552120112

280312BV00001B/137/P